LET THERE BE LIFE

LET THERE BE LIFE

J J Scarisbrick

First published by LIFE
LIFE House, Newbold Terrace, Leamington Spa
Warwickshire CV32 4EA

ISBN 978-0-9555507-0-6

A Cataloguing in Publication Record
for this title is available from the British Library

Typeset in Plantin
Printed in Great Britain by
Warwick Printing Co. Ltd

CONTENTS

FOREWORD

This small book is a personal memoir. It focuses on some of the major themes in the story of the struggle between the Gospel of Life and its opponents in Britain – as I have experienced it in the last 40 years.

It is not a straight history of the pro-life movement in this country. I speak mainly about LIFE because I know more about it than I do about other movements and inevitably see events and people through LIFE eyes. I also wanted to salute the courage and dedication of the many hundreds of LIFE supporters and workers who have borne the heat of the day over the years – running the LIFE Care Centres and National Helpline, leading its educational work and again and again rallying to plead in public for justice for human life before birth.

The views expressed herein are my own and not necessarily those of other Trustees of the charity or its supporters. I hope they are, of course.

J J Scarisbrick
Leamington Spa 2007

I.

A PROFILE OF THE PRO-LIFER

A pro-lifer is committed to converting society to the Gospel of Life. A pro-lifer yearns to be the occasion of enabling fellow-citizens to come to see that absolute respect is due to all human life from its beginning – fertilisation – and that all induced abortion, i.e. the deliberate destruction of unborn human beings, the artificial production of human life by *in vitro* fertilisation (IVF), all forms of human embryo abuse and all cloning using human materials are morally unacceptable.

That conversion must be freely made. There is no intention or desire to impose views on others, even if this were possible. A total conversion of society may never happen, of course. But if the great majority were won over and the full, equal protection of the law bestowed on all human life before birth, the victory would have been won.

But how is this near-miracle to be achieved, at least in modern Western societies?

One takes the advice of a lawyer on a legal matter or of a garage mechanic on repairing a car because they are experts. That is easy enough. But how and why we come to assent to others' views on moral issues which touch us personally, maybe deeply, and have conflicted with our own, how far we can know things without final proof of them, how belief and knowledge interrelate – these are much more difficult matters. Human beings are such complicated creatures: an often fluctuating amalgam of reason and emotion, idealism and self-centredness, self-confidence and self-doubt, openness and prejudice, goodness and sinfulness. And much more.

That explains an inescapable fact of life, namely, that objectively valid arguments are, alas, not always convincing ones. The pro-lifer knows that the arguments for the pro-life case are valid, indeed, invincible. But if they are to be convincing at least three things have to be remembered.

First, A should not expect B to begin to question, let alone abandon, deep-rooted views on a moral issue, unless persuaded that A has really tried to understand why B holds them. Unless A has listened carefully and, to use the vogue phrase, sincerely appreciates where B "is coming from", B's mind will remain closed. Secondly, B will not listen actively, positively, until persuaded that A's case is intellectually coherent, i.e. water-tight. Thirdly, what A says is often less important than what kind of person A is. Convergence, "conversion", occur both because what is said is increasingly perceived to be true but also, perhaps more so, because the listener is drawn by the speaker's integrity and wants to share in that liberating authenticity which bestows special authority on him. That is why the not saying of something may be the better way of helping the listener to discover what the sayer wanted to say. The conversion may take a long time, but it will always come from within. The convert discovers that the conversion has been taking place.

The pro-life activist is required to be a specially sensitive, patient and gentle person, therefore – and faces many challenges.

The first is to remain convinced of the enormity of killing the unborn, manufacturing human beings in IVF laboratories, scrutinising and discarding "substandard" human embryos and deep-freezing "spares", surrogacy, cloning and all the other ways in which the right to life and human dignity are violated – while yet having deeply-felt compassion for many of those caught up in all these misdeeds and hatred for none of them.

An unintended pregnancy, at least initially, can seem to be a disaster. This can be true even in a happy and stable marriage. How much more so if the circumstances are less favourable. For a young woman about to go to university or on the brink of a subsequent career, for instance, it will seem like a death. She may turn to abortion to spare boyfriend and siblings shame and loving parents heartbreak, as much as for any "selfish" reason. She does so because there does not seem to be any alternative. The idea of "going it alone" as an unsupported mother is unthinkable; and it is no use saying that she should have thought about this before becoming sexually active. She is the creature of the permissive society, of value-free sex education promoted by successive Governments since the 1960s and of the ruthless sex industry which dominates so much of today's culture.

It is wrong to portray all doctors and nurses engaged in the abortion trade as brutes. Some may be. Abortion is big business. Some of the private clinics are probably staffed by dregs of the medical profession who are making big bucks out of what they are doing, day after day. Abortion charities like BPAS and Marie Stopes have profitable "agency agreements" with the NHS by which abortions are done in the private sector at the taxpayers' expense. (These agencies are effectively given open cheques by the State in payment for their services; and GPs in turn receive commissions for referring patients to them.) Many women report that their abortion clinic was a callous place and they were treated almost as cattle. But pro-lifers have to accept that many abortion-providers are convinced that what they are doing is delivering women and girls from desperate plights – profoundly wrong-headed though they may be in so believing.

A pregnant woman diagnosed as carrying a severely disabled child will probably come under disgraceful pressure to abort; and only those who have been unable to conceive will fully know how desperate a couple may become to end their childlessness by seeking the IVF clinic. IVF doctors, like the pioneers, Steptoe and Edwards, may be convinced that theirs is a loving response to others' suffering.

Much of what claims to be compassion is no doubt bogus – because largely self-regarding. But that is beside the point. What follows from all this is that there is a moral duty on the pro-life movement to do all it can to provide the positive alternative to the wrongdoing happening around it. Unless accompanied by a pro-life pregnancy care service, anti-abortion preaching will sound hollow, if not sanctimonious. Pro-lifers cannot simply wring their hands over the evils of IVF; they must strive to provide a pro-life way of overcoming childlessness. And so on.

Pro-lifers rightly accuse their opponents of being obsessed with women's "rights" to the exclusion of others'. "Pro-choicers" in turn accuse pro-lifers of a similar tunnel vision: one which focuses only on the child. There is some truth in this second charge also. A false polarisation has sometimes damaged pro-life efforts. The authentic Gospel of Life is both pro-woman and pro-child, and regards mother and child as equally precious.

The old dictum about loving the sinner while hating the sin is of relevance here and brings us to a question which has long vexed the pro-life movement: how hard-hitting and militant should it be?

Marches, rallies and roadside chains may have value but only if organised on a large scale and conducted with dignity. As for picketing of abortion clinics, those taking part have to answer two questions: why am I doing this? and what impact will it have on passers-by, the clinic staff and its clients? The desire to threaten and punish, though subconscious, may be hard at work and it is easy for small handfuls of protestors to look like cranks. It is easy to *seem* to intimidate. It is difficult to ignore taunts.

We must ask similar questions about the use of shocking visual material – photos of aborted children, videos like *The Silent Scream* and *The Hard Truth*. These have their place in the pro-life armoury. But they must be used with great sensitivity. They may complete a conversion – and confirm existing pro-life convictions – but will they initiate one? Probably not. They must not be used indiscriminately or prematurely. If they do they will alienate, close minds and confirm the convenient belief that pro-lifers are misogynistic fanatics. Pro-lifers are naturally angered by the mass destruction and trivialisation of human life which is taking place all around them. But that anger must be contained. The desire to hit people hard and to shock is a way of venting it, exasperation and even hatred, and relieves those involved but damages their cause.

The sinner is not now being loved. To say this is not to have gone "soft": it is to have become wiser.

* * *

Anyone who has presented the pro-life case to a new audience will know that the same few questions (what about rape? what if the mother will die? what of the disabled child? what about backstreet abortion? isn't it a woman's right?)

come up again and again as if via some subliminal programming. It is difficult to deal patiently and courteously with them over and over again.

It is even more difficult to remain calm in the face of pro-abortionists' attempts to justify themselves: "the child is merely a dependent being", "the child is part of the mother", "most people agree with abortion therefore it is right", "pro-lifers do not have to have abortions so they cannot object" and so on. We will consider these claims later. For the present consider three examples of deviousness which, since they came from Establishment sources, are especially egregious.

First, around 1990 when IVF, etc was about to be legalised by the Human Fertilisation and Embryology Act we suddenly started hearing about the "pre-embryo", that is (presumably) a stage of human life which was even less deserving of respect than an embryo. Who first invented this we will never know. "Pre-embryo", however, was soon quickly assigned to the scientific trash can. It had done its work.

That 1990 Act was the direct fruit of the Committee chaired by Mary Warnock set up to review the issues surrounding new techniques of assisted reproduction and to provide the intellectual foundation for the later legislation. After promising in its introduction to engage in rigorous moral reasoning the Report soon had to turn to the question, the burning question, of whether the human embryo is truly a human being. "Although the question of when human life or personhood begin appear to be questions of fact susceptible of straightforward answers", the Report notes, "we hold that the answers to such questions are complex amalgams of factual and moral judgements". It then goes on to make this astonishing statement: "Instead of trying to answer these questions directly we have therefore gone straight to the question of how it is right to treat the human embryo". (*Report of the Committee of Enquiry on Human Fertilisation and Embryology* (1984), para 11.9) How could the distinguished members of this Committee be party to the absurd suggestion that one can know how something is to be treated without knowing what that thing is, i.e. what its moral status is? How can one begin to deal with such intellectual sleight of hand? Did the Committee believe it could get away with it?

A more brazen conjuring trick had already been performed in 1983. Worried lest post-coital contraception (so-called) such as the Morning-after-Pill – which the manufacturers concede had a "fail-safe" abortive action – could come within the scope of the Abortion Act, the Government, abetted by the pharmaceutical industry, decided to re-write an important portion of human biology.

The Offences against the Person Act 1861, which, it should be recalled, was still the central piece of legislation concerning abortion, had not spoken of the "abortion" but of "procuring a miscarriage". It was decided to take advantage of this fact in a remarkable way. As the Attorney General Michael

Havers explained to the House of Commons, miscarriage cannot occur before carriage, which is true enough. He went on to say something obviously untrue: there can be no carriage unless the thing carried is attached to the carrier. This, he claimed, was what "carriage" meant in common parlance – and it was patent nonsense. (The Attorney General was doubtless carrying some money when he made this statement, but that money was not attached to him). In the case of the human embryo "attachment" meant implantation; hence, he ruled, there could be no abortion before implantation and hence anything that prevented implantation, i.e. killed before it, was not abortive.[1] Thus post-coital contraception was merely contraceptive even though it could destroy life already begun and not merely prevent its beginning.

There was more to come. As the Minister for Health, Sir Gerard Vaughan, explained in several letters to LIFE, we must distinguish between fertilisation and conception. We have been wrong to believe for centuries that they were one and the same thing. Conception begins when the embryo attaches, i.e. begins to implant (even though it was already known as a *conceptus*). Pregnancy begins then, too, we were now being told. So for centuries we have erroneously supposed that the average pregnancy lasts 266 days. It lasts several fewer. Implantation is a process lasting several days but we were never told whether conception/pregnancy begins at the start or the completion of the process.

Amazingly, all this has now become official doctrine[2]. But gestational age, which all the English-speaking world except Canada and the USA reckon to be "real age" plus two weeks (i.e. from the last menstrual period), is still used to measure the length of a pregnancy for the purposes of the Abortion Act. So an unborn child who is really, say, 10 weeks old (that is, conceived ten weeks previously) is 12 weeks old for the purposes of the Act and, according to the "New Biology" is presumably only 9 weeks. We are in a muddle, thanks to this unblushing example of re-writing science to serve political purposes.

* * *

Much forbearance is required when greeted with the "seamless garment" argument. It is a favourite particularly of Christians who are not really pro-life but will not admit the fact. It runs thus: abortion is one of many urgent issues facing us: Third World poverty and neo-colonialism, economic exploitation by Big Business, social injustice, racism, religious intolerance, sexism, abuse of the environment and so on. It cannot be isolated from the rest because fundamentally these are all "justice" issues.

1. *Hansard* (Commons, Written Answers), 10 May 1983, cols 236-7.
2. Thus all the medical dictionaries quickly re-wrote their definitions of "conception", "fertilisation" and "pregnancy" (with varying thoroughness) in deference to the "New Biology". But gynaecologists and the general public ignored it. The story of this "con" is told with admirable gusto by John R Ling in *The Morning-after pill. Uncovering the truth* (2007), pp 22ff.

That, of course, is true. What is untrue is the implication that we cannot tackle the abortion issue until we have dealt with the others or that we should not prioritise. Because we cannot do everything should we do nothing? In fact, many well-known pro-lifers are also distinguished campaigners for other good causes precisely because their commitment to fighting the injustice of abortion leads them to challenge the injustice of, for example, persecution of Christians in much of Asia, Third World debt, sex slavery. But they, like the many other pro-lifers who have not the resources to be heavily engaged in other causes, rightly argue that the abortion issue and all that now goes with it, because it involves the destruction of human life on a massive scale and is happening here and now on our own doorstep, has a special urgency.

The "seamless garment" argument is as shabby a way of avoiding a politically incorrect cause as the "personally, I am against it, but I won't stop others getting it. I won't impose my views on others" line. This, too, is unacceptable. The reasons for being personally (i.e. privately) opposed are reasons for also being publicly opposed. How we would mock someone who said "personally I'm against rape but I won't stop rapists raping". We cannot compartmentalise ourselves morally like that.

Opponents of the pro-life cause try to demonise pro-lifers by accusing them of wanting to "impose their views" on others and persecute women. They do not and could not do so even if they did. They want their fellow-citizens to come to see that abortion is wrong, is unworthy of a civilised society, and freely to reject it. They want society to outgrow abortionism as it did, for example, the Atlantic slave trade. They want fellow-citizens to see that there is a better way of dealing with the crisis pregnancy and that abortion does not liberate women (far from it). They want Parliament to protect women and unborn children by imposing sufficient penalties for "procuring miscarriage" to deter any doctor or para-medic – not the woman – from engaging in illicit activity.

More sophisticated opponents – usually Christians (especially Catholics) who want to get off the hook – try to discredit pro-lifers with a bit of historical theology. They point out that it was in 1869 that Rome (Pope Pius IX) imposed an absolute ban on all abortion, that there had been toing and froing on the matter in previous centuries and that most of the Fathers of the Church, and most medieval theologians, including the mighty St Thomas Aquinas, believed in "delayed animation" that is, taught that the immortal rational soul enters the body several weeks after conception. In the latter's view, therefore, fully human life does not begin until then and abortion before the body is "formed", that is, ensouled, is not truly homicide. So pro-lifers are more Roman than Rome, it is claimed, and by failing to distinguish between life that is human but not yet humanised, i.e. not yet *personal*, are out of step with Tradition.

How much of this is true? Only some. Yes, Pius IX imposed automatic excommunication for all abortion in 1869 – or rather, re-imposed it. That had been the penalty for centuries until Sixtus V relaxed the law in 1591 and restricted the penalty to abortions of a "formed" child. One suspects that he, like some contemporary moral theologians, may have been wrestling with the case of a pregnancy which is threatening the mother's life and cannot be sustained until the child is viable – in which case, because the child is doomed, the doctor is not choosing between mother and child (as he does in therapeutic abortion), but between two deaths and one. But Pius IX "invented" nothing.

It is also true that many Fathers and scholastics believed in "delayed" rather than "immediate" animation. They did so largely under the influence of the Greek polymath Aristotle (and Galen) who, on the basis of empirical research using fetal corpses, concluded that what was destined to be human life received initially a vegetable "form," then an animal one and finally a rational one (the human soul). He also decided on the evidence before him that the male is finally ensouled around 42 days after fertilisation and the female some weeks later.

Such was Aristotle's authority as a scientist, and pretty well everything else, that his views were accepted by many of the Fathers and later Christian theologians such as Thomas Aquinas. But – and this is the crucial fact which is repeatedly missed by those who would use Aquinas and others as a stick with which to beat pro-lifers – it was never argued by these Aristotelians that abortion was permissible up to the moment of ensoulment (animation). Before that moment an abortion would not be exactly homicide, but it would be gravely sinful nonetheless. Ensoulment was not a dividing-line between permissible and impermissible abortion[3].

It is more than wearisome to have to explain this again and again to people who really should know better than to repeat errors which have been carefully pointed out to them.

As we shall see[4], the distinction between "human" and "humanised", "human life" and "personal life" is equally specious: too clever by half – but equally taxing of pro-lifers' patience.

* * *

Pro-life activism is not confined to refuting others. The most exciting challenge it faces is to take the initiative and proclaim themselves as tomorrow's people. They are the radical democrats, the ones who have seen a great light.

---

2. It is interesting that none of those who misinterpret Catholic theologians on this issue seems to have read Connery, *Abortion: the Development of the Roman Catholic Perspective* (Chicago, 1977). Though not the most readable of books, it is a comprehensive account of Catholic teaching down the centuries and a thorough refutation of those who claim that it has been inconsistent.

4. below pp 20f.

Today we marvel that, in the past, apparently ordinary, decent people could approve of slavery, serfdom or apartheid; could, indeed, even regard them as divinely ordained. We now deplore the idea of "Untermenschen" (human beings written off as sub-standard) or of "life unworthy of life". But it is not so long ago that many otherwise enlightened people assented to them. We now confidently denounce racism, but at the height of the British Empire every good Englishman was convinced of his racial superiority. We reject many other forms of discrimination which in the past were applauded or at least regarded as part of the natural order. We reckon that we have outgrown them and come to see that this is progress, because they were incompatible with our sense of natural justice and the unity of humankind.

Will we not outgrow abortionism for exactly the same reason? To exclude a whole segment of the human family – the unborn – from the protection of the law is as unjust as, say, slavery.

Abortion is yesterday's response to a problem: a bloody, violent one. We recognise instinctively that moral progress consists in finding non-violent ways of conducting our affairs. We are glad, for instance, that disputes can be settled in law courts and not with daggers and fists. We rejoice that bloody wars between England and Scotland or England and France, once endemic, are now behind us.

Pro-lifers are the really pro-women people. They have seen the truth of what abortion does to the dignity and integrity of a woman – and how the sexual revolution, of which abortionism is an essential element, has not so much given women control over their bodies as made them more available to men, more exploitable by the predatory male, than ever before. Radical feminists have betrayed their sisters. And pro-lifers are the only ones who are telling the truth about the mental and physical harm that abortion does.

There will come a time when people will rub their eyes and say of our fellow citizens, "How could they do it? How could they be so blind? How could they not see that what they were saying about unborn children (that they were not really human beings, have no souls, etc) echoed exactly what previous societies had said about those whom they wished to exploit? How could they proclaim their commitment to human rights and at the same time deny a whole section of society, the unborn, the most fundamental right – the right to life?"

It is only the Gospel of Life which will cure our age of such moral schizophrenia and create a society in which everyone can feel fundamentally safe because we have finally rejected the idea that there can be "sort of " human beings. And even as all human life has been accorded the full, equal protection of the law, so women will have achieved their full, unique dignity.

This is the message which the pro-lifer has to deliver, gently and patiently, to the world. The world will listen only if the people delivering it have themselves been made nicer people by it.

II.

THE PROGRESS OF LIFE

LIFE was founded in August 1970 to do two things for the first time; to take an absolutist stance against abortion, that is, to reject all abortion, and to set up a nationwide pro-life pregnancy care service. Unless abortion was rejected in principle there could be no intellectually coherent case against it. Unless refused to even the hardest of the hard cases, it would soon be permitted to most; and unless those who were taking such a bold (and, to some, heartless) stand were prepared to provide a positive alternative to abortion and to open their arms unconditionally to any woman facing a crisis pregnancy, their anti-abortion words would easily sound hollow, if not worse.

LIFE was from the start a non-denominational, lay movement. Its pro-life pregnancy care service was the first in the UK, probably the world. There were, of course, many mother and baby homes run by the Churches, lay charities and local authorities. But what LIFE set up was different, a counselling and support service inspired by the Samaritans. It was for long the only pro-life movement which combined educational/political *and* caring work. In the USA, for instance, the two were kept distinct and even at arm's length from each other. But LIFE's argument was that each needed the other. If there could on occasion seem to be (and maybe really was) a tension between them, this was a price that must be afforded.

LIFE chose its name long before the word "pro-life" was coined (in the USA). It was an inspired choice. As the saying goes, it says it all. And as the different forms of attack on human life multiplied remorselessly thereafter, the name became ever more apt.

Most of the first members of LIFE also supported the Society for the Protection of Unborn Children, set up in 1967 to counter David Steel's Abortion Bill. Its leading founders, Lord Barrington and Elspeth Chowdharay Best (as she later became on marrying), are the pioneers of the UK pro-life movement. LIFE was started with the full knowledge and generous approval of SPUC, which saw it as complementary, not a rival. Indeed, Lord Barrington chaired some of LIFE's earliest public meetings.

The movement grew rapidly. There were over fifty LIFE Groups by 1975 and 100 – most running a local care service – by 1980. Most care services were run from town- or city-centre premises and were staffed by volunteers. Most LIFE Groups had a local family or two who could take in girls who had been made homeless by pregnancy or wanted to keep their pregnancies secret (and to have their babies adopted). In 1973 LIFE acquired its first house – in Coventry. It was the gift of a Catholic priest whose generosity was legendary. In 1977 the Housing (Homeless Persons) Act was passed which imposed new responsibility on local authorities for tackling homelessness and required priority to be given to homeless pregnant women. This was a heaven-sent opportunity for LIFE. Dozens of local authorities, seeing that LIFE Groups could help them discharge their new statutory responsibilities, leased houses (usually with three or four bedrooms) to LIFE. Thanks to the same Act, LIFE even obtained a Government grant – admittedly a minuscule one over three years – to make possible the appointment of a national housing officer. At the same time LIFE Housing was set up as a registered charity, its trustees being the national officers of LIFE. LIFE Housing Trust was soon expanded to become the LIFE Care and Housing Trust, primarily so that the care centres could enjoy the mandatory 80 per cent local rates relief and donors to the care service could covenant their donations.

In 1981 LIFE was set up in Northern Ireland: a momentous event because from the start LIFE NI was – and has since always been – supra-sectarian, bringing together Christians of almost every denomination, some of whom had never even talked to one another, let alone worked together. The pro-life cause transcended confessional divides in an admirable way. Though the Abortion Act did not extend to the Province there was plenty of work to do, including countering the attempts of the pro-abortion lobby to capture this abortion-free zone. Belfast LIFE quickly acquired a handsome care centre in the city and a LIFE house, entered enthusiastically into educational work and nurtured new Groups across the Province.

There were soon LIFE Groups and care centres in almost all the cities and major towns of the UK, all wholly sustained by supporters' subscriptions. LIFE's first headquarters had been a bedroom in a private house. This was replaced by rented office accommodation (still in Leamington Spa) in 1977. In 1989 LIFE decided to own its HQ and acquired a stylish self-contained building in the centre of the town.

Meanwhile all LIFE Groups, with varying degrees of success, had been engaged in local pro-life educational work – an essential concomitant of their care service. A team of often heroic volunteers were taking the pro-life message to local schools and colleges, and any group who would have them, armed with an increasingly sophisticated range of visual aids: posters and slides, then videos, fetal models – as well as leaflets, LIFE pens and rulers and badges.

* * *

The pro-life movement in Britain seeks the repeal of the Abortion Act 1967. It is not intent on putting the clocks back to a pre-1967 time. It wants to put the clock forward to a society which has repudiated abortionism and come to see that the LIFE way of responding to the crisis pregnancy is the right way. Though in 1991 the LIFE Care and Housing Trust changed its name and became simply "LIFE" and the former non-charitable LIFE handed over all its assets to the "new" charity, this is still what LIFE sees as the ultimate fruit of its labours.

Two questions immediately arise. First, is it permissible to proceed step by step or must one go for the whole hog and nothing less? Secondly, if the step-by-step approach is chosen, what should those steps be?

It had always been supposed that, given the realities of the political scene, there was no alternative to gradualism and that any measure which saved even a few lives would be welcome. Of course, there was the danger that a minimal measure could make matters worse in the longer term because it would sedate the public conscience and postpone a more significant improvement to the law. So each case would have to be judged on its own merits – and the judgements would be political ones. But anything which really reduced the amount of injustice should be supported, even though it left things still seriously imperfect. Provided pro-lifers remained committed to achieving complete justice – the full protection of the law for human life from fertilisation – they would not have compromised their principles by working for piecemeal amendments. This is so obvious to most people that it scarcely needs to be explained. Recently, however, an attempt has been made to argue that, if pro-lifers accept anything less than an absolute ban, they are colluding in abortionism. This is far-fetched.

There were two possible kinds of amendment: making abortion less readily available by tightening the conditions under which abortion could be performed or by reducing the upper-age limits for abortion. The former was tried first.

In 1975 a Scottish MP, James White, made the first attempt to amend the law by replacing the most-invoked criterion of the Act (that "continuance of the pregnancy would involve risk, greater than if the pregnancy were terminated, to the physical or mental health of the woman,") with a clause requiring simply " a risk of serious injury to the woman". At first sight, this would have been an important improvement because that section of the Act (as no doubt its author had intended) had proved completely permissive. But there was a problem – and one which produced a sharp disagreement among pro-lifers. As LIFE warned, "risk of serious injury" would achieve nothing. There had to be a *substantial* risk of serious injury if the new criterion was to have any effect. The degree of risk as well as the size of the risk had to be quantified, otherwise the slightest risk would "qualify". James White, like others, failed to see this point.

In the event, the White Bill was sent – most unusually – to a Select Committee (to which LIFE gave evidence). This was the idea of the then minister for Health, Dr David Owen. He promised that, if the Committee had not completed its work by the end of the current session it would be immediately re-established at the beginning of the next. It did not complete its work by then. When Parliament re-assembled Dr Owen failed to honour his promise. Only after furious protest did he relent: a clear forewarning of the dirty tricks the pro-abortion lobby would be ready to employ.

The White Bill nonetheless failed. Several more attempts to tighten the law were made by pro-life (or more or less pro-life) MPs who had won a high place in the Private Members' Ballot, notably by John Corrie, another Scot, in 1979. This was the most ambitious measure, reviving the White clause (with the addition at last of "substantial"!) and requiring that pregnancy advisory services be financially separate from private-sector abortion providers. The Bill aroused intense, sometimes chaotic, debate. Though John Corrie was not a great orator or politically skilled, his Bill made steady progress to its committee stage, but then failed.

In 1987 the young David Alton, having won a high place in the Ballot, decided to enter the fray with a Bill to reduce the upper age-limit from 28 to 18 weeks. The two Davids (Steel and Alton) were both Liberals and both in their day had been the youngest MP in the House. There was therefore a special poignancy that one should now be challenging the other's work. The decision to go for a "weeks" Bill rather than attempt a re-run of Corrie *et al* was made because it seemed to have a much better chance of success. "Criteria" Bills had got nowhere and another one would see battle-lines immediately, predictably, re-drawn. It would suffer from the same difficulty as its predecessors: though "substantial" and "serious" were already used in the Act, they are inexact words. Since the 1967 Act had made play of the fact that its purpose was to *clarify* as well as amend the law, a new basic criterion using those words would be vulnerable to the charge that it re-introduced uncertainty – whereas an 18-week rule would be precise and objective. Since many MPs subscribed to the popular (but illogical) view that an unborn child should be protected once viability was reached and since, thanks to medical advances, the age of viability had been steadily coming down, there was a good chance that even the less hard-line pro-abortionists would accept a lowering of the upper age-limit. They might baulk at 18 weeks. But 20, 21 weeks would be better than nothing.

The BABY ("Back Alton's Bill – Yes") campaign was the most impressive of all LIFE's political efforts, thanks above all to the charismatic leadership which David Alton gave it. A compelling speaker, tireless and politically accomplished, he combined a highly professional campaign in Parliament with a whirlwind tour of Britain to address enthusiastic public meetings and deft use of friends in the media. Meanwhile MPs were bombarded with letters from their pro-life constituents to back the Bill or at least abstain from voting against it.

A controversial private member's Bill has little chance of success unless granted Government time, as was David Steel's twenty years previously. But no Government, certainly not Mrs Thatcher's, was going to give the Alton Bill that privilege and, despite all the enormous effort, it was talked out – ambushed, gunned down by a pro-abortion lobby determined that their sacred cow should suffer no let or hindrance.

Shortly after the Alton Bill had been defeated the Government introduced what was to become the Human Fertilisation and Embryology Act 1990.

Though this was concerned with licensing *in vitro* fertilisation and embryo research the Act emerged with significant amendments to the Abortion Act tacked on to it. These reduced the upper age-limit from 28 to 24 weeks – but excepted eugenic abortion and abortion to save the mother from serious permanent injury or to save her life. Abortion on these grounds could now be performed up to birth, a lamentable setback for the pro-life cause.

It would subsequently be claimed by some pro-lifers (not LIFE) that the disaster was a direct consequence of the Alton Bill's failure. That Bill, some said, had anyway been a misguided initiative by an inexperienced young MP who had been swayed by bad advice. But this is to re-write history. The truth is rather different – and more complicated.

In 1929 Parliament passed the Infant Life (Preservation) Act. This made it an offence (of "child destruction") deliberately to kill an unborn child "capable of being born alive". The Act stated that the fact that a pregnancy had lasted some 28 weeks or more constituted *prima facie* proof that the child was so capable. In other words, after 28 weeks the onus of proof would be on the defence to show that the child had not been capable of being born alive; before then the onus would be on the prosecution to show that the child had been. Since the Abortion Act 1967 left this earlier Act unaffected, the latter had provided the 28-week age-limit on legalised abortion after 1967.

Following the failure of complicated "criteria" Bills like John Corrie's it was generally agreed in pro-life circles that only a simple, one-clause bill had any chance of success. LIFE therefore proposed the following amendment to the Infant Life (Preservation) Act: "for the words 'twenty-eight weeks' are substituted 'twenty-four/twenty-two/twenty (according as deemed possible) weeks' ". This would not achieve much, but it would have been a start – and it would save a few lives. LIFE thereafter repeatedly argued that this could be the way forward, at first with the enthusiastic agreement of Sir Bernard Braine, MP, the chairman of the All-Party Parliamentary Pro-Life Committee (as it then was – now it is a Group).

In the mid-1970s a pro-life lawyer called Michael Bell formed the Association of Lawyers for the Defence of the Unborn (ALDU). He was a member of LIFE and had for a while thought about calling his venture "LIFE Lawyers" (to match LIFE Doctors and LIFE Anglicans) but it was eventually agreed that it would be better to have a free-standing association whose brief would be to mobilise pro-life opinion within the legal profession independently of any existing pro-life organisation. As well as joining in the debate on the legal status of the unborn child and the human embryo, ALDU gave close attention to the implications of that 1929 Act and was soon arguing that it provided the best weapon for the pro-life movement. Since the Act protected any child capable of being born alive and since, a child of 20, 15, 12 or even fewer weeks could live for a few minutes if prematurely ejected from the womb, most abortions done under the 1967 Act, ALDU argued, were unlawful. Therefore the right way forward for the pro-life movement was to get existing law enforced, not to strive to change it.

This became accepted doctrine among much of the pro-life movement, especially the senior pro-life political leaders whose constant cry became "let's just concentrate on simply getting the law (i.e. the 1929 Act) enforced." However, attempts to put this into practice were unsuccessful. On several occasions LIFE tried to challenge the lawfulness of abortions which had been carried out at 23 or 24 weeks in the courts, but the prosecuting authorities always refused to act on the ground that, since the presumption of the law was that a child was not capable of being born alive before 28 weeks, there was little chance of a successful prosecution[1]. Eventually, in a famous case in 1987 where a father tried to stop his 24-week unborn child from being aborted by invoking the 1929 Act the judge ruled that "capable of being born alive" meant capable of surviving outside the womb without artificial support and that the prosecution would have to show that this particular child was so capable. It would not be enough to claim that children of that age were normally viable.

That was that. ALDU's way forward proved to be a cul-de-sac. Furthermore, it had drawn much attention to the 1929 Act. No doubt the vigour of David Alton's campaign had alarmed its opponents – but by 1990 it was very much past history. However, "capable of being born alive" was not. The pro-abortion lobby had only just managed to contain the campaign launched with it. Since it was clear that viability had come down to 24 or 23 weeks, it was only a matter of time before the 1929 law would be changed to protect children of that age – or, to be safe, of 21 or 22 weeks. Moreover, if someone discovered how to enable the lungs of even younger children to function, there would be pressure to reduce the upper age-limit even further.

1. Thus, over the years, LIFE has reported to the police six cases of premature, but viable, children, having been denied food or care after birth in English hospitals, including one born live at 28 weeks after a prostaglandin abortion who survived unaided for 12 hours; but the prosecuting authorities always refused to act. LIFE also complained about a doctor who openly boasted about aborting children after 24 weeks but no action was taken against him. The most egregious case was in 1986, when a doctor in Luton aborted a child of over 30 weeks' gestation by prostaglandins. The child was afterwards heard crying in the sluice room in which she had been dumped, but the doctor sat on a commode outside to prevent anyone rescuing her. LIFE reported him to the police. He was arrested and charged – but acquitted at the committal stage on the ground that, because her mother had been overweight, he had misjudged the child's age (he had not done a scan – conveniently) and he had sat on the commode because exhausted by a hard day's work.

LIFE had also challenged the lawfulness of "selective pregnancy reduction" (i.e. the random stabbing to death of "surplus" children resulting from multiple insertion of embryos in the womb in IVF procedures). This was declared lawful in 1990. In 1983 LIFE had challenged the first use – by a London hospital – of the morning-after pill. LIFE had argued that, since this had an abortive function, its use should be subject to the Abortion Act; whereupon the Attorney General ordered the DPP not to proceed – and reported to Parliament – on the ground that miscarriage (i.e. abortion) could not be procured before implantation. This, he said (absurdly), was because something could not be carried unless it was attached to the carrier. As we have said (above p5), he asked us to believe that this was the "popular, ordinary and natural sense" of the word "carriage".

So what happened in 1990 was this. As a sop to public opinion and a "pre-emptive strike" against the pro-life forces, the age-limit for most abortions was lowered to 24 weeks. But the amended Abortion Act then went on to provide that the 1929 Act would henceforth not apply to doctors (and so would be deprived of its original purpose). Abortion of special-needs children, or where there was a grave threat to the mother's life or health, would have no time-limit, that is, could be performed up to birth. That they were indeed capable of being born alive and surviving without oxygen support would no longer provide any protection[2].

The dangerous Infant Life (Preservation) Act had had its teeth drawn.

* * *

Following the collapse of the Communist empire in 1989, LIFE worked hard to help fledgling pro-life movements to develop in Romania, the Czech Republic, Slovakia and Latvia. Individual LIFE activists travelled repeatedly to these countries to provide training in pro-life education and pregnancy care – usually in the "LIFEmobile", a Ford transit van, and delivered food, clothes and simple medical supplies (tens of thousands of aspirin tablets to Romania, for instance). Pro-lifers from Croatia, Russia and Romania, and elsewhere, were guests at LIFE National Conferences. More recently, LIFE has been helping further afield – in Malta and Sri Lanka, for example – and has trained counsellors from the Seychelles. All this has confirmed an important fact which relations with pro-life organisations in the USA, Australia, etc had long made clear: the pro-life movement is a worldwide groundswell, the work of ordinary, "little" people rarely supported by the great and good, and usually battling against much of the media and the Establishment. We have even heard recently of the first stirrings of pro-life activism in China.

The 1990s saw far-reaching changes to LIFE's inner workings. In the early days, for instance, its educational work was done by volunteers (members of local LIFE Groups). It was soon necessary to establish the rule that no one should speak in public in the name of LIFE in schools or on radio and TV who had not been "approved" and received training. But, like all

2. The detailed sequence of events is complicated but worth repeating. In January 1987 Hugh Montefiore, Anglican bishop of Birmingham, suddenly introduced a Bill into the Lords to amend the 1929 Act and reduce the abortion upper age-limit from 28 to 24 weeks. He had previously been no friend of the pro-life cause. The Government supported his measure. Frightened by this, the wily Lord Houghton (husband of Vera and ardently pro-abortion) managed to get the Bill sent to a Select Committee, to which he and leading pro-abortion peers, including Lady Warnock, were appointed. That Committee recommended in March 1988 that the Bill "should not proceed" and that there should be no time-limit for abortion at all as far as doctors were concerned. By remarkable sleight-of-hand, after the failure of the Alton Bill in May 1988, that recommendation was grafted on to the amended Abortion Act, which in turn was grafted on to the Human Embryology and Fertilisation Act 1990. The octogenarian Douglas Houghton and others used the Alton Bill as a smokescreen to cover his much deeper conspiracy to de-criminalise abortion at any age by emasculating the 1929 Act. It was the Montefiore Bill, not the Alton one, which had enabled him and his fellow "conspirators" to do so.

charities, LIFE was now finding that the supply of volunteers was drying up and they had to be replaced by paid workers. At the same time, as the team of young, carefully selected and trained Education Officers was forming – from around 2000 onwards – the scope and nature of LIFE Education work was undergoing profound development: abortion, designer babies, the epidemic of sexually-transmitted diseases remain at its centre, of course, but now set in the context of "relationships" – which asks young people to ask themselves what sort of person they want to be and what sort of society they want to live in, and to explore the nature of true happiness. It invites them to ask questions of themselves that they may have perhaps never confronted. It brings them to the Gospel of Life in an unexpected way. It enables them to discover the pro-life light within themselves. LIFE schools talks, especially the all-day school conferences, are helping to create a new, pro-life generation (but there is, of course, much more to be done than finances yet permit).

At the same time LIFE's care service has been undergoing similar professionalisation. Not least because opponents try to argue that LIFE's counselling is not and cannot be non-directive and would dearly love to have the authorities clamp down on any pro-life care services, but more importantly because clients deserve only the best, it has long been policy to require LIFE counsellors to undergo externally validated training courses. But standards rise inexorably. A fully professionalised service now requires diplomas and certificates, in-service training and supervision, and so on. At the same time, largely because people now expect to do so much by telephone, texting and online, there has been a marked shift in client behaviour: fewer women making first contact face to face in a LIFE care centre, more using the National Hotline (set up in 1991), email and texting.

A yet more radical change has overtaken LIFE Housing. Originally LIFE's houses were run by part-time volunteers (LIFE members) and overseen by local LIFE Housing Committees who were responsible for their day-to-day management, including their finances. But by 2000 things were very different. Thanks to the Government's Supporting People Programme, LIFE houses were offering much more than a roof over heads. The residents (or "service users", as the jargon has it) were to receive training in a wide range of life-skills (hygiene, cooking, budgeting, IT skills, etc) to prepare them for independent living and a new structure of trained, paid Support Workers and Life Skills Coordinators came into being to deliver this service to the clients during and after their residence – and to non-residents. All this was made possible by greatly increased Government funding and this inevitably meant more bureaucracy. Such was the complexity of making bids and returns that finances had to be centralised. As ever-more training and supervision were required – and ever-more appraisal and record-keeping – the day-to-day management of LIFE Housing inevitably passed from Groups to the centre. And as the amount of bureaucracy escalated, so LIFE Housing's staff expanded. LIFE houses are still an integral part of LIFE's care service and LIFE Groups still have an important pastoral contribution to make to them. But things have changed.

Over the years 1973 to 2000 more than 5000 women and their children, born and unborn, have been accommodated in these houses. The National Hotline and LIFE Care Centres have received over one and a half million serious calls for help.

Talk about how many unborn children have been "saved" is distasteful to many even if an accurate figure could be given. But it would not be vain boasting to claim that there are thousands of children and young people alive today who *might* not have seen the light of day if LIFE had not been "there" at a critical moment in their mothers' lives and many thousands of women who, if LIFE had not enabled them to escape panic and pressures of others and to discover what they really wanted, would probably have gone down the abortion road.

* * *

The cardinal principle of LIFE had from the first, as has been said, been that it is not enough to speak out against wrong-doing. We have to roll up our sleeves to provide a positive alternative to it. This had inspired the LIFE pregnancy care service. It inspired two more initiatives.

To a pro-lifer, IVF and all that goes with it – embryo scrutiny and selection, embryo freezing, throwing away of "spares, surrogacy, etc – are morally objectionable, because profoundly incompatible with the respect which is due to all human life, big or small. But unless pro-lifers recognise the anguish which childlessness can cause and are ready to strive to provide an alternative, those objections will remain "academic" and carry little weight.

It was therefore urgent that the pro-life cause should develop an alternative to IVF. A pro-life embryologist proposed a technique for overcoming blocked or non-existent fallopian tubes, later known as NEST – natural egg selective transfer – which involved using an ultra-sound scanner to pick up a newly-matured ovum, taking it past the blocked or non-existent tube and depositing it at the top of the uterine cavity. In 1994 a Catholic order of nuns, the Sisters of Mercy, gave LIFE a magnificent building in Liverpool which became the first LIFE Health Centre. Here NEST was first attempted. It was not successful. Soon afterwards, however, two midwives who had been key figures in the NEST programme, having heard about the Napro (Natural Procreation) Technology pioneered by an American gynaecologist, Dr Thomas Hilgers, raised money to begin training in a new treatment for female infertility. Eventually a team of US-trained "practitioners" and a physician had been assembled and the LIFE FertilityCare Programme (LFP) launched. There was now a truly pro-life alternative to IVF – one that was safer, "greener", successful and, morally speaking, completely acceptable. The first LFP baby was born in 1999.

The new LIFE Health Centre made possible another initiative: Zoë's Place. For years, indeed, since the trial of Dr Leonard Arthur in 1981[3], the conviction had been growing that it was not enough to denounce eugenic abortion and neonatal euthanasia. The pressures on a mother to abort an unborn child who had been diagnosed as seriously abnormal were enormous. The discovery that she had been delivered of, say, a child suffering from some mysterious syndrome or, say, spina bifida was increasingly hard to bear because prenatal screening had re-awakened old prejudices and fears which society in recent generations (before the coming of abortionism) had done much to overcome. The parents of a special-needs child had to cope not only with their grief and, all-too often, the primitive belief that they were being punished for something. There was now shame and the not always unspoken inference of others that they were irresponsible in bringing such a child into the world. A pro-lifer knows that the disabled have a prophetic role: to remind society of values which increased materialism and hedonism obscures. But a pro-lifer also knows that a disabled child can "disable" a whole family.

If LIFE was to be true to its foundation principle, a loving positive alternative to what the world provided – and one which would give support to parents who had the courage to defy the world – had to be found.

A Zoë's Place is a special haven for special-needs children aged 0 to 5 years. The "philosophy" behind it is that a children's hospice (which caters for young people up to18 years) may often not be the right environment for very small, vulnerable children. These need tailor-made provision. So do their parents. Simply because a Zoë's Place specialises in providing palliative care – respite and terminal – for the very young, parents can give and receive much mutual support and quickly be confident that their children are safe. Zoë's Place in Liverpool, the first baby hospice in the UK, probably in the world, opened a new chapter in the story of the hospice movement.

The opening of the second LIFE Health Centre (in Middlesbrough) made possible the arrival of Zoë's No 2 in 2005. By then LIFE had handed Zoë's to a separate charity, Zoë's Place Trust, a daughter of LIFE and a source of especial pride to the mother – as well as a sign of contradiction to the world to which the likes of David Steel and Leonard Arthur have belonged. The dream is that there should be a Zoë's Place in every major city/conurbation in the UK – even as the LIFE FertilityCare Programme becomes available throughout the UK. Indeed, as neonatal euthanasia gains ground in Holland and it is now seriously proposed in some secularist circles that children should not be granted the protection of the law (and birth certificates should not be issued) until several weeks after they have emerged from the womb – in order to give time for them to be thoroughly checked for "quality" – the Zoë's Place programme should extend beyond the shores of Britain.

---

3. See below pp 36 ff.

Philosopher Kim

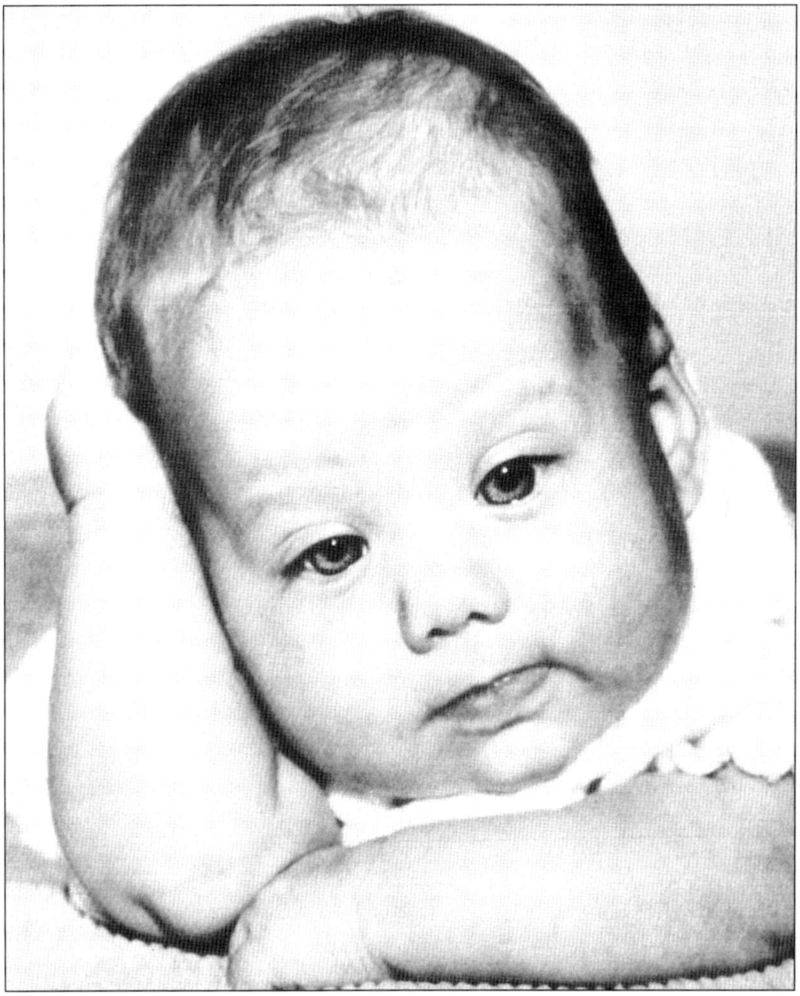

This is one of the first photos of a LIFE baby – and is still one of the best. It was used on early adverts of the LIFE Care Service in the 1970s with the caption "I'm glad my mum went to LIFE". 25,000 "Kim" postcards were sent to MPs, plus a petition, in 1979/80, urging them to support John Corrie's Abortion (Amendment) Bill – the third major (and unsuccessful) attempt to curb the abortion flood unleashed by the 1967 Act.

Papal Blessings for LIFE

Above: A newly-elected Pope John Paul II gives his blessing to LIFE at a General Audience in Rome in 1978, adding, "what you are doing is very important for the modern conscience." He had probably spoken in four or five other languages before he met this rather over-awed English pair.

Below: Twenty years later the same pope, by then author of the celebrated pro-life encyclical *Evangelium Vitae*, and never fully restored after the assassination attempt on him, repeats his blessing at the end of an international pro-life conference organised by the Pontifical Council for the Family. The latter's president, Cardinal Trujillo, looks on.

LIFE Care Centres galore

As the number of LIFE Care Centres grew (there were over 60 of them by the early 1980s) so did the ribbon-cutting opening ceremonies.

Left: Jill Knight, MP, as she was then (she is now in the House of Lords and still a doughty pro-lifer) opens the Northampton LIFE Care Centre on 20 August 1980, LIFE's tenth birthday to the day.

Mayors at work – in Sittingbourne *(above)* and Luton *(below)*

Later arrivals. *Left*: singer Dana, now an MEP, opens Bristol's first LIFE Care Centre in 1985;

Below: One of the oldest LIFE Care Centres – in Eltham, London – celebrates its silver jubilee in 1998. Margaret Clarkstone, doyenne of the Eltham LIFE Group, is at the centre, with her co-workers and their offspring, about to cut the cake.

Dumbarton's Centre opens in May 1998.
It includes a thriving LIFE shop.

Right: The mayor of Dartford helps NW Kent LIFE celebrate its 21st.

Some Important Speakers at LIFE National Conference

Cardinal Hume with members of LIFE Central Committee when he came to speak at the LIFE National Conference in 1977 in Leamington Spa. He came again in 1999, this time to Coventry. This was one of his last public engagements before he died. Though obviously in pain, he gave a lively talk and then spent the lunch-break being photographed with LIFE delegates from all over the UK, including *(below)* those from Stockport.

Sue Ryder *(right)* gave a memorable address to Conference in 1995. Her husband, Leonard Cheshire, VC, had been a patron of LIFE from early days. Lady Ryder recalled her pro-life efforts in the House of Lords and her work with post-War poor, especially in Poland. She is talking here to Nuala Scarisbrick, for some 30 years full-time (but unpaid) National Administrator and chief "animator" of LIFE.

Mary Kenny – author, playwright and journalist – has also been a frequent (and eloquent) speaker at LIFE National Conferences since the mid-70s.

Joel Brind, Professor of Human Biology and Endocrinology at City University, New York, and world expert on the abortion/breast cancer link, makes his third appearance at LIFE National Conference in 2007 – with an update on the continuing struggle to get the truth about the ABC link acknowledged by the Establishment.

And, of course, David Alton – LIFE patron and heroic political campaigner against the Goliath of abortionism – seen here at the National Conference in 1987.

Protests and Petitions

In the early days there were mass rallies organised by SPUC in Birmingham, Liverpool, London, etc and similar acts of witness in other cities, such as Leicester in 1980 (*right*) and Glasgow (*below*). Several LIFE Groups (e.g. Glasgow and Oxford) continue to hold annual walks through their cities; and London's Ten Bridges Walk is a regular act of witness as well as a fundraiser (it raised over £14,000 last time) attended by LIFE people from across southern England. The last big rally in London was in 1997 – to mark the 30th anniversary of the Abortion Act – organised by the Pro-life Alliance.

The first major effort by LIFE to secure Government funding for our care work was made in 1984 when 50 cyclists from all over the UK (even Scotland!) arrived at the Department of Health and Social Security – as it then was – at Elephant and Castle, in London to present a petition to the Secretary of State asking for financial support for LIFE's pregnancy care service and housing. *Above*: A DHSS official meets the LIFE cyclecade and is handed the petition. Needless to say, this was fruitless.

LIFE has repeatedly appealed for state support for its care service and, more recently, its educational work. Every attempt has been unsuccessful. The stock reply has been that the Government does not support any particular PSHE programme, which is more than suspect in view of the enormous sums it has poured into such agencies as the Family Planning Association, Marie Stopes, Sex Education Forum, etc, all of which have a very clear agenda.

The most ambitious bid yet for Government support for our work: on 27 October 1997, the 30th anniversary of the passing of the Abortion Act, Anne Dibb, LIFE trustee and Hon National Caring Officer (and major architect of the expansion and increasing professionalisation of LIFE Care Service over many years), presented a 150,000-signature petition to the prime minister asking for £7 million over five years to expand our Care Centres, National Hotline and Housing. With Anne (front row, second left) are representatives from LIFE houses across the country, including Northern Ireland. The prime minister's office referred the petition to the Department of Health. After many delays, a minister (Tessa Jowell), eventually agreed to meet a small LIFE delegation. When she did, in June 1999, it was clear that she had not read the document we had submitted to her setting out the LIFE case and had no idea why we had come to see her. A few desultory meetings subsequently with one of her officials got nowhere.

The TWO MILLION TOO MANY campaign

Launched in 1983 to mark the two millionth abortion carried out under the 1967 Act, the "Two Million Too Many" (TMTM) campaign delivered by post or by hand two million specially produced leaflets across the country. Here St Albans LIFE Group are enveloping hundreds of leaflets for distribution in the town. Many other LIFE Groups worked heroically to do likewise. Though doubtless now dated, the leaflet was one of the best (and most challenging) that LIFE has ever produced. And it contained no nasty pictures!

The Alton Bill, 1987-8

David Alton's attempt to curb abortionism by reducing the upper age-limit to 18 weeks was the keenest fought pro-life political effort ever and came nearer to success than did any other, before or since. It also aroused the most ferocious opposition inside Parliament and outside. During its "BABY" campaign ("Back Alton's Bill – Yes!") LIFE produced a powerful video – "18 weeks – dead or alive?" and organised a million-signature petition to Mrs Thatcher asking that, if necessary, the Alton Bill should be given Government time (as was David Steel's bill in 1967) to ensure that it got a vote at third reading. Hundreds of "BABY" cards went to MPs from LIFE members and doctors and nurses. Meanwhile David Alton was stomping the land holding public meetings in almost every major town to rally support. In the end, in May 1988, his Bill was talked out at third reading thanks to furious manoeuvring by opponents. In the following year Ann Widdecombe introduced an identical Bill which was scuppered by a 3-hour filibuster by the virulently pro-abortion Denis Skinner, often known as "the Beast of Bolsover".

Preparing for a public meeting in support of the Alton Bill in Sheffield on 18 April 1988.

Donations to the 'BABY' campaign gratefully received at address overleaf!

BABY
BACK ALTON'S BILL-YES!

Doctors for Alton

I am a member of the medical profession and support Mr. David Alton's Abortion (Amendment) Bill.

Signed: ....

Name (BLOCK LETTERS) ....

Address ....

.... Post Code: ....

....

Present position: ....

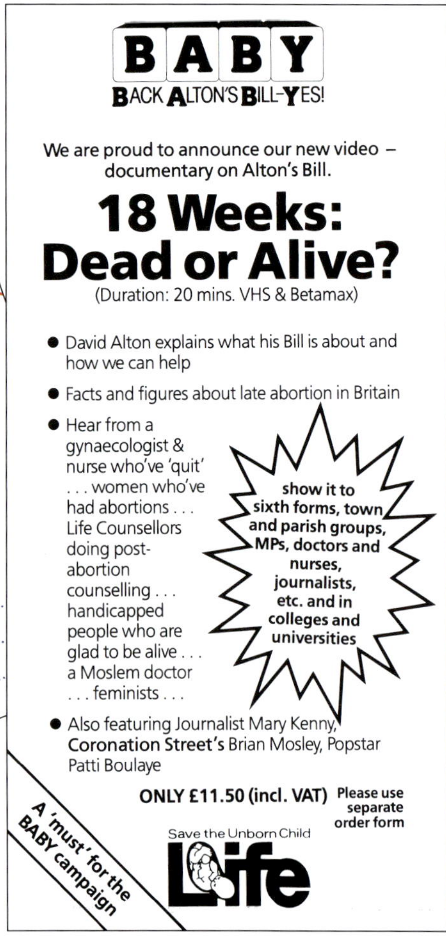

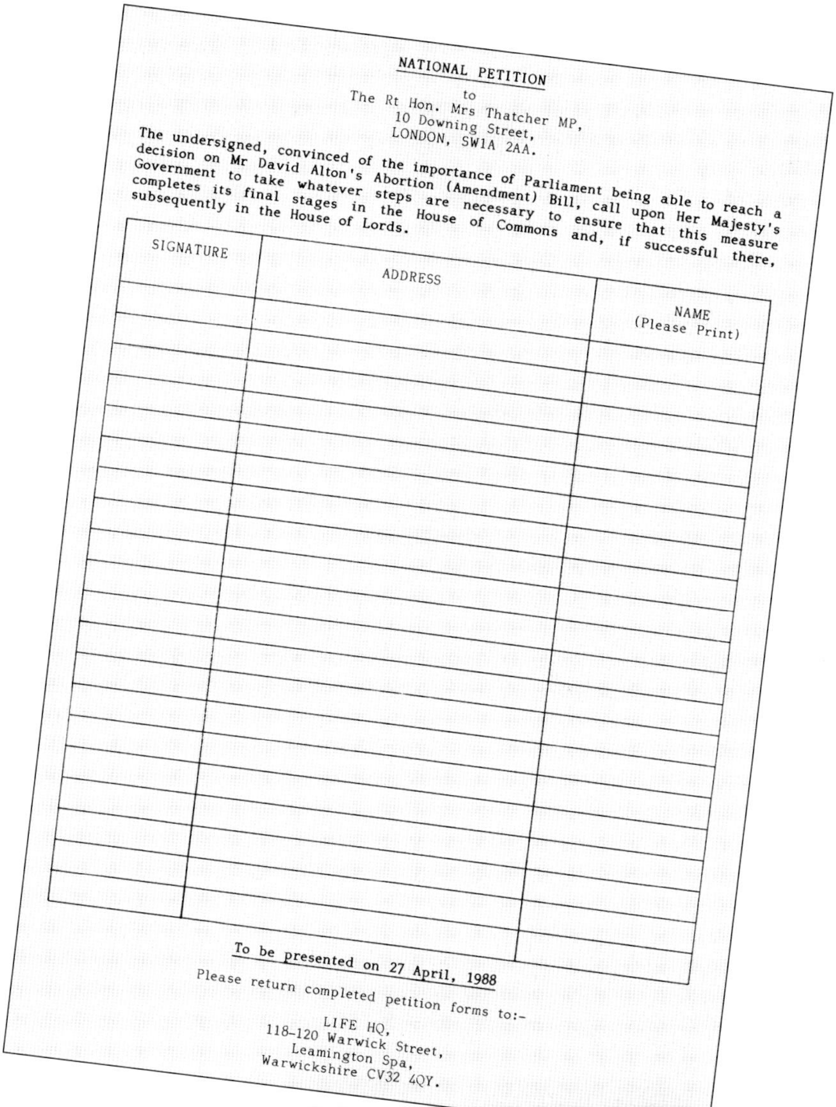

NATIONAL PETITION

to

The Rt Hon. Mrs Thatcher MP,
10 Downing Street,
LONDON, SW1A 2AA.

The undersigned, convinced of the importance of Parliament being able to reach a decision on Mr David Alton's Abortion (Amendment) Bill, call upon Her Majesty's Government to take whatever steps are necessary to ensure that this measure completes its final stages in the House of Commons and, if successful there, subsequently in the House of Lords.

SIGNATURE	ADDRESS	NAME (Please Print)

To be presented on 27 April, 1988

Please return completed petition forms to:-

LIFE HQ,
118-120 Warwick Street,
Leamington Spa,
Warwickshire CV32 4QY.

The opposition (which had mounted the "FAB" – Fight Alton's Bill campaign) turned out in force to picket Birmingham town hall, when David Alton spoke there on 19 January 1988. For a while the police lost control and were overwhelmed by a chanting, pushing mob. The BABY meeting in Leicester was nearly sabotaged by a phoney bomb-scare. While Alton was speaking at Central Methodist Hall in London, some screaming women rushed at the podium and tried to pull over tables and tear down microphones.

Defending the Human Embryo

Norman St John Stevas, MP (*left*) receives a package of petitions signed by over two million people calling upon Parliament to protect human embryonic life from all forms of abuse made possible by the new technique of *in vitro* fertilisation. Next to him is Raymond Johnson, then Director of CARE – which, with other pro-life organisations, had joined in the huge work of collecting signatures across the UK.

The petition was a direct response to the Warnock Report, published in 1984, which recommended approval of IVF and use of "spare" embryos in destructive experimentation, etc. The inspiration for this initiative had come from Bill Cash, MP, who, at the LIFE National Conference in 1985, had argued that Warnock could best be defeated by setting up a Select Committee of the House of Commons which would really get at the truth which Warnock had ducked or obscured – plus a nationwide petition calling for Parliament to give the full protection of the law to embryonic human life.

The first idea – launched with an Early Day Motion (no 868) – seemed likely to succeed until (lamentably) the leading pro-life MPs suddenly changed their minds and withdrew their support, on the ground that it would "let the Government off the hook". This was curious – because the Government was not on any hook.

But the second idea took off. Bill Cash said "nothing less than 2 million signatures will do." We did it! But Parliament paid little attention – except that Enoch Powell took up the challenge and attempted a private member's bill to protect lives generated by IVF from abuse. His Bill failed, however.

MMM – another effort to protect unborn life

In 1987 thousands of cards were sent to MPs by post or delivered by hand in Parliament or at their surgeries calling on them to give the protection of the law to the unborn. "Mail MPs a Mountain" the LIFE campaign was called. Here Marion Roe, MP for Broxbourne, receives a packet of MMM cards from constituents John and Vera Golden, two tireless pro-lifers. The MMM campaign provided the opening "broadside" on behalf of David Alton's Abortion (Amendment) Bill, published on 22 October 1987.

Some of the people who were doing the work

The founding members of LIFE Northern Ireland – who owed much to Jean Garland (second from the end) and her husband Sidney.

West of Scotland's splendid team have been led for many years by Robert Graham (back row, second from the end).

Chorley LIFE Group's AGM, October 1988. the Group owed so much to indomitable Annie Walsh (seated second on left) and then to Iris Norris (standing, fourth from left) and her husband.

A study-day in December 2004 for counsellors from the NE (Sheffield, Middlesbrough, Doncaster, Leeds, Newcastle) who help "man" the LIFE National Helpline from 9am to 9pm every day. Callers from any part of the country are automatically switched through to the counsellors (usually two) on duty – who themselves may be miles apart. The National Helpline is doing a roaring "trade".

The Bournemouth LIFE delegation to National Conference in 1992. the Group was founded twenty years previously and had long had Merville Pidgeon (top left) at the helm – looking after a LIFE house and very successful Care Centre. Three of its counsellors accompanied Merville.

Leading lights of the Reading LIFE Group

LIFE Houses

Bournemouth boasts the oldest LIFE house. Opened in the early seventies, it can accommodate seven residents (or "service-users", as they are now called). During the last 30-plus years LIFE Housing has undergone important changes, not least thanks to the Supporting People Programme, which enables us to provide much more than simply a roof over heads. A LIFE house is both a safe haven for women made homeless through pregnancy and unsupported mothers with small children and also provides training in a wide range of life skills to prepare them for independent living. LIFE Housing is an essential part of LIFE's Care Service and is unique. No other pro-life movement in the world has anything to match it.

The handsome LIFE house in Belfast.

Inside the Oxford LIFE house in 1982. Christopher Flynn (chairman) with some of the Caring team and resident mums and babies.

LIFE Education

Delivering the pro-life message to people of all ages, but especially the young has been a prime purpose of LIFE since its inception. In recent years LIFE's educational work has expanded hugely – in Northern Ireland and Great Britain – headed by a team of young regional Education Officers.

Above: a LIFE schools conference in progress

Below: Varria Russell-White, LIFE Education Officer in Yorkshire, conducts a class

Some more LIFE babies

Two young mothers and their children whom LIFE helped all the way.

LIFE workers with two babies and their mums residing in the LIFE House in Walsall.

A former archbishop of Birmingham, Maurice Couve de Murville, with plenty on his hands: two residents of the LIFE house in Warwick.

LIFE Shops

There are ten LIFE shops around the country – the oldest in Wisbech (opened in 1991), the most recent in Loden, outside Norwich. They are an important part of LIFE's Care Service, for three reasons: first, they provide high quality baby clothes and equipment at very good prices (often free to LIFE clients); secondly, most of them also contain the local LIFE Care Centre; thirdly, they raise funds to pay the rent of those Centres and for local advertising of their services. *Above*: the proud team who run the Weymouth LIFE shop with Joyce Fannon (second left), its chief architect. *Below*: Inside the very successful shop in Bloxwich (Walsall). There are four LIFE shops in Scotland, and others in St Helens and Ipswich.

Some more people who have mattered

Elspeth Chowdaray-Best – the co-founder of SPUC in early 1967 and the true founder of the pro-life movement in Britain. In recent years she has been particularly involved in the work of Alert in opposing euthanasia.

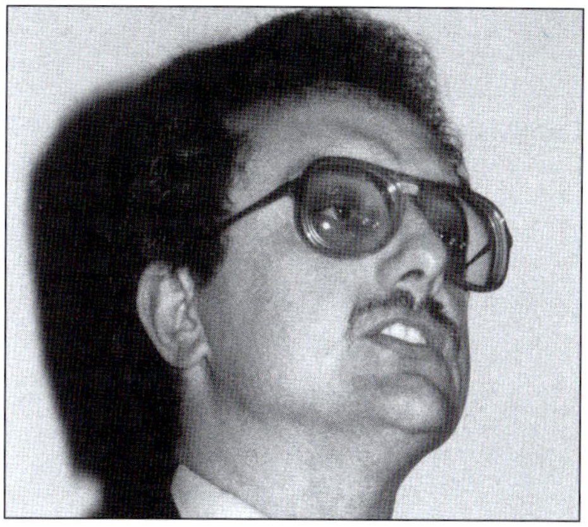

Keith Davies – a passionate servant of the cause who was the chief inspiration of LIFE's vigorous political activity in the 1980s, especially during the campaign in support of Enoch Powell's attempt to ban human embryo abuse in 1984/5, the Alton Bill and the events of 1989/90 which resulted in the Human Fertilisation and Embryology Act 1990. Keith's premature death in 1994 was a deep shock.

Pat Boyd – first worked with Scunthorpe LIFE Group, then (eventually) came to London and for many years was chief counsellor of the important LIFE Care Centre in the capital. Heaven only knows how many young people are alive today thanks to her skilled counselling. From 1990 onwards she played a major role in promoting LIFE's work in Eastern Europe after the collapse of the Communist empire, especially the Czech Republic. She is seen here (centre) receiving a gift from pro-lifers in Olomuoc, Poland.

Ron Norris FRCOG – a consultant gynaecologist who had never performed an abortion and a constant supporter of the pro-life cause. Co-founder of LIFE Anglicans, he became increasingly saddened by the corruption of the medical profession, especially his specialism, and the failure of his beloved Anglican Church to speak out against the relentless attack on human life.

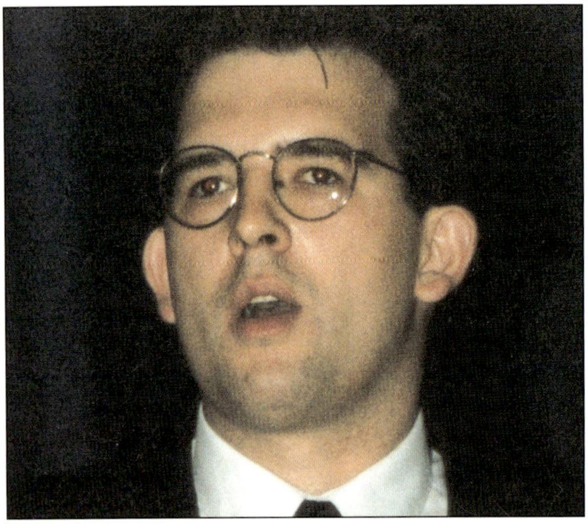

Peter Garrett – for eleven years LIFE's gifted Director of Education and Research who did much to develop LIFE's ever-growing educational work. Here he is addressing National Conference in 1995 when LIFE's Silver Jubilee Appeal was launched.

Virginia Griffin – a key figure at the first LIFE Health Centre (in Liverpool) and ardent LIFE worker in the North-West – and, with Margaret Parsons, the National Coordinator of the LIFE FertilityCare Programme (LFP). Indeed, she and Margaret are its chief architects. LFP, in providing the pro-life alternative to IVF, is a crucial ingredient in that "counter-culture" discussed in Chapter VI below.

III.

WHEN DOES HUMAN LIFE BEGIN?

Today we can answer the question about when human life begins with a certainty that would have been impossible fifty or a hundred, let alone two hundred, years ago. The modern sciences of genetics and embryology have established beyond doubt that it begins when the father's sperm penetrates the mother's ovum. This is the decisive, irreversible event which releases an explosion of highly complex, self-directing growth, i.e. multiplication and diversification of cells. Modern genetics shows that, as the two sets of chromosomes, inherited from ancestors via the parents, fuse, a new genetic blueprint (or genome) which is unique to that new being (but will be shared by an identical twin) is laid down and this will determine much of the future person's physical characteristics, aptitudes, psyche – and even diseases to which he/she will be prone.

Fertilisation (conception) is the only event to which I can point and say: "That's when I started being me and I have been me ever since. From that moment my life has been a continuous "becoming". Birth was simply an incident (admittedly an important one) in a life already begun – usually 266 days previously – and a change of environment; the beginning of my life outside the womb not the beginning of my life".

There is much that is still not clearly understood about the early days of life: whether the first cells multiply by constant doubling (1, 2, 4, 8, 16, etc) or by adding to themselves (I, 2, 3, 5, 8, 13, etc), for instance, or how identical twinning occurs. But for the modern scientist there is no uncertainty about when and how human life – like all animal life and, indeed, all living things – begins.

The pro-abortion and IVF lobbies have tried to overturn these findings, however. They have tried to do so in essentially three different ways. The first, and least impressive, is by claiming that, since gametes are alive, fertilisation is not the beginning of life – and in a sense, individual life has no beginning. But this is to ignore the fact that, though they are indeed alive, gametes cannot grow. Left alone they will die; if united, a third entity comes into being which did not exist before and an astonishing surge of growth is released. These are incontrovertible facts.

A second line of attack argues that life in the womb is *not yet* human until a certain point. What is that point? Here opinions have differed widely. One said syngamy – the final fusing of the inherited chromosomes about 18 hours after fertilisation began. Lady Warnock said at 14 days, with the appearance of the primitive streak. As we have seen, some theologians have plumped for

42 days or thereabouts (a throwback to Aristotle and the Middle Ages) and an archbishop of Canterbury chose quickening – absurdly[1].

But to say that human life begins at 18 hours, 14 days or 42 days after something is to provoke immediately the question: 18 hours, 14 or 42 days after what? The answer is: after the beginning! Exactly. To give her her due, Lady Warnock tried to be a bit more clever by arguing that, since monozygotic (i.e. identical twinning) could occur up to 14 days, we could not be sure that *individual* human life was present until then. But this was muddleheaded. There are two possible explanations of twinning: either the twin is a "bud" which grows out of the "branch" and is therefore younger than the sibling or, as seems more likely, twinning is genetically determined. In that case there have been two separate lives present from the start even though we have not been able to see them. In either case, however, what is growing in the womb is not pre- or "sort-of" human. It is "doubly" human. When challenged on this point, Lady Warnock was unable to defend herself. She is not the only person to get into a twist over twinning.

As we shall see, an archbishop of York was to argue that becoming human is a process (which is true in one sense) and that, since processes cannot have beginnings (which is untrue) human life has no precise beginning[2]. But this was a maverick's view. Much more substantial was the argument that life in the womb was only "sort-of" human because not yet *personal* life, that is, was human but not yet humanised. It was not personal or humanised because not yet fully conscious or capable of self-knowledge, self-determination, choosing – which are distinctive of personal, fully human life. Some theologians argued thus. Their views were quickly taken up by secular ethicists and have become their stock-in-trade.

But, using those criteria, one could conclude that children do not deserve to be admitted to full membership of the human race until years after birth. A babe in arms is not yet capable of self-knowledge and choosing, and so on – and it will be months before he/she will be in any meaningful sense. And are we less human when we are asleep or under an anaesthetic and hence not fully self-conscious or choosing anything? The decisive fact is that a human being has the *radical* ability to know, think, choose, and so on from the beginning, otherwise it could never fully do these things later on. At fertilisation a being is "launched" into a life-path that has knowing, thinking, choosing, etc, as its distinctive features. It does not receive these abilities from outside. They are radically present from the time when his/her genome is established, that is, from fertilisation: so human life is always truly personal, even if there is a long way to go before the distinctive features of personhood become fully realised.

There is a further objection. The claim is that we know a being is a real human person because we know it thinks, chooses and so on. But is this true?

1. See p. 44.
2. Below, pp 46 f.

I recognise a being as a human person because he/she looks like one. Walking down the street I intuitively distinguish between, say, a car and a pillar-box and any human being I see. I do not need proof that he/she therefore thinks, chooses or whatever to recognise him/her as human. I have abstracted an idea of what human beings look like from my experience of them and identify them immediately, instinctively. If I were shown a being who was incapable of ever thinking, choosing, etc I would have to change my mind about his/her moral status, but it is physical appearance which has first led me to conclude that he/she is a member of the human race – and not a "sort-of" one, not a "not-yet" one.

When I see a picture of, say, a 28-week-old unborn child I immediately recognise it as a human being – because it looks like one. Further reflection will lead me to conclude that one day it will be thinking and choosing as I do. If I were told that he/she would never be able to do these things I would have to revise my opinion of the child's moral status. The same would be true if I were shown a picture of a 15- or 10- week-old unborn child. If I am shown one of a 2-week-old I might not recognise him/her as human because I have had little experience of human beings at that age. In fact, that small creature looks exactly what human beings look like at that age. Why should we expect otherwise? It is my ignorance that is the problem. If I were an obstetrician or embryologist I would immediately know that I was looking at a very young human being and that it is as human to look like that as it is to look like a 28-week-old or a newborn child – or an adolescent, adult, or senior citizen, for that matter. If I were told that this small creature would never be able to think or choose, etc, I would have to change my mind about his/her moral status. But a scientist would tell me that that creature is already beginning to develop the ability to think and choose – and will one day do so, as I do.

The "not yet" argument chooses the wrong criteria. It is too Platonic. It is defective for another reason.

To claim that an unborn child does not have a right to life because not yet able to think or choose, etc, overlooks the fact that he/she has the radical ability to do these things one day, if allowed to live long enough, by virtue of his/her own inner dynamism. Nothing has to be added from outside. The potential is within. But to take away the ability to achieve what would otherwise be achieved in the future – in this case the right to life – is to do something as harmful and therefore wrong as denying or taking away what has been achieved. If it is wrong to castrate healthy males it is as wrong to castrate a healthy small boy as it is to castrate a healthy adult; and it is no defence to say that the boy was not yet sexually mature. His age is irrelevant. Similarly, if it is wrong to deny a grown person's right to life it is equally wrong to take away the ability of an unborn child (of any age) to live long enough to qualify as a full human being (which he/she would have done if allowed to do so). And it is no defence to say that the child was not yet capable of thinking and choosing, and therefore not a person. He/she would have become one if allowed to.

So, even if it were true that an unborn child or human embryo in the IVF clinic is not yet truly human (and it is not true), it would not follow that it has less right to life, that is, is morally inferior to a fully developed one. The "not yet" argument does not work[3].

It may be objected that we have been talking about the injustice of denying the right to life to the preborn and that, since injustice can be done only to human beings (not to animals or plants), the question has been begged as to whether the preborn are truly human. But the word injustice has not been used – we have spoken only of the *harm* that is done by killing. This has been called wrong, i.e. morally wrong. That may be the same as calling it unjust. The defence would be that a being which, though not yet fully human, is on the way to being so, is in a unique moral category and can be the victim of moral wrong, i.e. injustice.

Pro-lifers are among those who take the simple view that things begin at the beginning. It is a striking fact that those who claim that human life does not begin at fertilisation disagree among themselves about where the starting-point is and how we know that it has been reached. They produce convoluted reasoning to support their case and are persistently guilty of evasion and *non-sequiturs.* That is why pro-abortionists increasingly say, "Yes, of course it's a human being, but so what?"

When people say that what they are really saying is, "it's a human being but it can't call the police and can't hit back." So ...

It's not yet in sight and therefore not yet in mind.

---

3. LIFE has boasted, not unreasonably, that its refutation of the "not yet" argument was its most important contribution to the debate on the moral status of human life before birth.

IV.

THE ANATOMY OF ABORTIONISM

The Abortion Act 1967 conferred no right to abortion and imposed no duty to perform one. It simply provided that the existing law which forbade abortion would not apply if certain conditions were met. If an abortion were performed without these conditions having been met a criminal offence would be committed.

Of course, at that time it would have been politically impossible to have had all abortion declared lawful. Parliament would never have done what the USA's Supreme Court did in 1973, that is, declare that abortion is a woman's right. Instead Parliament left the law in an extraordinary muddle. Either abortion is right or it is wrong. If it is wrong in some circumstances it must be wrong in all circumstances because the only reason why it is wrong is that it involves destroying innocent human life – and that will be true on every occasion. In other words, it is a question of all or nothing. The middle way, Parliament's way, is intellectually incoherent.

Arguably, the pro-abortion lobby would have been well advised, then and since, to focus exclusively on an appeal to compassion. It should have argued simply that unwanted pregnancy can cause intense human anguish, can ruin relationships and careers and break hearts; that the single mother is most likely to descend into the bottom of the poverty trap; that every case is a hard case. It should have argued that women do not want abortions and doctors and nurses do not like doing them – any more than, say, people "like" having teeth extracted or dentists "like" extracting them – but, alas, these things sometimes have to be done. They are regrettable facts of life. To refuse abortion to a desperate woman is to be intolerably heartless. Only a religious fanatic or arrant misogynist would do so. A true Christian would reach out to that woman in unconditional love and say that Christian love required that the burden be lifted off her. The modern secularist would say that a liberal abortion law was the mark of a civilised society.

That is the only way in which the pro-abortion case should have been presented.

But instead of settling for this appeal to the heart, the pro-abortion lobby from the start tried to rationalise their position. That immediately got them into difficulty.

Thus when his bill was going through Parliament, David Steel argued that abortion is permissible because the unborn child is merely a "dependent" being. This is true but, since dependence implies duties on the person depended on rather than rights over the dependent, it did exactly the opposite to what was intended. Then there was the familiar claim that the unborn child is merely part of the mother, which is patently untrue. The child has a separate set of limbs and blood supply as well as being genetically distinct. Either mother or child can die independently of the other. And if the child were part of the mother the latter would be incomplete after birth. Nor is the child merely a potential human being, as some claimed. He/she is a being with a lot of potential, a potential adolescent and adult, but already actually a growing human being.

For the feminists, of course, the nub of the matter is that "It's a woman's right to choose". This was to become the chief battle cry of the pro-abortion lobby. If one asked "where does this right come from? who gives it to women?" no convincing answer is forthcoming. More importantly, perhaps, what is the answer to this question: "Is it ever right to take another (innocent) human being's life?" The pro-lifer would want to go on to say that, since a woman has no right to have a born child put to death, she can have a right to destroy an unborn child only if it can be shown that the latter is morally inferior to the former. But the only way that one can argue that human life before birth is morally inferior to born life is by saying it is dependent or only potentially human or that the unborn child is merely part of the mother. And none of these statements is valid.

Whenever a debate on abortion takes place it is never long before the "backstreet" argument – and the horror stories of women butchered with knitting needles, etc – make their appearance. Wherever the pro-abortion campaign is waged, frightening statistics of illegal abortion and a huge toll of women's lives are produced – most of them wildly exaggerated. In 1967 estimates of the "backstreet" trade ranged from 15,000 to 25,0000 a year. That most of the unlawful activity was in Harley Street rather than backstreets was quietly overlooked. So, too, was the fact that, since maternal death rates from all abortion, procured and spontaneous, had been declining dramatically in the previous decade, if there really were a quarter of a million illegal abortions a year the "backstreet" trade had become remarkably skilful and safe. The pro-abortion propagandists could not have it both ways.

Nor, though they chanted the slogan "Keep it safe, keep it legal", could they answer the objection that wrongful actions do not cease to be wrongful by becoming hygienic. If old ladies are being battered to death in filthy backstreets shall we have NHS clinics where they can be battered to death in hygienic conditions? So, before long the "backstreet" argument was re-tuned to run thus: "There has always been abortion and always will be. Desperate women will always find a way. Face facts, therefore, and at least bring abortion under control and make it safe." But you could also argue that there will probably always be rape, racism, burglary, bad driving, etc. Should we therefore face facts and legalise these things? No. We may never stamp out these wrongdoings completely, but we can strive to do so.

The more the pro-abortionist talks, the worse things get. They are at their very worst when academics enter the lists. Thus a distinguished moral philosopher in Yale could seriously argue as follows: since most people think that abortion is right it must be; and since pro-lifers do not have to have abortions themselves they have no right to object. Another American academic, a woman, produced the following ludicrous analogy: if you woke up one day and found that a very sick, world-famous violinist was being kept alive by having been "plugged into" your kidneys without your consent, you would not be morally bound to continue to sustain him. No one can be forced to be a Good Samaritan. Similarly, a woman who finds herself pregnant and does not want to be, cannot be required to continue to sustain the unborn child "plugged into" her[1].

⋆ ⋆ ⋆

Pro-lifers have always found it very difficult to engage in reasoned discussion with their opponents. This is not primarily because they have been talking from different premises. Rather, it is because those opponents do not listen and do not answer questions. Of course, they in turn accuse pro-lifers of having closed minds. No doubt, some have. But the carefully constructed pro-life case is rarely answered. Pro-lifers listen carefully to what the opponents say and when they challenge them – that is, produce reasoned criticism of what they have heard – they receive no response. A genuine desire for orderly debate encounters only slogan-mongering or evasion. The pro-lifer will say that this is inevitable, since their opponents are trying to defend the indefensible. He/she will also quickly discover that no issue turns otherwise calm, rational people into unreasonable ones as does abortionism.

David Steel has been unfazed by the fact that his talk about "dependence" was an own goal; and when his promise that the floodgates would not open proved wrong he not only did not show remorse but voted against attempts to stem the flood. The Warnock committee's decision to bypass the question of the moral status of the human embryo and "to proceed immediately to considering how it should be treated" has caused Lady Warnock no blushes. The Attorney-General Michael Havers was not ashamed to make the absurd claim that, to carry something required that it be attached to someone.

Pro-lifers have argued that the increasingly explicit, value-free sex education which has been imposed on the young since the 1960s, far from reducing teenage promiscuity, pregnancy and sexually-transmitted infection,

1. Eileen McDonagh, *Breaking the Abortion Deadlock* (New York & Oxford, 1996) esp. pp 6 ff. Other academics who have attempted to provide a philosophical basis for abortionism include Jeffrey Reiman in *Critical Moral Liberalism: Theory and Practice* (1977), who simply states as a given that unborn children have no rights (and nor do mentally disabled born people), John Rawls who "argued" in *Political Liberalism* that, since "all reasonable people" agree with abortion those who disagree can be ignored, Peter Singer of Princeton and John Harris in Manchester. Most produce no substantial argument but simply treat pro-lifers as obscurantists, "traditionalists", Luddites, etc who can be conveniently ignored.

has increased it. This is a thesis which any reasonable person would at least find plausible and worthy of exploration. But successive Governments, i.e. the Department of Health and its ministers, have dismissed it – not after careful study or reflection, but out of hand, *a priori*. The question did not need a reasoned answer because it should never have been asked.

Over the years British governments have poured millions into the United Nations Fund for Population Activities and International Planned Parenthood Federation, both of which are dedicated to a programme of mass sterilisation and forcible abortion in Africa, South America, the Indian subcontinent and China. British taxpayers' money has also streamed into national bodies like the Family Planning Association and Brook, which work under the umbrella of those international agencies, and into the private abortion industry, notably BPAS and Marie Stopes. These other "pro-choice" pressure-groups are abetted by, and have made a creature of, the Royal College of Obstetricians and Gynaecologists (RCOG).

Like the Royal College of Nursing, the RCOG in 1967 was opposed to David Steel's Bill and still committed to the traditional view that, when looking after a pregnant woman, an obstetrician had two patients who merited equal care. But in a lamentably short time old values were cast aside and, while professing to be officially neutral, the College had become an engine of abortionism.

The clearest proof of this has been its refusal to entertain the idea that abortion can do serious harm to a woman. Thus the official doctrine is that infertility is not associated with induced abortion. This is obviously untrue. Leave aside the clear evidence that, if chlamydia is present, an induced abortion can carry the infection to the top of the uterus and the resulting pelvic inflammatory disease can cause tubal blockage (if this is not the case, why is precautionary treatment for chlamydia before abortion recommended and widely practised?). There is the very simple fact that "retained products of conception" are an acknowledged cause of damage to the fallopian tubes and hence infertility: and incomplete abortion which leaves behind some "products of conception" is a known hazard. How often it happens is not the point. The RCOG has denied that it happens at all.

There is now a large literature on the subject of post-abortion syndrome. The evidence has been gathering from all over the world that any pregnancy loss, but especially induced abortion, can leave a trail of guilt, anger, and grief, and that post-abortion women can suffer grievously. But the Establishment in general and the RCOG in particular deny this. They say the evidence is inconclusive. In the first place they allege that the evidence is merely anecdotal, not the fruit of rigorous, scientific research. This is untrue. A major study published in the UK in 1992, for instance, reported that at least 10 per cent of women suffered serious mental illness after abortion; and two studies from Finland showed that abortive women are three times more likely to attempt suicide than women who go to term[2]. Yes, much of the remaining reports of post-abortion trauma are anecdotal, that is, individual testimonies. But "anecdotal" is not the same as "untrue" or "insignificant". It cannot be proved that what the women concerned report is typical. But it cannot be proved that it is not. What is perhaps atypical is that those women have chosen to tell their stories – not what they tell. Certainly, there comes a point when individual testimonies cannot be brushed aside as insignificant. If post-abortion syndrome is largely a myth, why do even abortion agencies like BPAS offer post-abortion counselling and why do LIFE counsellors spend many hours a week listening to women tell their stories about how abortion devastated them?

The official line is that the women who suffer thus have had a history of mental illness, i.e. were already mentally unstable. This is convenient but irrelevant. If an abortion has triggered a recurrence of mental disease the woman is a post-abortion victim nevertheless. Moreover, it is simply untrue. Many of the victims had previously been healthy, normal women. Unabashed, the RCOG even claims that women who are refused abortion also suffer distress and that this could outweigh or match the damage occasionally done by a "termination". In concluding that the evidence for PAS is inconclusive, the College relies almost exclusively on a study published in 1991 – a meta-analysis of the existing literature which concluded that post-abortion trauma was not a significant event[3]. But many of the studies it reviewed had had remarkably small samples and most covered a very short period of time (some only a few weeks and none more that three years). Since it can be many years after the event that women are "hit" by post-abortion guilt and grief and so on, the conclusions of this allegedly definitive analysis are more or less worthless.

Since abortion has now been widely available for decades and since is one of the most common of operations, one would have expected the RCOG to decide that it was their duty to commission a thoroughly professional, up-to-date study of the mental and emotional sequelae of what many of their fellows and members had been heavily engaged in for most of their professional lives. The College declares the evidence to be inconclusive. Should they have been satisfied with inconclusiveness? Should there not have been a definitive verdict? It was safer, of course, to leave the issue unresolved in a scientific limbo.

---

2. Zolese and Blacker, "The psychological complications of therapeutic abortion", *British Journal of Psychiatry*, 1992; 160: 742-9; Gissler *et al*, "Suicides after pregnancy in Finland", *British Medical Journal,* 1996; 313 and in *Acta Obstet Gynecol, Scand.* 1997;76. Their findings have been confirmed by Ferguson *et al*, "Abortion in young women and subsequent mental health", *Journ. Child Psychology and Psychiatry,* 2006; 47: 16-24.

3. Dagg, "The Psychological Sequelae of Therapeutic Abortion, etc." in *American Journal of Psychiatry*, 1991; 148: 578-585. RCOG: *The Care of Women Requesting Induced Abortion. Evidence-based Guidelines No 7* (2000), p 31.

That is where the College want to put the debate about the abortion/breast cancer (ABC) link, too. The evidence, once again, is "inconclusive" and those who argue that induced abortion is a significant risk factor for breast cancer are simply scare-mongering. At the same time the RCOG declared that a meta-analysis of the ABC literature published by Joel Brind *et al* in 1996 had "no methodological flaws and could not be disregarded"[4]. Since Brind, a professor at Baruch College, City University of New York, and a formidable authority on the ABC link, had shown that 26 out of 32 studies from around the world indicated that the link existed, it was difficult to see how the verdict of "not proven" could be passed without disregarding him.

There are two distinct elements to the ABC debate. First, it is now widely accepted that a full-term pregnancy, especially if followed by breastfeeding and especially if this is the first pregnancy, provides protection against breast cancer in later years. So, if a woman or girl has her first pregnancy "terminated" she forgoes that protection. Subsequent full-term pregnancy may make good the loss in part, but her defences have been weakened. But that is not all. Studies from around the world suggest that she will have increased the risk of attack, especially if hers is a nulliparous abortion, that is, if she had no full-term pregnancy previously. Since the majority of abortions in Britain are nulliparous, abortion must be playing a part in the alarming and steady increase in the incidence of breast cancer since the late 1970s. That is the Brind argument.

Moreover, there is a clear biological explanation of the ABC link. In early pregnancy a huge surge in oestrogen levels causes the cells of the breast to proliferate. Later in pregnancy these cells differentiate to enable them to produce milk. If this differentiation does not occur the cells become vulnerable to carcinogens. This will happen if the child is born very prematurely. It does not happen if the abortion is spontaneous.

The RCOG – and the pro-abortion lobby as a whole – has counter-attacked, arguing that the studies which prove the ABC case are flawed because of "recall bias": that is, they are based on retrospective interviews/questionnaires and women who have breast cancer, it is alleged, are more likely to report that they have had an abortion than are those who have not developed the disease. Only record-linked prospective studies, that is, studies using official statistics which record an abortion before breast cancer is reported, are reliable. And so on. This was a rather feeble rearguard action. But then in 2004 a team led by Dr Valerie Beral of the Cancer Research UK in Oxford published a new meta-analysis of the ABC data, a study which the RCOG had long proclaimed would be definitive[5].

---

4. *ibid*, p 30.
5. Beral *et al*, "Breast Cancer and abortion: collaborative reanalysis, etc, *Lancet*, 2004; 363: 1007-16. It claimed to re-analyse 53 (actually 52 – they miscounted) studies from 16 countries around the world.

Beral *et al* predictably found that at least the record-linked prospective studies disproved the ABC link conclusively. But this was emphatically not so. Out of 83,000 breast cancer cases contained in this review no less than nearly 34,000 came from three studies: one from Denmark, one from Oxford and the third from Sweden. All three had been shown to be egregiously defective by Brind: the first because it mistook the date when abortion was legalised in Denmark and missed 60,000 abortions as well as including excessive numbers of women young enough to have had abortions but not yet old enough to have suffered their full incidence of breast cancer; the Oxford one because it included only abortions done in the NHS and hence misclassified as non-abortive breast cancer victims a large tranche of women who had had abortions in the private sector; the third because of quite arbitrary handling of the data. Brind's devastating criticism of the three articles had been published in learned journals. They were ignored by Beral and co. Though entitled a "collaborative reanalysis" of the literature, Brind was not invited to take part in it.

This is the true face of abortionism. It is, of course, asking much of any professional to admit that he has been actively doing harm to those who he claimed to be helping. It is not easy for the medical profession to admit that they are actively generating mental disease and are the chief reason why a horrible disease like breast cancer is now the commonest form of cancer.

When a study commissioned by LIFE appeared in 2001 showing that breast cancer rates had risen in the UK exactly as would have been expected if increasingly available abortion was at least partly to blame[6], the RCOG simply refused to begin to consider that there was even an *association* between the two. Instead, they produced other explanations – increased obesity, later menopause, binge-drinking – without any statistical evidence and usually without any possible biological explanation for it. When David Alton initiated a debate in the House of Lords on the ABC, he encountered an angry, almost hysterical, refusal even to consider the question.[7]

How long will heads remain in the sand?

* * *

This, then, is abortionism. It cannot engage in reasoned debate. It is incoherent. It can offer only slogans, assertions and old myths. It evades and fudges. It will break the most basic rules of scientific research and not hesitate to ignore norms of academic discourse.

* * *

6. Patrick Carroll, *Abortion and other pregnancy-related risk factors in female breast cancer* (2001).
7. *Hansard* (Lords), 29 October 2003, cols 335 ff.

Many people have never heard of Francis Galton (1822 – 1911). But he was one of the most influential Englishmen of modern times. He was a professor at University College London. He coined the word eugenics and founded what eventually became the Eugenics Society. He effectively established the modern "science" of eugenics. A cousin of Charles Darwin, with whom he exchanged many ideas, he argued that, just as we breed plants, race-horses and foxhounds, etc, to produce the best specimens, so is it our duty, almost a "religious" one, to strive to produce ever better, i.e. fitter, human beings. Left to herself, Nature would eventually ensure the survival of the fittest; but Nature's ways are slow and painful. Why not intervene in her processes to accelerate the emergence of a "nobler", "fitter" society – or at any rate "abler commanders, statesmen, thinkers, inventors and artists"? In his biometric laboratory and during extensive travels he studied ways in which scientific breeding could transform society. To encourage the fitter to intermarry (positive eugenics) was one thing. But what about discouraging the less fit to reproduce themselves (negative eugenics)? Here Galton himself hesitated. But most of his followers did not.

His ideas spread quickly all over the world, especially in the USA (where large-scale non-voluntary sterilisation of "feeble-minded" women – it was called "mental hygiene" – soon became widespread), Australia, South Africa, France and especially Germany, where a Society for Racial Hygiene was set up in 1905. In 1912 the first International Eugenics Congress was held. In 1924 a book appeared in Germany advocating euthanasia for the physically and mentally defective. It first used the chilling phrase "Life unworthy of Life" (*lebensunwertung Lebens*). The idea of the "*Untermenschen*" and "useless mouths" were being born.

The founders of the London School of Economics, Sidney and Beatrice Webb, were keen members of the Eugenics Society (as well as members of the influential left-wing Fabian Society). So was the LSE's first director, William Beveridge – later famous as the father of the Welfare State – and his successor. Soon the Eugenics Society could number leading members of the intelligentsia and political life – including John Maynard Keynes, Bertrand Russell, H G Wells and Neville Chamberlain, as well as churchmen like Bishop Barnes of Birmingham, and numerous professors of anthropology, biology and public administration.

Thanks especially to the LSE, eugenics had finally established itself in British politics. And this was *negative* eugenics. Beveridge in 1906 had urged that unemployable men should be forbidden to procreate. In 1910 Winston Churchill had approved a bill to allow sterilisation of lower class women, but thought better of it. In 1930 a Fabian MP introduced a bill to legalise eugenic sterilisation. Even more revealingly, 29 members of the nascent Abortion Law Reform Association, who spearheaded the campaign for liberalising the law on abortion, were members of the Eugenics Society.

The eugenics movement had long since formed an uneasy alliance with the Neo-Malthusian League, founded in 1884 by the free-thinker MP, Charles Bradlaugh. Named after the influential parson – Rev Thomas Malthus (1766-1834), who had argued that, unless curbed, the population would always outgrow the food supply – the Neo-Malthusians campaigned strenuously to promote birth control throughout society. The eugenicists were also keen on contraception – but they wanted it to curb the birth-rate of the "lower" classes i.e. less fit, not the healthier members of society (who should be encouraged to breed). Both eugenicists and Neo-Malthusians, with varying degrees of openness, argued that abortion would be a concomitant of contraception.

It is important to appreciate that the early feminists, whose sights were set on achieving the vote and equal education for women, and on campaigning against such things as wife-beating, were deeply opposed to this campaign for artificial birth control, sterilisation and abortion. They were mainly high-principled women who rightly saw that the contraception campaign was being waged by men for the benefit of men and would demean women. It would also undermine marriage by making it easier for unfaithful wives to have affairs with married men without being found out. There was similar opposition from the young Labour Party – because the latter understandably resented the Neo-Malthusian argument that the poor had only themselves, that is, their irresponsible fecundity, not unjust economic and social structures, to blame for their poverty, and because the birth control crusade was so obviously aimed at them. The large Catholic presence in the early Labour Movement also helped to explain the party's antipathy. Nor could the eugenicists disguise the fact that the "inferior" stock was found among the deprived slum-dwellers more often than among the affluent classes and that people like the Webbs had disapproved of poor relief on the ground that it encouraged the lower orders to multiply. As the notorious Anglican Bishop Barnes of Birmingham (1924-53) elegantly put it, female sterilisation was to be encouraged because "we must get rid of the slovenly, vicious, idle wasters of the community. Unfortunately the welfare state is only too likely to encourage their increase."

The birth control movement certainly made great strides in the inter-war years, thanks above all to the ceaseless campaigning of women like Marie Stopes, who opened her first birth control clinic in 1921, Dora Russell (wife of philosopher Bertrand), Vera Houghton (founder of the Family Planning Association, which brought together most of the birth control groups under one umbrella in 1939) and Edith Summerskill – whose efforts were matched in America by the indefatigable Margaret Sanger (1897 –1966) founder of the IPPF.

What admirers of these women tend to overlook, however, is that they were not really feminists in today's sense; they were primarily eugenicists.

They were directing their efforts at the "feckless" poor – to stop the "unfit" from multiplying, and being a burden on society. Most would have favoured compulsory contraception and eugenic sterilisation to secure population "quality, not quantity". Margaret Sanger said it all when she denounced those misguided women who were unwittingly making wars possible (by producing surplus males to be recruited into tyrants' armies), filling slums, prisons and asylums, and inflicting on the world the insane, the disabled, the ignorant and prostitutes. Jews, Blacks and Catholics were her especial targets[8].

Abortionism lurked behind this eugenicist "family planning" crusade. It became more overt in 1938 when an ALRA gynaecologist, Dr Aleck Bourne, gave himself up after aborting a young woman who had allegedly been made pregnant after rape by soldiers in London. In the ensuing trial, the judge argued that, since the Offences against the Person Act 1861, the basic law on abortion, spoke only of *unlawful* procuring of miscarriage as a crime, there must be some induced abortions which are lawful. He ruled that what Dr Bourne had done was one of these. This celebrated test case, carefully planned by ALRA, prised open the door only slightly. In 1967 the door was pushed wide.

How this came about is still not entirely clear. But some factors are. First, by 1967 the Labour Party was very different from the party of a saintly George Lansbury or even Clement Attlee – men with a sincere concern for social justice. It had been taken over by the likes of RHS Crossman and Roy Jenkins (who, as leader of the House of Commons and Home Secretary, respectively, played a crucial role in steering David Steel's Bill through Parliament). They were direct descendants of the eugenicist/neo-Malthusian tradition. They had contempt, not mercy, for the poor. Secondly, the post-war baby boom, which peaked in 1964, greatly strengthened the panic about over-population and the need to curb the birthrate by whatever means.

Then there was an extraordinary fact: the feminist movement was completing an about-turn to become pro-contraception and pro-abortion. How precisely this happened has not yet been fully explained.

Thanks to Marie Stopes and Margaret Sanger, not to mention so-called "sexologists" like Havelock Ellis, the birth control movement had usually preached sexual permissiveness – romantic "free love" – for bourgeois women. The latter, it was argued, should rejoice in and enjoy their feminine spirit and sexuality, while ensuring that their fertility was under strict control (thereby setting a good example to the "unfit" working class women). Birth control would allow them to make reproductive choices: to have small, healthy families and escape the "servitude" of relentless childbearing or to enjoy promiscuous sexual activity without commitment of the sort increasingly promoted by the left wing, Hollywood and much of the other liberal media.

8. See, especially, Ann Farmer, *Prophets and Priests. The Hidden Face of the Birth Control Movement* (2002) for a brilliant account of all the above – to which I am much indebted – and John Cavanaugh-O'Keefe, *The Roots of Racism and Abortion* (1999).

World War II, and the new responsibility it gave to hard-line socialist ideologies, intensified the assault on traditional values regarding the family and sexual behaviour. By the early 1960s a Marie Stopes/Margaret Sanger "Female Liberation" movement – which had little to do with votes or political rights but was about "gender" equality – had been born.

The Pill was a final factor, because, for the first time, it gave women apparently safe, painless and almost complete control over their fertility – which led some to demand that free abortion "on demand" would allow them to achieve what was the logical conclusion of this story, namely, complete control. Covert abortionism could come out into the open and claim respectability. The extraordinary ferment of the Sixties and the failure of those who could and should have spoken out on behalf of sanity and tradition abetted the Western World's version of a Cultural Revolution. By the late 1960s hard-line feminists has become militant abortionists.

There is a last, decisive twist to this story. In 1963 John Ehrlich's book, *The Population Time Bomb* was published, which was sweet music to the birth-controllers and abortionists because it predicted a Doomsday far more terrible than nothing that Malthus could have forecast: a world population crisis. The "population explosion" was now not just a British thing. It was a crisis which threatened our whole planet with mass starvation by the year 2000. Drastic action was required at once, especially in the Third World, successors to the "feckless" poor of the First World.

So there was unleashed on the hapless inhabitants of Africa, Asia (especially India and China) and South America a ruthless population control campaign: forcible contraception, sterilisation and abortion. The eugenics movement had always been overtly racist. It preached white supremacy. Now that doctrine had a new face and a new virulence. The fast-growing populations of South America and China, for example, had to be culled because, before long, they would challenge the West and ask why they had so small a share of the world's wealth when they constituted so much of the world's population. The West's – particularly the USA's – economic and political dominance was at stake.

From the late 1960s onwards, the might of the West, especially the USA, was devoted to population control programmes in the Third World. The United Nations – through its Fund for Population Activities (UNFPA) and World Health Organisation (WHO), in close collaboration with International Planned parenthood Federation (IPPF – an international offspring of the Family Planning Association) – was its catspaw. But if these agencies failed to persuade local governments to promote their programmes there was always the direct approach: much-needed aid (financial and other) would be withheld until the appropriate population policies had been introduced. Thus was the East (and South) won, i.e. seduced, by Western Neo-Colonialism.

As far as Britain was concerned, an important lesson had been taught: what we were doing to ourselves was what was being done everywhere by sensible people. We were part of a righteous worldwide struggle against over-population. It was our duty to lead the way: another form of the "white man's burden", one might say.

As they forced their unwelcome policies on Third World women, IPPF, UNFPA and Marie Stopes International tried to disguise their true purposes by claiming that they had come to rescue women from the horrors of backstreet abortion, relentless childbearing, disease and so on. Wildly unreliable figures of women butchered to death every year by quack medicine-men and unqualified nurses in often squalid conditions would be their stock-in-trade – together with equally tendentious claims about infanticide and deaths in childbirth. That these were pure guesswork (because no accurate statistics were available) was rarely noticed.

The myth of over-population had initially been accompanied by the claim that the world would soon not be able to produce enough food to feed itself. When this was shown to be untrue, there came the warning that supplies of minerals and fossil fuels would soon be exhausted[9]. Meanwhile the "Green" cause had been born, which taught that human beings were doing irreparable damage to the environment, indeed, to our whole planet, by their wanton emission of greenhouse gases, destruction of rainforests, factory-farming etc. Eventually a new menace loomed: global warming alongside the energy crisis.

Politicians need crises and causes. These help them to feel important. But the population controllers needed these crises even more – because it is becoming increasingly clear that what the world faces is a population implosion, not that (mythical) explosion. Just as the AIDS crisis has given respectability to the condom culture so the new doom-mongers provided the IPPF, UNFPA, Marie Stopes International and all who abetted their works with a new camouflage.

There have been many more incongruities or contradictions within the population control movement. For example, the truly shocking stories of forcible sterilisation and abortion of women in china and South America have evoked little protest from Western feminists. Many of those most concerned for the environment causes would be of the Left politically, and instinctively suspicious of the USA and big business (if not openly hostile); yet they fail to see how their support for world population control serves both. Many of those who believe that Third World women are being liberated and their "reproductive health" and "reproductive rights" (the code words for ever more available contraception, sterilisation and abortion) are being promoted would regard

9. Thus in 1972 the Club of Rome, the EEC's forum, predicted in a report entitled *Limits to Growth* that there would be no copper left to mine by 1993, no natural gas by 1994, no petrol by 1992, no tin by 1987. One suspects that the threat of global warming is being hyped in a similar way.

themselves as bitter opponents of racism and committed democrats. But they fail to see the eugenic racism which drives agencies like Marie Stopes and have not yet seen that democracy is based on the supposition that all human beings are equal, while eugenics is based on the supposition that they are not.

The most obvious victory of the abortionists is the provision in the Abortion Act, as amended in 1990, allowing abortion up to birth of special-needs children. This has produced ever-more ruthless pre-birth screening techniques for "weeding out" defectives – the "useless mouths". Eugenics has captured genetics. Modern genetics is eugenics. IVF permits (in effect requires) scrutiny of embryos and discarding of sub-standard ones. Pre-implantation diagnosis allows parents to have children who have been "screened out" for genetic disorders or who can supply genetic material for repair of siblings. The Human Genome Project (which has much potential for good) and the imminence of human cloning (which will mean further commodification and exploitation of human life and is morally unacceptable) are bringing genetics, genetic engineering and eugenics into the centre of daily living.

Eugenics drives the euthanasia campaign. Outwardly (and for many) it is "about" compassion and dying with dignity. Really (and for the powerful forces behind it) it is "about" getting rid of the unfit, and the burdens on families, pension funds, the NHS, Social Services – the "useless mouths". Though it has not yet achieved a major victory in Parliament, it has won a momentous victory in society: the slogan "quality of life" has become part of everyday discourse. Gone from public policy-making and public discussion the age-old principle of "sanctity" or "inviolability" of human life, the belief, that is, that the right to life belongs absolutely to every human being by virtue of his/her humanity and is not conferred from without. Instead, there is a criterion for measuring the value of every human life. "Quality of life" means different things to different people, but what it is meant to mean by those who have most promoted it is sinister. "Quality of life" is a short step away from *lebensunvertung Lebens,* "life unworthy of life". It enables us to_deceive ourselves into thinking that there are some people – "unwanted" children in the womb, for example, special-needs born children, seriously ill or disabled people of all ages, the old and the senile – of such low "quality" that their interests would be served by killing them.

Eugenics is the chief begetter of the Culture of Death and the most bitter opponent of the pro-life cause.

V.

EUTHANASIA – NEONATAL AND ADULT

On 5 November 1981, Dr Leonard Arthur, a consultant in Derby City Hospital, was found not guilty by Leicester Crown Court of the attempted murder in June 1980 of John Pearson, a newborn child suffering from Down's syndrome.

During the 1970s LIFE received at least eight reports from around the country of newly-born disabled children, mainly suffering from spinal bifida or Down's syndrome, who were being, or had been, "sedated to death", i.e. filled with sedative drugs so that they would not demand food or drink and would therefore quietly starve to death. In every verifiable case, LIFE called in the local police. But the latter always found either that the corpse and often the records of the case had disappeared or that, by a coincidence, their arrival coincided with the discovery that the child, after all, loved milk and was gulping it down.

Decent people would have been shocked to hear that this sort of thing was happening in British hospitals, as it undoubtedly was – and almost routinely. But if they had paused for a moment they should have seen that this "weeding out" of "substandard" children after birth was an obvious extension of the practice of eugenic abortion licensed by the Abortion Act 1967. If it was permissible to kill a child *in utero* when there was a "substantial risk that, if born, it would suffer such physical or mental abnormalities as to be seriously handicapped" (to quote the Abortion Act) what was more logical than to kill immediately after birth a disabled child who had previously eluded detection? Same child; same unworthiness of life. And since prenatal "search and destroy" techniques became ever more efficient, i.e. ruthless, and doctors faced the possibility of litigation if a disabled child slipped through the net, it was becoming almost a duty to dispose of any special-needs child who had had the good fortune to be born. Postnatal euthanasia was the predictable product of pre-natal euthanasia.

Dr Leonard Arthur was a distinguished citizen of this Brave New World. Kindly and "deeply" Christian (he read the New Testament during his trial), he had devoted much attention to despatching, quickly and quietly, Down's children who had eluded ante-natal screening and been born in his hospital. It transpired after his trial that at least thirty had been taken to the corridor, the death alley, where this Angel of Mercy dealt with them. Arthur was a member of the Eugenics Society. He had simply been putting into practice a fundamental eugenic principle: some human beings are unfit to live. One woman who had known she was carrying a Down's child and, with her husband, had accepted this as God's will, was so frightened by the sinister man who came to her bedside after the birth and urged her to let him "take care" of her baby, that she immediately discharged herself. She had exceptional courage. Many a mother, still in a state of shock on hearing that she had given birth to a seriously stricken child and perhaps exhausted by labour, would have succumbed to the quietly spoken, apparently compassionate advice of so esteemed an authority figure as a consultant.

John Pearson's mother did. He was born on 28 June 1980. When Down's syndrome was diagnosed Dr Arthur quickly took him into his control and started pumping him with the powerful sedative DF118, a drug widely used as a painkiller for adults after surgery and listed by the manufacturers as not suitable for small children. LIFE was alerted to what was happening by an anonymous phone call and immediately informed Derby CID. Despite repeated attempts thereafter by the media and police to get us to reveal who it was – nurse, doctor, or whoever – who phoned us, we never broke the promise to reveal nothing about his/her identity. On the afternoon of Friday 1 July the police arrived at Derby City Hospital. The baby was dead (he had died a ghastly, slow death) but the police found his corpse in the sluice room and took it, and the case notes, away. Analysis showed that the child had been given three times the amount of DF118 sufficient to kill an adult. On 5 February 1981 Dr Arthur was arrested and charged with murder. When the police first interviewed him they asked the drug had been used. He made the following reply: 'It is a sedative which stops the child seeking sustenance'.

Yes, he had drugged the baby to ensure that he could not seek or take nourishment and would starve to death – and he openly confessed that this had been his intention.

* * *

It is worth dwelling on the subsequent trial, not least because it revealed how poisoned the legal and medical professions, and the general public, already were by the elitist eugenics of abortionism, and how corruptible British justice could be. The trial was a travesty of justice.[1]

There were three chief actors: the judge, Mr Justice Farquharson, prosecuting council, Douglas Draycott, QC, and defence council, George Carman, QC. Leonard Arthur scarcely figured. Knowing how easily his client would incriminate himself (he had already been dangerously frank to the police, as has been said), Carman decided that he would not let him be exposed to cross-examination. The defendant was tucked away and Carman left to deploy his customary tactic – to confuse everyone as much as possible. He was no great

1. Its story was told in detail in LIFE booklet *Regina* v *Arthur* (1982) and *LIFE News* 10(1982). What follows here is a synopsis of these reports

orator or brilliant legal mind. He won cases by producing red herrings and generating complexity. Douglas Draycott was no match for him. As for the judge, the following soon became apparent. First, he had excessive deference for the medical profession, especially for such eminent witnesses for the defence as Sir Douglas Black, president of the Royal College of Physicians. At the same time, he had an equal and opposite prejudice against Down's children (speaking disparagingly in his summing up of their "oriental" features and "lolling tongues", etc). Secondly, he got himself into a hopeless tangle, as no lawyer should do, over the distinction between intention and motive. Finally, it soon became clear that he was determined that Arthur, like him a distinguished member of an ancient profession, should not be found guilty.

All that prosecutor Draycott had to do was to keep on asking the same question: "what therapeutic (i.e. positive) purpose had that DF118 been intended to serve?" There was no other issue. And there was only one answer to that question. Arthur had already given it implicitly to the police. It was "none". The drug had been intended to procure death. What Arthur's motive had been was irrelevant.

The Crown's case, which relied on the evidence of the police and the pathologist from Sheffield who had examined Baby Pearson's body, was made potentially even more damning when the defence started calling other paediatricians as witnesses. These, like Sir Douglas Black, agreed that sedating disabled newborns to death was accepted practice, though one doctor observed that DF118 was not the drug that he would use. So the defence was apparently to be that Leonard Arthur had only been doing what any good doctor would do: the so-called Bolam principle, i.e. that if enough doctors are doing something, it must be lawful. But then Carman threw the trial into a new direction by producing out of the blue another doctor – a paediatrician – also from Sheffield, who had slides of Baby Pearson's organs showing that, as with all Down's children, his respiratory system was vulnerable and that he had a heart condition. After much complicated medical evidence Carman was able to imply that the child would have soon died a natural death anyway. This was, of course, irrelevant as well as untrue. But prosecutor Draycott allowed the court to be bamboozled and the judge to change the charge against Arthur from murder to attempted murder. Much confusion ensued. Draycott had allowed the proceedings to get completely out of his control. Since this was new evidence which the Crown's pathologist had not seen, he should have asked for an adjournment to enable his expert witness to examine it. He did not. He not only failed to focus on that one simple question about why Arthur had prescribed that drug for Baby Pearson, that is, what had been his *intention* i.e. purpose. He missed the point that, if the baby was as badly afflicted as was now being alleged, the last thing he had needed was a heavy dose of DF118! Arthur's purpose had clearly been murder.

It was now for Mr Justice Farquharson to deliver the *coup de grace*. He ruled, as a matter of law, that to administer a drug which was intended to procure death to a child who was already close to dying would be merely a "holding operation" and lawful. He directed the jury that, if they decided that Arthur's regime for Baby Pearson was a "holding operation" it could not amount to attempted murder, because it would be revocable, merely negative non-action and designed to let Nature take its course. This was verging on the grotesque. A "holding operation" is something neutral, the maintenance of the status quo. But what Arthur did was to administer a drug to Baby Pearson whose purpose was not to keep him going – in a "steady state", so to speak – but to kill him. He had foreseen, willed and intended death and had actively procured it. That the judge could fail to see that he had acted criminally defies belief. Nonetheless he directed the jury that, if they decided that Arthur's regime for Baby Pearson had been a "holding operation", as now defined by him, they should find him not guilty of attempted murder. This they quickly did.

The media had been largely on Arthur's side (the *Guardian* for example, commending the "negative care" and the "sleepy peaceful passing" of Baby Pearson). The Christian bishop of Derby deplored the ordeal which Arthur had had to endure. A close friend, MP for Derby, wrote angrily in *The Times* about how a saintly man had been persecuted by LIFE, forgetting that it was the prosecuting authorities, not LIFE, which had brought Arthur to trial. Arthur died some months later. The same MP then accused LIFE of killing him. Graham Greene had written to *The Daily Telegraph* defending him. A member of The Guild of Catholic Doctors rebuked LIFE.

* * *

The verdict in the Arthur trial could have seemed a major victory for the euthanasia lobby. Interestingly, it was not. Most people knew in their hearts that Arthur was guilty. He had been proud of what he done. Mr Justice Farquharson's idea of a "holding operation" was obviously absurd. The revelation that neonatal killing was widespread shocked people, despite what the *Guardian* and *Times* might say, and resulted in an unprecedented statement by the attorney general to Parliament effectively conceding that Arthur had been wrongly acquitted.[2] This in turn led the British Paediatrics Society to issue guidelines which implicitly condemned what Arthur had been doing and what Sir Douglas Black, soon to head up a body to promote medical ethics, and other doctors had commended. At least for a while, newly-born special-needs children were safer in British hospitals than they had been before. An apparent defeat had become a modest pro-life victory.

2. In a written answer to Mrs Jill Knight, MP, he said: "The law relating to murder and attempted murder is the same now as it was before the trial." But he had refused LIFE's request to seek the Court of Appeal's ruling on the lawfulness of that "holding operation".

* * *

There was another pro-life success, equally unexpected, in 1992 where a committee of the House of Lords set up to consider the question of voluntary (adult) euthanasia came out strongly against it – despite the fact that its chairman was reputedly unsound on the issue and its membership included the recently ennobled Lady Warnock and an eager understudy, Baroness Jay, daughter of former prime minister Jim ('Sunny') Callaghan. That the committee concluded as it did was largely due to two pro-life initiatives: a magisterial submission by the Linacre Centre (which surpassed anything else which the committee received) and a visit to Holland to see what really happened once the law against so-called "mercy" killing was relaxed. It was thanks to the efforts of Alert, an anti-euthanasia campaigning group set up by two pro-life veterans, Elspeth Chowdharay-Best and Dr Peggy Norris, that this visit took place. It opened eyes. The committee recommended that the law should not be changed. There, one would have thought, the matter would have rested for a considerable time. A mere four years later, however, that same House of Lords – in the persons of the law lords – gave a pro-euthanasia judgement which matched Mr Justice Farquharson's "holding operation" for intellectual incoherence.

* * *

Tony Bland had been severely hurt in a football crowd stampede at Hillingdon, Leeds, and left in a "permanent vegetative state", a pejorative term against which LIFE had protested in its submission to that previous House of Lords committee. Eventually, after many months of hospitalisation and several rescues from pneumonia, the doctors sought leave to withdraw food and fluids and to starve the young man to death. The case was taken all the way to the Lords, where the doctors were finally granted their wish.

It should be said at once that, if poor Tony Bland had been correctly looked after, he would probably not have survived as long as he did and the House of Lords judgement would never have been necessary. After several bouts of pneumonia doctors should have concluded that further intervention was futile and that he should be allowed to die naturally. Only a vitalist, (i.e. someone who insists that every effort should always be made to keep alive a dying person for as long as possible and never to admit defeat) would have argued otherwise. Opponents of pro-lifers like to accuse them of vitalism; but the pro-life position is that there can come a time when it will not only be right to withdraw treatment but even wrong (because it would be futile and overburdensome) to persist with it.

No, it was not the fact that Tony Bland's death was sanctioned that was morally objectionable but the intellectually vacuous ground on which this was done and the implications of the Law Lords' ruling. Despite what the media persisted in saying, Tony Bland was not "allowed to die" as he would have been if carried off by a final, overwhelming attack of pneumonia. He was caused to die by being starved (and since death by starvation is a horrible way to go, probably his departure was speeded by a doctor's syringe). The Law Lords ruled that the treatment which could be withdrawn included food and fluids when these were administered "artificially". But providing one's neighbour with food and drink is an act of common humanity, not medical treatment; and why is tubal feeding any more "artificial" than, say, using a knife and fork or a baby's bottle? But most egregious of all was the Lords' central reason for granting the doctors their wishes. The latter asked them to rule that it was in Tony Bland's "best interests" to be dead. And this they did.

Let us ponder that ruling. I can reasonably claim that a decision or action would be in someone else's best interests (or my own, for that matter) if I can know (and only if I can know) pretty well what the consequences of that decision or action are likely to be. Thus I can decide that it is in my best interests to go to bed or that it is in my child's best interest to be put to bed because I know that sleep will restore mind and body and prepare both for tomorrow. The Law Lords could therefore rule that it was in Tony Bland's best interests to be dead only if they knew what would happen to him after death. But, even if they believed in life after death, they could not know what that life would be.

Their verdict therefore was absurd. That has not prevented it from becoming enshrined in the Common Law.

* * *

Encouraged by the Bland judgement and despite the report of the committee only a few years previously, the euthanasiast lobby in parliament, abetted by the Voluntary Euthanasia Society, pressed on relentlessly. They were much encouraged by the arrival on the scene of the Mass-going Mr Blair, whose utilitarian government dedicated much effort to accelerating the paganising of British society. It quickly set to work on eroding the law which protected the old and lonely and incapacitated (who have been a steadily growing burden on the National Health and Social Services) and, in particular, focusing on the role of living wills, a complex issue which was an obvious Trojan horse for the euthanasia lobby. A consultation document, always an ominous sign, from the Office of Constitutional Affairs, led the way and eventually a draft of the Mental Incapacity Bill was published. Both before, during and after, it was repeatedly and categorically stated that the Government was not in favour of euthanasia and intended no legislation which would open the door to it. How honest these assurances were was revealed by the story of the evolution of the Mental Incapacity (subsequently re-named "Capacity") Bill. The original text had said nothing about a doctor deliberately causing a patient's death by omission or otherwise. Thanks to the vigilance and vigour of the Bill's critics, led by Archbishop Peter Smith, Catholic archbishop of Cardiff, and Cardinal Murphy O'Connor's appeal to the prime minister, the lord chancellor promised the archbishop in writing that an addition would be made which forbade a doctor to take any action with the intention of causing death. This crucial concession, won at the eleventh hour, greatly helped the Bill to pass its second reading in the Commons. But when the new text appeared "with the intention of" had become "with the desire to". Since it is possible to intend but not actually desire something, such sleight of hand could be significant and was a measure of how devious the Government could be.

Time will tell how important the Mental Capacity Act has been as a stepping-stone towards a totally "liberalised" law on euthanasia and how effectively the defeat in the Lords of the much more dangerous Joffe Bill has halted those hell-bent on legalising assisted suicide. Predictably, guardians of the integrity of the medical profession such as the BMA have betrayed the cause, as the Royal College of Obstetricians and Gynaecologists did in the wake of the Abortion Act. But those who are committed to the hospice movement and know how much progress has been made by palliative medicine in enabling "last days not to be lost days" (and how much would be undone if the euthanasiasts and so-called "death with dignity" lobby had their way) have mobilised themselves. And Catholic bishops have become more proactive and more outspoken on behalf of the pro-life cause than ever before.

Just as abortionism "triumphed" at a time when there was less real need for it than there had ever been in our history, so the euthanasia lobby has become most aggressive precisely as the remarkable expansion of the hospice movement has been showing a much better, more civilised way of caring for people in their last days on earth. This fact poses a double challenge: to expand hospice provision and to ensure that the hospice care is not corrupted by those who preach the spurious doctrine of "quality of life". Overuse of diamorphine, together with denial of food and fluids to incapacitated patients, is a constant threat and may already be producing "euthanasia from within" – not just in overstretched NHS geriatric units and senior citizens homes but in the hospices dedicated to enabling the dying to die worthily.

There is one small part of it which should be an especial source of pride to pro-lifers, namely, Zoë's Places. The idea of a baby hospice – as distinct from a children's' or adult one – was conceived in 1982 thanks to Regina v Arthur. It took a long time to become a reality but is now thriving. A new form of hospice care has been pioneered, inspired initially by the trauma of the career and acquittal of Leonard Arthur.

* * *

The adult hospice movement must be ever more vigilant in the face of alarming evidence that the distinction between administering palliative drugs which could, but are not intended to, hasten death and ones which are intended to do so is being quietly eroded.

What is happening in Holland, where euthanasia and doctor-assisted suicide are now rampant, should warn us of the dangers of yielding to the – at first hearing – plausible arguments of the euthanasia lobby for a modest relaxation of the law to allow mercy killing for the hard cases. The exception quickly becomes the norm.

We must be equally on our guard against the so-called Gröningen Protocol. This governs the treatment of newborn children judged to be too small to be worth trying to save because they will have a "very poor quality of life". Gröningen Hospital authorities have decided that such children should be "allowed to die" and have accordingly authorised the despatch of spina bifida and other special needs babies who have come to them for care. No official action has been taken against the hospital which claims that, with the consent of parents, doctors routinely kill such children, So far there have been no prosecutions and it is generally believed that there will not be any. So the way is cleared for the legalisation of paediatric euthanasia before long.

If this happens, Britain and eventually the whole of Western society could "go Dutch" (or continue to do so), and the merciless mercy-killer of Derby – Leonard Arthur – become a martyr to his cause.

The need for an authentic adult and children's hospice movement is as urgent as the need for a national provision of Zoë's Places.

VI.

THE CHURCHES AND THE GOSPEL OF LIFE

With some important exceptions, Britain's Christian leaders have given little public support to the pro-life cause. Many have ignored it. Some have actively opposed it.

John 'Honest to God' Robinson, Anglican bishop of Woolwich, and the celebrated Methodist leader Donald (later Lord) Soper were vice-presidents of the Abortion Law Reform Association (ALRA), the hard-line pressure-group whose campaign to de-criminalise abortion in Britain climaxed in David Steel's Abortion Act 1967. They were direct heirs to Church leaders like Bishop Barnes of Birmingham, a keen supporter of the Eugenics Society in the 1930s.

In June 1967, as the debate on the Steel Bill entered its last phase, Geoffrey Fisher, archbishop emeritus of Canterbury, wrote a letter to *The Times* (an unusual thing for a retired Primate of all England to do) which asserted that human life begins at quickening, that is, when the mother first feels the child moving in her womb, and that abortion would be permissible up to that moment. That *The Times* should have given space to a letter from the former *de facto* head of the Anglican Communion is not surprising – since that paper was then the Establishment's deferential mouthpiece. What is surprising is that a man of Geoffrey Fisher's stature could have produced such a silly statement. Quickening, like viability, tells us nothing about the moral status of the child growing in the womb. What the archbishop wrote was irrelevant to the debate; and the conclusion he drew from it illicit.

When the Steel Bill reached its final stages in the House of Lords, Geoffrey Fisher's successor, Michael Ramsey, spoke passionately in its favour. A mannered, spell-binding speaker, he argued that the law on abortion was so shot through with uncertainty that doctors were having to cope with impossible dilemmas. This was the official line (the Steel Bill's subtitle was "a Bill to amend *and clarify* the law on abortion") and was tendentious. The prevailing law was not full of uncertainties. To procure an unlawful miscarriage "by any means whatsoever" or to attempt to do so (even if the woman was not pregnant) was forbidden by the Offences against the Person Act 1861, but, following the ruling in Rex *v* Bourne in 1938, a test-case stage-managed by ALRA, abortion was not unlawful if done in certain cases, for example, to save the mother's life or after rape. In truth, abortion was generally available in Harley Street and private clinics, but the fact that the law was being quietly flouted was not proof that it was unclear. There was no need for new legislation unless one's purpose was to make abortion more available. So, when the archbishop of Canterbury proclaimed the urgent need for abortion law reform he was implicitly pleading for relaxation, not clarification, of the law. And since he was a respected, if slightly eccentric, figure, his verdict carried considerable weight.

Some may think that the archbishop was simply naïve and had swallowed David Steel's assurances that his Bill would merely tidy up things and not open the floodgates. Ramsey was no pro-abortionist, it would be claimed. He could never have foreseen and, if he had, would never have approved of, the mass destruction of unborn life which that Bill unleashed. Much of that is surely true.[1] But the archbishop was not entirely innocent.

In 1965, well before the Steel Bill saw the light of day but when abortion law reform was being widely mooted in liberal circles, Ramsey had set up a committee to review the Church of England's position on the issue with, one suspects, the clear (but unspoken) purpose of finding a way of reducing traditional Judaeo-Christian teaching without appearing to do so too openly. It was chaired by another Ramsey, Ian, who was Michael Ramsey's successor as bishop of Durham: a clever, ex-Cambridge chaplain who liked to remind Christians that "the Church is in a learning situation". The secretary to the committee was one Gordon Dunstan, whose training had been in art history but had somehow been enlarged to include moral theology and who occupied the FD Maurice chair of social and moral philosophy at King's College London. From there he waged a campaign against the pro-life cause. What animated him is unclear; but, encouraged no doubt by an English Jesuit (his successor as FD Maurice professor), he never tired of arguing (wrongly) that papal teaching on pro-life issues had been inconsistent. Like that Jesuit, who followed American dissenters such as Richard McCormick, SJ, and Charles Curran, Gordon Dunstan would persist in the claim that Catholic teaching on abortion did not harden until the time of Pius IX in the mid-nineteenth century and that absolutist pro-lifers were more absolutist than Catholic tradition itself. As we have seen, these ideas were to have a long life because gratefully picked up by others who wanted to abandon the Gospel of Life when the debates on embryo research and cloning arose.

But this is to anticipate. The committee which Dunstan served in 1965 did what had been expected of it. It produced a report which professed commitment to upholding the sanctity of all human life while allowing that abortion in various circumstances would be the lesser of two evils and hence a morally licit, compassionate act[2]. The archbishop was off the hook.

Ramsey retired in 1972, by which time the abortion rate had soared to over 150,000 a year. It is a striking fact that, if he had sincerely intended only

---

1. Ramsey wanted abortion only to protect the mother's life *or health* and opposed other criteria (e.g. fetal disability) as separate grounds. *Hansard* (Lords), 19 July 1967, cols 276 ff. But he said "we do not know at what stage a foetus becomes a human being." *Ibid*, col 277.
2. Church of England Board of Social Responsibility, *Abortion: an ethical discussion* (1965).

that the law should be clarified, he failed to protest when, after all, the floodgates opened.

To give him credit, his successor, Archbishop Coggan, did. He spoke of abortionism as "a runaway bus". But he did nothing to bring it under control. Nor did his successors Robert Runcie and George Carey. They simply looked the other way[3]. Lambeth made no comment on successive attempts from 1975 onwards to curb that "runaway bus". There were undoubtedly some more or less pro-life Anglican bishops but none was prepared to speak out in his diocese or the Lords, and only one – Nigel McCulloch, bishop of Wakefield – was an active supporter of the pro-life cause (together with a retired missionary bishop, Anselm Genders, CR). Pro-life Anglican lay people found the Board of Social Responsibility, chaired for years by liberals like Hugh Montefiore of Birmingham and then Richard Harries of Oxford, determined to brush the issues under the carpet.

It was an Archbishop of York (rather than Canterbury) who led the next offensive against the Gospel of Life. John Habgood, primate of England from 1983 to 1995, played a decisive role in securing the passage through Parliament of the Human Fertilisation and Embryology Act 1990 which licensed *in vitro* fertilisation (including the production of human embryos solely for destructive experimentation) and amended the abortion law to permit abortion up to birth if the mother's life was in danger or the child was a special-needs one.

This Act, it will be recalled, implemented the recommendations of the committee chaired by Mary Warnock which had made the startling claim that personal human life does not begin until the appearance of the "primitive streak" on day 14 and that any form of embryo abuse was morally permissible up to that time (a doctrine which did not prevent its author, a professional philosopher and by then Lady Warnock, from subsequently voting in the Lords for abortion up to birth).

Professor Dunstan had argued that human life does not begin until the nervous system has been established – at about 42 days. This was essentially a throwback to a medieval idea (indeed, a pre-medieval, Aristotelian one) and patently at odds with the findings of modern genetics and embryology. Archbishop Habgood had a more radical message – and one which he hoped would satisfy all-comers: becoming human is a process, like becoming middle-aged, and has no precise beginning. Processes cannot have beginnings, he said. So we have a choice. Either we can play safe and treat all

3. One Anglican bishop did try to face it openly, but in an unexpected way. In 1971 the then bishop of Winchester proposed a prayer to the General Synod to be said after an abortion which contained the following: "into your hands we commit in trust the developing life we have cut short. Look in kindly judgment on the decision that we have made." This was matched by a "staunch" Christian gynaecologist who in 1972 wrote in a book entitled *Abortion: the personal dilemma* that, when he "terminated" an unborn child he told himself that that was a life which "God had let slip." *God!*

human life from fertilisation as sacrosanct or we can say that the embryo has no human value and may be used to serve a higher good than itself. He preferred the latter.

But it was manifestly wrong to assert that a process cannot have an exact beginning – which is the essence of the Habgood case. For example, a cricket match is a "process" which can last hours, even days. But it has a precise beginning nevertheless: when the umpire calls "play". At that moment two previously separate teams "fuse" irrevocably to become a unique new cricket match, just as at human fertilisation sperm and ovum fuse to become a unique new human being. Like a cricket match, that new human being thereafter needs only time and a favourable environment in order to develop.

The archbishop claimed, and received, attention because, as he reminded his fellow-peers, he was a scientist (he had studied pharmacology) as well as an archbishop. He also did some philosophising. We can distinguish, he said, between what something is and what it is morally worth, that is, we can name a thing without making a value judgement on it. So something can be human, i.e. look like one, without having any human value.[4]

But this kind of word-play, in vogue when the archbishop was an undergraduate, has long such been discredited. When we identify something – dog, kettle, or whatever – we are evaluating it at the same time. When we call someone a hero we are saying that he is a man and a brave one. When we identify a life as human we are making a moral statement about it. Knowing what it is immediately leads us to how it ought to be regarded.

The measure which John Habgood eagerly supported, the Human Fertilisation and Embryology Act 1990, was at odds with Judaeo-Christian moral tradition in two ways (and thus represented a double assault on the Gospel of Life). In the first place, it licensed the manufacture of human beings in laboratories by technicians carrying out impersonal professional procedures: a further commodification of human life which opened the way to discarding "substandard" embryos, storing "spares" in deep freezers and a "pick `n` mix" use of gametes (donated or purchased – even Online) to produce customised offspring. From "sex without kids" we have reached "kids without sex". Secondly, again for the first time in our history, Parliament approved the use of human material in destructive research and experimentation. Hitherto civilised countries cherished the principle, enshrined in the Helsinki Declaration, that experiments on human beings should be carried out only for their benefit. Another moral Rubicon had been crossed.

That Act would no doubt have reached the Statute Book without John Habgood's support because it had passed the Commons with a large majority, thanks not least to a two-line whip imposed by the then Government (Mrs Thatcher's) – contrary to the tradition that, on moral issues, MPs should

4. *Hansard* (Lords), 7 December 1989, cols 1019 ff; 8 February 1990, cols 955 ff.

enjoy a free vote. But the archbishop was a major force in the Lords and influenced that vote as decisively as Michael Ramsey had done in 1967. As Keith Joseph (by then a peer) wrote to LIFE explaining how he had come to vote for a measure which at first hearing would have offended his high-minded Jewish reverence for life, "having listened to the archbishop of York, my mind was made up". An unusually full House heard the archbishop's speech – many peers then repairing to dinner and returning only to vote later in the evening without having heard any further speeches.

* * *

There is a final chapter in this catalogue of Anglican failure. It brings us to the story of how Britain became the first European (and English-speaking) country to licence human cloning in 1998 and thus depart yet further from its Judaeo-Christian past.

Of course, after Dolly the sheep, it was almost inevitable that the scientific imperative ("I can therefore I must") would prevail. The race was on to enter forbidden territory, break taboos, taste power of which no Renaissance wizard could have dreamed – namely, the creation of a genetically identical replica of a living person by taking a nucleus of one of his/her cells, placing it inside the emptied shell of someone else's ovum and jerking this new human construct into life by passing an electric shock through it. Thus a new kind of human being – produced asexually and without mother or father in the traditional sense – would have been manufactured.

Prime Minister Tony Blair greeted this enthusiastically, expressing the remarkable idea that Science should not be subject to ethical restraints. His Government led the way in claiming that stem cells taken from cloned embryos could revolutionise medicine and enable the conquest of terrible diseases such as Parkinson's, diabetes, Alzheimer's, etc. The media lapped up all this (mostly forgetting that we had heard similar claims a few years previously for fetal tissue transplants which had proved ill-founded and then for research using "spare" embryos produced by IVF). At least for a while they fell for what was a shocking example of deliberate official dis-information: the claim that only birth cloning, i.e. placing a cloned embryo in a womb and allowing it to be born, constituted real cloning, and that nuclear cell replacement (NCR) for therapeutic purposes, which would allow harvesting stem cells from cloned embryos up to fourteen days (after which they would be destroyed), was not cloning at all. Only this procedure, therapeutic NCR, would be permitted. Birth cloning was morally repugnant and would never be permitted, so we were categorically informed.

But this was shameless deception. Therapeutic NCR and birth cloning involve identical procedures. Both produce clones of the person from whom the replacement nucleus is taken. The difference between the two procedures is in their outcomes. Birth cloning results in a birth. Therapeutic cloning results in death, two weeks after life has started.

There was a further dishonesty: the refusal of the pro-cloning lobby to accept that umbilical cords provide an almost inexhaustible supply of stem cells with which to develop stem cell therapy techniques and that cells taken from the patients themselves were likely to prove as successful in treating degenerative diseases of all kinds as embryonic ones, not least because they would be a perfect genetic match and would not encounter problems of rejection. Indeed, almost every week new evidence has been coming to light that the future lies with adult stem cell therapy and that the embryo cloning lobby is chasing a chimera.

The pro-life case was and is simple. We should not want cloning because it involves yet more manipulation, exploitation and trivialisation of human life. Human beings are ends in themselves and should not be used or produced simply to supply spare parts for others, and so on. Moreover, we do not need cloning. The way forward lies elsewhere.

But the pro-cloning propaganda campaign, led by the Government, thrust ahead inexorably, brushing the pro-lifers aside. What the latter least needed at this point was a distinguished Anglican bishop to appear on the scene who would argue that pro-life objections were misplaced and that cloning up to fourteen days was morally permissible. But this is what they got.

Bishop Harries of Oxford, chairman of the Board of Social Responsibility and a utilitarian bioethicist, quickly became a major apologist in the House of Lords for cloning and embryonic stem cell research. Intellectually, he was, so to speak, Gordon Dunstan's clone. Like him – and equally revealingly – he invoked what he claimed was Catholic teaching, repeating the same misrepresentation of what Church Fathers and medieval Aristotelians had said about ensoulment and the same misinterpretation of the history of papal teaching on abortion of an "unformed" child[5]. This was once more sweet music to anti-life peers (and liberal Catholics: *The Tablet*, for example, gave him generous space); and it greatly helped Parliament to lead Britain yet further into the moral abyss.

* * *

British Methodists, Baptists and the United Reform communities have, alas, remained largely uncommitted to the pro-life cause. Thankfully the same is not true of those who belong to the Evangelical tradition. Their pro-life awakening, begun in the USA, spread to Britain in the late 1970s and, as the

5. *Hansard* (Lords), 22 January 2000, cols 35 ff. Bishop Harries chaired the subsequent Lords Select Committee on cloning which was almost entirely filled with peers in favour thereof. So were the 26 experts which it called to give evidence. Only two scientists who had contrary views were heard – and then only because Lord Alton sacrificed much of the mere hour granted to him to enable them to do so. The then archbishop of Canterbury refused to censure Harries (as LIFE asked him to do) or to distance himself from the latter's views. After retiring, the bishop became a member of the Human Fertilisation and Embryology Authority – the "watchdog" established to oversee the IVF industry, etc.

presence of such enterprises as CARE, the Christian Institute and Education remind us, have been very fruitful of pro-life witness and action ever since. But perhaps precisely because "hierarchy" is alien to authentic Evangelicalism, the latter has produced a groundswell of popular pro-life enthusiasm rather than any major pro-life prophets.[6]

It may be painful for some to hear the story of how the Catholic bishops of England and Wales conducted themselves as the Steel Bill made its way through Parliament in 1967. They were silent: deliberately so. They were persuaded by the heroic few who were trying to mobilise opposition to the Bill in Parliament that any statement or action by them would be inflammatory and play into the pro-abortionists' hands. The then archbishop of Westminster, John Carmel Heenan, and his brother-bishops duly held their peace. The cardinal would later express deep regret that he had taken the advice of those Catholic MPs (Norman St John Stevas being the most prominent). It was typical of him that he should have had the courage to confess an error of judgement. It was perhaps also typical of him that he did not make a full confession. In the first place, it was not the Catholic MPs' advice alone which was to blame. As late as June 1967 he was still convinced that the Steel Bill would never pass and was confident that, if it threatened to do so, he would be able to get to the prime minister, Harold Wilson, and persuade him to ditch it by refusing it Government time[4]. Secondly, and much more importantly, Cardinal Heenan overlooked the fact that, though the Steel Bill received the Royal Assent on 27 October 1967, it did not come into force until 27 April 1968. There was a six-month delay to enable the necessary preparation to be made. It may or may not have been right to be silent while the Bill was completing its last stages in Parliament in October 1967, but there was nothing to be lost, and much to be gained, by speaking out six months later. The Hierarchy could and should have broken their silence then. As it happened, on 22 to 24 April 1968, just before the Act was unleashed, the bishops of England and Wales were gathered at Westminster for their regular Low Week meeting. Ironically, the Abortion Act came into force while the Race Relations Act, 1968 was being debated: a profoundly anti-Christian piece of legislation coinciding with a profoundly Christian one. Here was a wonderful opportunity for the bishops to speak out and give leadership – not just to the Catholic flock. How powerfully could they have shown the contradiction between these two measures.

Instead, they said nothing. Nothing about either. That was the real failure. Nor had they done anything in those previous six months to rally such agencies as the Catholic Nurses Guild or the Guild of Catholic Doctors to

6. But I do not forget the admirable work of the Christian Institute and the growing pro-life influence of the Christian Medical Fellowship – among other important Evangelical movements.

7. I know this because he said it to me and his words are etched deeply on my memory.

prepare for the coming storm. In the event, two organisations which could have done much to make to make the Abortion Act inoperable (at least in the NHS, given especially its large proportion of Catholic nurses) proved to be feeble.

It was not, of course, that the bishops were disloyal to the Church's teaching on abortion. Their failure was due to other things – about which one can only speculate.

The Second Vatican Council (1962-65) had, among much else, required bishops to undergo what was, in effect, a personality change – from remote, sometimes autocratic, administrators and builders who paid little attention to the laity and the outside world and were responsible only to Rome, to accessible pastors who served and listened to the Faithful, acted collegially with brother-bishops, sought dialogue with the World, and were actively committed to ending the scandal of Christian disunity. For those brought up under the pre-Vatican II dispensation all this was profoundly unsettling, all the more so since the Church everywhere was in ferment after the Council and secular society, thanks to increased affluence and the so-called sexual revolution of the Sixties, was becoming increasingly hedonistic and de-Christianised. As well as having to come to terms with all this, the bishops of England and Wales were now in 1967/8 challenged to do something they had never done before: to take a very public stand on a moral issue and confront not just their own flock but society as a whole. Hitherto the Established Church had been the official guardian of the nation's conscience, but, as far as sexual issues were concerned, it had been steadily surrendering that duty since the Lambeth Conference of 1930 gave way on the issue of artificial birth control. Would the Catholic bishops now take on a national role by denouncing the Abortion Act? Would they have the vision to do so? If they did, would they be acting according to the spirit of Vatican II, and, in particular, serving the cause of ecumenism?

To be fair to them, many may have believed David Steel's assurance that his Act would not result in much more abortion than was already happening. A pious bishop might never have thought possible the mass destruction of human life which in fact ensued. It is easy to be wise after the event. There was another consideration. The commission recently set up in Rome to consider the Church's teaching on contraception (especially the Pill) was about to report. Many believed that Paul VI would accept the increasingly strident demands of the liberals and declare chemical contraception – if not barrier methods, too – to be licit. At least one English bishop was so sure this would happen that he had thousands of leaflets printed which explained the change in teaching to the Faithful. Since it would have been difficult to speak about abortion without dealing also with the explosive subject of contraception, until Rome had spoken on the latter, the bishops would have had another reason for silence.

In the event, of course, *Humane Vitae* reaffirmed traditional Catholic teaching and condemned all forms of artificial birth control as well as abortion. The heroic papal statement was issued in July 1968. It intensified the challenge facing English bishops: would they openly and actively confront the World (and the dissidents within their community) and openly and actively promote the papal teaching on two crucial moral issues – abortion and now contraception?

The answer was no. They did not publicly defy Rome, of course. They exhorted obedience to *Humane Vitae* – but in most cases *sotto voce*. There was no fight in them. They fell back from the parapets.

The middle months of 1968 – from April to the Autumn – were a turning-point in the history of the Catholic Church in Britain: a great might-have-been. Had the bishops risen to the occasion they would no doubt have caused uproar (at least for a while) but in the longer term they would have emerged with unique new authority. Their failure – "lack of vision" might be more charitable – in those crucial months cost them dear. Since their silence was not easy to break thereafter, most seem subsequently to have turned their backs on *Humane Vitae* and the abortion issue, and simply hoped that they would somehow go away. Most gave little public encouragement to the growing pro-life movement or to those who courageously continued to promote natural fertility management – against most of the odds.

It was not until 1981, fourteen years too late, a pro-lifer might have cried, that they spoke out against abortion – on the eve of the historic visit to Britain of Pope John Paul II. A cynic might suggest that their strong pro-life message would not have appeared if a papal visit had not been imminent. It was an excellent statement – lucid, orthodox and compassionate. But there was one curious feature about it. It went out in the names of only the archbishops, not the whole hierarchy – apparently because a much-respected bishop who had been seduced by clever talk about the distinctions between "human" and "humanised" and "human being" and "person" (and was allegedly hung up on the alleged "problem" of twinning) could not accept the document's statement *tout court* that human life begins at fertilisation. Over-awed, brother-bishops held back and so what had been intended to be a pro-life declaration by the whole British episcopate took on the reduced form of a message from only the country's archbishops.

Cardinal Heenan's successor at Westminster, Basil Hume, graciously spoke twice at LIFE National Conferences (first in Leamington Spa in 1977, shortly after he became archbishop) and then in 1999 in Coventry shortly before he died of cancer and when he was already in obvious discomfort. Not long before, Glasgow's Cardinal Winning launched a much-publicised initiative promising financial support for pregnant women who had chosen the pro-life route. But few of the numerous private MPs' attempts to curb abortionism, from James White's in 1975 to David Alton's in 1987, received the public blessing of England's Catholic bishops.

It was not that they doubted that abortion was profoundly wrong. It was that they did not take seriously what that same Thomas Winning himself had said: "The pro-life cause is not *an* issue. It is *the* issue."

So it was a question of priorities. Which was more important: the mass destruction of preborn life, IVF, embryo freezing, cloning, etc here at home or politically correct issues such as the Third World poverty and peace issues or the Environment?

It would not be fair to leave matters there, however. In the 1990s an Episcopal Bioethics Committee was set up (uniquely) by the hierarchies of England and Wales, Scotland and Ireland which, though it fell short of the high-powered secretariat for pro-life affairs established by the US bishops, helped to give Catholic leaders courage at last to speak out against the latest assaults of the neo-pagans – cloning and then, of course, adult euthanasia. A hierarchy that had been silent in 1967/8 and 1990 had found a voice by the time the new Millennium arrived.

The Church's condemnation of human cloning did not, alas, halt Parliament's rush to legislate it (albeit therapeutic cloning only) in 2001. But a dogged counter-attack against what was eventually entitled the Mental Capacity Bill, led by Archbishop Peter Smith of Cardiff and vigorously supported by Cardinal Murphy O'Connor, undoubtedly resulted in an Act that, though far from perfect, was a good deal less menacing than it would otherwise have been. The policy of "hanging on in there" and fighting every inch of the way saved a little ground, which was more than the policy of outright condemnation and refusal to negotiate, advocated by some pro-lifers, would have secured.

It was a partial victory. The defeat in May 2006 of Lord Joffe's Bill, always, as has been said, a more sinister measure than the Mental Capacity Bill (because it provided for assisted suicide not simply voluntary euthanasia), was a significant victory which owed much to the ably-led All-Party Parliamentary Pro-Life Group, the vigorous response of pro-life groups and the efforts of Archbishop Smith. But the danger has been scotched, not killed.

* * *

In its early LIFE had always half-hoped (perhaps naively) that there would one day be a message from Cardinal Heenan which ran something like this: "Yes, I know you are a non-denominational organisation but all that you say and do in your educational and care work accords completely with the Church's teaching and mission. Perhaps more to the point, the Catholic Church is so committed to the pro-life movement has so much to offer it – with its children's societies, adoption services, care homes, and hospitals, not to mention its huge number of schools and extensive property – that we should surely make common cause, work together at least informally, and thereby maximise our impact". But the message never came. Though the cardinal had the vision to found the Linacre Centre, which was especially charged with giving guidance to the bishops on bioethical issues, he was not capable of – or did not see the need for – such a leap of imagination.

Shortly after it was founded, LIFE wrote to the Catholic bishops asking if we could at least have their help in promoting its work in their dioceses. Some, most notably Derek Worlock (then bishop of Portsmouth), responded warmly. Others made no reply. One, the bishop of Shrewsbury, made a dramatic announcement that any pregnant woman who refused abortion would receive material support through his Children's Society, a gesture that attracted much media attention but was short-lived and, like Cardinal Winning's initiatives in Glasgow some thirty years later, perhaps distracted attention and resources from a wider (and in Glasgow's case, existing) pro-life programme.

Then, in 1991, an important thing happened. The Pontifical Council for the Family – at short notice – invited pro-lifers from all over the world (and regardless of religious allegiance) to an international get-together in Rome. Hundreds came. Whether it was ever capable of being more than a large talking-shop is not clear. But at the end there was an open forum (preceded by a memorable meeting with Pope John Paul II) to which spokespersons of the several workshops into which delegates had been divided reported on their discussions. LIFE had put forward the following ideas: that the Church Universal should mark 25 March as a holy 'Day for Life', that on that day homilies (better, joint pastoral letters from local hierarchies), and Bidding Prayers, etc should focus on the Gospel of Life, as we would later call it, and that there should be a collection at all Masses that day for pro-life work.

It was with special delight, therefore, that, when the papal encyclical *Evangelium Vitae* appeared in 1996, LIFE read the pope's words commending the idea of an annual Day for Life to his brother-bishops worldwide. It would be vainglorious to suggest that LIFE's proposal had somehow reached Pope John Paul and was the inspiration for his words. He did not pick up the idea of making the feast of the Annunciation (for many Christian societies for centuries the first day of the year) or LIFE's other ideas. But at least he had given a powerful lead.

LIFE wrote at once to Cardinal Hume putting to him all that we had proposed in Rome years before and citing paragraph 73 of *Evangelium Vitae*. He replied that the bishops would surely want to discuss the matter at their next meeting. We repeated our proposals regularly thereafter to bishops whenever we sent them *LIFE News*. Those who replied agreed that these were important ideas which the bishops would surely consider.

Then suddenly, in late 2002, it was reported that the bishops had at last agreed to launch a Day for Life programme. This would be held on a Sunday in early July and there would be a national collection for pro-life causes.

Moreover, since the initiative had come from the Bioethics Committee set up jointly by the hierarchies of Scotland and Ireland, as well as England and Wales, the Scottish and Irish Bishops were holding their Days, too. A committee was set up to plan the event. Pro-life organisations were invited to make suggestions about what form it should take. LIFE urged that there should be a joint pastoral letter from the Bishops to launch the first Day, that there should be posters about it in schools and churches, etc, etc. and that all Catholics should be urged to become actively involved in the pro-life apostolate in one way or another.

In the event, the Day for Life committee adopted the "seamless garment" approach and, instead of focusing on the pro-life cause in the strict sense (and as it is understood in *Evangelium Vitae),* decided that the annual Days should "celebrate" childhood, family life and old age, etc, in turn. Much of the money collected has gone to the Linacre Centre – an excellent cause which had always been on the "shopping list" – and some to hospices.

2007 has produced good news, however. Pro-life charities are at least to benefit from the Day. So the story has a happy ending.

VII.

TOWARDS A PRO-LIFE COUNTER-CULTURE

LIFE's way is the right way because it is the way of truth and compassion. Abortionism, like most wrong-doing, cannot hold out against these.

Like most wrong-doing, abortionism must implode from within.

More than any other in history, today's society professes commitment to universal human rights – yet, at the same time, denies the fundamental right, the right to life, to a whole section of the human family. Society proclaims the unity of that family – and then excludes a whole category of human beings from it. As has already been noted, society denounces all forms of discrimination (sexism, sizeism, ageism, etc) and fails to see how it discriminates against the youngest and smallest among us. Society shows the greatest concern for the born disabled while devising ever more ruthless ways to search out and destroy special-needs unborn children. Society deplores violence – and yet approves of the utter violence of abortion. Society cannot live forever with these contradictions. Something has to "give".

Our world is increasingly peopled with women severely wounded by abortion, but the Establishment still denies that there is such a thing as post-abortion trauma. Sooner or later, the truth will out. Sooner or later it will become impossible to say any longer that the soaring rates of breast cancer across the world have nothing to do with the increased supply of abortion. The truth about the ABC link will out.

One day politicians will have to admit that the explicit, value-free sex education which has been foisted on ever-younger children is a direct cause of the promiscuity, high pregnancy and abortion rates, and the record levels of sexually-transmitted infections among teenagers. By abetting agencies like the Family Planning Association, Brook and Marie Stopes, licensing school nurses to distribute condoms, morning-after pills and abortion advice even to under-age children (without parental permission or knowledge), the Department of Health has done all it can to corrupt the young – as well as to undermine parental authority. They purport to deplore all this. But they remorselessly promote it. Short-term quick fixes – which are what politicians usually provide – have had disastrous long-term consequences.

In 1967 the likes of David Steel and RHS Crossman promised a gullible nation that abortion law reform would strengthen marriage and family life, reduce illegitimacy and improve the health of women and children. How hollow those promises seem now as we face ever more divorce (and much less marriage) than ever, over 50 per cent of births outside marriage (compared with 5 per cent in 1967) and STI rates at epidemic levels in many of our towns and cities.

Abortionism is a god that has failed.

It has also corrupted. Abortion is profoundly divisive. It is an "unmentionable". Others do not want to know. The woman grieves alone. There will be a no-go area between parents and daughters, husbands and wives, women and partners.

Born children often intuit, even if they are not told, that a sibling is missing. Since young children assume that parents exist solely for their well-being and have no other raison d'être, this discovery can devastate trust between offspring and parents.

So every abortion represents a failure of, and/or threat to, human relations.

Abortionism is both a cause and an effect of the relentless debauching of society by much of the media (and Government) in recent years that has licensed public vulgarity and indecency at a level which would have been unthinkable 20 or 30 years ago. Today's western society has come closer to publicly sweeping aside a basic code of sexual conduct than probably any previous one in history. Abortionism is a major cause and effect of this current hedonism, i.e. sexual consumerism.

It is women who must say this most clearly because it is they who have suffered most. As older feminists now increasingly agree, the Sexual Revolution, of which "liberalised" abortion is a key element, has not liberated women. On the contrary, it has made them ever more available to the predatory male. Every abortion is a profound affront to a woman's dignity, integrity and femininity. Probably most women know this in their hearts.

It is women who suffer most from post-abortion trauma. It is they who are affected by accelerating breast cancer rates. Women yearn to be cherished. But modern womanhood has lost much of its dignity and "mystery" and hence male respect. It is difficult to cherish that which is not respected.

Women have much to do with "civilising" males. But they have surrendered much of their authority to do so. Reportedly, gangs of feral teenage girls now prey on the most forlorn housing estates and female drunkenness, drug use and yobbishness are an all-too familiar sight in most towns at weekends. One has only to see the provocative gangs of young women who throng streets on Friday and Saturday evenings or pour out of pubs and nightspots at closing times to see how much of what Christianity and the original feminist movement earned for their sex has been thrown away.

Love poetry is a thing of the past. Swains do not have to swoon any more. The young have been engulfed (largely) by a pop culture which is anarchic at best and nihilistic at worst, by a sex industry which assaults them via all the media ever more blatantly and by the "condom culture" vigorously promoted by many Governments worldwide. There is no place for poetry and not much for chivalry in that "culture".

Women must lead the protest against all this. So too, of course, parents, teachers, decent males, religious leaders.

* * *

More than one moral philosopher has warned that the professions are de-professionalising themselves. The following is meant by that statement. A profession is a body of trained people dedicated to serving the common good and to abiding by certain transcendent principles. They receive, develop and in turn pass on to the next generation knowledge and skills which they inherited from their elders. Admission, training and regulation of the profession's affairs are the responsibility of a regulatory body – an incorporated society or "college" or similar – appointed to guard the integrity of the profession and the best interests of its members.

Lawyers are committed to promoting justice. That is an "absolute". Doctors are committed to healing and saving life. "First do no harm" was the crucial command of the Hippocratic Oath which they used to swear. That a doctor should never use his knowledge and skills deliberately to harm, let alone kill, was also an "absolute". Of course he must respect a patient's autonomy, including the right to refuse treatment; but he must never do or be party to any action which conflicted with his duty to preserve human life. He does not simply do what patients or their relatives ask for. He is not customer-led. He is more than a technician – who is someone who does what he is told. He does what his professional principles tell him.

When a doctor authorises or does an abortion he is guilty of two things. He is breaching the fundamental principle of his profession (his duty to protect life) and, since well over 90 per cent of abortions (at any rate in Great Britain) are "convenience" abortions, he has allowed "customer choice" to override professional judgment. Of course he may well claim that what he has done will do more good than harm, that is, that the gains will outweigh the losses, and that more "pleasure" than "pain" will result from his decision. But if he thinks that he is the victim of a kind of moral thinking – utilitarianism – which is bogus. It is bogus for several reasons, not the least being that it is impossible to know the full consequences of an action and secondly, even if one could, it would be impossible to determine whether the good results outweighed the bad (the "pleasure" over and against the "pain") because there is no common unit of measuring these two things. So there can be no conclusion. One might just as well flip a coin. But a professional does not do the equivalent of flipping coins – and certainly not in order to placate outside self-interest.

When the Royal College of Obstetricians and Gynaecologists promotes abortionism, as it now does – eagerly – it is betraying the profession. When it refuses to heed mounting evidence of the damage being done by it to women (its patients) and to investigate the complaints thoroughly, it is acting unprofessionally, because failing to monitor what its members are doing and it is encouraging. It is being driven by hard-line abortionism, not principles.

A doctor who sedates a newborn disabled baby to death or abets an adult suicide is acting unprofessionally, as well as unlawfully. When doctors say that it is in the "best interests" of the a patient to be denied food and fluids (and to die a horrible death) or claim to judge "quality of life" they are talking outside their professional expertise and making statements that are intellectually incoherent – just guesses. So, too, are judges who go along with all this – the Law Lords in the Bland judgement, for instance. They were being led by political correctness, not jurisprudence.

Consumerism is rotting professionalism.

* * *

All is not lost. Far from it. There are still a lot of good, generous, sensible people around – even though many are cowed (or simply bewildered) by the prevailing culture. Human beings are idealists, in the sense that they have, and yearn for, ideals. Only humans have them. Animals do not. They cannot be eradicated – as the repeated collapse of unjust political regimes reminds us – however much external forces may try. Human beings are ineradicably committed to truth and justice. They also have an ineradicable sense of right and wrong, however much these are overlaid by false values or self-interest. The natural order has been and is continuing to be overturned in many areas of life ("natural" here meaning much more than merely "instinctive" or the opposite of artificial). But we know intuitively what that right order is. It is written on hearts. It makes sense. It is holistic and dynamic. It enables us to begin to understand the dignity of our bodies and provides the environment in which the human spirit can flourish.

LIFE's pregnancy counselling and care service, its housing and FertilityCare Programmes, together with its educational work among the young, are modest first stages in creating a pro-life counter-culture and rallying people of goodwill to the cause. LIFE is not alone, of course, in this apostolate.

We must look to the day when businesses, major stores, banks and the like publicly proclaim their pro-life commitment as they now do to their "green" and Fairtrade credentials.

We must look to the day when hospitals and doctors' surgeries openly espouse pro-life values, and they and hospices display notices over their doors promising that no one who enters will be in danger of being sedated or starved to death.

The re-professionalising of the medical profession must come from within – from those who have clung to the high ideals of yesterday and have the courage to make them tomorrow's. Perhaps there has to be an "alternative" medical profession, an alternative structure from which to mount this rescue.

There is certainly an urgent need for pro-life research in genetics, embryology, adult stem cell therapy, etc – to challenge and provide an alternative to what so may Governments and the major grant-making foundations fund. (LIFE has long yearned to be able to set up a Research Centre to begin to do just that!)

We must look to the day when all Christians have come to see the enormity of destroying innocent life before birth – as well as after – and those non-Christian communities which have retained a strict moral code have learnt to temper their condemnation of abortion with mercy for the "fallen" woman – else they will unwittingly drive the latter into desperate action.

The law of England stubbornly refuses to recognise the unborn child as a legal person. This was perhaps forgivable 50 or 100 years ago when so much less was known about life before birth. But now that we can look through the "window on the womb" and watch children grow, suck thumbs, stretch limbs, now that we know about genetics and the continuity of human life from fertilisation onwards, it is forgivable no longer. It is now so evident that birth is simply an incident in a developing human life – a change of environment, not of moral status – that it can only be a matter of time before the law, if it is not to continue to be an ass, has to confer legal personhood on the unborn human being.

In recent decades secular humanism has been waging a ruthless campaign against Judaeo-Christian teaching on marriage and the family, with the disastrous consequences we see all around us. It can only be a matter of time before all but the most doctrinaire politicians come to see this and, having accepted the evidence that children thrive best – physically, emotionally and academically – in the traditional family environment, accept the need to rehabilitate family life and heterosexual marriage.

It can only be a matter of time before Governments recognise that the population-controllers got it badly wrong and that the widespread collapse in the birth-rates requires immediate action, such as pro-natalist policies, to stave off the demographic disaster. Abortion will then become unpatriotic and large families politically correct.

We must look to the day when a new feminism has liberated women from the idea that they must be the same as men and equally competitive, and can rejoice in their complementarity, knowing that they are equal but different; when the young have recovered their adolescence from the clutches of the sex industry and the family planners; when parents have fully re-discovered their unique responsibility and dignity as procreators; and when, as has been said, society has simply "outgrown" abortionism and all that it underpins, recognising that it is incompatible with justice and the respect which is due to all human life.

We must look to the day when we have helped our fellow-citizens to see that in proclaiming moral absolutes and arguing that absolute respect is due to all human life, even at its smallest and weakest, we are wanting to create a world in which everyone will feel safer – one in which we would all prefer to live.

We look to the day when the coherence of our case, the compassion with which we present it and the conviction we carry as authentic human beings have won the consent of at least the majority of those fellow-citizens. Then the pro-life counter-culture will have become the prevailing culture.

* * *

All the above is just a beginning. There is no doubt much more to say and do.

Sepp Fischer (Hrsg.)

BUSHCRAFT

DAS BUCH VOM WALDHANDWERK

Mit Beiträgen von:

Michael Blaumeiser, Markus Graßmann, Rocco Hartwig, Detlev Hoppenrath, Oliver Lang-Geffroy, Peter Nietz, Johannes »Joe« Vogel und Susanne Williams

pietsch

Einbandgestaltung: Patricia Braun, www.patriciabraun.de

Titelbilder: Detlev Hoppenrath, Sepp Fischer, istock/AlexStar

Bildnachweis: Sepp Fischer (U4), Michael Blaumeiser (U4), Joe Vogel (Kapitelbild Grundlagen), Detlev Hoppenrath (Kapitelbild Wasser und Nahrung), Rocco Hartwig (Kapitelbild Waldhandwerk konkret). Sämtliche anderen zur Illustration dieses Buches verwendeten Aufnahmen stammen – wenn nicht anders vermerkt – vom Verfasser des jeweiligen Beitrags.

ISBN 978-3-613-50843-9

1. Auflage 2017

Sie finden uns im Internet unter:
www.pietsch-verlag.de

Lektorat: Susanne Fischer

Innengestaltung: Patricia Braun, www.patriciabraun.de

Druck und Bindung: Graspo CZ, 76302 Zlín

Printed in Czech Republic

INHALT

VORWORT

Liebe Leserin, lieber Leser,

vielen Dank dass Du Dich fürs Bushcraften interessierst! Ich freue mich, dass die Begeisterung für die Natur weithin zunimmt und zu einem wachsenden Trend geworden ist. Bushcraft-Techniken sind Helfer in allen Outdoor-Angelegenheiten, aber das Bushcraften ist auch ein eigenständiges Hobby.

Egal ob Einsteiger, Fortgeschrittene oder Experten – ich hoffe, in den nächsten Kapiteln finden sich für jeden von Euch viele interessante Hinweise, Kniffe und Tricks, damit Ihr mit mehr Spaß und mehr Professionalität draußen unterwegs sein könnt. Jeder hat es verdient, dass ihm die Freiheit der Natur, der Wälder, der Flüsse und Seen (wieder) nähergebracht wird.

Eigentlich aus den Bergen stammend, später in der Großstadt tätig, war ich selber eine ganze Weile lang naturabstinent – mittlerweile eine anerkannte Diagnose: »Naturdefizit«. Mit 36 Jahren erkannte ich endlich wieder, was mir die Natur bedeutet und

wieviel es mir bringt, draußen zu sein. Ich denke, es hing mit dem Ausgebranntsein zusammen, dass ich mich nach Stress im Geschäftsleben und privaten Problemen am Fluss sitzend und Kiefernnadeltee kochend wiederfand. Und wieder zu Hause, merkte ich sofort, wieviel Kraft und Schwung mir diese kurze Auszeit gegeben hatte.

»Wenn Dich das Leben anekelt, geh hinaus in den Wald, geh hinaus auf die Wiese, geh hinaus zum See und atme.« Das gibt meine Gefühle so ziemlich wieder. Oder auch: »Bushcraft ist etwas im Herzen, das etwas im Kopf öffnet«.

Bushcraft bedeutet für mich reine, ungetrübte Lebensfreude, draußen in der Natur eins zu sein mit allem Geschaffenen. Bushcraft gibt mir Kraft, Zuversicht, Entspannung, Freude, Genügsamkeit, Zufriedenheit und so manches Mal Erinnerungen für's Leben.

Und viele gute Leute durfte ich durch das Waldhandwerk schon kennen lernen, nicht nur aus Deutschland, Österreich und der Schweiz, sondern auch Gäste und Besucher aus so unterschiedlichen Ländern wie Rumänien, England oder den USA. Bushcraft ist ein sehr friedliches Hobby, das Menschen weltweit miteinander verbindet. Alle sind wir sehr an der Gemeinschaft und am Teilen (von der Ausrüstung bis hin zum Erlebnis) interessiert. Der Bushcrafter ist ein eigener Schlag. Und vor allem die Bushcrafterin, denn glücklicherweise erfreuen sich auch immer mehr Frauen am Leben draußen.

Jedem Bushcraft-interessierten Menschen, den ich bisher getroffen habe, war unser gemeinsames Hobby schon mal eine Hilfe und Stütze im Leben. Nicht nur als Freizeitgestaltung, sondern auch und besonders in schwierigen Lebenssituationen. Wenn man seinen Mitmenschen die Freude an kleinen Dingen wiederbringen kann, ist das eine schöne Sache. Bushcraft kann das schaffen, und das nicht als jahrelanger Prozess mit ungewissem Ausgang, sondern als Ergebnis im Hier und Jetzt.

Bushcraften erdet, es eröffnet ganz neue Möglichkeiten, die Natur und das Draußensein zu genießen; es macht freier und zuversichtlicher, wenn man sich in der Natur bewegt. Und gleichzeitig lehrt es einen auch wieder, klar zu erkennen und sehr zu schätzen, was unsere Zivilisation alles zustande gebracht hat.

Bushcraft ist ein Life-Style aber auch eine Family-Affair, hier können Alt und Jung gleichermaßen Freude haben. In der Natur wird man wieder Zeit-reich und lernt, mit Spaß das ganze Jahr über draußen sein zu können und die Natur zu respektieren.

Mein größter Dank gebührt meiner Familie, die mich immer wieder rauslässt oder sogar ins Freie schickt. Er gilt meinen lieben Bushcraft-Freunden und Autoren dieses Buches: Michael Blaumeiser, Markus Graßmann, Rocco Hartwig, Detlev Hoppenrath, Oliver Lang-Geffroy, Peter Nietz, Susanne Williams und meinem Freund und Trainingspartner Joe Vogel. Er gilt auch meinen Zuschauern auf YouTube, dem Pietsch Verlag mit m(s)einer ausgesprochen fleißigen und geduldigen Lektorin Susanne Fischer und natürlich allen Lesern dieses Buches, welche hoffentlich die Freude am Draußensein weiterverbreiten.

So, nun aber viel Spaß beim Lesen und Ausprobieren! Geht's Ausse!

Euer Sepp Fischer

GRUND-
LAGEN

WAS DU WISSEN MUSST

WAS IST BUSHCRAFT?

Bushcraft ist ein Begriff, der in den USA geprägt wurde; er beschreibt die Fähigkeit oder Kunst, in der Wildnis zu überleben (abgeleitet von *bush* = dem Lebensraum der australischen Aboriginals und *craft* = Fertigkeiten/Handwerk). In Großbritannien wird eher von Woodcraft (von *wood* = Wald) gesprochen. Immer mehr Europäer erfreuen sich mittlerweile dieses Hobbys. Es vereint das Wissen über unterschiedlichste Themen: vom Bau eines Unterschlupfs bis hin zur Bestimmung von essbaren Wildpflanzen oder der Zubereitung tierischer Notnahrung (z.B. Nagetiere oder auch Insekten).

Und was ist dann der Unterschied zwischen Bushcraft und Survival? Na ja, Bushcraft würde ich als ein freiwilliges und naturverbundenes sowie langfristiges Draußensein beschreiben, wohingegen Survival sich eher mit der Thematik des Überlebens mit absoluter minimaler Ausrüstung oder in Katastrophenfällen beschäftigt. Aber natürlich haben beide Themen gewisse Überschneidungspunkte. Als »Bushcrafter« ist es Dir ein Anliegen, natürliche Ressourcen zu nutzen, aber sie nicht bis zur Erschöpfung auszunutzen, wohingegen jemand, der sich in einer Survivalsituation befindet, wahrscheinlich aufgrund der absoluten Notsituation eher weniger auf Nachhaltigkeit achten würde. Ein gemeinsames Interesse von Bushcrafter und »Survivalist« ist es, auch mit natürlichen oder traditionellen Methoden Dinge herzustellen, die ein gutes Leben oder eben auch ein Überleben möglich machen.

Sepp Fischer und Michael Blaumeiser auf einer Winter-Bushcrafttour in der Jachenau.

Links: **Traditionelles Feuerkit mit Flint, Steel und Zundermaterial.** ***Rechts:*** **Eine Tasse Tee gekocht auf der EDC-Bushbox.**

Viele nehmen das Thema Bushcraft schon fast zu ernst und machen es zu einer Art Religion – für mich stehen dabei der Spaß und der Erfahrungsaustausch an erster Stelle. Es ist ein Fakt, dass wir als Bushcrafter (und auch als Menschen überhaupt) nie auslernen; so gibt es immer noch Dinge, wo ich heute sage: »Was, so geht das auch?« Wenn es dann zu mir und zu meinem Stil passt, versuche ich, dieses Wissen in mein »System« zu integrieren – toll, was Neues gelernt! Ich glaube, das ist auch der Hauptunterschied zum Survivalisten, der nur ein Ziel verfolgt: **ÜBERLEBEN**.

Sepp hab ich mal sagen hören:

»Technisch gesehen ist Bushcraft eine Schnittmenge aus drei großen Teilbereichen:

1. *modernes Camping, Hiking, Bergtouren, Kanufahren; eigentlich sämtliche Outdooraktivitäten*

2. *Expeditionen, Extremreisen, langes Überdauern außerhalb der Zivilisation*

3. *überlieferte Techniken von der Steinzeit über das Mittelalter bis zur frühen Moderne.«*

Ich denke, das trifft es sehr gut: Unterm Strich benutzen wir heute genauso moderne Materialien wie steinzeitliche und überlieferte Methoden, um uns ein Feuer zu starten oder einen Unterschlupf zu bauen. Und warum sollte jemand ein schlechterer Bushcrafter sein, nur weil er im Zelt schläft – dafür ist er vielleicht besser am Bowdrill oder in anderen Techniken.

VON WEM STAMMT ES?

Streng genommen, kommen viele der noch heute benutzten Techniken eigentlich aus der Steinzeit bzw. der Prähistorischen Zeit, z.B. das Benutzen eines Handbohrers wie eines Bowdrills oder die Verwendung von Schlageisen und Feuerstein, um mit diesen ein Feuer zu machen. Diese Techniken werden auch heute noch von Naturvölkern benutzt, wenn es ums Feuermachen geht, und der Fallenbau ist bei diesen Völkern ebenfalls noch heute präsent. Der Begriff »Waldläufer« ist einer der geläufigsten Begriffe, der auch heute noch gerne verwendet wird, wenn es um Bushcraft geht.

Klassische Ausrüstung: der italienische Gebirgsjäger-Rucksack gepackt für eine 1-Tages-Tour.

Ray Mears sowie Mors Kochanski sind für mich die prägendsten Personen im Bereich Bushcraft, die in ihrer Herangehensweise sehr traditionell sind. Der Satz »*The more you know, the less you carry*« ist ein Beispiel, das sich ins Hirn brennt. Ich denke, das macht wirklich die Kunst aus: mit wenig zurechtkommen und das Beste aus der Situation machen, bedächtig und im Kopf vorbereitet sein sowie sich selbst und seine Grenzen kennen.

Ray Mears und seine »*12 Woodlores*« sind für mich noch immer von großer Bedeutung. Sätze bzw. Regeln wie »*Aim to achieve maximum efficiency for the minimum effort*« (was im konkreten Fall z.B. mal heißen kann: »Warum ne Axt nehmen, wenn ich den Ast auch absägen kann?«) sind, so denke ich, eine gute Anleitung für ein gutes und »bequemes« Leben in der Natur. Hier kann ich das Thema nur anreißen, ich empfehle Dir aber, mal z.B. in Ray Mears »The Survival Handbook« zu blättern. (Auch wenn das auf den ersten Blick merkwürdig klingen mag; Bushcraft und Survival gehen doch enger Hand in Hand, als so mancher denkt.)

Ich habe Euch die 12 Woodlores oder »Waldregeln« mal übersetzt – ein toller Leitfaden für Bushcrafter und Survivalisten, wie ich finde:

RAY MEARS' »WOODLORES«

1. Fordere nicht die Natur heraus, sondern Dich selbst.

Gelegentlich hörst Du Leute darüber reden, dass sie die »Elemente besiegen«, indem sie einen Berg besteigen oder die Polkappen oder indem sie andere, ach so mutige Taten vollbringen. Die Wahrheit ist aber, dass die Herausforderung in jedem selbst liegt. Hast Du die nötigen Fähigkeiten? Kannst Du Deine Angst überwinden? Niemand kann die Elemente besiegen; wer so dumm ist, die Warnzeichen nicht zu beachten oder mit dem Kopf durch die Wand zu gehen, stirbt dabei. Anstatt unnötige Risiken zu einzugehen, musst Du die Herausforderung annehmen, zu wissen, wann Du Dich zurücknehmen musst, Dich selbst besser kennenzulernen und zu verstehen, wie die Natur funktioniert.

2. Wenn es sich zu »hart« anfühlt, machst Du was falsch.

Jeder Dummkopf kann es sich schwer machen; man bekommt keine Fleißpunkte für das Tragen eines schweren Rucksacks oder für irgendwelche unnötigen selbstauferlegten Aufgaben. Natürlich kannst Du für eine Expedition trainieren und es Dir dabei etwas härter machen – denk aber immer auch darüber nach, ob es nicht eine Möglichkeit gibt, es Dir bequemer zu machen, ohne dass dies zum Nachteil wird. Insbesondere in Notsituationen, wenn Du schon demoralisiert bist, kann eine kleine Schwierigkeit der Tropfen sein, der das Fass zum Überlaufen bringt.

3. Gib immer 100 Prozent beim ersten Versuch.

Ob Unterschlupf, Feuermachen oder was auch immer – wenn Du es nicht gleich beim ersten Mal richtig machst, verschwendest Du Deine Energie und wirst noch einmal von vorne anfangen müssen.

4. Versuche, den geringstmöglichen Aufwand zu betreiben und möglichst effizient zu sein.

Um zu arbeiten, brauchst Du Energie; für Energie brauchst Du Nahrung. Draußen Nahrung zu finden ist Arbeit. Wenn Du Feuerholz sammelst, trägst Du dann gleich große Mengen oder nur eine Hand voll?

5. Verpasse keine Gelegenheit.

Dies ist sehr wichtig. Wenn Du unterwegs geeignete Wasser- oder Nahrungsmittelvorräte bzw. Materialien zum Feuermachen findest, sammle sie sofort – es kann sein, dass sich später, wenn Du sie brauchst, keine Gelegenheit mehr dazu ergibt. Dies gilt besonders für Feuermaterialien bzw. Zunder. Am Ende eines Tages kann es immer noch regnen, oder es hat schon vorher geregnet, und alles ist durchnässt. Viele meiner alten Hemden und Jacken haben Birkenrindenstücke in den Taschen, die ich vor einigen Jahren gesammelt habe, um sie dort zu trocknen.

6. Passe soweit wie möglich Deine Erwartungen an die gegebenen Umstände an.

Wenn Du keinen bequemen Riesen-Shelter bauen kannst, dann gib Dich mit einem kleinen Schutzraum zufrieden. Wenn keine Riesen-Auswahl von Wildpflanzen zur Verfügung steht, sei dankbar für die eine Art, die Du essen kannst. Lass die Psychologie für Dich arbeiten. Sei realistisch – mach es Dir bequem, aber überarbeite Dich nicht, um dies zu erreichen: Es bringt nichts, Dir einen Palast zu bauen, wenn Du dann erschöpft darinnen zusammenbrichst. Aber unterschätze auch nicht, was Du erreichen kannst.

7. Iss nur das, was Du sicher identifizieren kannst.

Vertrau nicht auf Geschmackstests und verwende nicht auf gut Glück unbekannte Pflanzen als Nahrungsmittel. Der einzige

Ein rustikales Frühstück auf einer Bushcraft-Tour in den Schweizer Voralpen.

Edelstahlbehälter eignen sich hervorragend, um auf Feuer zu kochen.

Weg, um sicher zu essen, ist es, bevor Du aufbrichst zu lernen, was man essen kann und wie man die entsprechende Nahrung zubereitet. Wenn Dir das zu schwierig ist, dann solltest Du nicht versuchen, Dich von Wildpflanzen zu ernähren.

8. Betrachte jedes Wasser als verschmutzt.
Sogar das sauberste, schnell fließende und verlockende Wasser könnte verunreinigt sein; Du kannst das nicht auf den ersten Blick erkennen. Koche oder reinige jedes Wasser – und überprüfe es insbesondere auf Anzeichen einer chemischen Verschmutzung!

9. Dein Feuer verhält sich proportional zu Deinem Gemütszustand.
Wie auch immer Dein Gemütszustand sein mag: Wenn Du ein Feuer anzünden kannst, wird er sich verbessern, aber wenn Du es vergeigst, wird Deine Motivation wie ein Kartenhaus in sich zusammenfallen. Wenn Du nicht genügend Vertrauen in Deine Fähigkeiten hast, ein Feuer im Regen zu starten, dann ist es möglicherweise besser, Du versuchst es erst, wenn der Regen aufgehört hat.

10. Wenn Du natürliche Ressourcen sammelst, orientiere Dich an der natürlichen Selektion – das ist der »Weg« der Natur.
Lass die Starken stehen, ernte die Schwachen; beim Sammeln von Pflanzen bzw. Nahrung solltest Du immer darauf achten, genügend gesunde Pflanzen, Schalentiere oder was auch immer übrigzulassen, die den Bestand fortsetzen können. Hierdurch werden stärkere, gesunde Pflanzen und Lebewesen die besten Chancen haben, zu überleben und sich in Zukunft zu vermehren.

11. Nimm nur Erinnerungen mit und hinterlasse nur Fußabdrücke.
Minimiere Deine Einwirkungen auf die natürliche Umwelt, wann immer es Dir möglich ist. Dein Ziel sollte immer sein, Deinen Lagerplatz in einem besseren Zustand zu verlassen, als Du ihn angetroffen hast.

12. Sei fit, bereit zu schwimmen und gib niemals auf.
Jede einzelne nützliche Fertigkeit oder Technik ist leichter zu erlernen und zu beherrschen, wenn Du fit bist. Die Wildnis ist voller Risiken und unvorhersehbarer Umstände. Dein körperlicher Zustand und Deine Fitness kann unter solchen Umständen überlebenswichtig sein.

WAS BRINGT ES?

Die Frage, was Bushcraft bringt, kann nur jeder Einzelne für sich selbst beantworten. Für mich ist es im Wesentlichen ein Zurückkommen zur Natur und auch zu sich selbst, eine Art der Entschleunigung in einer sich viel zu schnell drehenden und bewegenden Welt bzw. Gesellschaft. Sich in der Natur zu bewegen, sich selber wieder spüren zu lernen und einfach mit wenigen Mitteln zurechtzukommen, erscheint manchem am Anfang bestimmt unmöglich bzw. undenkbar. Aber wenn Du einmal festgestellt hast, wie viel es einem bringen kann, kannst Du regelrecht süchtig danach werden. Ein einfacher Kaffee, ein Essen, ein ganzer Tag draußen. Ein Wochenende, wo Du Dir vielleicht ein eigenes Lager baust, wohin Du Dich zurückziehen kannst, ist ein Antrieb, der einen wirklich beflügeln kann.

Ein Punkt, den ich in den letzten Jahren allerdings am meisten zu schätzen gelernt habe, ist gar nicht so offensichtlich: Es sind die Freundschaften, die sich aus diesem Hobby ergeben haben – eine Verbindung, die sich schwer beschreiben lässt, aber ein Gefühl, das sich sehr schnell ergibt. Menschen, die ich heute nicht mehr missen möchte, alle kennengelernt durch dieses eine Wort: **BUSHCRAFT**.

ZEIT FINDEN ZUM BUSHCRAFTEN

Ach ja, das leidige Thema Zeit ... Ich sag Dir ganz ehrlich: Zeit hab ich nicht immer soviel wie ich will, aber ich bemühe mich, die gegebenen Möglichkeiten so gut es geht zu nutzen. Ein kleines Feuer im Garten mit den Kindern, angezündet mit einem Feuerstahl, einem Flint-und-Steel-Kit, dieser »magische« Moment, wenn sich das Zundernest in ein Feuer verwandelt – einfach toll und für mich Entspannung pur. Einen Löffel zu schnitzen oder sich einfach ein, zwei kleine Bushcraft-Projekte vorzunehmen. Das geht auch, wenn man nur wenig Zeit hat, und ist trotzdem wertvoll als Vorbereitung für größere Unternehmungen. Übungen, wie ein Feuer bzw. eine Glut mit einem Handbohrer oder Bowdrill mit den eigenen Händen zu erzeugen, lassen sich mit den richtigen Vorbereitungen auch in den eigenen vier Wänden einfach machen. Auch das kann Bushcraft sein.

GEEIGNETE PLÄTZE FINDEN: WO KANN ICH? WO DARF ICH? AUF WAS SOLLTE ICH ACHTEN?

Sicher fragst Du Dich auch: Wo darf ich meinem Hobby überhaupt nachgehen? Na ja, dies ist in der Regel, zumindest in Deutschland, Österreich oder auch der Schweiz, leider nicht immer ganz so einfach. Zum einen haben wir in Deutschland ein Gesetz, was ganz klar regelt, ob und wo Du Feuer machen darfst und kannst, aber

Bushcraft-Lager in England bei meinem guten Freund Simon.

auch wie und wo Du z.B. in einem Wald übernachten bzw. wild campen darfst. Jedes Land bzw. in Deutschland sogar jedes Bundesland regelt dies etwas anders – also bitte informiere Dich, wie die Gesetzeslage im jeweiligen Land bzw. Bundesland ist. Hier als Beispiel ein paar Auszüge aus dem Landesforstgesetz für das Land Nordrhein-Westfalen:

§ 2 (Fn 42) Betreten des Waldes

(Zu § 14 Bundeswaldgesetz)

(1) *Das Betreten des Waldes zum Zwecke der Erholung ist auf eigene Gefahr gestattet, soweit sich nicht aus den Bestimmungen dieses Gesetzes oder aus anderen Rechtsvorschriften Abweichungen ergeben. Das Betreten des Waldes geschieht insbesondere im Hinblick auf natur- und waldtypische Gefahren auf eigene Gefahr. Zu den natur- und waldtypischen Gefahren zählen vornehmlich solche, die von lebenden und toten Bäumen, sonstigem Aufwuchs oder natürlichem Bodenzustand ausgehen oder aus der ordnungsgemäßen Bewirtschaftung des Waldes entstehen.*

(2) *Absatz 1 gilt sinngemäß auch für das Radfahren, ausgenommen die Benutzung motorgetriebener Fahrzeuge, und das Fahren mit Krankenfahrstühlen auf Straßen und festen Wegen.*

(3) *Wer den Wald betritt, hat sich so zu verhalten, daß die Lebensgemeinschaft Wald und die Bewirtschaftung des Waldes nicht gestört, der Wald nicht gefährdet, beschädigt oder verunreinigt sowie andere schutzwürdige Interessen der Waldbesitzer und die Erholung anderer nicht unzumutbar beeinträchtigt werden. Im Wald dürfen Hunde außerhalb von Wegen nur angeleint mitgeführt werden; dies gilt nicht für Jagdhunde im Rahmen jagdlicher Tätigkeiten sowie für Polizeihunde.*

§ 47 (Fn 33) Waldgefährdung durch Feuer

(1) *Im Wald oder in einem Abstand von weniger als einhundert Meter vom Waldrand*

Teile der Reflektorwand meines »alten« Bushcraftlagers, das leider von Fremden zerstört wurde.

ist außerhalb einer von der Forstbehörde errichteten oder genehmigten und entsprechend gekennzeichneten Anlage das Anzünden oder Unterhalten eines Feuers oder die Benutzung eines Grillgerätes sowie das Lagern von leichtentzündlichen Stoffen nicht zulässig. Die Forstbehörde kann auf Antrag eine Befreiung von dem Verbot erteilen.

(2) *Absatz 1 Satz 1 gilt nicht für*

1. *den Waldbesitzer und die Personen, die im Wald oder auf den angrenzenden Grundstücken beschäftigt werden,*

2. *Personen, die aufgrund sonstiger Vorschriften zulässige oder behördlich angeordnete oder genehmigte Maßnahmen durchführen und*

3. *die zur Jagdausübung Berechtigten sowie die Imker während der Ausübung ihrer Tätigkeit.*

(1) *Im Wald darf in der Zeit vom 1. März bis 31. Oktober nicht geraucht werden. Dies gilt nicht für den in Absatz 2 genannten Personenkreis.*

Für Dich heißt das: Offenes Feuer ist nicht erlaubt, solange Du keine »angelegte« Feuerstelle vorfindest oder den Waldbesitzer kennst und dieser Dir das Feuermachen erlaubt.

Andere Möglichkeiten sind hier z.B. Bushcrafter-Treffen oder auch Bushcraft-Kurse, wie sie z.B. mit Sepp Fischer, Joe Vogel oder Peter Nietz auch einige der Autoren dieses Buches abhalten: Für gewöhnlich hat hier der Veranstalter eine Erlaubnis, z.B. um Feuer zu machen, bzw. hier kann den Bushcraft-Aktivitäten im vollen Umfang nachgegangen werden, und das meist ohne Einschränkung.

Nun willst Du als Bushcrafter natürlich auch im Wald übernachten. Selbst wenn man sich tiefer in die Gesetze einliest, findet man aber keine einschlägigen Texte oder genauere Regelungen für eine oder mehrere Übernachtungen. Was man jedoch sehr wohl findet, und das in den Gesetzestexten eines jedes Bundeslandes, sind Aussagen zum Zelten.

Stockbrot am Lagerfeuer im Garten mit den Kindern – auch das ist Bushcraft.

Hier kann man allgemein sagen, dass das Zelten im Wald nicht erlaubt ist. Dies schließt auch schon das Aufbauen eines Zeltes mit ein. Für die freie Landschaft gibt es jedoch keine Erwähnungen, somit ist das Zelten in freier Landschaft nicht explizit verboten. **Jedoch Vorsicht! Das Zelten auf fremdem Besitz ist ohne Erlaubnis natürlich verboten!**

Sehen wir uns im Vergleich dazu mal skandinavische Länder, sprich Norwegen oder auch Schweden, an sowie z.B. Schottland, so ist hier eigentlich alles anders: Das »Wildcampen« wird in diesen Ländern bzw. Kulturen eher als normal angesehen und wird dort ganz anders ausgelebt, was uns auf Reisen natürlich entgegenkommt.

Aber Achtung! Das heißt nicht, dass hier einfach mal frische Bäume umgeschlagen werden sollten, nur um einen Shelter zu bauen oder ein Feuer zu machen. Stattdessen solltest Du dort genau wie hier den eigentlichen Bushcraft-Gedanken leben und für ein Feuer z.B. nach Totholz suchen bzw. Ressourcen sinnvoll nutzen.

AUSRÜSTUNG

Die, so glaube ich, meistgestellte Frage zum Thema »Bushcraften« lautet: Was brauch ich, wenn ich rausgehen will? Und, na ja, die Antwort ist eigentlich ganz einfach: Nix! Das mag auf den ersten Blick komisch klingen, aber einen Rucksack, eine Regenjacke sowie ein Paar Schuhe, die sonst für Waldspaziergänge benutzt werden, hat eigentlich jeder zu Hause.

Bei der Zusammenstellung Deiner Ausrüstung kommt es natürlich auch darauf an, wie lange Du draußen bleiben und was Du draußen machen möchtest. Eventuell willst Du ja sogar draußen übernachten. Im Folgenden möchte ich Dir drei verschiedene Ausrüstungs-Varianten für unterschiedliche Bedürfnisse zeigen.

1-TAGES-TOUR

Als Beginner brauchst Du außer einem Rucksack und einem Messer noch wasserfeste Kleidung, die auch mal schmutzig werden darf, sowie ein paar leichte Wanderschuhe. Willst Du Dir eine Mahlzeit zubereiten, wirst Du außerdem noch einen kleinen Kocher, einen Topf und eine Trinkflasche benötigen, sowie ein einfaches Besteck, wobei ein selbstgeschnitzter Löffel schon was besonders Feines ist. Eine Plane aus dem Baumarkt sowie eine einfache Schnur oder ein paar Meter Paracord zum Aufbau eines Sonnen- oder Regenschutzes sind ebenfalls wichtig. Im Einzelnen gilt:

Rucksack: Hier kannst Du einfach einen alten Rucksack nehmen, den Du zuhause hast; für einen Anfänger muss er keine besonderen Anforderungen erfüllen. Ich empfehle eine Größe von 20–25 Litern. Die Rucksäcke gibt es von verschiedenen Herstellern in komplett wasserdichter Ausführung. Falls Du nicht so viel Geld ausgeben möchtest, kannst Du Deine wichtigsten Habseligkeiten auch in Plastiktüten oder wasserdichte Beutel verpacken.

Messer: Des Bushcrafters liebstes Spielzeug – aber ganz ehrlich: Ein umgebautes Küchenmesser tut es eigentlich ebenfalls; auch einfache Klappmesser wie ein Victorinox oder ein einfaches Opinel reichen für leichte Schnitzarbeiten oder um sich z.B. Essen zuzubereiten. (Beachte bei der Auswahl bitte unbedingt den §42a des Deutschen Waffengesetzes, weitere Infos bekommst Du im Kapitel » Arbeiten mit dem Messer«.)

Bekleidung: Hier ist die Wahl ziemlich einfach: Zieh das an, was draußen schmutzig werden kann und was Dich warmhält. Alternativ kannst Du auch Deinen lokalen Army Shop besuchen (oder Dich auf *www.asmc.de* oder *www.truman.de* umsehen) – gebrauchte Militärkleidung ist immer nützlich und kostet nicht viel.

Schuhe: Diese sollen vor allem bequem und der Jahreszeit angepasst sein. Wichtig ist, dass Du sie in einem Fachgeschäft kaufen solltest. Lass Dich hier bezüglich Deiner persönlichen Anforderungen beraten – nicht immer ist ein steigeisenfester Schuh von Nöten. Hast Du einen Schuh gefunden, solltest Du ihn vor größeren Wanderungen auf jeden Fall »einlaufen«, um spätere Blasen zu vermeiden. Passend zum Schuh solltest Du Dir ein oder zwei Paar vernünftige Wandersocken zulegen. Auch hier empfehle ich Dir, Deinen Berater anzusprechen. Meine Tendenz geht zu den Herstellern Falke oder Smartwool. Wenn Du kälteempfindlich bist, sind letztere sicher die beste Wahl: Wolle wärmt und atmet extrem gut, und diese Socken haben mich bisher nie im Stich gelassen.

Kochen etc: Wenn es um die Zubereitung von Essen oder auch Heißgetränken geht, eignet sich z.B. ein einfacher 500-ml-Edelstahlbecher etwa von Tatonka oder auch GSI. Passend zu diesen Bechern/Kochtöpfen empfehle ich eine 1-Liter-Trinkflasche, z.B. von der Firma Nalgene. Diese passen in die Becher und bilden somit einen Teil Deines Kochsets. Bei den Kochern eignen sich z.B. Trockenbrennstoff-Kocher wie ein Esbitkocher oder auch der M71-Gelkocher der Schweizer Armee; beide sind günstig zu bekommen und reichen für den Anfang mehr als aus. Einen weiteren beliebten Kandidaten hab ich hier zum Schluss: den klassischen Spirituskocher, z.B. einen Trangia. Als Besteck reicht ein einfacher Spork aus BPA-freiem Kunststoff. Du hast natürlich noch deutlich mehr Möglichkeiten, draußen zu kochen – vom Edelstahl-Kochtopf über den Dutch Oven bis zu Schmiede- und Gusseisenpfannen. Genaueres zu diesem Thema findest Du im Kapitel »Draußen kochen«.

Unterstand/Shelter: Wie gesagt, zum Anfang tut es die Plane aus dem Baumarkt oder vom Discounter. Ich empfehle hier eine Größe von 2 x 2 bzw. 2 x 3 Metern. Zum Befestigen und Abspannen brauchst Du noch ein paar Meter Schnur oder etwas Paracord, und schon hast Du einen Schutz vor Regen, Sonne oder Schnee. Was alles möglich ist, erfährst Du im Kapitel »Lager und Unterstände«.

First Aid: Zur Standardausrüstung sollte, egal wie lange und wie oft Du unterwegs bist, unbedingt ein Erste-Hilfe-Set gehören. Such dieses nach Deinem persönlichen Know-how aus und ergänze es z.B. um passende Kopfschmerztabletten, Kohle-Tabletten, Durch-

Ausrüstung für eine 3-Tages-Tour in den Schweizer Voralpen.

fallmittel etc. Wenn Du Dich intensiver für das Thema interessierst, schau in das Kapitel »Sicherheit«.

1-3-TAGESTOUR

Dieser Punkt unterscheidet sich von der 1-Tages-Tour vor allem dadurch, dass Du nun eine Übernachtung einplanst und dafür natürlich die richtige Ausrüstung dabeihaben musst. Außerdem solltest Du an Deinen Essensvorrat bzw. Deine Versorgung denken. Ein Tipp: Wenn Du Deine ersten Nächte draußen verbringst, nimm Dir ruhig jemanden mit, der dies schon einmal gemacht hat. So wird es die ersten Male einfacher für Dich – und: »Geteilte Angst ist halbe Angst.« Zu den einzelnen Ausrüstungsgegenständen ist das Folgende zu beachten:

Rucksack: Der wichtigste Hinweis für den Kauf eines passenden Rucksacks: Geh in ein Fachgeschäft, wo Du diesen anprobieren kannst – denn wenn Dein Rucksack Dich »ärgern« sollte, weil er nicht passt, ist die ganze Tour für die Katz. Ein geeigneter Rucksack wird sicherlich größer ausfallen als Dein Tagesrucksack. Mein aktueller Rucksack für diese Art von Tour ist beispielsweise ein 5.11 Responder mit einem Volumen von ca. 40–50 Liter, damit ich meine Ausrüstung darin unterbringen kann und nicht alles draußen dranbinden muss, oder ein LK 35 der schwedischen Armee. Es gibt natürlich auch viele andere gute Hersteller. Als erstes musst Du Dir darüber klarwerden, was Du transportieren willst und vor allem wie, also: Wie schwer wird es, und wie komfortabel möchtest Du das Ganze bewegen. Eine Faustformel, nach der Menschen x Prozent ihres Körpergewichtes tragen können, ist meiner Erfahrung nach wenig hilfreich. Fakt ist: Es macht nicht viel Spaß, einen 1000 g leichten Rucksack zu besitzen, wenn ich eine Ausrüstung bewegen bzw. tragen möchte, die 15 kg oder schwerer ist. Die Tragesysteme sind bei diesen Rucksäcken nun mal nicht für diese Art von Last gedacht. Ich bevorzuge die robuste Variante, wie z.B. den oben erwähnten 5.11 oder die Rucksäcke der in Deutschland ansässigen Firma Tasmanian Tiger bzw. Tatonka. Die meisten Rucksäcke in der Größe um 40–50 Liter und darüber haben gewöhnlich mindestens eine Zweikammer-Aufteilung, d.h. Hauptfach oben sowie Nässe- oder Schlafsackfach unten. Dies hilft Dir, Dich zu organisieren. Leicht bis mittel-wasserfest ist heutzutage eigentlich jeder Rucksack bzw. ist teilweise eine Regenhaube integriert. Nichtsdestotrotz verpacke ich meine Wertsachen und mindestens einen Satz Wechsel-Bekleidung in einem Drybag, damit ich mich, falls doch mal was schiefgeht, zumindest nachts trocken schlafen legen kann. Auch wenn es verrückt klingt, so würde ich fast raten, den Rucksack für solche Touren als letztes zu kaufen – so hast Du in etwa eine Idee, was Du mitnehmen möchtest und welches Volumen Du brauchst; manchmal ist es weniger das Gewicht als der Platz, den Du brauchst. Von Anfang an einen »zu großen« Rucksack zu kaufen, davon würde ich abraten, denn wenn Du den 100-Liter-Rucksack zuhause hast, machst Du ihn sicher auch voll.

Messer/Werkzeuge: Bei Touren, die mehr als einen Tag dauern, solltest Du überlegen, ob Du neben Deinem Hauptmesser auch ein kleines Beil oder eine Klappsäge mitnimmst, z.B. um kleine Bauten zu errichten oder für ein kleines Lagerfeuer. Wenn es um Beile oder Äxte geht, bevorzuge ich die Firma Gränsfors Bruks aus Schweden, aber auch Firmen wie Hultafors oder Fiskars bauen gute Werkzeuge für etwas weniger Geld. Bei Äxten/Beilen gilt für mich: Lieber eine mittelgroße Axt als ein kurzes Beil, da ich diese auch »kurz« greifen kann wie ein Beil, wogegen ich ein kurzer Beil nicht verlängern kann und so deutlich mehr Kraft brauche als nötig. Wenn Du nur an ein Messer als One-Option-Tool denkst: Ja, kann man machen, allerdings sollte dieses Messer dann mindestens 4 mm dick und mindestens 12 cm lang sein. Eine Ausnahme macht meiner Meinung nach in Bezug auf die Klingendicke z.B. das Mora Garberg; dieses Messer ist einfach ein »Beast« und dank seiner Full-Tang-Konstruktion beinah unzerstörbar. Bedenke jedoch, dass Du unter Umständen Deinem einzigen Messer bei falscher Nutzung erheblichen Schaden zufügen kannst. Bei Sägen bin ich nach einigen Tests von anderen Geräten immer noch mit meiner Bako Laplander unterwegs und kann diese doch günstige Säge nach wie vor empfehlen. Es gibt natürlich auch effizientere Alternativen wie z.B. die Silky Katana oder auch Sägen von der Firma ARS sowie Klappsägen der Firma Fiskars, die aber im Schnitt auch etwas teurer sind. Wie bei den meisten Dingen empfehle ich Dir auch hier eine Beratung im Fachhandel.

Bekleidung: Für Mehrtagestouren solltest Du wenigstens einen weiteren Satz Bekleidung dabeihaben, z.B. für den Fall, dass Du aufgrund von extremem Wetter wieder etwas Trockenes zum Anziehen brauchst. Glaub mir: Nass schläft es sich nicht gut. Deine Bekleidung sollte natürlich an die gewählte Jahreszeit angepasst sein. Hier gilt ebenfalls: Du kannst natürlich am Anfang auf die günstige Armeebekleidung zurückgreifen, allerdings ist Funktionsbekleidung deutlich leichter und trocknet schneller. Bei Hosen achte ich darauf, dass sie robust und aus einem wasserfesten oder schnelltrocknenden Material sind. Es gibt kaum etwas Schlimmeres als nasse Klamotten. Gehen wir einfach mal durch, was ich selbst trage und wieso. Bei warmer Unterwäsche ist Merinowolle (etwa von der Firma Woolpower) einfach ein fantastisches Material für den Outdoor-Bereich: Sie wärmt ungemein, und selbst im feuchten Zustand fühlt sie sich extrem gut an. Außerdem nimmt sie relativ schwer Gerüche an, was draußen ein enormer Vorteil ist. Das gleiche gilt für Socken. Als Oberbekleidung verwende ich gerne ein Funktionshemd, z.B. von Fjällräven. Bei Jacken bin ich mit dem Lodenstoff der deutschen Firma Roughstuff sehr zufrieden. Dabei handelt es sich um Wolle mit einer extremen Dichte, die also auch bedingt wasserabweisend ist und super wärmt. Ihr größter Vorteil gegenüber klassischen Fleecejacken besteht darin, dass sie nicht schmilzt, wenn Du mal am Feuer sitzt oder schläfst. Feuerfest wie eine Löschdecke ist sie natürlich nicht. Günstige Alternativen hab ich in diesem Bereich noch nicht wirklich gesehen. Bei Hosen bin ich ein großer Freund der Firma Fjällräven. Sie verwendet ein Baumwollmischgewebe, das unter dem Namen G1000 bekannt ist, dieses wird mit einem passenden Wachs behandelt und ist somit so gut wie dicht und atmet dabei trotzdem. Bei den meisten meiner Aktivitäten kommen solche Hosen zum Einsatz. Eine günstige Variante stammt von der Marke Frilufts. Bei Regenbekleidung sind meine erste Wahl Jacken aus einem Trilaminat, auch Hardshell genannt. Ob die nun von Mammut, Arcteryx oder wie in meinem Fall von der Britischen Armee sind, musst Du für Dich bzw. muss Dein Geldbeutel entscheiden. Das wichtigste ist, dass Du Dich nach dem Zwiebelprinzip kleiden solltest, soll heißen: Schicht für Schicht bis zur Regenjacke. Dieses Prinzip funktioniert aber nur, wenn Du Funktionsbekleidung über Funktionsbekleidung trägst. Wenn Du z.B. ein Baumwoll-T-Shirt unter Deiner Regenjacke anhast, wirst Du schnell feststellen, dass Dein Shirt nass wird. Das ist aber nicht die Jacke: Die Membranen sind nur so groß, dass sie Wasserdampf durchlassen sollen, Dein Baumwoll-T-Shirt speichert aber leider Nässe, und die Jacke macht das, was sie tun soll: nämlich dicht sein. Bei Winter-Touren solltest Du besonders darauf achten, dass Du Dich durch diesen Effekt nicht unterkühlst. Aber wie gesagt, ein Satz Bekleidung zum Wechseln gehört sowieso dazu.

Schuhe: Auch die Schuhe sollten wie Deine übrige Kleidung an die Jahreszeit angepasst sein. Für die meisten Aktivitäten draußen bevorzuge ich knöchelhohe Schuhe, da hier die Gefahr des Umknickens deutlich geringer ist. So verringerst Du das Risiko, dass Du aufgrund einer Verletzung Deine Tour abbrechen musst. Natürlich brauchst Du keine steigeisenfesten Bergstiefel, wenn Du in den heimischen Wäldern unterwegs bist. Dein Schuhwerk sollte aber auf jeden Fall dem Terrain angepasst sein. Bei den Materialien bevorzuge ich Leder mit Membran. Auch wenn es schwerer ist, habe ich das Gefühl, dass trotz einer Goretex-Membran mein Fuß besser atmen kann als in einem Textilschuh mit gleicher Membran. Aber das ist wie vieles Andere Geschmacks- bzw. Erfahrungssache. Klar kannst Du auch einen Lederschuh wachsen oder ölen, bis er dicht ist; dann ist aber die Atmungsfähigkeit quasi dahin. Leder ist in den meisten Fällen deutlich stabiler und langlebiger als ein »Stoff«schuh – meinen ersten Lederstiefel hatte ich fast 20 Jahre lang, und selbst dann habe ich ihn nur ausgetauscht, weil er nicht nochmal neu besohlt werden konnte. Diese Stabilität hat natürlich ihren Preis in Form von Gewicht. Ein Textilschuh gleicher Machweise ist einfach leichter. Bei einer Beratung im Fachgeschäft kannst Du dem Berater Dein Vorhaben schildern, und zusammen werdet Ihr sicher den richtigen Schuh finden. Ich verwende z.B. aktuell neben einem Meindl-Lederstiefel (Kategorie A/B) einen Lowa Zephyr mit Goretex und im Winter einen Schneestiefel der Firma Salomon.

Kochen etc.: Wenn das in der 1-Tages-Tour beschriebene Kochset für Dich passt, ist das super. Du kannst überlegen, die Kunststoffflasche durch eine Edelstahlflasche auszutauschen, um Wasser direkt in der Flasche zu kochen. Neben den genannten Dingen habe ich fast immer einen Titanteller der Firma Snowpeak (funktioniert für mich auch als Pfanne) und ein BPA-freies Nylon-Besteck von Humangear dabei, bestehend aus einem Löffel und einer Gabel. Ein Messer haben wir ja eh mit – also warum noch eines mitschleppen? Die Unterschiede zwischen der Ausstattung für 1- oder 3-Tages-Touren hängen natürlich stark davon ab, was Du essen möchtest (siehe hierzu das Kapitel »Draußen kochen«).

Unterstand/Shelter: Wenn Du mit der oben genannten Baumarktplane zufrieden bist, kannst Du diese auch weiterhin benutzen. Ich bevorzuge ein Tarp, was etwas leichter ist. Auf jeden Fall solltest Du auch einige Meter Schnur oder Paracord einpacken. Gehen wir kurz auf die einzelnen Materialien sowie deren Vor- bzw. Nachteile ein. Die Baumarktplane ist mit Sicherheit die günstigste Variante, dafür ist sie im Packmaß leider groß und außerdem nicht unbedingt leise beim Aufbauen. Bei Tarps kannst Du Dir überlegen, ob Du eher traditionell oder doch leicht und modern unterwegs sein möchtest. Zu den traditionellen Tarps gehören Canvas- bzw. Baumwoll-Tarps, z.B. von Jurtenland. Diese sind für gewöhnlich unzerstörbar feuerfest und geben Dir durch diverse Schlaufen unterschiedliche Möglichkeiten des Aufbaus. Nachteil ist hier ganz klar das Gewicht und das Packmaß. Handelsübliche Tarps bestehen für gewöhnlich aus einem PU-beschichteten Ripstop Nylon. Sie wiegen im Schnitt ca. 200–500 g, etwa ein Viertel eines Canvas-Tarps. Auch Nylon-Tarps lassen sich durch diverse Schlaufen zu ganzen Zelten aufbauen; die Variationen sind quasi unerschöpflich (siehe hierzu das Kapitel »Lager und Unterstände«). Ob Du dazu die Baumarktschnur oder Paracord benutzt, liegt bei Dir, die Nylonschnur aus dem Baumarkt kostet sicher weniger, ist aber meiner Meinung nach nicht so »schön« zu knoten. Ich bevorzuge nach wie vor Paracord in einer 550er- bzw. 5-mm-Stärke. Mit diesem könntest Du quasi ein Auto abschleppen, also reicht es auch, um einen Unterschlupf zu bauen. Grundsätzlich empfehle ich Dir aber, mit verschiedenen Reepschnüren oder auch Paracord zu testen, was Dir eher liegt. Zur Länge des verwendeten Seils kann ich nur

Mein Schlaf-Setup: Hängematte und Tarp.

sagen: Je länger, desto besser. Ich habe für gewöhnlich mindestens ein Paracordbündel von 15 m Länge dabei (meistens als Firstleine) und diverse kleinere Reste von Längen um die drei Meter als Abspannleinen oder für andere Knoten etc.

Schlafen: Wenn Du ein oder zwei Übernachtungen einplanst, brauchst Du neben Deinem Shelter einen passenden Schlafsack sowie eine zur Jahreszeit passende Isomatte. Die einfachsten Isomatten, die Du für wenig Geld bekommst, sind sicher diejenigen der Bundeswehr. Diese isolieren aber nicht unbedingt gut, und recht dünn sind sie außerdem. Dennoch lohnt sich der Kauf, da Du sie auch als Sitzmatte nutzen kannst. Passende Isomatten, die wenig Platz wegnehmen, sind hingegen recht teuer. Dafür sind sie aber nicht nur platzsparend und leichtgewichtig, sondern auch für deutlich interessantere Temperaturbereiche geeignet. Ich nutze eine thermarest xtherm, aber auch Modelle wie die Exped Downmat sind hervorragende Matten für Temperaturen unter null Grad. Am robustesten sind – auch wenn sie deutlich mehr Platz wegnehmen – die klassischen Schaumstoffmatten. Sie können keine Luft verlieren und sind so quasi unzerstörbar; auch das Gewicht ist meistens hinnehmbar: Eine Matte in der Größe 1,90 x 1,9 cm wiegt 950 g und hat ein Packmaß von ca. 60 x 25 cm. Die meisten »Luftmatten«, z.B. der Firma Thermarest, haben eine Nylonoberfläche – diese sind empfindlich, und Du solltest Deinen Untergrund z.B. nach spitzen Steinen oder auch Ästen absuchen. Dafür sind sie um einiges kleiner und leichter: Eine vergleichbare Matte in der Größe 1,83 x 51 cm und einer Höhe von 6,3 cm hat ein Gewicht von gerade noch 356 g und ein Packmaß von 23 x 10 cm. Nachteil ist, wie erwähnt, das Material dieser Matten; die Oberfläche ist entsprechend dünn und muss geschützt werden. Nichtsdestotrotz bevorzuge ich diese kleineren und leichteren Matten und lege dafür z.B. eine »Elefantenhaut« als Schutz vor Nässe und Beschädigungen drunter.

Bei **Schlafsäcken** gilt: Kunstfaser-Modelle haben den Vorteil, dass sie durch die Füllung selbst dann wärmen, wenn sie feucht sind, wohingegen Daunenschlafsäcke etwas, sagen wir mal, problematischer sind. Es gibt durchaus Hersteller, die relativ unempfindliche Daunenschlafsäcke herstellen – diese sind zwar teurer, aber um das Vielfache kleiner und leichter bei gleicher oder teilweise höherer Wärmeleistung wie günstigere Modelle. Klassische Hersteller für den Bereich Bushcraft sind mittlerweile Firmen wie Carinthia, Mountain Hardware, Deuter oder Yeti. All diese Schlafsäcke decken einen unterschiedlichen Temperaturbereich ab, und es ist wichtig, diese Zahlen richtig zu verstehen. Nehmen wir als Beispiel den Deuter Treklite-2 Daunenschlafsack; hier werden drei Temperaturen angegeben: Komforttemperatur 5 °C, Grenztemperatur –2 °C, eine Extremtemperatur –16 °C. Bequem und warm schläfst Du also bei einer Außentemperatur von 5 °C, ab einer Temperatur von –2 °C sollte es eine ungemütliche Nacht werden, in der Du sicher das eine oder andere Mal aufwachen wirst, und ab einer Temperatur von –16 °C ist ein Überleben zwar möglich, aber ich würde es, ehrlich gesagt, nicht darauf ankommen lassen. Beim Kauf eines Schlafsacks solltest Du auf jeden Fall in einem Fachgeschäft schildern, was Du vorhast und mit welchen Temperaturen Du rechnest. Natürlich spielt daneben auch Dein persönliches Kälteempfinden eine wichtige Rolle. Mit all diesen Informationen solltest Du einen passenden Schlafsack für deinen Overnighter finden. Ach ja, eine Sache darf bei mir nie fehlen: ein Kissen … :-)

Hängematte/Tarp/Lavvu: Tja, wenn es um die Art und Weise des Draußenschlafens geht, ist für mich eins klar: Hängematte! Ich benutze aktuell ein für mich gebautes Modell der Firma Danstuff, hab aber mit einer klassischen DD Frontline Hammock angefangen, die ich bis heute auch empfehlen kann. Ein Moskitonetz sowie die Möglichkeit, eine Isomatte in eine Art zweiten Boden einzulegen, sind für mich absolut essenziell. Damit diese auch im Winter funktioniert, falls Du planst, wie ich ganzjährig in einer Hängematte zu schlafen, empfehle ich Dir, neben einer guten Isomatte auch einen Underquilt (auch Underblanket genannt) zu benutzen; dann sind selbst Minusgrade kein Problem. Das Schlafen in einer Hängematte ist etwas anders als gewöhnlich, denn hier liegst Du leicht diagonal in Deiner Matte. Diese Art zu schlafen eignet sich vor allem für Seiten-, aber auch Bauchschläfer. Eine andere Art, die ich total gern mag, ist die Polnische Zeltbahn: wenn Du zwei davon besitzt, lassen sie sich zu einem kleineren Tipi bzw. einem Lavvu zusammenknüpfen. Diese Art von Unterschlupf ist fast wie ein Wohnzimmer, und es gibt sie in diversen Größen. Ich habe für mein Lavvu z.B. auch einen kleinen Zeltofen – damit ist es im Winter quasi unschlagbar.

Ein kleiner Klapp-Hobo, ein Trangia-Spirituskocher sowie ein Feuerstahl sind immer dabei.

Beachte zum Zelten unbedingt die Gesetze Deines Bundeslandes, einen Auszug findest Du im Kapitel »Was Du wissen musst«.

First Aid: Egal, ob Du nun einen Tag oder drei Tage draußen sein möchtest, nimm auch hier ein Erste-Hilfe-Set mit, das auf Deine persönlichen Bedürfnisse angepasst ist. Ein wichtiger Hinweis, weil es mir auf einem Treffen schon mal passiert ist: Falls Du eine bestimmte Medikation benötigst, z.B. falls Du Diabetiker, Allergiker oder auch Bluthochdruckpatient bist, dann lass dies bitte Deine Mitbushcrafter wissen. Wenn Du mit Menschen unterwegs bist, die Du noch nicht lange kennst oder die Deine Situation nicht kennen, werden sie Dir ansonsten im Notfall nicht helfen können, einfach weil sie nicht Bescheid wissen. Also informiere Deine Mitwanderer über Deine Medikamente und/ oder einen eventuellen Notfallplan, den Du bei Dir trägst.

ODER MEHR

Der Hauptunterschied zwischen 3-Tages- oder 2-Wochen-Touren liegt eigentlich in der Menge der Nahrung oder des Wassers, die Du benötigst. Die Ausrüstung und Bekleidung dagegen bleibt im Wesentlichen gleich. Ob Du nun noch ein Paar Socken oder ein T-Shirt mehr mitnehmen möchtest, liegt bei Dir – ich würde in jedem Fall aus Gewichtsgründen das Waschen der Kleider vorziehen: Je mehr Du einpackst, desto schwerer wird Dein Rucksack; logisch, oder?!

Wie Du Wasser finden oder Deinen Wasservorrat wieder auffüllen kannst, erfährst Du z.B. in Johannes Vogels »Trinkwasserversorgung in Extremsituationen«; Informationen über essbare Insekten oder Pflanzen, um eine Durststrecke zu überbrücken, findest Du in seinen Titeln »Tierische Notnahrung« bzw. »Pflanzliche Notnahrung«. Gerade am Anfang solltest Du Deine Touren so planen, dass Du alle 3 Tage an einem Ort vorbeikommst, wo Du Deine Nahrungsmittelvorräte wieder auffüllen kannst. Für autarke Touren empfehle ich Dir einen Wasserfilter wie den Sawyer Mini oder auch den MSR Trailshot. Beide sind nach Herstellerangaben in der Lage, 99,999% aller Bakterien und Protozoen zu filtern. (Natürlich solltest Du darauf achten, was für Wasser Du filterst; siehe hierzu das Kapitel »Trinkwasser beim Bushcraften«.) Die beiden genannten Filter sind zwar leicht, aber dafür relativ schwierig zu reinigen. Ich empfehle sie für den Gebrauch durch maximal zwei Personen, für alles andere solltest Du Dir im Fachgeschäft die Filter von Firmen wie Katadyn oder MSR ansehen. Diese gibt es in unterschiedlichen Größen, Gewichten, Ausstattungen und natürlich Liefer- sowie Filterleistungen. Wie bei fast jedem Ausrüstungsgegenstand sind hier preislich keine Grenzen gesetzt – überleg Dir gut, was Du für die Zukunft haben bzw. machen möchtest.

Beim Essen (siehe hierzu das Kapitel »Draußen kochen«) gibt es die Möglichkeit, auf gefriergetrocknetes Essen zurückzugreifen – es wiegt wenig und muss im Regelfall mit ca. 500 ml heißem Wasser aufgegossen werden. Bezüglich der Frage »Was soll ich denn nehmen?« kann ich nur mit dem Sprichwort antworten: »Was der Bauer nicht kennt, das frisst er nicht«. Das soll aber natürlich nicht heißen, dass Du auf keinen Fall etwas Neues probieren solltest! Aber Du musst es nicht auf Teufel komm raus auf einer Tour probieren; halt Dich an das, was Dir sonst auch schmeckt, dann wird es passen.

Was auf keinen Fall fehlen sollte, sind kleine Energielieferanten wie z.B. Nüsse, Trockenfrüchte usw. Ich bin normalerweise kein Rosinenfreund. Aber auf Touren schmecken mir Trockenfrüchte plötzlich – ich bin, was das Essen angeht, draußen offensichtlich deutlich aufgeschlossener als in der heimischen Umgebung. Ansonsten hab ich auch gerne ein Stück Hartkäse, Salami oder Trockenfleisch wie Beef Jerky dabei; sie halten sich quasi ewig und liefern Energie, die Du auf Touren brauchen kannst.

AUFMERKSAMKEIT & NATURWAHRNEHMUNG

WO IST DAS ROSA EICHHÖRNCHEN?

Da wir in unserer modernen Gesellschaft nicht mehr als Jäger und Sammler leben müssen, scheint es nicht mehr so wichtig, in der Natur aufmerksam zu sein. Es klopft einem beim Schnitzen kein Bär auf die Schulter, man kocht nicht mehr täglich am offenen Feuer oder muss gewisse Punkte bei der Schlafplatzwahl beachten. Dennoch ist Aufmerksamkeit und ein Bewusstsein für die Umgebung auch heute noch sehr wichtig, sei es beim Spazieren im Wald oder in der Stadt, beim Autofahren oder eben beim Bushcraft- und Survivaltraining. Aus den von unserem Körper wahrgenommenen Reizen müssen wir relevante Informationen extrahieren, erkannte Muster interpretieren und mit unseren Erinnerungen abgleichen, um dann situationsabhängig zu handeln. Dabei ist zu beachten, dass unsere Erinnerung nicht dem entspricht, was »wirklich geschehen« ist, sondern lediglich unserem Blickwinkel. Man sollte stets wahrnehmungs-, planungs- und handlungsfähig sein. Fällt eine dieser drei Säulen weg, muss man Glück haben, was das Beispiel Fahrradfahren leicht verständlich illustriert.

Eine Voraussetzung, um mit den meisten Situationen klarzukommen, ist es, Ruhe zu bewahren und nicht in Panik auszubrechen. Dynamische Systeme können sich unter Umständen schnell verändern; die Prinzipien, die sich daraus ergeben, lassen sich mit etwas Übung leicht verinnerlichen: Vereinfacht gesagt muss zuallererst die Situation wahrgenommen und eingeschätzt werden **(Observieren)**. Danach werden weitere Schritte und notwendige Aktionen bedacht **(Planen)**, worauf die Ausführung des Plans erfolgt **(Agieren)**. Dann sollte man wieder vorne anfangen und wahrnehmen, was sich aus der eigenen Handlung ergibt *(siehe Abb.)*. Dieser Vorgang kann sehr schnell ablaufen, z.B. beim Skifahren, oder eher langsam, z.B. beim Schach. Man spricht von »Situation Awareness« oder »situativem Bewusstsein«. Der Bereich der Aufmerksamkeit ist durch die Ansprüche der digitalisierten Gesellschaft allerdings oft auf Bildschirmformat reduziert. Wir sind übersättigt und nahezu abgestumpft. Da unser Gehirn permanent alle möglichen Arten von sensorischen Eindrücken verarbeitet und gerade die Werbung unsere Aufmerksamkeit fangen und binden will, ist unsere heutige Lebensweise nur mit Hilfe vieler »Filter« möglich. Sonst würden wir unter einer permanenten Reizüberflutung leiden. Außerdem wollen wir stets ein Ziel vor Augen haben und erwarten ein ganz

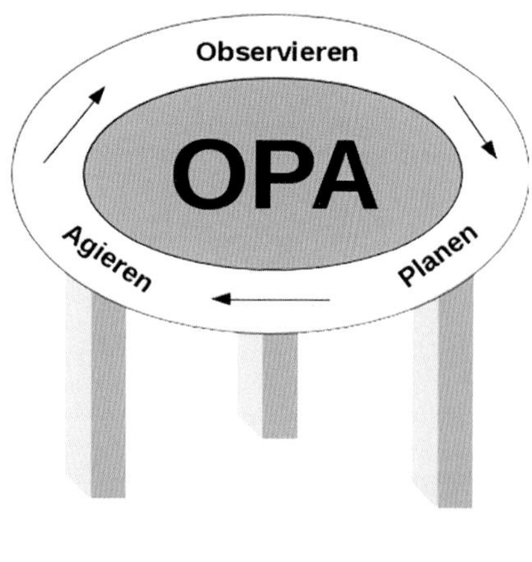

bestimmtes Muster oder Ergebnis; andere Eindrücke blenden wir dadurch aus. Unsere »Hardware« kann aber eigentlich auch peripher viel mehr wahrnehmen. Du kannst ein sehr detailliertes Bild Deines Umfelds erhalten, auch ohne direkt hinzuschauen oder konkret etwas zu suchen.

Wie bei allem gilt hier die goldene Regel: Übung macht den Meister. Man muss observieren, worin man besser werden will, dann planen und sich beispielsweise mit Hilfe von Videos, Artikeln und Tutorials weiterbilden, um dann auch das Handeln nicht zu verpassen. Es gilt also anzufangen, sich regelmäßig die Finger schmutzig zu machen und ruhig und fleißig zu üben. Dabei stets **observieren** (»War das gut?«), **planen** (»Was kann man verbessern?«) und **handeln** (»Neuer Versuch oder regenerieren!«).

ALLE RICHTUNGEN

Um die Aufmerksamkeit in alle Richtungen wieder zu trainieren, solltest Du Dir zuallererst etwas Zeit nehmen und draußen einen Platz suchen, den Du regelmäßig aufsuchen kannst. Der Termindruck muss rausgenommen werden, Du musst »entschleunigen« und den Blick wieder nach oben heben. Es geht darum, den Geist zu klären und sich selbst mal nicht mehr zuzuhören. Es gilt, Geduld zu haben und die Hektik, die Du aus dem Alltag mitbringst, abzulegen. Meditationserfahrung kann helfen, allerdings findet diese nur selten auf nassem, kalten Boden bei Wind und Wetter statt. Direkt in der Natur gibt es ungewohnte äußere Eindrücke, die die Situation zu Beginn ungemütlich und unkomfortabel machen, aber auch wahrnehmbare Informationen darstellen. Der Schlüssel liegt dabei, wie beim Meditieren, in der Atmung. Die Konzentration und das Auseinandersetzen mit der Atmung helfen uns, schnell den Geist zu klären und die Umstände zu akzeptieren. Es geht nun darum, sich vor dem geistigen Auge ein Bild der Umgebung zu schaffen und dabei weiter ruhig zu atmen.

Übung 1 (leicht): Verharren

Such Dir einen relativ ungestörten Platz in einem Garten, Park oder Wald in Deiner Umgebung (nicht in Deinem Lager an einem Feuer) und verharre dort für etwa 30 Minuten. Versuche, Deine Umgebung wahrzunehmen und einfach nur dazusein, ohne etwas Wichtiges tun zu müssen – außer atmen natürlich: einatmen – ausatmen ...

DIE SINNE REAKTIVIEREN

Das **Sehen** mit beiden Augen ist unser Primärsinn. Es bindet die meiste Aufmerksamkeit und wird auch am meisten beansprucht. Will man die anderen Sinne schulen, sollte man sich daher am besten die Augen verbinden. Das Sehen erlaubt uns, grob gesagt, Objekte zu unterscheiden und Entfernungen bei verschiedenen Lichtverhältnissen abzuschätzen. Heute ist unser Sehen meist auf Bildschirmformat beschränkt, und die meiste Zeit sind wir auf etwa 0,5–2 m vor uns fokussiert, wobei die Umgebung gut ausgeleuchtet ist.

Dabei sind unsere Augen für andere Aufgaben gemacht, und eine dauerhafte Belastung dieser Art kann ihnen schaden. Deshalb solltest Du immer wieder zwischendurch die Augen entspannen. Dazu hebst Du den Kopf und schaust einfach vor Dich hin, ohne etwas bewusst zu fixieren oder zu fokussieren. So können die Muskeln am Auge sich entspannen. Außerdem haben wir eigentlich nicht nur eine Blickrichtung, sondern ein ganzes Blickfeld, welches peripher nahezu 180° beträgt. Dabei reagieren die Außenbereiche besser auf Bewegung und die Innenbereiche eher auf Farben, Kontraste und Kanten. Um Dein eigenes Blickfeld zu bestimmen, streckst Du beide Arme vor Dir aus, hebst den Kopf, blickst gerade auf die gehobenen Daumen und beginnst, mit diesen zu wackeln. Jetzt werden die Arme nach links und rechts außen geführt, wobei Du den Blick weiter geradeaus hältst. Wenn die wackelnden Daumen am Rand kaum noch zu sehen sind, hast Du den maximalen Blickwinkel erreicht *(siehe Abb.)*.

Auf der Netzhaut des menschlichen Auges befinden sich drei Typen von sogenannten Zapfen für die Wahrnehmung von verschiedenen Wellenlängen des Lichts. Diese ermöglichen es also, Farben im Hellen zu sehen. Diese Zapfen sind allerdings nicht sehr lichtempfindlich und reagieren daher nur bei ausreichender Helligkeit. Die sogenannten Stäbchen dagegen reagieren schon bei viel geringeren Lichtintensitäten und relativer Dunkelheit, sind also in Bezug auf die Lichtstärke viel empfindlicher. Außerdem hat jeder Mensch nur einen Typ von Stäbchen, welcher besonders stark auf Licht mit hohem Blau- oder Grünanteil reagiert. Daher entsteht für uns nachts mit nur sehr schwachen Lichverhältnissen kein Farbeindruck. Dass unser Auge ausschließlich Stäbchen nutzt, ist heute meist nur morgens beim Aufwachen erreicht. Auch bei nur kurzer zu starker Lichtintensität sind diese sofort überreizt, und es dauert eine gewisse Zeit ohne starke Reize, bis sie wieder ihre volle Kapazität erreichen. (*Fun Fact: Die Anpassungszeit fürs Nachtsehen entspricht etwa der Dämmerung.*) Wenn sich die Augen also an die Dunkelheit gewöhnt haben, sollte man nicht auf grünes oder blaues Licht zurückgreifen. Es empfiehlt sich, schwaches rotes Licht zu nutzen, da es zwar die Umgebung ausleuchtet, aber die Nachtsichtfähigkeiten des eigenen Auges weniger beeinträchtigt. Beim Bushcraft- oder Survivaltraining kann man damit sehr einfach experimentieren, indem man sich mal in der Dunkelheit mit dem Rücken zum Feuer setzt und abwartet, wie sich der visuelle Eindruck verändert. Aber Vorsicht: Nur einmal ins Feuer schauen oder die Taschenlampe benutzen, und man muss wieder von vorn anfangen.

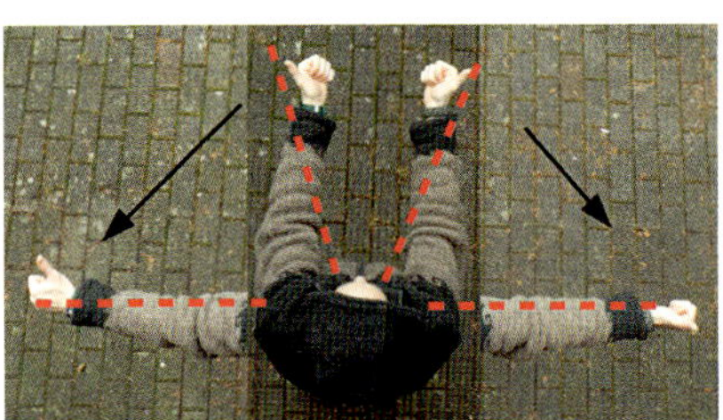

Des Weiteren ist das **Hören** mit zwei Ohren für die Wahrnehmung der Umgebung und das Prägen eines Gesamtbilds entscheidend. Es erlaubt uns, grob gesagt, ebenfalls das Unterscheiden von Objekten und das Abschätzen von Entfernungen, allerdings mit Hilfe von Schall. Viele Sehbehinderte beispielsweise sind durch Geräusche zu einer räumlichen Wahrnehmung fähig und können sich so sicher durch dunkle Räume bewegen. Hierfür brauchen sie ein besonderes Gespür für das Abschätzen von Entfernungen und Einfallswinkeln. Auch Nichtblinde können dieses Werkzeug – ähnlich wie Musiker das Gehör – wieder feiner einstellen. Kurze, knackende, hohe Töne sind allgemein besser geeignet als tiefe Töne, die aufgrund der Frequenz keine Richtungsbestimmung zulassen. Um dies zu üben, kannst Du mit geschlossenen (oder noch besser: verbundenen) Augen vor einer Wand stehen und einen möglichst immer gleich lauten, schnalzenden Ton mit der Zunge erzeugen. Jetzt gilt es zu beachten, wie sich die verschiedenen Facetten des Gehörten verändern, wenn Du langsam die Position wechselst. Du kannst Dich setzen, drehen, nach links, rechts, vorne oder hinten bewegen. Mit etwas Übung und Geduld wirst Du ein Gespür dafür entwickeln, wie es sich anhört, vor einem großen Objekt zu stehen und wie weit Du davon entfernt bist.

Riechen und **Schmecken** gehören hier zusammen, denn Dinge riechen anders, wenn man z.B. gerade etwas Scharfes gegessen hat, und Nahrung schmeckt ganz anders, wenn man gerade eine Zigarette geraucht hat oder am Feuer im Rauch sitzt. Grundsätzlich können wir auch hier in gewisser Weise Objekte unterscheiden. Heutzutage haben wir jedoch eine gewisse Scheu entwickelt. Es müssen schon auserlesene Gewürze, Weine oder Destillate sein, in die wir unsere Nase stecken. »Unangenehme Gerüche« werden nach Möglichkeit überdeckt, oder man hält sich die Nase zu. Für mich ist dagegen unbeschreiblich, wie intensiv Duschgel nach zehn Tagen draußen im Wald riechen oder sogar stinken kann. Daher öfter mal die Nase bewusst einsetzen! Ziel soll es nicht sein, jeden, dem man begegnet, wie einen Hund zu beschnuppern, sondern Dinge des alltäglichen Lebens wieder bewusster mit der Nase wahrzunehmen, z.B. das Kaffeepad, bevor man es in die Maschine packt und vielleicht danach. Man wird wahrscheinlich nach kurzer Zeit schon merken, wenn einem jemand eine andere Sorte unterschieben will. So spielen auch das Riechen und das Schmecken eine entscheidende Rolle für den Gesamteindruck unserer Umgebung.

Fühlen nach innen können wir z.B. die Atmung oder den Herzschlag. Nach außen haben wir unser größtes Sinnesorgan, die Haut. Sie kann allgemein Schmerz, Wärme- und Druckunterschiede wahrnehmen, z.B. wenn man vom Schatten ins Sonnenlicht tritt. Außerdem erlaubt sie uns das Tasten, womit wir im Allgemeinen Objekte unterscheiden können. Diese Wahrnehmung kannst Du im ersten Schritt üben, indem Du Dir der Kleidung am Leib bewusst wirst. Die haptische Wahrnehmung über die Hände kannst Du durch das gezielte Erfühlen von Gegenständen, aber auch beispielsweise durch das Schnitzen trainieren. Auch die Füße sind hierfür sehr wichtig, was Du beim Barfußgehen lernen kannst. Es darf allerdings kein kontrolliertes Fallen sein, wie wir es heute mit Schuhen gewohnt sind. Du musst das Gewicht beim Schritt auf dem hinteren Bein lassen und solltest locker in den Knien stehen. Jetzt musst Du üben, mit dem vorderen Fuß zu tasten und dann erst den Schritt zu machen *(siehe Abb.)*. Dazu muss ein Gang rausgenommen werden, und Du musst wieder lernen, langsam zu gehen. Außerdem solltest Du immer wieder kurz verharren und

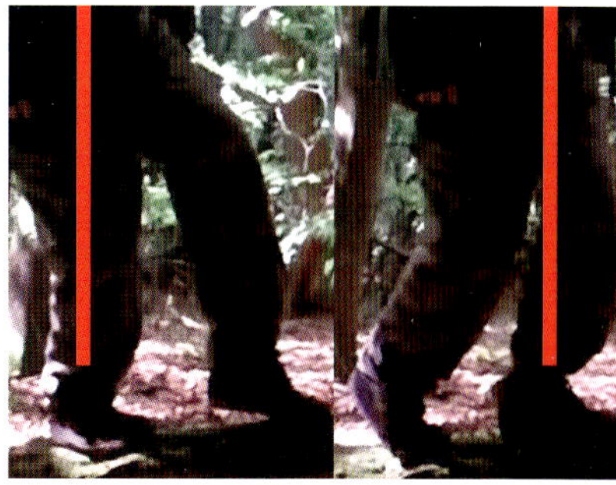

Tasten mit den Füßen, locker in den Knien, Gewichtsverlagerung trainieren

den Blick umherschweifen lassen und dabei auch nach oben schauen. Du kannst auch üben, Dinge wie z.B. einen Stift mit dem Fuß aufzuheben, besonders falls Du zu Beginn Probleme mit der Balance hast. Um besonders den Gleichgewichtssinn zu trainieren, kann diese Übung mit geschlossenen oder verbundenen Augen absolviert werden.

Als nächstes ist es wichtig, sich aller hier genannten Sinne unbewusst bewusst zu sein und diese zu nutzen. Es geht darum, aus den Sinneseindrücken das Gesamtbild des dynamischen Systems im »Fluss« wahrzunehmen, ohne an einem einzelnen Eindruck zu haften. Dabei hilft es, zuerst nacheinander jeden Sinn zu erfahren und zu aktivieren, um sich danach der Umgebung bewusster zu sein und sowohl das Gehirn als auch die Sensorik durch die Einzeleindrücke zu schulen.

Übung 2 (mittel): Verharren mit Anleitung – alle Sinne erfahren

Geh zu Deinem Platz aus Übung 1 und verharre zu Beginn mit geschlossenen Augen. Nimm Dir für jeden Sinn ein paar Momente Zeit. Atme ruhig und denke das Atmen nicht, sondern versuche, es in seinen Eindrücken wahrzunehmen. Fühle, wie sich der Brustkorb hebt und senkt, wie das Herz dazu schlägt. Nach außen kannst Du z.B. mit dem Spüren der Kleidung oder dem Wind auf der Haut beginnen. Rieche und schmecke Deine

Umgebung. Höre auf leise und laute Geräusche, deren Richtung und Rhythmus. Beim Sehen angekommen, öffnest Du die Augen und kannst mit der peripheren Wahrnehmung oder dem Fokus spielen.

DAS GESAMTBILD ALS TEIL DAVON

Zuerst muss man realisieren, dass die Natur eigentlich überall um uns herum ist und wir selbst ein Teil davon sind. Auch wir sind in einem Biotop integriert und leben in Symbiose mit anderen Lebewesen, selbst wenn wir vieles davon nicht bemerken. Wir müssen wieder zum »Einheimischen« werden, der die Zusammenhänge kennt und respektiert. Die Schwierigkeit liegt darin, eine Balance zwischen Detailverliebtheit und Gesamtaufmerksamkeit zu finden. So ist es zwar wichtig, zum Erlernen der Muster fokussiert im Kleinsten zu arbeiten, man sollte sich dabei aber auch des Gesamtbildes und der Umgebung bewusst sein. Die gewonnenen Eindrücke muss man mit einbeziehen und in einen Kontext bringen. Andererseits darf auch der gewonnene Gesamteindruck nicht die Wahrnehmung der feinsten Details beeinträchtigen. Das immerzu neu geprägte Gesamtbild soll lediglich als Schablone dienen, die ständig mit den aktuellen Reizen abgeglichen und sozusagen darüber gelegt wird.

Die allgemeinen Umstände und Veränderungen, die vor der eigenen Haustür herrschen, können jetzt weiter mit einfließen. Sei es das Wetter und das eigene Empfinden der Temperatur oder die Stärke der Sonneneinstrahlung und Mondphase mit den verschiedenen Lichtverhältnissen. Daraus folgen klar die Uhrzeit und das Datum beziehungsweise die Jahreszeit. Ein grundsätzliches Gespür für die Himmelsrichtungen und Richtungen zu markanten Punkten ist ebenfalls wichtig. So ist es ein Leichtes, sich die Himmelsrichtungen in den eigenen vier Wänden über genau diese und den Verlauf der Sonne zu verinnerlichen. Man beobachtet einfach, in welchen Fenstern die Sonne am Morgen, Mittag und Abend steht. Dieses geprägte Bewusstsein kann man dann auf ein immer größeres Gebiet übertragen. Ist nun beispielsweise im Wetterbericht von Wind aus Richtung Westen die Rede, hat man, auch ohne auf einen Kompass zu schauen, eine Vorstellung von der Richtung. Als weiterer Punkt bestimmen jetzt die anderen Lebewesen um uns herum unsere Wahrnehmung, von Menschen über Tiere zu Pflanzen, die eben auch Teil des Biotops sind und unser Verhalten und Gesamtbild mit beeinflussen.

So erstellst Du Stück für Stück eine Karte der Umgebung in Deinem Kopf und beginnst, immer mehr Details zu integrieren. Um mit der Zeit auch die zunächst unbekannten Bereiche abbilden zu können, musst Du so oft wie möglich draußen sein, mit dem Umfeld interagieren, Fragen stellen und weiter Dein Grundbild prägen. Wie ein Künstler zeichnest Du dieses und lernst selbst feinste Muster und Strukturen kennen. Durch Erfahrungen mit allen Sinnen können dann Abweichungen von den bekannten Strukturen schnell unterbewusst wahrgenommen und erkannt werden, wodurch die Aufmerksamkeit sofort darauf gerichtet wird. Daher einfach mal beim Schnitzen oder Feuerbohren am Holz riechen oder mit den Lippen fühlen, denn solche kleinen sensorischen Details erlauben es unserem Gehirn, Muster besser zu festigen und somit besser zu lernen.

Übung 3 (schwer): Gesamtbild prägen

Führe Übung 2 ein Jahr lang regelmäßig mindestens einmal pro Woche aus. Erstelle des Weiteren eine Karte der Umgebung und dokumentiere darin Himmelsrichtung, Wege und Wildwechsel, andere Spuren, Pflanzen, gefühlte Temperatur, Regen oder Schneefall, Windrichtung, Bedeckungsgrad des Himmels, ob Sonne oder Mond sichtbar sind, Tageszeit und kurz Deine derzeitige persönliche Konstitution.

SICHERHEIT

Bushcraft bedeutet, mit den Mitteln der Natur zu leben und sich auf die Natur einzulassen. Dazu sollte man aber auch eine realistische Einschätzung davon haben, was Natur eigentlich bedeutet. Die Natur gibt uns alles, was wir zum Leben brauchen, aber sie verzeiht auch keine Fehler. Die Fähigkeit, die Natur richtig einschätzen zu können und ihr richtig zu begegnen, macht den Unterschied aus zwischen einer entspannten Zeit draußen und einer lebensbedrohlichen Katastrophe.

Wir haben uns angewöhnt, uns jederzeit auf das Sicherheitsnetz unserer Zivilisation stützen zu können, wenn wir in eine unangenehme Lage kommen. Wir brauchen nur das Handy zu zücken, und der Hubschrauber kommt, wenn es nötig ist. Als Bushcrafter wirst Du aber in Situationen kommen, in denen es dieses Netz nicht mehr gibt. Im Wald oder im Gebirge ist Handy-Empfang nicht immer gewährleistet, schon gar nicht, wenn Du zum Beispiel in einer Schlucht steckst und vom Hochwasser überrascht wurdest. Oder wenn einfach Dein Handy die letzte Flussüberquerung nicht heil überstanden hat.

Bushcraft bedeutet deshalb auch: Verantwortung übernehmen, in erster Linie für Dich selbst. Wenn Du in der Natur bist, dann wird es immer Situationen geben, in denen Du vollkommen auf Dich alleine gestellt bist, in denen es keine Möglichkeit gibt, Hilfe zu holen. Bushcraft bedeutet nicht nur, bei schönem Wetter mal in der Natur zu übernachten, sondern die Natur so gut zu verstehen, dass man auch mit ihren rauen und unnachgiebigen Seiten so gut klarkommt, dass man weder sich selbst noch andere gefährdet.

AUSRÜSTUNG, ERFAHRUNG UND VORBEREITUNG

Ausrüstung, Vorbereitung und Erfahrung sind die Ecksteine aller Bushcraft-Aktivitäten. Mit dem Begriff Ausrüstung ist dabei nicht eine quantitative Aussage gemeint, also dass Du mit einem Riesenrucksack voll mit allen möglichen Ausrüstungsgegenständen herumläufst. Vielmehr ist das qualitativ zu verstehen: Wichtig ist, dass Du die *richtige* Ausrüstung mitnimmst und auch weißt, wie Du sie richtig verwendest (was Erfahrung voraussetzt).

Einem erfahrenen Bushcrafter reicht es, Messer und Feuerstahl dabeizuhaben. Ohne Übung und Erfahrung dagegen hilft Dir auch ein riesiges Arsenal an Ausrüstung überhaupt nichts, wenn Du nicht weißt, wie Du es verwendest. Das fängt schon bei scheinbar trivialen Dingen an: Wenn ich das Feuermachen unter widrigen Bedingungen (strömender Regen, starker Wind etc.) nicht geübt habe, dann werde ich vielleicht trotz bester Ausrüstung einige sehr kalte und vielleicht sogar lebensbedrohliche Stunden in einer kalten, windigen Regennacht verbringen müssen. Das ist der Grund, warum Ausrüstung und Erfahrung der erste Punkt im Kapitel Sicherheit sind.

Ausrüstung

Persönliche Sicherheit fängt also bei der richtigen Ausrüstung an. Nichts ist gefährlicher, als mit inadäquater oder schlechter Ausrüstung unterwegs zu sein. Schon Kleinigkeiten können hier den Unterschied zwischen unbeschwertem Spaß in der Natur und lebensgefährlichen Abenteuern ausmachen. Aber: Alleine einen Ausrüstungsgegenstand zu haben, nützt nur sehr wenig. Du musst auch den Umgang damit trainieren, und das möglichst konstant und immer wieder.

Und Du wirst sehen, dass sich Deine Ausrüstung ständig Deiner Erfahrung anpasst. Am Anfang wirst Du mit ziemlich viel (wahrscheinlich zu viel) Ausrüstung unterwegs sein. Mit zunehmender Erfahrung wirst Du immer mehr dieser Ausrüstung weglassen oder gegen andere Ausrüstungsgegenstände austauschen. Du wirst Qualität schätzen lernen, und Du wirst sehen, dass Du draußen nur sehr wenig brauchst und zudem vieles davon improvisieren oder direkt aus der Natur nehmen kannst.

Wichtig sind vor allem die richtige Kleidung und das richtige Schuhwerk. Zieh Dir Schuhe an, in denen Du trittsicher und bequem gehen kannst, die robust und fest sind und die Deinen Fuß stabilisieren (also vor dem Umknicken schützen). Eine Fußverletzung draußen kann ausgesprochen unangenehm sein – einmaliges Umknicken reicht, um sich einen Bänderriss zuzuziehen, was Deinen Aktionsradius ganz erheblich einschränkt. Und abseits der ausgetretenen Wege wirst Du auch in Situationen kommen, in denen Du zum Beispiel balancieren oder ein bisschen klettern musst – mit anderen Worten: wo Trittsicherheit ein wichtiges Thema ist.

Deine Kleidung sollte zweckmäßig sein. Hinter diesen einfachen Worten verbirgt sich vieles, das Du Dir nur durch Erfahrung aneignen kannst. Du wirst zum Beispiel in der Praxis schnell feststellen, dass eine vorgebliche Hightech-Jacke aus Kunstfaser zwar vielleicht ganz gut gegen Wind schützt, aber keineswegs so atmungsaktiv ist, wie ursprünglich angenommen – und auch nicht richtig wärmt, insbesondere nicht, wenn Du nass bist. Außerdem ist sie nach einer halben Stunde am Lagerfeuer voller Löcher von den Funken. Eine solche Jacke sieht im Laden gut aus, aber wenn Du nachts bei Regen irgendwo sitzt und erbärmlich frierst, dann würden Dir zwei Schichten Wolle sehr viel besser helfen, weil sie Dich auch dann noch warm halten, wenn Du klitschnass bist.

Ein Beispiel: Letztes Jahr musste die österreichische Bergwacht zwei Leute aus Bergnot retten, die mit unzulänglicher Kleidung und nur mit einer Rettungsfolie ausgerüstet im Hochgebirge übernachten wollten. Es stellte sich heraus, dass es sich um zwei Bushcraft-Anfänger handelte, die ein paar YouTube-Videos von bekannten Bushcraftern gesehen hatten und das nun selbst ausprobieren wollten. Der Unterschied: Die beiden hatten ungeeignete Kleidung an und zudem zwar große Begeisterung für die Sache, aber keinerlei Erfahrung.

Erfahrung

Du hast gesehen, dass schon im Abschnitt »Ausrüstung« immer wieder die Erfahrung angesprochen wurde. Das liegt daran, dass Erfahrung und Ausrüstung teilweise Äquivalente sind – Du kannst (in Grenzen) Ausrüstung durch Erfahrung ersetzen und umgekehrt. Erfahrung hat aber den Vorteil, dass sie sich weder abnützt noch verloren gehen kann – sie steht Dir auch dann noch zur Verfügung, wenn Du gerade zusehen musst, wie all Deine Ausrüstung den Berg runterkullert oder im Fluss weggetrieben wird.

Um sich in der Natur sicher zu bewegen, ist neben der richtigen Ausrüstung also vor allem die Erfahrung ausschlaggebend. In der Natur gibt es Situationen, in denen Du vielleicht nur eine sehr geringe Entfernung von potenzieller Hilfe entfernt bist – und doch ist sie so unerreichbar, als seist Du auf dem Mond.

Erfahrung erwirbst Du nur Schritt für Schritt. Geh es also langsam an, damit Du lernen kannst, die Dinge richtig einzuschätzen, Gefahren zu erkennen und ihnen rechtzeitig und richtig zu begegnen. Trainiere die Fertigkeiten, die Du draußen brauchen wirst, zunächst in sicherer Umgebung: Lerne, Feuer unter widrigen Umständen zu machen und sicher mit Axt und Messer umzugehen, beschäftige Dich mit Erste-Hilfe-Techniken und übe sie auch, übe den Bau von Unterständen auch bei schlechtem Wetter und in kalten Jahreszeiten.

Vorbereitung

Erfahrung muss gelegentlich aufgefrischt werden. Trainiere deshalb Deine Fähigkeiten und Techniken regelmäßig – das machen auch (und ganz besonders) die Profis so. Auch Deinem Körper schadet es nicht, wenn er regelmäßig Bushcraft-Situationen trainiert. Durch diese Vorbereitung weißt Du, wie Du auf bestimmte Situationen reagierst, wie Du mit Kälte und Hitze klarkommst, wo Deine Grenzen sind und wo es gefährlich wird. Und wenn Du Dich oft draußen bewegst, bekommst Du mehr Gefühl für Gleichgewicht, eine bessere Körperspannung, mehr Trittsicherheit – und das sind Faktoren, die Deine Sicherheit erhöhen und Gefahren reduzieren.

Durch Vorbereitung kannst Du mit Gefahrensituationen besser umgehen oder ernsthaften Gefahren ganz aus dem Weg gehen. Ein paar wesentliche Gefahrenquellen werden in den folgenden Abschnitten behandelt, aber es gibt auch sehr viel alltäglichere Dinge, die in der Natur schnell eine Situation kippen lassen können, so dass Du Dich plötzlich in großer Gefahr befindest. Einer der wohl erfahrensten Bushcrafter und Survival-Experten Deutschlands kam zum Beispiel bei einer scheinbar harmlosen Bootsfahrt in eine akut lebensbedrohliche Situation, die er nur auf Grund seiner Erfahrung und seines Trainings überlebte. Unter anderem hatte er sich auf Kenter-Situationen vorbereitet, indem er immer und immer wieder geübt hatte, sich unter Wildwasserbedingungen aus einem kenternden Kajak zu befreien. Das rettete ihm das Leben.

Zum Thema Vorbereitung gehört auch eine Technik, die gerade im Umgang mit Gefahren sehr hilfreich ist: »Was-tun-wenn?« Wann immer Du Dich in eine potenziell gefährliche Situation begibst, überleg Dir, womit Du konfrontiert werden könntest und wie Du darauf reagieren wirst. Wenn Du beispielsweise einen Fluss durchwaten willst, dann mach Dir klar, was alles passieren kann, triff entsprechende Vorkehrungen und mach einen Plan, wie Du der Situation begegnen wirst. Mit anderen Worten: Hab immer einen Plan (und am besten auch noch einen Plan B).

DIE RICHTIGE PLATZWAHL

Häufig unterschätzt wird die Wahl des richtigen Ortes. Dabei ist es draußen (und insbesondere, wenn Du übernachtest) essenziell, den Ort, an dem Du Dein Lager aufbaust, sehr sorgfältig auszuwählen. Folgende Punkte sind wichtig:

- → *Bevor Du Dich irgendwo niederlässt, sieh Dir die Umgebung sehr genau an. Sind im Boden Tiere, die Dir gefährlich werden können (Ameisen, Wespen, Bienen, Skorpione etc.)? Ist über Dir ein morscher Ast oder neben Dir ein toter Baum, der beim kleinsten Windstoß umfällt? Bist Du an einem lockeren Hang, der bei Regen abrutschen könnte? Besteht Gefahr von Steinschlag? Ist die Gegend sturmsicher? Es ist wirklich wichtig, dass Du diese Überlegungen anstellst – Du wirst trotzdem noch genügend lehrreiche Überraschungen erleben.*
- → *Selbst kleine Wasserläufe können (besonders im Gebirge oder in sehr trockenen Gegenden) bei Regen innerhalb allerkürzester Zeit zu reißenden Flüssen werden – halte Abstand!*
- → *Leg Dein Lager niemals in einer Senke an – bei Regen sitzt Du im Wasser oder gerätst gar in Lebensgefahr.*
- → *Wenn Du Dein Lager auf einem Wildwechsel errichtest, kannst Du eventuell in allergrößte Schwierigkeiten kommen. Halt Dich fern davon.*
- → *Achte darauf, dass in Deiner Umgebung die benötigten Ressourcen vorhanden sind (Schutz, frisches Wasser, Feuermaterial, Material für Lager).*

→ *Bestehen andere Gefahren?*

→ *Lass Deine Ausrüstung nicht herumliegen und lagere so, dass Du im Notfall sehr schnell aufbrechen kannst, ohne dabei wichtige Ausrüstung zurücklassen zu müssen (Messer und Feuerstahl habe ich zum Beispiel immer am Körper; wenn ich mich nachts davon trennen sollte, habe ich beides immer direkt neben mir liegen).*

TIERE

Wildtiere

In Mitteleuropa wirst Du kaum Probleme mit Wildtieren haben. Dennoch solltest Du Dich auch hier immer adäquat verhalten und dieses Verhalten trainieren, es wird Dir eines Tages helfen:

→ *Lass keine Nahrungsmittel im Lager herumliegen, insbesondere nicht über Nacht.*

→ *Erledige Dein Geschäft windabwärts vom Lager, vergrabe Deine Hinterlassenschaften.*

→ *Verstau Deine Schuhe an einem sicheren Ort (insbesondere Lederschuhe, manche Tiere interessieren sich dafür) und sieh hinein, bevor Du sie wieder anziehst.*

→ *Übernachte nicht in der Nähe von Wildwechseln und halte Dich von Orten fern, an denen Aas oder gerissene Tiere liegen.*

Insekten, Parasiten und Kleinstlebewesen

In unseren Breiten gibt es nur wenig Kriechzeug, das Dir ernsthaft gefährlich werden kann (es sei denn, Du bist allergisch gegen Insektengifte). Dennoch solltest Du Dich insbesondere bei längeren Aufenthalten in der Natur vor Insekten und Parasiten schützen. Zum einen kann auch die heimische Zecke sehr unangenehme Folgen haben (Du wirst trotzdem wahrscheinlich als Bushcrafter jedes Jahr mehrere davon haben), andererseits gibt es eine Reihe von Parasiten, die zum Beispiel in stehendem Wasser vorkommen und Dir erhebliche Probleme bereiten können. Andere Parasiten wie Läuse oder Flöhe können Krankheiten übertragen, beispielsweise Fleckfieber. Aber auch schon ein durch verdorbenes Wasser ausgelöster schwerer Durchfall kann bei einem längeren Aufenthalt in der Natur ohne Zivilisationskontakt lebensbedrohlich sein (da hilft dann die Kenntnis der Pflanzen und das Wissen, dass zum Beispiel gerbstoffreiche Pflanzen wie Eichenrinde oder Brombeerblätter gut gegen Durchfall eingesetzt werden können).

Die wichtigste Maßnahme ist Hygiene: Halte Dich auch draußen sauber – das heißt nicht, dass Du nicht ohne Dusche und Seife leben kannst, sondern vor allem, dass Du Dich regelmäßig wäschst oder auch mal in einem sauberen Gewässer badest. Wenn Du stehendes Wasser verwendest, dann reinige es vor dem Gebrauch (siehe Kapitel »Trinkwasser beim Bushcraften«). Suche abends oder nach einem Marsch durch hohes Gras Deine Kleidung und/oder Deinen Körper nach Zecken ab.
Tipp: *Alles, was sich abbürsten lässt, ist keine Zecke, alles andere musst Du Dir genau ansehen.*

Falls Dich eine Zecke erwischt (und das wird, wie gesagt, häufig passieren), dann ist auch das kein Grund zur Panik. Es ist hilfreich, wenn Du eine sogenannte Zeckenkarte dabei hast (wesentlich besser als Zeckenzangen), damit lassen sich Zecken sehr einfach und vor allem komplett entfernen. Wichtig

Mit einer Zeckenkarte lassen sich Zecken sehr einfach entfernen.

ist, dass das innerhalb der ersten 24 Stunden nach dem Biss passiert, andernfalls besteht die – sehr geringe – Gefahr, dass Du an Borreliose erkrankst.

WETTER

Sehr häufig unterschätzt wird, dass das Wetter extrem schnell umschlagen kann, auch in unseren Breiten. Aus einem warmen Hochsommertag kann binnen einer Stunde eine Gewitterfront werden, die einen ganzen Wald umlegt. Im Gebirge kann man binnen Minuten plötzlich orientierungslos im dichtesten Nebel stehen und einen lebensbedrohlichen Wetter- und Temperatursturz erleben. Ausrüstung, Vorbereitung und Erfahrung machen auch hier den Unterschied aus.

Persönlich war ich zum Beispiel bereits mehrfach im Wald, als ein schwerer Sturm aufkam. Das erste Mal kam völlig unvorbereitet – es kamen Wolken auf, andere Anzeichen waren im Wald nicht zu erkennen. Dann frischte der Wind auf und entwickelte sich binnen sehr kurzer Zeit zu einem orkanartigen Sturm, in meiner Umgebung begannen Bäume umzufallen.

ORIENTIERUNG / RÄUMLICHES BEWUSSTSEIN

Du bewegst Dich draußen erheblich sicherer, wenn Du Deine Orientierungskünste und Dein räumliches Bewusstsein trainierst. Das ist nicht nur deshalb wichtig, weil Du Dich dann nicht mehr verirrst, sondern es hilft Dir auch, Gefahren besser zu begegnen. In der oben erwähnten Situation der umfallenden Bäume reduziert man z.B. die Gefahr, wenn man eine mentale Landkarte der Umgebung hat (das ist das, was ich räumliches Bewusstsein nenne) und deshalb weiß, wohin man ausweichen kann oder wo man Sicherheit findet, beispielsweise auf einer vor Kurzem passierten Lichtung (siehe Kapitel »Aufmerksamkeit & Naturwahrnehmung«).

Wenn Du Dich in der Natur bewegst, dann solltest Du zu jeder Zeit wissen, wo Du Dich befindest, wo die Himmelsrichtungen liegen, und Du solltest ständig mental mitkoppeln. Das hört sich am Anfang vielleicht kompliziert an, aber Du wirst sehen, dass es Dir sehr schnell zur zweiten Natur wird. Du wirst ein Bewusstsein für die Gegend entwickeln, in der Du Dich bewegst. Ein erfahrener Bushcrafter registriert ständig seine Umgebung, er nimmt die Ressourcen wahr, die sie ihm bietet, erkennt die Gefahren und die Möglichkeiten, die sie ihm gibt. Du wirst sehen, dass es auch abseits der von Menschen angelegten Wege ein Wegenetz gibt, das seinen eigenen Gesetzen gehorcht und auf dem man sich ebenso gut und sicher bewegen kann. Lass Dich auf Deine Umgebung ein und auf die Geschichten, die sie Dir erzählt – das ist ein ganz wesentlicher Teil des Waldhandwerks.

GELÄNDEBEDINGTE GEFAHREN

Wenn Du Dich in der Natur bewegst, gibt es immer wieder Gefahren, die durch das Gelände bedingt sind. Auch hier hilft situatives und räumliches Bewusstsein: Nimm die Gegend, in der Du Dich bewegst, bewusst wahr. Das ist wie beim Autofahren: Als Fahranfänger ist es schwierig, alle Eindrücke zu verarbeiten und einzuordnen, aber mit der Zeit wird das ein Automatismus, man registriert Gegebenheiten und Gefahren automatisch.

Du musst in der Lage sein, Gefahren zu erkennen und auszuweichen. Als Bushcrafter wirst Du mit vielen Geländeformen konfrontiert sein, von denen eine zumindest potenzielle Gefahr ausgeht – die nur dann eine Gefahr ist, wenn Du sie nicht erkennen und nicht darauf reagieren kannst. Beispiele dafür sind zum Beispiel Sümpfe, Steinschlag oder Lawinengebiete. Sie haben das Folgende gemeinsam: Die drohende Gefahr ist mitunter sehr schwer erkennbar, aber in ihren Auswirkungen elementar und/oder akut lebensgefährlich.

Sehr häufig geht es neben dem Erkennen der Gefahr darum, abschätzen zu können, wann es Zeit ist, umzukehren. Man ist in vielen Fällen in Versuchung, sich eher in Gefahr zu begeben als umzukehren, insbesondere wenn die Umkehr mit großen Unannehmlichkeiten verbunden ist: Soll ich nicht doch versuchen, durch den Sumpf zu kommen, statt den langen Rückweg anzutreten und einen riesigen Umweg in Kauf zu nehmen? Soll ich nicht doch dieses kleine Schneefeld überqueren, auf dessen anderer Seite ein idealer Biwakplatz wäre, wenn die Alternative eine stundenlange Kletterei ist?

UMGANG MIT DEM MESSER

Dieses Kapitel wird Dir vielleicht überflüssig erscheinen. Mit einem Messer kann doch jeder umgehen, oder? Aber: Bushcrafter arbeiten in der Regel mit extrem scharfen Messern und üben dabei außerdem meist sehr viel Kraft aus (beim Batoning zum Beispiel, dem Spalten von Feuerholz mit dem Messer). Deshalb solltest Du unbedingt die folgenden Grundregeln zum Thema Messersicherheit verinnerlichen (siehe Kapitel »Arbeiten mit dem Messer«).

Messersicherheit

→ *Immer vom Körper weg arbeiten.*

→ *Messer nie herumliegen lassen.*

→ *Messer nach Gebrauch immer sofort wieder in die Scheide.*

→ *Nie mit blankem/offenen Messer in der Gegend herumlaufen. Falls das dennoch unvermeidlich ist: Messer locker (so dass man es sofort loslassen/wegschleudern kann) und weit vom Körper weg halten, Spitze und Klinge ebenfalls vom Körper (und anderen Personen) wegzeigend.*

→ *Klingt komisch, ist aber so: Nur ein scharfes Messer ist ein sicheres Messer, also halte Dein Messer scharf.*

→ *Wenn Du Dein Messer weiterreichst, dann immer mit dem Griff voran.*

→ *Achte auf Deine Umgebung (und vor allem auf Personen im Arbeitsbereich Deines Messers).*

ERSTE HILFE

Zu diesem Thema gibt es ganze Bücher – und jeder Bushcrafter sollte sich in medizinischer Nothilfe möglichst gut auskennen und deshalb zumindest eins dieser Bücher aufmerksam durchlesen und auf jeden Fall einen Erste-Hilfe-Kurs besucht haben.

Als Bushcrafter wirst Du sehr häufig mit dem Thema Wundversorgung bzw. Behandlung von Schnitten, Quetschungen, Entzündungen und Splittern konfrontiert werden. Dafür bietet uns die Natur sehr viele interessante Hilfsmittel an, die sich sommers wie winters draußen finden lassen. Fichten- und Tannenharz haben antibiotische und antimykotische Eigenschaften (Ameisen setzen Harz übrigens gezielt gegen Bakterien

Improvisierter Natur-Verband einer tiefen Schnittwunde mit einer antibakteriellen pflasterähnlichen Auflage aus Tannenharz, einem Verband aus Spitzwegerich, der mit Grashalmen fixiert wurde.

und Pilze ein), dasselbe gilt für die meisten Moose und Flechten und einige Pflanzen, die auch unter dem Schnee zu finden sind, wie etwa der Spitzwegerich. Mit Rinde lassen sich sehr gut Verbände improvisieren.

Ich persönlich helfe mir nahezu ausschließlich aus der Natur, aber gerade am Anfang ist es empfehlenswert, wenn Du ein kleines, handelsübliches Mini-Erste-Hilfe-Set dabei hast. Es enthält in der Regel in etwa Folgendes:

Inhalt Erste-Hilfe-Set

- → *Wundkompressen*
- → *Verbandstuch/Dreieckstuch*
- → *Binden*
- → *Wundschnellverband, Pflaster, Heftpflaster*
- → *Handschuhe (bushcraftmäßig auch als Not-Wasserbehälter verwendbar)*
- → *Desinfektionstupfer*
- → *Schere, Sicherheitsnadeln*

Zusätzlich solltest Du dem Set noch ein hochwirksames Schmerzmittel und ein paar Wasserentkeimungstabletten hinzufügen. Trainiere aber zunehmend Dein Wissen über Pflanzen – nicht nur die medizinischen Anwendungen, sehr viele Pflanzen haben auch einen sehr hohen Nährwert, isolieren gut oder vertreiben Schädlinge und können deshalb in vielerlei Hinsicht (und auch in Notsituationen) hilfreich sein.

INFORMATION

Mit einer einfachen Maßnahme, die jeder Bergsteiger kennt, möchte ich das Kapitel beschließen: Informiere nach Möglichkeit andere über Deine Vorhaben. Das ist die beste Versicherung, die Du haben kannst. Wenn Dein Partner, Deine Familie oder Deine Freunde wissen, was Du vorhast, dann wissen sie im Notfall auch, wo sie nach Dir suchen müssen. Auch wenn das beim Lesen dieses Buches vielleicht ein bisschen überdramatisch klingt – aber wenn Du mit einem gebrochenen Bein irgendwo liegst und die Nacht bricht an, dann ist es ein sehr gutes Gefühl zu wissen, dass Hilfe bestimmt schon unterwegs ist.

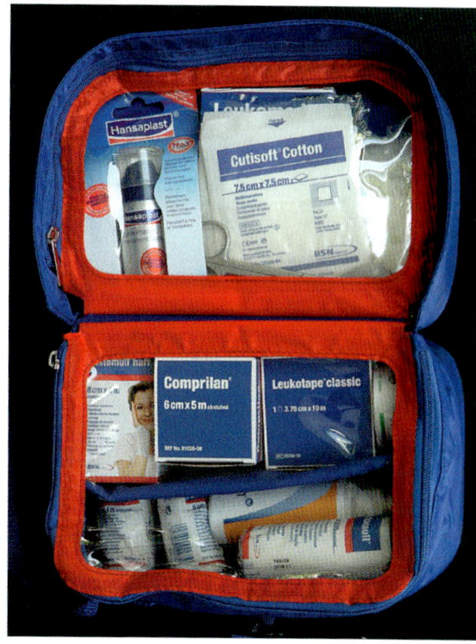

Bushcraft-Einsteiger sollten ein professionelles Erste-Hilfe-Set mit sich führen.

Unterrichte also andere über die folgenden Punkte:

Wann: *Wann willst Du aufbrechen und wann willst Du wieder zurück sein?*

Wo: *Was ist Dein Ziel?*

Wie: *Welche Route willst Du einschlagen, welche Besonderheiten gibt es?*

Du kannst das ganz undramatisch und beiläufig machen, indem Du Deinem Partner oder einem Freund von Deinem bevorstehenden Abenteuer erzählst und dabei die wichtigen Details (wann, wo, wie) erwähnst.

Wichtig: *Melde Dich zurück, wenn Du heil heimgekehrt bist!*

WASSER UND NAHRUNG

TRINKWASSER BEIM BUSHCRAFTEN

Wenn Du zum Bushcraften in den Wald gehst, solltest Du natürlich wissen, wie Du an Trinkwasser kommst. Denn selbst für zwei Tage im Camp ist es schwierig, neben der notwendigen Ausrüstung und der Nahrung das gesamte Wasser mitzunehmen. Ein Liter Wasser wiegt bekanntermaßen ein Kilogramm, zwei wiegen das Doppelte und so weiter. Das summiert sich ganz schön.

Da Du als Bushcrafter in aller Regel nicht »ultraleicht« unterwegs bist und die Zeit im heimischen Wald nicht zu einem Überlebenstrip verkommen soll, ist es also immer sinnvoll, ein paar Liter Wasser dabei zu haben. Für den Rest gibt es einige einfache Techniken, die es Dir erlauben sollten, ohne Wassermangel draußen eine gute Zeit zu verbringen.

Eine gefüllte Feldflasche aus Metall sollte immer dabei sein – manche besitzen sogar ein integriertes Kochsystem oder einen Becher, der das Abkochen erleichtert.

Das hier ist ist kein »Survivalbuch« – deshalb beschränken wir uns bei den Techniken auch auf Mitteleuropa. Bananenblätter, ausgequetschte Würmer und Bambustöpfe fallen also weg – damit aber auch die üblen Krankheitserreger und Verunreinigungen, die es teilweise schon südlich der Alpen und natürlich in Entwicklungsländern in Bachläufen und Seen gibt.

Die Trinkwasserbeschaffung besteht prinzipiell aus drei Aufgaben: Finden, Einschätzen und Aufbereiten von natürlichen Wasserquellen. Das Finden ist in gemäßigten Regionen meist kein großes Problem. Deutschland, Österreich und auch die Schweiz sind sehr wasserreich. Außerdem regnet es häufig – am Tarp abgelaufener und gesammelter Regen ist immer genießbar.

Auch das Einschätzen ist hier nicht so riskant, da es in Mitteleuropa beispielsweise keine gefährlichen Parasiten gibt, die Dich schon beim Betreten des Gewässers befallen können.

Zur Aufbereitung werden wir wichtige »bushcraftige« Methoden anschauen. Denn einfach nur Wasser sammeln oder einen Wasserfilter bzw. Chlortabletten zu verwenden, wäre dann doch etwas zu einfach. Um das Wasser ohne technische Hilfsmittel sicher aufzubereiten, werden zudem einige spannende handwerkliche Skills benötigt.

Gewässer in Mitteleuropa sind in aller Regel ohne Aufbereitung trinkbar.

Die wichtigsten Stellen zum Finden von Wasser sind überlappende Berghänge und Täler.

FINDEN VON WASSER

»Wenn Du in einer Wüste Wasser suchst ...« soll hier ebensowenig Thema sein wie das Anzapfen von Bäumen. Das sind Techniken für den Notfall, die entweder in Europa nicht relevant sind oder sich nur auf den echten Notstand beziehen. Um in Mitteleuropa oder Skandinavien auf einer Bushcrafttour zu dehydrieren, muss man schon eine Menge falsch machen. Wer dagegen am ersten Bushcraftabend ohne Not eine Birke anbohrt, um sich Birkenwasser abzulassen, muss sich nicht wundern, wenn er vom Ortspolizisten einen Platzverweis und vom Förster eine Rechnung bekommt.

Wir suchen also Tümpel, Quellen, Bäche und kleine Flüsse – eben solche Gewässer, die in »Bushcraftregionen« auch verfügbar sind. Dazu schaust Du Dir zuallererst die Umgebung an: Wasser fließt nach unten – also suchst Du generell an der tiefsten Stelle. Handelt es sich um hügeliges Gelände, suchst Du an der Stelle, an der zwei Berghänge aufeinander treffen und einen gemeinsamen Ablauf bilden (beispielsweise ein Tal oder eine Klamm). Hier fließt Regen (und den gibt es häufig – auch im Hochsommer) nach unten ab und hinterlässt ein kleines Flussbett. Selbst wenn schon länger kein Tropfen mehr gefallen ist, findet man in Biegungen und an Senken genügend Wasser.

Manchmal sind im Wald auf Rückegassen, in denen Baumstämme transportiert wurden, auch kleine Pfützen stehen geblieben. Das liegt daran, dass hier der lehmige Boden verpresst wurde und das Wasser nicht mehr versickern kann (dass es hier Lehm gibt, kann für die Aufbereitung hilfreich sein). Zu guter Letzt findest Du in der Ebene diverse Gewässer wie Entwässerungsgräben, Seen und Tümpel. Meist flankiert durch Schilf und Rohrkolben und damit von weitem sichtbar.

Diese Pflanzen sind neben einer Reihe von weiteren Gewächsen wichtige sogenannte »Wasserzeiger«. Wo Du sie findest, kannst

Wichtige Pflanzen, die Gewässer anzeigen

Binsen

Zeichen für: Staunässe, feuchten Boden

Beschreibung: Die praktisch nur auf staunassem, zumindest aber sehr feuchtem Boden wachsenden Binsen bilden dicke, auch im Winter grüne Polster. Ihr Stängel ist innen schwammig ausgefüllt.

Schilf

Zeichen für: Kleine Gewässer, Gräben, langsam fließende Flüsse, Seen

Beschreibung: Schilfrohr wächst in dichten Beständen an den schlammigen und kiesigen Randregionen von dauerhaften Gewässern. Seltener ist Schilf an ausgetrockneten Gräben und Tümpeln zu finden.

Rohrkolben

Zeichen für: Seen, Tümpel, Teiche

Beschreibung: Verschiedene Arten von Rohrkolben haben sich auf sumpfiges, also meist etwas trüberes Wasser angepasst. Aus der Ferne ist bis zum Herbst zu erkennen: Sattgrüne Farbe – Wasser vorhanden, Beige – Gewässer trocken.

Weiden

Zeichen für: Seen, große Flussläufe, Überschwemmungsgebiete

Beschreibung: Weiden, aber auch andere schnell wachsende Laubbäume benötigen große Mengen Wasser. Ihre Wurzeln brauchen ständigen Kontakt mit Flüssigkeit. Sie wachsen deshalb oft an Seen und Flüssen.

Du davon ausgehen, dass der Boden zumindest staunass ist und mit ein wenig Graben Wasser oder Schlamm gefunden werden kann.

ERKENNEN DER WASSERQUALITÄT

Hast Du erst einmal Wasser gefunden, geht es darum zu erkennen, ob es einfach so getrunken werden kann oder ob es aufbereitet werden sollte.

Die Fragestellung, die am wichtigsten ist: Werden Fäkalien in das Gewässer eingeleitet?

Mit den Fäkalien gelangen nämlich Keime und einzellige Darmparasiten in das Wasser. Das kann dann zu starken Durchfällen und Bauchweh führen – damit ist das Bushcraftwochenende natürlich erstmal gelaufen.

Fäkalien gelangen entweder aus Siedlungen mit schlechter Abwasseraufbereitung in das Gewässer, durch Weiden und ausgebrachte Gülle oder aber durch Wildtiere. Solange Du Dein Wasser nicht aus einer Hirsch- oder Wildschweinesuhle entnimmst, spielen Wildtiere in Europa aber nur eine untergeordnete Rolle. Jeder kleine Bach spült tausende von Litern Wasser in der Stunde hinunter. Da müssten sich die Tiere zu hunderten in Reih und Glied stellen und nacheinander erleichtern, damit eine erhebliche Verunreinigung entsteht.

Auch einzelne, hunderte Meter flussaufwärts liegende verendete Tiere sind unproblematisch (sofern es sich nicht um einen im Harz verendeten Elefanten handelt). Im Laufe der Zersetzung wird der Kadaver von Millionen Litern Wasser umspült. Die Verdünnung ist viel zu groß für relevante Keimkonzentrationen.

Das sieht bei Weiden anders aus – hunderte Kuhfladen oder abertausende Schafköttel liegen hier konzentriert auf den Wiesen, und mit einem Regenguss landet ein großer Teil davon im Bach. Zusätzlich spielen natürlich die Einleitungen von Klärwerkswasser eine Rolle. Dabei ist es vor allem die Addition von hunderten dieser Anlagen, die Rhein und Elbe leicht belasten.

Durch diesen Quellbach fließen mehrere Kubikmeter Wasser je Stunde. Ernsthafte Verunreinigungen würden sich nur durch größere Dörfer ohne Abwasseraufbereitung ergeben.

Grundsätzlich sind die Klärwerke heute so ausgereift, dass die Gewässer nur noch gering mit gefährlichen Keimen versetzt werden – vorausgesetzt, Du holst Dein Wasser nicht direkt aus dem Ausfluss.

Eingeleitete Fäkalien lassen sich wenige Meter nach dem Eintritt nicht mehr sehen. Allerdings gibt es Indikatoren, die darauf hinweisen können. Denn Fäkalien sind Dünger – und gedüngtes Wasser wird algig und grün. Wenn Du einen stark trüben See hast, bei dem der Untergrund schweflig riecht, kannst Du davon ausgehen, dass hier erheblich mehr Keime vorhanden sind als in klarem Wasser. Also reinigst Du das Wasser in diesem Fall vor dem Trinken.

Bei Flüssen ist das nicht ganz so einfach zu erkennen. Durch das Algenwachstum werden Nährstoffe abgebaut. Sauerstoff geht dabei verloren. Sind (viel) zu viele Nährstoffe darin, sinken die Algen ab, sterben und bilden einen schleimigen Film. Diesen Schmier fressen manche Tiere, andere können durch ihn und die verringerte Sauerstoffmenge nicht mehr atmen und sterben. Deshalb erkennt man anhand verschiedener Kleintiere ziemlich gut, wie stark das Wasser durch Dünger – also Fäkalien und damit Keimen – belastet ist.

Sonderfälle

Ja, es gibt sie, die Sonderfälle, auch in Europa. Aufgelassene Erzgruben, zugeschüttete Deponien in den neuen Bundesländern oder aber großflächige Verunreinigung des Landes mit Müllresten aus der Papierproduktion (zum Ausgleich in einem alten Bundesland: Baden-Württemberg). Hier ist es tatsächlich nicht so einfach, gefährliche chemische Verunreinigungen zu erkennen, wenn man nicht spezielle Techniken zur Verfügung hat und bestimmte Erkennungsmethoden übt. Diese sind aber nicht Gegenstand des vorliegenden Buches.

Herden, die am Wasser stehen, können für erhebliche und vor allem gefährliche Verunreinigungen verantwortlich sein. Generell ist Widerkäuerlosung gefährlich.

Indikatorarten in Fließgewässern (unter Beachtung weiterer Hinweise)

Stein- / Eintagsfliegenlarven | **Köcherfliegenlarven** | **Bachflohkrebse** | **Egel** | **Wasserasseln**

ungereinigt trinkbar – **empfindliche Personen sollten aufreinigen** – **aufreinigen**

Generell gilt: *Ist Wasser ungewöhnlich gefärbt, schmeckt es stark bitter oder metallisch oder ist bekannt, dass durch Umweltskandale entsprechende Verunreinigungen in der Umgebung vorliegen, solltest Du das Wasser nicht als Quelle nutzen. Die betroffenen Regionen können im Allgemeinen vor der Planung eines Bushcraftabenteuers erfragt werden und sind in Mitteleuropa sehr selten.*

Neonfarbenes Wasser kommt in der Natur nur bei Verunreinigung mit Schwermetallen und Mineralien wie Eisen, Kupfer und Chrom vor.

AUFBEREITEN

Hast Du Flüssigkeit gefunden und eingeschätzt, geht es an die Aufbereitung. Tatsächlich ist genau diese Aufgabe eine der kompliziertesten. Denn um zu entscheiden, welche Art der Aufbereitung notwendig ist, solltest Du genau wissen, wie Dein Körper reagiert, wenn Du Baggersee- oder Flusswasser in größeren Mengen getrunken hast. Der eine verträgt es, er hat »einen robusten Magen«, der andere verträgt es nicht oder muss sich erst daran gewöhnen und bekommt Bauchgrummeln. Viele improvisierte Aufbereitungsmethoden reduzieren die Anzahl der im Wasser enthaltenen Keime auf ein solches Maß, dass zumindest für robustere Naturen keine Infektion zu erwarten ist.

Andere Techniken zählen zu den »sicheren Methoden« – mit ihnen kannst Du Wasser aus den allermeisten Quellen trinkbar machen, auch wenn es stark verkeimt war und Du einen eher empfindlichen Magen hast. Von diesen sicheren Methoden betrachten wir diejenigen, die für Bushcrafter in Mitteleuropa interessant sind. Ich gehe davon aus, dass die wenigsten von Euch eine Autobatterie für die elektrische Umkehrosmosepumpe mitschleppen möchten – diese erzeugt tatsächlich steriles Wasser. Aber wollen wir das auch? Trinkwasser soll nicht krank machen, steril muss es bei weitem nicht sein.

Vorbereiten

Das Aufbereiten des Wassers beginnt schon vor den eigentlichen Reinigungstechniken. Denn alleine schon die Auswahl des Entnahmeorts ist wichtig. An der Oberfläche eines Gewässers treiben nämlich alle möglichen Materialien: Insekten, hineingefallenes Laub und so weiter. Am Grund dagegen ist auch bei sauberen Gewässern der Boden bedeckt mit von Insekten und Kleintieren zerkleinerten Abbauresten. Deshalb versucht man, das Wassergefäß in einer mittleren Schicht zu befüllen. Dazu wird es bei fließenden Gewässern mit der Öffnung stromabwärts, bei stehendem Wasser nach unten eingetaucht, dabei zugehalten und erst etwa 10 Zentimeter unter der Oberfläche befüllt.

Zusätzlich ist es nicht immer sinnvoll, an dem am stärksten strömenden Ort Wasser zu entnehmen. Dort sind Schwebestoffe und Sedimente aufgewirbelt. Etwas flussabwärts ist schon vieles abgesunken. Ist das Wasser dennoch trüb, lässt man es einfach

Das Wasser soll erst unterhalb der Oberfläche in das Gefäß strömen. Soll ein Topf oder ein ähnlich großes Gefäß befüllt werden, taucht man es mit der Öffnung nach unten ein und dreht es.

Durch Absinken klärt sich das Wasser schon von selbst. Der klare Überstand kann einfach abgekippt werden. Wird zusätzlich vorgefiltert, ist das Wasser schon erheblich weniger trüb.

Gibt es eine Massenvermehrung von Algen im Wasser, sollte es nicht gekocht werden, bis die meisten Algen abgetrennt worden sind.

Einmaliges Aufkochen ist als sichere Aufbereitungsmethode zu bewerten. Bis das Wasser wieder Trinktemperatur hat, ist alles Gefährliche tot.

eine Weile stehen und gießt den klaren Überstand in ein anderes Gefäß. Alternativ kann es auch durch fest gepresste Fasern von Rohrkolben etc. geleitet werden. Ein Shirt oder Stofftaschentuch ist zu grobmaschig und zum Klären nicht geeignet. Das Gewebe hält aber zumindest schon mal Pflanzenteile und Algen zurück. Was nach 20 Minuten Standzeit oder Filtern durch dichtes Gewebe noch im Wasser als Trübung zu sehen ist, wirst Du nicht so einfach wegbekommen. Diese winzigen »Kolloide« sind etwa so groß wie Bakterien und schwimmen durch die Wärmebewegung des Wassers auf.

Auch wenn das Wasser grün und trüb ist, hilft Abstehenlassen nicht. Das sind einzellige Algen, die sich aktiv fortbewegen können. Hier hilft es, das Wasser langsam zu erhitzen, ohne es jedoch zum Kochen zu bringen. Dabei sterben die Algen und sinken nach dem Abkühlen ab; dann können sie durch Abkippen abgetrennt werden. Beginnt das Wasser zu kochen, schütte es lieber weg. Algen können Gifte produzieren, die beim Platzen der Zellen im Kochwasser freigegeben werden.

Abkochen

Das Erhitzen des Wassers ist die simpelste und eine der sichersten Möglichkeiten. Nicht umsonst gibt es weltweit Teezeremonien. Erhitztes Wasser ist sicher. Sobald Du Deinen Finger nicht mehr hineintauchen kannst, ist es so heiß, dass die allermeisten Keime sterben. Damit Du Dir nicht bei jedem Liter Wasser den Zeigefinger verbrühst, lässt Du es einfach einmal aufkochen und abkühlen. Bei einem Liter Wasser liegt die Temperatur dann etwa 10 bis 15 Minuten über 70 Grad Celsius.

Das häufig empfohlene zehnminütige Kochen ist völlig unnötig. Du möchtest keine tiefen Wunden mit dem Wasser spülen (das wäre mit gekochtem Wasser auch nach 2 Stunden Kochen nicht ratsam – Überdauerungsstadien der Keime überleben das), sondern es trinken. Was die kurze Sprudelphase überlebt hat, ist *im Magen* ungefährlich. Das zu wissen, ist vor allem auch hilfreich, wenn Du in einem improvisierten Topf aus Laubblättern kochen möchtest – 10 Minuten lang kochendes Wasser hält der nicht aus.

Filter

Du kennst sicher die improvisierten Filter aus Dreieckstüchern oder Socken, Kies, Sand und Kohle, wie sie in jedem Pfadfinderbuch beschrieben sind. Die meisten von ihnen sind wirkungslos, weil Wasser seitlich hinunterlaufen kann. Die einzige Möglichkeit ist, mit dichten Gefäßen zu arbeiten und einen Schichtwasserfilter zu bauen. Allerdings brauchst Du für den sicheren Einsatz dieses Keimreduktionsfilters sehr viel mehr Vorwissen, als ich hier vermitteln kann. Es gibt aber noch einen anderen, sicheren Filter, der außerdem ziemlich »bushcraftig« ist.

Dazu suchst Du zuallererst Lehm. Je fetter er ist, desto besser. Wenn der Lehm mit etwas Wasser angemischt wird, merkst Du, ob die Masse zäh und fest (fett) oder brüchig und bröselig (mager) wird. Der magere Lehm wird einfach so verarbeitet, der fette dagegen wird in Portionen geteilt, die jeweils in unterschiedlicher Dosierung mit Sägespänen, Grassamen oder vergleichbaren brennbaren Partikeln vermengt werden. Die etwa hühnereigroßen Knödel werden gepresst und gedrückt, zu einer Tasse geformt und am Feuer getrocknet (das dauert etwa eine halbe bis Dreiviertelstunde). Nach dem Trocknen kommen sie in die direkte Glut des Feuers und werden gebrannt.

Dabei entsteht Terrakotta, eine wasserdurchlässige Keramik, die in der Lage ist,

Tonbrandfilter: (1) Lehm lässt sich an vielen Stellen in Mitteleuropa sammeln. Mit ihm können Kochgefäße und Filter getöpfert werden. (2) Sehr fetter Lehm wird mit brennbarem Pulver versetzt, sonst ist der Filter zu dicht. (3) Fertiger Wasserfilter: Weil Lehm beim Brennen manchmal springt, macht es Sinn, gleich mehrere Filter vorzubereiten. Undichte Filter lassen sich immer noch als Sammelgefäß für Früchte und dergleichen nutzen.

Keime zurückzuhalten. Nach dem Abkühlen wird durch Kratzen mit dem Fingernagel getestet, ob die Hitze ausreichend war. Hört es sich hell und klingelnd an, ist der Tonfilter fertig. Die Tassen aus fettem Lehm werden durchgetestet: Du verwendest diejenigen mit der Lehm/Partikelmischung, bei dem das Wasser gerade noch hindurchsickert. Die Filter aus magerem Lehm müssen dagegen sorgfältig auf Sprünge und Risse kontrolliert werden.

Der fertige Filter kann mit etwas Sand zum Abfiltern größerer Partikel gefüllt werden. Danach kommt Wasser hinein, und das Wasser tropft langsam, aber stetig hindurch.

Diese Technik lädt besonders zum Improvisieren und Experimentieren ein!

Destillieren

Mit dem Wissen, dass die folgenden Beschreibungen von dem einen oder anderen Bushcrafter abends genutzt werden, um den im Rucksack vergorenen Apfelsaft zu einem »Kurzen« zu recyceln, möchten wir uns noch kurz die Destillation als Aufbereitungsmethode anschauen. Destillation ist die Trennung von Stoffen mit unterschiedlichen Siedepunkten über Hitze. Das ist vor allem in Regionen interessant, in denen es nur Salzwasser oder stark mit Metallen und Mineralien versetztes Wasser gibt. In unserem Fall ist die Destillation aber nicht nur eine recht spannende technische Spielerei, sondern kann genutzt werden, wenn das Wasser wirklich stark verunreinigt ist oder überhaupt kein Wasser gefunden werden konnte, dafür aber feuchte Erde oder Schlamm. Wenn diese Masse erhitzt wird, verdampft das Wasser, zurück bleiben die trockenen Erdreste.

Der Wasserdampf muss aber wieder in die flüssige Form zurückgebracht werden. Dazu muss er an einer kalten Oberfläche kondensieren. Im Rucksack hat man normalerweise einen Kochtopf und einen passenden Deckel dabei. Damit lässt sich schon einiges anfangen. Zur Destillation wird der Topf zur Hälfte mit Schlamm gefüllt und langsam erhitzt. Der Topfdeckel wird schräg darüber gelegt, so dass er aber noch möglichst viel abdeckt.

Eine improvisierte Destille ist schnell gebaut. Allerdings ist ihre Effizienz nicht sonderlich hoch. Den Deckel durch Wedeln zu kühlen, hilft aber schon.

Wenn feuchte Erde auf dem Deckel platziert wird, ist die Destillation etwas effektiver. Allerdings sollte kein Schmutz in das Auffanggefäß fallen.

Am Deckel kondensiert das verdampfte Wasser. Noch besser funktioniert die Technik, wenn Du den Deckel mit Pflanzenteilen bedeckst, die immer dann ausgetauscht werden, wenn sie anfangen zu dampfen. Man kann auch dem Topfdeckel Luft zufächeln oder etwas Schlamm darauf platzieren (wenn die Destillation Mineralien oder Giftstoffe abscheiden soll, darf natürlich nichts davon in das Sammelgefäß gelangen). Bei dieser Destillation sollte man etwa 10:1 rechnen: auf einen Liter Wasser im Schlamm erhält man etwa 100 ml Destillat, das ohne weitere Behandlung getrunken werden kann.

Uferfilter

Während es nicht ganz so einfach ist, sich einen funktionellen Filter aus Schichten in einer Flasche oder einem anderen Gefäß herzustellen, liefert die Natur eine ganz natürliche Filtermethode: Das Filtern des Wassers durch horizontales Sickern im Ufersediment.

Wasseraufbereitung

Beim Aufbereiten von Wasser gilt generell: Würdest Du im Wasser schwimmen, kannst Du es und solltest es auch unbearbeitet trinken.

Denn: Du bekommst ständig noch schmutzigeres Wasser in den Mund: beim Paddeln, Geschirrspülen oder nach dem Händewaschen. Bist Du nicht ein wenig mit »normalem Wasser abgehärtet«, kannst Du davon schon krank werden.

Um ein Gewässer fällt der Grundwasserspiegel leicht ab. Sofern der Fluss nicht in Felsenschluchten strömt, findest Du also in 20 bis 30 Metern noch dicht unter der Erdoberfläche den Grundwasserspiegel. Wenn Du dort gräbst, merkst Du recht schnellt, ob hier sauberes Wasser zu finden sein kann:

Ist der Sand frei von schwarzen Verfärbungen und riecht nicht faulig, bist Du richtig. Das Wasser, das sich hier sammelt, ist effektiv 30 Meter durch dichten Sand geströmt – so weit kommen kaum gefährliche Keime. Riecht der Untergrund aber unangenehm, kann es daran liegen, dass der Wasserspiegel bei Hochwasser bis an diese Stelle gelangt.

Dann gräbst Du entweder weiter vom Wasser entfernt oder gehst bei kleineren Gewässern an die andere Seite: Oft treibt auflandiger Wind Laub und andere auf der Oberfläche treibende Pflanzenreste, teilweise auch Hinterlassenschaften von Wasservögeln und anderen Tieren ans Ufer. Spätestens wenn Du ein Loch bis unter den Grundwasserspiegel gegraben hast und am Wasser riechst, merkst Du, ob es sauber ist. Es sollte kaum noch abgestanden oder muffig riechen, und es ist von Natur aus gefiltert und trinkbar.

Sollte das Sediment allerdings so dicht sein, dass von alleine kein Wasser kommt oder es sehr lange dauert, kannst Du den Prozess beschleunigen. Hierzu nimmst Du ein Röhrchen (Schilf, Zeltgestänge etc.) und

Links: **Ist der Sand am Ufer schwarz und faulig, sollte weiter entfernt nochmal gegraben werden.**
Rechts: **In aller Regel sammelt sich das Wasser innerhalb kurzer Zeit von selbst im kleinen Filterbrunnen. Ist das nicht der Fall, kann Unterdruck aufgebaut werden.**

platzierst es im Loch auf etwas Fasermaterial wie Rohrkolben oder Stroh und dichtest alles wieder mit Erde oder feuchtem Lehm luftdicht ab. Dann saugst Du am Röhrchen und verschließt es mit dem Finger. Durch den Unterdruck wird die Flüssigkeit in die Fasern gezogen, von wo aus sie dann mit dem Röhrchen abgesaugt werden kann.

Mit den beschriebenen Techniken solltest Du in der Lage sein, in Mitteleuropa genügend Wasser zu finden. Wenn Du ins Ausland fährst oder in Regionen unterwegs bist, die eher stark verunreinigt sind (Altrheinarme, kleine Tümpel), solltest Du Wasser immer besonders genau einschätzen.

Dazu musst Du immer mehrere Indikatoren beachten, niemals nur einen Hinweis als ausreichend ansehen. Am besten übst Du das regelmäßig an heimischen Gewässern.

DRAUSSEN KOCHEN

Buchstäblich ist nichts so sehr vom Geschmack abhängig wie das Lieblingsgericht. Egal, ob Du besonders gerne Pasta isst, Wiener Würstchen mit Kartoffelsalat oder einen knackigen Feldsalat mit Croutons – nicht alleine die verwendeten Zutaten, sondern die oftmals spezielle Zubereitung und der richtige Rahmen entscheiden darüber, ob ein Gericht bei Dir oder bei Deinen Freunden punkten kann. Nichts ist schlimmer, als wenn man nach einem Tag in der nassen Kälte bibbernd am Feuer sitzend den Abend bei einem tollen Gericht ausklingen lassen will – und dann ist das Gemüse zu Matsch zerkocht und die Nudeln sind angebrannt.

Um solche Erfahrungen zu vermeiden, beschäftigen wir uns in diesem Kapitel nicht nur mit einzelnen Rezepten, sondern allgemein damit, wie Lebensmittel draußen sinvoll und besonders schmackhaft zubereitet werden. Dies zeige ich an einfachen Beispielen.

Mit wenig Ausrüstung am Feuer zu kochen, muss nämlich nicht bedeuten, dass die Mahlzeit ein bis zur Unkenntlichkeit kohlrabenschwarz gekokeltes Stück Fleisch ist, das mit Mengen von Met hinuntergespült werden muss. Kochen am Feuer kann tatsächlich »Sterne-Küche« im wörtlichen Sinn sein:

Wer den Outdoortag mit am Feuer Gekochtem beendet – möglicherweise auch noch aus Zutaten, die er selbst gesammelt oder erlegt hat – dem schmeckt es immer besser. Und: Ein satter Blick durch die von den Flammen beschienenen Baumkronen in den Nachthimmel entschädigt Dich für den ein oder anderen handwerklichen Fehler bei der Zubereitung.

Lebensmittel-Qualität

Das Kochergebnis ist bekanntermaßen immer von den Zutaten abhängig.

Ich habe mich auf manchen Bushcrafttreffen schon ein wenig gewundert: Da sitzen die Recken in Leinen und Leder um das Feuer, packen ihren taktischen Rucksack aus.

Es erscheinen: das Holzbesteck, eine selbst gebrannte Kuksa, eine feuerfeste Emailkanne (die jeden stilechten Cowboy vor Neid erblassen ließe), Gusseisentopf und das teure Bushcraftmesser.

Und dann kommen die Zutaten: ein Tetrapack »Pennerglück«, 600 Gramm Nackengrillsteaks in Marinade vom Discounter (respektive ein mit Hefeextrakt totgewürzter Block Tofu), Aufbackbrötchen und Tabasco – nicht selten militärische Ein-Mann-Packungen; Tütenfutter.

Dabei ist das Kochen draußen viel mehr als die einfache Absättigung. Kochen am Feuer ist Bohème, etwas, für das man sich Zeit lässt, das zelebriert wird. ***Etwas Besonderes.***

Also spricht nichts dagegen, frisches Gemüse wie Kartoffeln, Tomaten oder Sellerie einzupacken. Gutes Olivenöl, Wildfleisch, frische Eier und dergleichen; Fisch und Kräuter lassen sich unterwegs besorgen. Das schmeckt nicht nur besser, es eignet sich zudem besonders gut zum Kochen am Feuer. Moderne Behältnisse und Kühlakkus ermöglichen es, Hochwertiges draußen zu kochen.

Von Gusseisen bis zu Aluminium – es gibt zahlreiche geeignete preiswerte Küchenutensilien für das Kochen draußen. Auschlaggebend für die Auswahl sind persönliche Präferenzen, geplantes Kochsetting, Reiseart und Aufenthaltsdauer.

AUSRÜSTUNG

Wir verwenden für unsere Zubereitung die Klassiker der Outdoorküche. Es gibt heute unzähliges Zubehör für das Kochen draußen. Vom faltbaren Silikontopf über mehrflammige Campingkocher bis hin zu gefriergetrocknetem Gulascheintopf kannst Du alles kaufen – und bestimmt ist auch der erste handkurbelbetriebene Thermo-»Küchenautomat« in Planung. Ich finde aber: Das ist alles Schnick-Schnack! Über der Glut in Gusseisen oder einer verbeulten Blechdose zubereitete Gerichte aus frischen Zutaten schmecken immer noch besser als High-Tech-Food aus der Tüte.

Billy Can

Zum Erhitzen von Wasser, zum Kochen kleiner Suppen – und natürlich für den morgendlichen Kaffee – ist die Billy Can der richtige Begleiter. Der kleine, dünnwandige Topf war ursprünglich natürlich eine einfache Dose. Auch heute verwenden viele Bushcrafter alte Konservendosen aus Blech, die auf einer Seite geöffnet und mit einem Draht als Bügel versehen werden. Idealerweise verwendet man einen Dosenöffner, um die Falznaht aufzutrennen – damit hat man auch gleich einen passenden Deckel. Konservendosen aus Blech müssen vor dem ersten Verwenden ausgeglüht werden, um die Kunststoffbeschichtung zu entfernen. Außerdem gibt es leichte Billy Cans auch fix und fertig aus dem Zubehör-Laden.

Multi-Wasserkocher: Eine einfache Billy Can ist dünnwandig und wiegt nur wenige Gramm.

(1) Benötigt werden etwas Draht und zwei Blech-Konservendosen: eine hohe, unbeschichtete als Billy Can, eine etwas breitere als Deckel. (2) Der Dosenboden wird mit einem Rand von etwa einem Zentimeter Höhe mit einem alten Messer oder einer Blechschere abgetrennt. (3) Der Schnittgrat muss unbedingt abgeschliffen werden. Er ist sehr scharf. (4) In den Deckel der Billy Can machst Du ein einzelnes Loch – das Gefäß erhält zwei Löcher für die Aufhängung. (5) Mit Draht werden Aufhängung und Deckelgriff gefertigt – sie können individuell gestaltet und geschmückt werden. (6) Die Billy Can wird über dem Feuer hängend verwendet. Traditionell sollte bei jedem Lagern eine »Billy« mit heißem Kaffee gemacht werden – *falls Besuch kommt.*

Dutch Oven

Mittlerweile dürfte der Dutch Oven oder »Camp Oven« jedem ein Begriff sein. Der gusseiserne Topf ist speziell für das Kochen in der Glut ausgelegt: Der Boden ist flach, bei manchen Modellen sogar mit Füßen versehen, und der dicht schließende Deckel ist für eine gleichmäßige Hitzeverteilung ideal.

Man benötigt nicht unbedingt die teure Version von Petroleumlampenherstellern und auch keine spezielle Kohle dafür. Jeder unbeschichtete gusseiserne Topf kann hierfür eingesetzt werden. Die Aluminiumtöpfe, die es als »Gulaschtopf« gibt, sind nicht ganz so gut wie Gusseisen, bieten aber einen recht guten Mittelweg zwischen Wärmeverteilung und Gewicht. Mit dem Topf kann gekocht, geschmort und gebacken werden, selbst alleine mit dem Deckel lässt sich allerlei zubereiten.

Gusseisenware ist dick und verhältnismäßig schwer. Diese Materialstärke hilft, die Hitze der Glut gleichmäßig zu verteilen.

Gusspfanne

Vor allem diejenigen, die mit dem Rucksack unterwegs sind, haben wenig Stauraum für zusätzliche Ausrüstungsstücke. Aber immer häufiger wandert bei mir eine gusseiserne Platte – zumindest ein Dutch-Oven-Deckel oder eine kleine Pfanne mit klappbarem Griff – in den Rucksack. Sie sind gute Al-

Der Dutch Oven im Einsatz: Mit wenig(!) Glut auf dem Deckel entsteht im Topf Ober- und Unterhitze. Ideal für eine lecker Kruste.

Pflege und Einbrennen von gusseisernem Kochgeschirr

Kochgeschirre aus Gusseisen sind die Elefanten unter den Stahlwaren. Damit ist nicht nur ihr deutlich höheres Gewicht gemeint, vergleicht man sie mit Titan- oder Alupötten, sondern auch ihre Gutmütigkeit bei Anwendungsfehlern und vor allem: ihr Gedächnis. Gusseisen »merkt« sich in seinen Milliarden feinen Poren und Rissen, was lange Zeit davor darin gekocht wurde. Fett zieht ein und nimmt damit Gewürz- und Geschmacksstoffe mit. Das mag für den Hausmann oder die Bushcrafterin erst einmal befremdlich wirken, aber genau das macht den besonderen Geschmack des »Eisenkochens« aus. Nach einigen Malen Kochen bekommt der Topf eine ölige Patina, die außerdem verhindert, dass etwas anbrennt. Das wirkt viel effektiver als Teflon- oder Steinbeschichtungen. Voraussetzung ist allerdings die richtige Pflege. Gusseisen ist ab Werk meist mit Paraffin vor Rost geschützt. Das Wachs muss entfernt werden. Dazu werden Topf und Deckel in starke Glut gelegt. Es beginnt zu qualmen und zu stinken. Nach einiger Zeit ist das Paraffin verdampft. Nach dem Abkühlen wird der Topf von innen mit ordentlich viel, außen nur mit etwas Öl (ich verwende Olivenöl) bestrichen und nach einigen Minuten wieder auf die Glut gelegt. Diesmal wird langsamer erhitzt, bis das Öl raucht. So bleibt der Topf einige Zeit heiß. Im heißen Zustand wird er mit Gras oder einem Küchenpapier ausgewischt. Fertig. Der Topf muss sein gesamtes Leben (hunderte Jahre) lang nicht mehr gespült oder gar mit Seife gereinigt werden. Nach dem Kochen wird er einfach trocken oder mit etwas Öl ausgewischt.

ternativen zu einem Dutch Oven, wenn auf offenem Feuer Speck mit Zwiebeln und Eiern für das Frühstück gebraten werden soll, Wurzeln zu Kaffee geröstet oder Bannock und Fladen gemacht werden. Während das Kochen über dem Feuer auch mit einem einfachen Stahl- oder Aluminiumtopf funktioniert (wenn auch mehr schlecht als recht), gibt es bei der Pfanne keine Alternative zum Guss. Wer einmal auf einem Teflon-beschichteten Topfdeckel aus Aluminium versucht hat, ein Spiegelei am Feuer zu machen, weiß, was ich meine. Die gleichmäßige Verteilung der Hitze ist beim Braten und Rösten besonders wichtig. Zweite Wahl zum Braten sind schmiedeeiserne Pfannen, die es mittlerweile auch günstig bei Discountern gibt. **Hinweis:** *Beschichtet sollten die Pfannen jedoch allesamt nicht sein. Wird beispielsweise Teflon zu heiß, entstehen sehr giftige Dämpfe.*

Wer oft und gerne über dem Feuer brät ist mit einer Gusspfanne *(links)* gut beraten. Allerdings gibt es sie kaum auf dem deutschen Markt und sie müssen importiert werden. Alternativen sind Crêpespfannen aus Guss oder schmiedeeiserne Pfannen.

Hobo-Kocher

Wer draußen am Feuer kocht, sollte sich im Klaren darüber sein, dass dies an vielen Stellen nicht erlaubt ist. Der Jahreswechsel zu 2017 hat in Bayern plakativ gezeigt, dass auch im Winter Feuer außer Kontrolle geraten kann. Zum vielmals verbotenen offenen Feuer zählen nicht nur Lagerfeuer, sondern auch Gaskocher, Spirituskocher und Hobo-Öfen. Letztere bieten allerdings die Möglichkeit, ein Brandrisiko erheblich zu *verringern*, soll auf offener Flamme gekocht werden.

Ein Hobo-Kocher besteht entweder aus einer einfachen großen Blechdose mit Luftlöchern oder ist zusammenfalt- bzw. -steckbar und bildet einen kompakten Brennraum. Da Brennmaterial in aller Regel in Massen vorhanden ist, ist die Effizienz der Hobos egal, weshalb es kein »Holzvergaser« sein muss. Du möchtest ja nicht Wasser »turbokochen«, sondern in Ruhe Deine Nahrung zubereiten. Im Hobo-Kocher wird ein Kamineffekt erzeugt, und Hitze sowie Glut werden kompakt gehalten.

Wirst Du allerdings mit einem brennenden Hobo im Wald erwischt, blühen Dir prinzipiell dieselben Strafen wie bei offenem Feuer – obwohl er, richtig eingesetzt, das Risiko eines Brandes reduziert.

Dabei kann das korrekte Verhalten die Gefahr durch Feuer erheblich reduzieren. Du solltest darauf achten, dass der eingesetzte Hobo-Kocher ein Ascheblech besitzt, also einen abgeschlossenen Boden, durch den keine heißen Verbrennungsrückstände fallen können.

Ein solcher Hobo ist auch dem ursprünglichen Hobo-Kocher am ähnlichsten: Er war

Hobo-Kocher gibt es in unterschiedlichen Größen und Ausführungen. Eine Auswahlhilfe bietet der Hersteller Bushcraft Essentials unter *www.bushcraft-essentials.com/german/kocher-auswahlmatrix*.

die Koch- und Wärmestelle von amerikanischen Wanderarbeitern und Landstreichern (»Hobos«) und bestand aus einem alten Ölfass oder einer für den besseren »Zug« durchlöcherten Blechdose.

Ebenso wie auf den modernen Hobo-Kochern aus Stahl- oder Titanblech war diese Art zu kochen effizienter und vor allem besser »regelbar« als eine offene Feuerstelle.

Letztendlich dürfte ein Grund für die Verwendung damals wie heute gewesen sein: Auch wenn es sich ähnlich wie bei Gaslaterne und Spirituskocher um ein offenes Holzfeuer handelt, wird es nicht als »Lagerfeuer« wahrgenommen. Es bleiben weniger Spuren zurück, und der Bau der Kochfeuerstelle entfällt beim »schnellen Kaffeekochen« in der Mittagspause.

Das kleine Hobo-Einmaleins

Auswahl des richtigen Hobo-Kochers

Bei der Auswahl des richtigen Hobos solltest Du nicht alleine auf das Gewicht achten – das sparst Du schon beim Brennmaterial. Viel wichtiger ist ***die passende Größe****.*

Kleine Kocher sind zwar leicht und handlich, das geringere Volumen speichert aber weniger Hitze, der Kocher zieht nicht so gut und hat auch eher Schwierigkeiten, feuchtes Holz sauber zu verbrennen. Kleine Kocher sind für heißes Wasser ausreichend oder wenn mal eine Suppe aufgewärmt werden soll. Kocher ab dem Volumen von ca. einem Liter können dagegen zum Kochen aufwendiger Gerichte genutzt werden – sie halten auch ein wenig Glut vor und lassen sich so auch besser regeln.

In jedem Fall sollte der Kocher ein Ascheblech haben und ***sich nicht bei Hitze verziehen****. Daneben stellt sich die Frage, ob der Kocher gelegentlich auch zum Kochen mit einem Spiritusbrenner genutzt werden soll.*

Anfeuern – Befeuern

Bevor mit dem Hobo gekocht werden kann, muss er erstmal brennen. Da solltest Du nicht den Fehler machen, den Brennraum vollzupacken, sondern mit einem kleinen Feuer aus trockenem Reisig beginnen, damit die Thermik beginnt zu ziehen. Stückchen für Stückchen kann dann Holz nachgelegt werden.

Brennt der Kocher erstmal, können ***ein paar*** *dickere Stückchen aufgelegt werden. Sie brennen länger und genügend heiß zum Kochen. Dünnes Material flammt schnell ab.* ***Je kleiner der Brennraum ist, desto häufiger muss auch nachgelegt werden****.*

Es sollte allerdings nicht dieselbe Menge in den kleinen Brennraum gepackt werden, wie in einen großen Kocher – beginnt das Holz zu qualmen und zu rußen, hast Du zu viel Brennstoff benutzt, und die Verbrennung läuft nicht mehr optimal. Mit ein paar Kochsessions hat man schnell ein Gefühl dafür entwickelt.

Auswahl des Kochgeschirrs

Ein Hobo-Kocher wird heiß. ***Richtig heiß!*** *Vor allem, wenn der Kamineffekt richtig zum Tragen kommt, kann es schnell passieren, dass Dir ein leerer Alutopf durchbrennt oder beschichtetes Kochgeschirr kaputt geht. Da die Hitze des stark* ***brennenden*** *Hobos auch seitlich um den Topf geführt wird, kann das nur verhindert werden, indem der Topf voll mit Wasser ist.*

Ideal sind natürlich die oben beschriebenen gusseisernen oder schmiedeeisernen Töpfe. Wer ein wenig Gewicht sparen will, kann auch Edelstahl verwenden.

Wer Speck mit Eiern anbraten oder Suppe simmern möchte, lässt den Hobo-Kocher erst brennen, bis sich ein Glutbett gebildet hat, setzt den Topf auf und kann dann einzelne Holzstücke zugeben, um die Hitze vorsichtig zu steuern, ohne dass Flammen um den Topf schlagen. Auf diese Weise lässt sich auch Alu- oder Titangeschirr verwenden.

DIE KOCHSTELLE

Egal, ob Du auf offener Feuerstelle oder über dem Hobo kochst – die Feuerstelle muss gut gesichert sein, damit das Feuer nicht außer Kontrolle gerät. Außerdem sollte immer etwas Sand, lockere Erde, ein Topf Wasser oder ein Löschspray greifbar sein. Du wärst nicht der erste Bushcrafter, dem das Feuer außer Kontrolle gerät.

Generell gilt bei Kochfeuern: Es muss klein sein. Wenn Du am Wärmefeuer kochst, nimmst Du ein wenig Glut beiseite und nutzt diese. Die Energiemenge, die einige kleine Scheite Holz freigeben, reicht zum stundenlangen Schmoren. *Der häufigste Anfängerfehler ist zu viel Hitze!* Wenn Du nur Wasser kochen möchtest, ist das nicht so schlimm. Soll Reis auf kleiner Flamme simmern, hast Du dagegen schnell einen verkohlten Klumpen in der Billy Can. Gut ist es, wenn die Feuerstelle zentrale Hitze abgibt. Das lässt sich durch eine schmale Grube (natürlich nur in nichtbrennbaren Untergründen – niemals auf Torf, Tannennadeln oder trockenem Humus) sicherstellen. Hier kannst Du außerdem Glut sammeln, wenn Du mit dem Dutch Oven oder einer Gusspfanne kochst. Dadurch wird die Feuerstelle geteilt: In der Grube wird die Flamme gehalten, über ihr kann in Wasser gekocht werden – in der daneben liegenden flammenlosen Zone wird die Hitze über Glut genauestens gesteuert.

(1) Eine flache Kuhle wird in den gewachsenen Boden gescharrt und mit einer Steineinfassung und einem Topfgestell versehen. (2) Ein wenig dünnes Holz wird abgebrannt. (3) Holz wird auf einer Seite verbrannt, Glut in die flammenlose Zone gefegt. (4) Durch Hinzufügen und Wegnehmen von Glut lässt sich die Hitze steuern.

Auf drei Punkten können Töpfe, Pfannen und dergleichen sicher und wackelfrei aufgestellt werden – ein sicherer Stand des Geschirrs ist beim Kochen Pflicht!

Topfgestell

Wenn Du einen Topf oder eine Gussplatte erhitzen willst, nimmst Du am besten drei kantige Steine von etwa Faustdurchmesser. Sie werden um Glutzone oder Flammenzone so verteilt, dass sie ein Dreieck bilden, wobei jeweils eine *Ecke* des Steins nach oben zeigt. Nur bei drei punktförmigen Auflagen kann wackelfreies Abstellen sichergestellt werden. Und das Gefäß *muss* sicher stehen! Du willst in ihm später rühren, schaben, wenden und Glut austauschen, ohne dass Dein Essen im Feuer landet oder schlimmer: Du Dich verbrennst. Auf einer Kochgrube wird der Topfhalter nicht zentral, sondern etwas versetzt aufgebaut. Dadurch kannst Du Holz nachlegen und die Glut schüren, ohne den Topf abnehmen zu müssen.

Holzwerkzeuge

Um Essen zuzubereiten, brauchst Du das eine oder andere Werkzeug, das Du auch schnell improvisieren kannst. Ich stelle Dir hier die einfachsten Formen vor, die immer gebraucht werden und die Du in wenigen Minuten schnitzen kannst.

Schaber/Wender

Zum Rühren und Wenden benötigst Du einen einfachen Spatel. In der Praxis hat sich eine Breite von etwa 3 bis 5 Zentimetern als ideal erwiesen. Er lässt sich auch aus härterem Holz noch einfach herstellen. Hierfür wird ein Ast auf 30 Zentimeter gekürzt. Ein Drittel wird mit dem Power-Cut auf zwei Seiten zu einer glatten Fläche verjüngt, der Rest wird auf vier Seiten zu einem Stiel ausgearbeitet. Die Spatelspitze wird je nach Bedarf flach und gerade geschnitten oder abgerundet.

Über dem Feuer oder dem Wasserdampf lässt sich der Schaber zu einem Wender in die gewünschte Form biegen. Auf diese Weise hergestellte Werkzeuge halten viele Kochsessions aus.

Wird der Spatel dicker ausgearbeitet, lässt sich außerdem zügig ein einfacher Kochlöffel herstellen.

Zange

Beim Kochen über der Glut ist die Zange oft ein unersetzbarer Helfer. Mit ihr werden große Glutstückchen versetzt oder ins Feuer gefallene Lebensmittel geborgen. Dazu kürzt

Schaber: (1) Für einen einfachen Schaber wird ein Stock abgeflacht und (2) der Stiel ausgearbeitet. (3) Die Vorderkante wird angeschrägt und (4) die Form des Spatels in der Hitze gebogen und unter Spannung abgekühlt.

Zange: (1) Eine Astgabel wird geschnitten und (2) mittig mit einer Kerbe versehen. (3) Unter Hitze lässt sich die Zange nun biegen, so dass sie (4) wie eine Pinzette zum Halten von Gegenständen geeignet ist.

Du Dir einen Ast mit kleiner Gabel auf etwa 50 Zentimeter, erhitzt ihn mittig und knickst ihn ab. Diese schnell improvisierte Zange ist ausreichend stabil. Natürlich kann sie auch mit Hilfe eines Zweibeinbundes und eines Keils als Federzange ausgearbeitet werden, die rudimentäre Form ist aber in aller Regel ausreichend.

Haken

Mit einem simplen Haken aus Holz wird vor allem die Billy Can und der Dutch Oven plaziert und korrigiert. Hier ist ein einfacher Stock mit kleinem Seitenast am besten geeignet. Geschnitzte Haken brechen unter Hitze eher aus.

Ein simpler Holzhaken ist wichtig zum Öffnen von heißen Deckeln, Verstellen von Töpfen oder Verteilen der Glut.

LEBENSMITTELZUBEREITUNG AM FEUER

Kochen mit der Billy Can: Tee, Kaffee, Suppe

Es soll Hobbyköche geben, die sogar Wasser anbrennen lassen. Das ist sicherlich nicht einfach. Wasser beim Kochen in das Feuer zu verschütten, ist dagegen ein häufiger Fehler. Bevor mit der Billy Can gekocht wird, musst Du Dich entscheiden, ob direkte Hitze der Flamme besser geeignet ist oder ob fein justierte Wärme der Glut benötigt wird. In hohen und schmalen Töpfen zu kochen, birgt die Gefahr des Siedeverzugs, bei dem das Wasser aus dem Topf schießt.

Um einfach einen Liter Wasser für den Kaffee zu machen, gehst Du folgendermaßen vor:

Es wird mit dem Haken oder der Zange aus der Feuerstelle genügend Glut für ein kleines Häufchen gescharrt. Auf das Häufchen wird ein kleines Stückchen Holz gelegt, das noch nicht vollständig zu Glut verbrannt ist. Nun wird etwas glühende Kohle verteilt, so dass die Billy Can wackelfrei stehen kann. Die maximal zu drei Vierteln mit Wasser gefüllte Dose wird *ohne Deckel* auf die dünne Glutschicht gestellt. Die Kohle erlischt unter der Dose relativ schnell - sie dient ohnehin nur zur Isolation.

Nun wird auf *einer* Seite der Billy Can Glut und Kohle angehäufelt, so dass sie bis zur Hälfte der Dose reicht. Darauf wird das brennende Holzstückchen gelegt - es sorgt für etwas Durchzug durch die Kohle. Von einer Seite erhitzt, beginnt das Wasser innerhalb von weniger als 5 Minuten zu simmern. Nun kann man Tee, Kaffee (oder klein geschnittenes Gemüse und Fleisch) zugeben.

Simmert das Wasser wieder, wird Glut durch Einblasen so weit erhitzt, bis das Wasser kocht, ohne überzusieden.

Kochen mit der Billy Can: Reis und Nudeln

Etwas schwieriger wird es, wenn über einem Feuer Getreideprodukte zubereitet werden sollen. Diese brennen nämlich schnell an oder bilden Schaum und kochen über den Topfrand. Der häufigste kulinarische Supergau ist nicht ohne Grund der Versuch einer Zubereitung von Dosenravioli während eines Festivals auf dem Camping-Gasbrenner der Eltern.

Die Hitzequelle muss zur Zubereitung von Getreideprodukten sehr genau geregelt werden. Am Feuer gekocht, gibt es außerdem das Problem, dass nicht ständig gerührt werden kann. Aus diesem Grund ist hierfür neben einem Hobo-Kocher, der sich über die

Die Wände der Billy Can werden durch die Flammen bzw. Glut sehr heiß, wodurch beim Kochen von Kaffee oder Suppe immer etwas »Schaum« anröstet, was den besonderen Geschmack der Lebensmittel aus diesem Kochgeschirr ausmacht.

Brennstoffzufuhr gut regeln lässt, ein Kochgestell für die Billy Can unerlässlich. Die einfachste Version besteht aus einem etwa zwei bis drei Zentimeter dicken Ast, der unten mit einer Vierkantspitze, oben mit einer flachen Kante versehen, schräg und fest neben der Glutstelle in den Boden gerammt wird. Ein weiterer Ast (nach Möglichkeit mit Seitenast) wird auf der gesamten Länge mit mehreren geschnitzten flachen Haken versehen, die sicher in die flache Kante des ersten Stabs fassen. Der Reis wird so bemessen, dass mindestens die doppelte Volumenmenge Wasser im Topf Platz hat (für Nudeln deutlich mehr Wasser einplanen).

Nun kann die Billy Can am Haken mit der gewünschten Menge von leicht gesalzenem Wasser direkt über der Hitzequelle platziert werden. Es wird genügend Glut unter dem Topf platziert, damit die Hitze auch den Kochvorgang durchhält, ohne abzukühlen.

Sobald das Wasser siedet, wird der Haken so weit nach oben versetzt, bis das Wasser nur noch leicht simmert. Man wartet etwa eine Minute und beobachtet, ob sich an diesem Zustand etwas ändert. Ist die Wassertemperatur stabil, können der Reis bzw. die Nudeln eingefüllt werden.

Der Deckel wird aufgesetzt und etwa 10 bis 12 Minuten später ist der Reis perfekt – ohne anzubrennen oder noch hart zu sein. Nicht einmal Wasser muss abgekippt werden.

Wasser abkippen

Wenn ein Überschuss an Wasser abgekippt werden soll, wird der Topf im geschlossenen Zustand vom Feuer genommen. Der Deckel wird leicht geöffnet und ein kleines Hölzchen zwischen Deckel und Topfrand geklemmt. Mit Handschuhen oder etwas Gras als Hitzeschutz kann der Deckel gehalten werden. Mit Hilfe des Henkels und des Holzhakens wird das Gefäß an einer Kante auf einen Stein abgestellt, am Henkel nach vorne gezogen, während der Deckel aufgedrückt bleibt. Auf diese Weise lässt sich Wasser abkippen, auch wenn kein Sieb verfügbar ist. ***Achtung:*** *Der Wasserdampf kann sehr heiß sein!*

Schmoren im Dutch Oven

Der schwere gusseiserne Topf ist eigentlich ohne ernsthafte Alternative, wenn Gerichte gebacken oder geschmort werden sollen. Der häufigste Fehler dabei ist, wie schon angesprochen, dass viel zu viel Hitze verwendet wird. Darum wird oft auch zartes Fleisch darin zäh wie eine Schuhsohle.

Um zu kochen, wird zuallererst die Feuerstelle vorbereitet: Auf die Glutstelle werden drei kleine Steine gelegt, auf die später der Topf gestellt wird. Sie sollen für ein wenig Luftzug sorgen – vor allem sollen sie den Topf von der Bodenkälte isolieren. Aus der Feuerstelle entnommen, wird Glut zwischen den Steinen angehäuft. Der Topf wird aufgestellt und erhitzt sich. Hinein kommt etwas Öl, Speckwürfel sowie eine kleingeschnittene Zwiebel. Die Zwiebeln werden mit dem ausgelassenen Speck glasig gebraten. Während dieser Zeit bekommt man auch etwas Gefühl für die Hitze der jeweiligen Feuerstelle.

Nun wird die Glut mit einem Stock unter dem Topf verteilt, bis sich das Bratgeräusch zu einem leisen Brutzeln reduziert hat. Nach Belieben werden nun ganze Möhren, Kartoffeln und Paprika hineingegeben und der

(1) Frische Lebensmittel sollten erst unmittelbar vor dem Kochen zerkleinert werden. Sie schmecken erheblich besser als Gefriergetrocknetes und halten sich ohne Schwierigkeiten 2 Tage. (2) Ausgelassener Speck und Zwiebeln bilden im Topf ein deftiges Fundament zum Schmoren. (3) Das Gemüse wird in möglichst großen Stücken hinzugegeben, mittenrein ein Stück gutes Wildfleisch (hier die Nuss aus der Rehkeule). Dazu etwas Wein und Kräuter. Deckel drauf – fertig. (4) Es kann stundenlang geschmort werden. Dazu darf das Gefäß aber nicht heißer als ca. 90 Grad Celsius werden – lieber zu wenig Glut als zu viel!

Boden mit etwa einem Zentimeter Rotwein bedeckt. Hierauf werden das Fleisch (im Beispiel Rehkeule) sowie Gewürze in den Dutch Oven gelegt und der Deckel verschlossen.

Nun werden wenige (!) Stückchen Glut auf den Deckel gelegt. Nach etwa 10 Minuten wird die Hitze mit einem befeuchteten Finger am Topfrand und auf dem Deckel getestet. Ist ein helles Zischen wie bei einem Bügeleisen zu hören, ist der Topf zu heiß. Befeuchtet sich dagegen das Eisen etwas und trocknet innerhalb von 2-3 Sekunden wieder, ist die Hitze genau richtig. Alle halbe Stunde wird so »gemessen« - bei Bedarf wenig Glut nachgeschoben. Innerhalb von ca. 2-3 Stunden bekommt man das Fleisch butterzart, während das Gemüse noch Biss hat.

Backen im Dutch Oven

Für das Backen von Brot und Kuchen ist der Dutch Oven ideal. Allerdings ist es nicht einfach, wenn man wenig Erfahrung mit der richtigen Hitze, der Wärmeverteilung und der benötigten Glutmenge hat. Für Einsteiger ist das Backen von süßem Brot eine gute Übung. Das Aroma, das der Dutch Oven an das Essen abgibt, passt ideal dazu. Für zwei Personen werden 300-400 Gramm Mehl mit etwas Trockenhefe, einem Esslöffel Zucker, einer guten Handvoll Sultaninen vermengt und mit Milch (wenn man sich eine Mischung vorbereiten möchte, Milchpulver und später Wasser) verknetet, so dass ein recht trockener Teig entsteht.

Der Laib wird beiseite gestellt und der Dutch Oven auf der Glutstelle platziert. Hinein kommen gereinigte flache Steine, die den direkten Bodenkontakt verhindern sollen. Der Topfdeckel wird aufgesetzt und mit etwas Glut bedeckt.

Ist der Topf so heiß, dass ein feuchter Finger beim Darüberstreifen keinen feuchten Film hinterlässt, es aber noch nicht zischt, wird der Deckel abgehoben und der Teig auf den Steinen platziert. Darauf kann noch etwas Zucker gestreut werden.

Nach etwa 15 bis 20 Minuten ist das Buschbrot fertig und der Zucker karamellisiert.

Tipp: *Um das Anbacken zu verhindern, wird der Teig auf flache Steine im Topf gelegt.*

(1) Die Hitze sollte beim Backen vor allem von der Seite und von oben kommen. Deshalb sollte nur wenig Glut unter dem Ofen sein. (2) Das Brot kann als weiches Frühstücksbrot ausgebacken werden - oder mit einer knusprigen karamellisierten Kruste.

Trapperfrühstück aus der Gusspfanne

Die flache Gusspfanne fürs Feuer ist im europäischen Raum noch kaum verbreitet. Dabei ist sie ideal, um auf der Glut zu braten – von Fleisch über Ei mit Speck bis Pfannkuchen lässt sich damit wirklich praktisch alles zubereiten. Der Vorteil der Gusspfanne ist: Es kann wirklich heiß gebraten werden, also auch bei Temperaturen, bei denen Alutopfdeckel sprichwörtlich die »Biege« machen würden. Hierzu wird die Platte entweder auf der Flammenseite der Feuerstelle, auf der »Nebenkochstelle« mit viel Glut oder auf einem Hobo platziert und erhitzt. Sobald die Pfanne beginnt zu rauchen (das ist das in den Poren gesammelte Fett), wird die Hitze etwas reduziert. Nun werden einige Streifen Bauchspeck auf die Pfanne gelegt, dazwischen Zwiebelringe. Ohne zu wenden, verbleibt alles in der Hitze, bis Speck und Zwiebeln glasig werden. Nun können Eier zentral in die Pfanne geschlagen werden. Sie verteilen sich auf dem Speck, und etwa 3–4 Minuten später ist das beste Trapperfrühstück fertig, das Du je probiert hast.

Tipp: *Wenn Du die Pfanne vorher umdrehst und über der Feuerstelle etwas »einräucherst«, bekommt das Gericht einen großartig rauchigen Geschmack.*

(1) Die Gusspfanne wird mit der Oberseite ans Feuer gestellt, um Räucheraroma aufzunehmen. (2) Dünne Streifen Bauchspeck werden auf die heiße Pfanne gegeben und ausgelassen. (3) Hierauf kommen dicke Zwiebelringe und pro Person (4) zwei Eier.

BACKEN UND BRATEN IN DER GLUT

Natürlich lassen sich viele Gerichte auch ohne jeden Topf und Kocher zubereiten. Allerdings geht es beim Bushcraften ja immer auch um ein wenig »Waldluxus«.

Wenn man sich die gängigen Gourmet-Zubereitungsmethoden anschaut, sieht man, dass man am direkten Flammenkontakt kaum vorbeikommt. Ob Gasgrill, Smoker oder Räucherpulver für den Backofen – hier wird das Grillen auf dem Feuer bzw. auf der Glut nur simuliert.

Dabei musst Du für ein gutes Ergebnis keinen besonderen Aufwand treiben. Die Hitze über der Glut ist direkter und heißer als in der Pfanne oder auf dem Rost. Außerdem ist die Wärmeverteilung nicht gleichmäßig, wodurch manche Bereiche am zubereiteten Essen stärker geröstet sind als andere, die weniger knusprig werden. Die richtige Mischung macht es häufig aus. Denn beim Grillen über Glut werden über die Maillard-Reaktion besonders viele »Röststoffe« gebildet, was sonst erst bei intensivem Braten in der Pfanne geschehen würde.

Wer nicht jede Malzeit aus der Glut zu sich nimmt, muss auch keine Sorge wegen Giftstoffen haben – Gutes über der Glut zubereitet und mit Freu(n)den genossen ist erheblich weniger schädlich, als dauerhaft (und vielleicht sogar schlecht gelaunt) auf dem Weg zur Arbeit den Smog der Innenstadt einzuatmen.

Fladenbrot aus der Glut

Wer einen Brotlaib backen möchte, kann das besonders einfach im Dutch Oven machen. Was jedoch wirklich besonders gut schmeckt, sind Brotfladen, die direkt in der Glut gebacken werden. Hierbei ist aller-

Glut und kein Gewürz – Du brauchst nicht viel, um Schmackhaftes zu kreieren. Die hohe Hitze der Glut und etwas Rauch zaubern ein wunderbares Aroma – ganz ohne Gasflamme und Alufolie.

dings besonders wichtig, dass auch wirklich Glut verwendet wird – sie brennt nicht mehr und qualmt auch nicht. Ansonsten wird das Ergebnis gewöhnungsbedürftig sein.

Aus einer Backmischung oder aus Mehl mit Trockenhefe, Nüssen, Rosinen und dergleichen wird ein zäher, nicht klebriger Teig gemischt und geknetet. Die Konsistenz ist am besten, wenn er beim Zerreißem auf breiter Fläche abbricht, ohne Fäden zu ziehen. Während der Teig einige Minuten liegt, wird Glut vorbereitet. Hierzu wird möglichst dünnes Holz bis Fingerstärke abgebrannt, bis in der Feuergrube eine ordentliche Menge Glut und Kohle liegen. Ein Teil davon wird auf die Glutstelle überführt und verteilt.

Vom Teig wird nun eine etwa eigroße Menge abgerissen. Daraus wird ein flacher Fladen geformt. Dieser kommt auf die Glut und wird nur dreißig Sekunden später wieder herausgeholt (da der Griff schnell erfolgt, geht das auch mit der Hand).

Nun wird der Fladen *noch* flacher gedrückt und gewendet wieder auf die Glut gelegt. Wieder etwa eine halbe Minute später erfolgt das nächste Plätten und Wenden. Nach etwa 3–5 Minuten sind knusprige Fladen fertig, die wider Erwarten weder in der Glut anbrennen noch mit Kohle oder Asche paniert sind.

Die richtige Glut

Wenn etwas in der Glut zubereitet wurde und sonderbar schmeckt, hast Du meist nicht lange genug gewartet: ***»Echte« Glut qualmt nicht mehr*** *und bildet auch keinen Flammensaum, wenn man hineinbläst. Wenn eine dünne weiße Ascheschicht aufliegt, ist sie genau richtig.*

(1) Mit Wasser, Mehl und Rosinen oder Wildfrüchten wird ein zäher, eher trockener Teig hergestellt und gut durchgeknetet. (2) Lassen sich Stücke »abbrechend« herausziehen, ist er genau richtig. (3) Flach gedrückt kommt er in die direkte Glut und wird regelmäßig gewendet. (4) Regelmäßig gewendet, bleiben weder Glut noch Asche hängen, noch verbrennt der Teig.

Steckerlfisch

Ein Highlight eines Abenteuertages ist es, wenn Du Dir unterwegs selbst Essen beschaffen und dieses am Feuer zubereiten kannst. Während selbst gesammelte bzw. gefangene Würmer, Insekten und Nagetiere meines Erachtens ganz klar zum »Survivalfutter« gehören, sind die Grundzutaten beim Bushcraften natürlich ziviler. Vor allem Fischfang gehört hier zum kleinen »Einmaleins« der Nahrungsbeschaffung. Wer etwas Leine und einen Haken mitnimmt, hat kaum Schwierigkeiten, am See oder Bach den einen oder anderen Fisch anzulanden (Genehmigungen natürlich vorausgesetzt!).

Dabei unterscheide ich grundsätzlich zwischen zwei Klassen: Alles, was unter Handtellergröße ist, kann am Stock zubereitet werden, was darüber liegt, in der Glut. Als Sakrileg empfinde ich dagegen das Zerkochen eines Fischs in Wasser – sofern Du nicht gerade eine Bouillabaisse mit entsprechenden Fischarten und Gewürzen zubereitest.

Insbesondere kleine, gräten- und stachelreiche Fische wie kleine Meeresfische, Barsche oder Weißfische brauchen Feuerhitze und Rauch. Sie lassen sich besonders einfach als Steckerlfisch am Feuer zubereiten. Dazu werden die Fische nur geschuppt, ohne Kopf ausgenommen und am Stöckchen unter regelmäßigem Wenden über die Glut gehalten. Das ist nicht nur eine tolle Beschäftigung auch für Kinder, sondern röstet den Fisch im Eigenfett so stark durch, dass Stachelstrahlen und feine Gräten beim Essen einfach zerknuspern. Nur die Hauptgräten und die Wirbelsäule bleiben übrig. Durch das »scharfe« Grillen wird außerdem der manchmal etwas schlammige Geschmack von Weißfischen reduziert.

(1) Fische werden vom Schwanz zum Kopf geschuppt. (2) Direkt hinter den Kiemen wird das Messer angesetzt und etwa bis zur Mitte des Fischs geschnitten. (3) Der Kopf wird fixiert und der Fisch nach hinten gezogen. Die Organe werden dabei entfernt. (4) Der Fisch kommt auf einen kleinen Spieß und über die Glut.

Fisch aus der Glut

Etwas anspruchsvoller ist das Zubereiten eines größeren Fisches auf – oder besser gesagt: in – der Glut. Natürlich lassen sich Forellen, Doraden oder Karpfen auf einem Grill zubereiten. Allerdings benötigt das Fleisch relativ lange Garzeiten. Dabei darf die Hitze nicht zu hoch sein, sonst verbrennt der Fisch außen und ist innen noch roh. Ist die Hitze zu gering, bildet sich keine Kruste, und der Fisch wird trocken.

Eine ganz gute Lösung ist deshalb das Verpacken in Blätter und das Vergraben in der Glut. Dabei wird ausreichend Hitze erzeugt, das Fleisch bleibt dennoch saftig – vorausgesetzt, Du hast das Gefühl für das richtige Timing. Ansonsten gibt es noch einen weiteren Trick: Entweder wird der Fisch nicht ausgenommen, oder die Bauchhöhle wird mit Kräutern und grünen (natürlich ungiftigen!) Pflanzen gefüllt. Danach wird der Fisch zusammengebunden und in mehrere Lagen aus großen Laubblättern eingeschlagen.

Auch hier solltest Du darauf achten, dass Du nichts Giftiges nimmst. Ideal sind Brennnessel-, Kletten- und Wegerichblätter, die teilweise erst etwas überlappend angeordnet werden müssen, damit Du eine ausreichend große Fläche erhältst.

Nachdem Du in einer Grube genügend Glut erzeugt hast, vergräbst Du darin das Paket und bedeckst es mit heißer Asche und Glut. Der Fisch im »Blätterteig« bleibt darin etwa 15–20 Minuten, bis die äußeren Blätter verkohlt sind. Darin: krosse Haut und unglaublich saftiges Fleisch!

Tipp: *Solange noch unverkohlte Blätter vorhanden sind, kann der Fisch selbst nicht anbrennen.*

(1) Den küchenfertigen Fisch auf ein Bett von essbaren Blättern legen. (2) Damit das Fleisch saftig bleibt, wird auch die Bauchhöhle gefüllt. (3) Alles wird fest eingewickelt und verschnürt. (4) Das Paket kommt auf die Glut und wird mit Glut, heißer Asche und brennendem Reisig bedeckt.

KOCHEN MIT DEM HOBO-KOCHER

Mit einem Hobo-Kocher kann unterschiedliches Material sehr effizient verbrannt werden. Man neigt allerdings dazu, den Kamineffekt, wenn er nun schon mal vorhanden ist, voll auszunutzen. Das ist nicht immer sinnvoll. Anhand des folgenden Hobo-Rezepts für zwei Personen möchte ich die wichtigsten Techniken beim Kochen mit dem Hobo darstellen.

Pasta con Origano

Der Hobo-Kocher wird mit Reisig angefeuert und ein Topf mit ca. einem Liter Wasser aufgesetzt. Bis das Wasser kocht, kann ordentlich gefeuert werden – die Flamme sollte aber nicht stark rußen. Kocht das Wasser, werden ca. 80–100 Gramm Nudeln zugegeben (kleine Nudeln lassen sich übrigens besser portionieren). Immer wieder werden kleine Mengen von Holz zugeführt, so dass das Wasser ca. 10 bis 15 Minuten simmert. Nach dem Abgießen des Wassers belässt man nur noch die Glut, und es kommen mindestens 2 Esslöffel Olivenöl in den Topf mit den Nudeln, klein gehackte Zwiebeln sowie Blüten und zerkleinerte Blättchen des wilden Majoran *(Origanum vulgare)*, der auf vielen Wiesen Mitteleuropas wuchert.

Alles wird ca. 5 Minuten auf der noch im Hobo befindlichen Glut gewendet, bis die Nudeln angebraten, die Zwiebeln glasig sind.

(1) Der Hobo wird befeuert, (2) die Nudeln in kochendes Wasser gegeben. (3) Ist das Wasser abgekippt, wird alles 5 Minuten mit Olivenöl, (4) Zwiebeln und geschnittenem wildem Majoran gewendet.

Selbst gesammelte Gewürze machen das Kochen draußen zu einem Erlebnis.

Einfach draußen kochen mit dem Hobo

Gutes Essen ist draußen besonders wichtig. Es kann die Motivation heben und die Leistungsfähigkeit erhalten. Aber vor allem macht es Spaß! Dieses Buch zeigt Dir, wie Du mit dem Hobo für Dich und Deine Mitreisenden kochen kannst – mit einfachen, auch selbstgesammelten Zutaten, vor allem aber mit der richtigen »Strategie«.

Verlag pietsch, ISBN: 978-3-613-50851-4
ca. 192 Seiten, 19,95 EUR

WALD-
HANDWERK
KONKRET

FEUER

FEUER IST LEBEN

Das Feuer war schon immer ein wichtiger, wenn nicht sogar einer der wichtigsten Bestandteile der menschlichen Zivilisation. Ohne das Feuer wären wir heute nicht da, wo wir jetzt sind. Im Laufe der Jahrhunderte entwickelten die Menschen verschiedene Methoden, um ein Feuer zu entfachen. Diese Methoden haben sich bis heute bewährt und werden zum Teil immer noch angewandt. Einige dieser Methoden beschreibe ich in diesem Buch.

Ein Feuer hat seit jeher einen hohen psychologischen Wert. Es bietet Geborgenheit, Sicherheit, Licht und Wärme. Im dunklen Wald alleine zu stehen, ist keine schöne Vorstellung. An einem hellen, wärmenden Feuer zu sitzen, dagegen schon. Feuer kann Leben retten, aber auch alles zerstören. Denken wir nur an Hausbrände oder Brandrodungen, ob sie gewollt sind oder nicht. Sicherlich hatten die Menschen früher ein hohes Wissen darüber, welche Hölzer zum Feuermachen gut geeignet sind. Die Auswahl der richtigen Hölzer ist genauso wichtig wie die Technik des Feuermachens. Das setzt voraus, dass ich einige Bäume oder Sträucher richtig bestimmen kann.

In Zeiten des Feuerzeugs sind solche Kenntnisse nicht mehr selbstverständlich. Wenn sich ein Mensch der Natur wieder nähert, ist dies wie eine Zeitreise in die Vergangenheit, auf der unbewussten Suche nach den eigenen Wurzeln.

WICHTIGE GRUNDLAGEN

Als Bushcrafter haben wir natürlich ein besonderes Interesse daran, ein Feuer in freier Natur zu machen. Einerseits ist es ein schönes Gefühl, an einem wärmenden Feuer zu sitzen, hineinzusehen oder etwas zu kochen. Andererseits kann ich im Notfall mit einem Feuer Wasser abkochen, mich wärmen und habe Licht.

In unseren Zeiten, in denen offene Feuer selten geworden sind und eine Heizung den Ofen ersetzt, ist es wichtig, die Menschen wieder mit dem sicheren Umgang mit einem Feuer vertraut zu machen. Brandschäden entstehen nämlich meist durch Unkenntnis oder Leichtsinn.

Damit wir unser Hobby so gut wie möglich ausüben können, müssen wir Dinge wie das Feuermachen immer wieder üben. Dazu benötigen wir eine geeignete und sichere Feuerstelle. Einfach ein Feuer im Wald zu machen, ist in Deutschland grundsätzlich verboten. (Es gibt einige Ausnahmen: So dürfen z.B. Forstarbeiter oder Jäger unter bestimmten Bedingungen ein Feuer im Wald machen.)

Wer das Feuermachen üben möchte, kann sich nach Feuerstellen oder Grillplätzen in seiner Region erkundigen. Hier ist es ratsam, das zuständige Forstamt im Voraus zu fragen. Naturschutzgebiete sind im Bezug aufs Feuermachen natürlich ein absolutes Tabu. Und bei höchster Waldbrandstufe darf auf keinen Fall im Wald ein Feuer gemacht werden. Auch auf dem eigenen Grundstück kann man das Feuermachen gut üben. Bitte sprich es vorher mit Deinen Nachbarn und der zuständigen Behörde ab. Hier helfen auch die Feuerwehren. Ein Steinboden mit Feuerschale ist ideal zum Üben auf dem eigenen Grundstück. Stelle unbedingt sicher, dass immer genügend Löschmaterialien wie Wasser, Sand, Feuerlöscher oder Löschdecken vorhanden sind.

<u>**Ansonsten gilt:**</u> *Jede offene Flamme außer Zigaretten ist auf einen Abstand von 100 m vom Waldrand fernzuhalten. Weitere Tipps zur Feuerstelle findest Du im Kapitel »Was Du wissen musst«.*

ANZÜNDER UND HILFSMITTEL

Anzündhilfen liegen im Wald, Du musst sie nur erkennen und mitnehmen. Nutze Deinen Weg! Es hat sich bewährt, zwischendurch zu sammeln, was man findet, und nicht erst damit anzufangen, wenn der Lagerplatz erreicht ist. Das spart Zeit und Energie, weil ich ja nicht im Voraus weiß, ob ich an meinem Lagerplatz etwas Geeignetes finde.

Birkenrinde: Der beste Anzünder ist für mich die Birkenrinde, die auch bei nassem Wetter brennt. Birken sind in unseren Breiten sehr häufig und durch ihre weiße Rinden-Farbe leicht zu finden. Birken sind oft Erstbesiedler und sterben leicht ab. Wenn Du aufmerksam im Wald unterwegs bist, findest Du immer Birkenrinde, die am Boden liegt oder an toten Bäumen hängt. Obwohl sich der Baum mit ätherischen Ölen in der Rinde vor Pilzen und Bakterien schützt, ist er doch sehr anfällig für den Befall. Die Substanzen allerdings, die den Baum schützen sollen, lassen die Rinde recht einfach, gut und lange brennen. Also immer etwas trockene Birkenrinde in der Hosentasche haben. Aber denk dran: Bushcraft heißt auch, nicht die Bäume zu töten. Also zieh bitte keine Rinde von frischen Bäumen ab!

Zapfen und Harze: Ein weiteres gutes Hilfsmittel sind die mit Harz besetzten Zapfen von Nadelbäumen. Die wurden früher als Anzünder für das häusliche Feuer benutzt. Am besten funktionieren sie, wenn sie trocken vom Baum fallen, schön weit geöffnet sind und jede Menge Baumharz an ihnen klebt. Baumharz ist ein hervorragendes Brennmaterial. Eingewickelt in Blätter, lässt es sich leicht in einer Tasche verstauen und mitführen. Es dient nicht nur zur Brandbeschleunigung oder als Brandhilfe, es brennt sogar ohne andere Materialien. Du findest es an Nadelbäumen wie Kiefer, Fichte, Lärche. Wenn ein Nadelbaum irgendwo verletzt wird, schickt er Harz an diese Stelle, um sie zu schützen und zu heilen. Frisches Harz kannst Du direkt an kleine Äste oder Rindenstücke streichen. Je kleiner sie sind, desto besser.

<u>**Hinweis:**</u> *Wenn Du kleine **Harzbeulen**, ausgehärtetes Harz, am Baum findest, dann kannst Du diese absammeln und anzünden. Harz brennt auch bei Nässe.*

Feuerbaum/Featherstick: Mit einem Feuerbaum lässt sich ein Feuer gut anzünden. Such Dir unterwegs ein Stück Holz, etwa 20–25 cm lang. Achte dabei darauf, Totholz von Bäumen zu verwenden. Holz, das auf der Erde liegt, zieht Nässe an und ist meistens feucht. Im Baum kann das Holz durch die Luft gut trocknen. Die Rinde wird komplett entfernt. Ist es draußen feucht oder hat es gerade geregnet, musst Du die äußeren Holzschichten entfernen, bis Du an das trockene Innenholz kommst. An einer Seite machst Du eine Spitze, die später in die Erde gesteckt wird. Stell den Stock so hin, dass die Spitze nach oben zeigt. Dann schneidest Du mit Deinem Messer kleine längliche Späne in das Holz. Das erfordert etwas Übung. Die Späne sollten möglichst am Stock bleiben, d.h., Du musst das Messer wieder rausziehen, kurz bevor Du den Span abschneiden würdest. Dabei gilt: Je feiner die Späne sind, desto besser. Die feinen Späne bieten dem Feuer eine größere Angriffsfläche. Einen dicken Ast kann ich nicht entzünden. Aber wenn ich ihn ganz fein in hauchdünne Späne schneide, brennt er leichter an. Es lässt sich nicht vermeiden, dass ein paar Späne abfallen, sei es, weil ich zu tief geschnitten habe oder weil sie zu dünn sind. Diese Späne solltest Du auf jeden Fall aufheben und zum Anzünden benutzen. Beim Einschneiden musst Du von unten nach oben arbeiten. Dabei drehst Du den Stock und arbeitest Dich langsam bis zur Spitze. Wenn Du jetzt den Stock umdrehst, sieht das Ganze aus wie ein Tannenbaum.

Die Spitze des Feuerbaumes kommt in die Erde, und Du kannst vorsichtig kleines, dünnes Holz an den Baum lehnen. Unten angezündet, kriecht das Feuer von ganz alleine nach oben und vergrößert sich dabei. Das feine Holz, das am Feuerbaum lehnt, trocknet und entzündet sich leichter. Dabei kommt genügend Sauerstoff an das Feuer. Wer sich die Zeit nehmen möchte, kann auch mehrere kleine Feuerbäume ohne Spitze machen: Einfach trockene Äste von einem Baum nehmen, wieder die Rinde entfernen und auf zwei Seiten kleine Löckchen einkerben. Die können dann einfach mit auf das entstehende Feuer aufgelegt werden.

Zeitungsanzünder: Zu Hause kann man sich sehr einfach selber ein paar Anzünder basteln oder vorbereiten. Das Gute bei diesem Anzünder ist, dass er fast nur aus Dingen besteht, die sowieso in den meisten

Herstellung eines Feathersticks/Feuerbaums.

Feuerstelle mit Feuerbaum, *oben:* aufgebaut, *unten:* entfacht.

Hilfsmaterialien, um ein Feuer herzustellen: Birkenrinde *(oben links)*, Kiefernzapfen *(oben Mitte)*, Zeitungsanzünder, gerollt *(Mitte)*, Baumharz *(unten Mitte)*, Feuerbäume *(rechts)*.

Haushalten zur Verfügung stehen: eine alte Zeitung, ein paar Wachs- oder Kerzenreste und ein wenig Schnur. Öffne die Zeitung und leg sie auf den Boden, drei bis fünf Seiten übereinander. Jetzt nimmst Du die Kerzenreste und träufelst das Wachs auf das Papier, so wie Regentropfen auf Steine fallen, bis der Boden einigermaßen gleichmäßig gut bedeckt ist. Dann wird die Zeitung locker zusammengerollt. Nicht zu fest, sonst brennt sie nicht gut, aber auch nicht zu locker, sonst fällt das Wachs wieder raus. Am Ende solltest Du eine etwa 50 cm breite Rolle vor Dir liegen haben. Träufle etwas Wachs am Ende auf die Zeitung, so dass sie zusammenhält. Jetzt kannst Du mit einem Stift alle 5–8 cm einen Strich auf die Rolle machen und an diesen Stellen eine Schnur darum binden. Die Schnur ziehst Du schön fest, so dass sie sich nicht wieder löst. Du hast jetzt mehrere gleich große Stücke, die aber noch an der Rolle sind. Nun schneidest Du auf einer Unterlage mit einem scharfen Messer zwischen den Schnüren die Rolle durch. Die selbstgemachten Anzünder füllst Du in ein Glas, damit sie trocken bleiben. So beseitigst Du Deinen Müll, sparst Dir das Geld für Anzünder aus dem Supermarkt und kannst bei Bedarf einfach darauf zugreifen.

Trockene Äste und Planzen: An Nadelbäumen, insbesondere bei Fichten, gibt es immer kleines, abgestorbenes, trockenes Holz. Direkt am Stamm lassen sich im unteren Bereich die kleinen nadellosen Äste abknicken. Sie sind dünn und lassen sich leicht sammeln. Der Baum schützt diese Äste durch sein Nadeldach, dadurch sind sie fast immer trocken und brennbar. Im Herbst lassen sich auch trockene abgestorbene Pflanzen leicht entzünden. Beispielsweise eignen sich Knoblauchrauke, Distel und Brennnessel hervorragend dafür.

DIE VORBEREITUNG

Wie Du wohl schon bemerkt hast, ist Geduld und vor allem eine gute Vorbereitung ein sehr wichtiger Bestandteil des Feuermachens. Erst wenn ich alle Materialien zusammenhabe, fange ich an, ein Feuer zu machen. Manchmal haben wir nur einen Versuch, und der muss dann klappen. Zu einer guten Vorbereitung gehören:

- → *genügend Feuerholz (großes und mittleres Holz)*
- → *kleines Anzündholz (Zweige)*
- → *Zunder*
- → *Zundernest*
- → *Feuerbohrhölzer.*

Zu meinen Feuerbohrhölzern gehören:

- → *ein Bohrbrett*
- → *ein Bohrer oder Spindel*
- → *ein Druckstück*
- → *ein Bogen mit Schnur.*

DER ZUNDER

Zunder sind leicht brennbare Materialien, mit denen ich einen Funken oder eine Glut aufnehmen, sichern und vergrößern kann.

Natürlicher Zunder

Als pflanzliche Zunder haben sich besonders die Flugsamen verschiedenster Pflanzen bewährt, z.B. Löwenzahn, Distel, Rohrkolben, Waldrebe und das Weidenröschen. Bei den Bäumen sind es Pappel, Weide und Platane. Aber auch trockenes Moos oder das zerriebene Pulver von trockenen Flechten funktionieren. Das Pulver, das Borkenkäfer beim Fressen unter der Rinde eines Baumes hinterlassen, kann ebenfalls als Zunder dienen. Bei allen gilt: je trockener, desto besser.

Selbstgemachter Zunder

Seile und Schnur aus pflanzlichen Materialien: Ein guter Zunder aus pflanzlichen Fasern, den Du Dir selber herstellen kannst, besteht aus Seilen und Schnüren. Solche, die z.B. aus Hanf, Baumwolle oder Kokosfasern gedreht sind, kannst Du einfach wieder aufdrehen, so fein wie möglich zerreiben und zu einem festen Knäuel in Deiner Hand formen. Synthetische Fasern funktionieren nicht. Das kannst Du ganz leicht überprüfen: Wenn Du eine kleine Flamme, etwa vom Feuerzeug, an das synthetische Material hältst, brennt es nicht gut, sondern tropft und fließt zusammen. Zündest Du hingegen einen ausgefransten Strick aus Naturmaterialien an, brennt dieser oder glüht stark (wie ein Lampendocht ohne Öl).

Verkohlte Baumwolle, Hölzer und Pilze: Eine recht einfache Variante, sehr guten Zunder herzustellen, ist das Verkoken oder Verkohlen. Der Begriff Verkoken kommt aus der Kohlebranche und bedeutet, dass ein Stoff mehr oder minder unter Luftabschluss erhitzt und alle verbrannten Stoffe abgeführt werden. Was übrig bleibt, wird verwendet. In unserem Fall ist es die Baumwolle in verarbeiteter Form, wie sie in Kleidungsstücken zu finden ist.

Wichtig dabei ist, dass das Kleidungsstück aus 100 % Baumwolle besteht. Also wenn Du wieder mal eine alte Unterhose oder ein altes T-Shirt entsorgen musst, vergewissere Dich, dass es aus Baumwolle besteht. Dann kannst Du daraus sehr gut funktionierenden Zunder machen. Außerdem ist Baumwolle zum Beispiel auch in Mullbinden enthalten.

Eine alte Dose, die nicht groß sein muss, z.B. eine Dose für Lederfett zum Schuheputzen, sollte vorher gereinigt werden und innen sauber sein. Jetzt stößt Du ein kleines Loch in den Deckel, damit alles, was qualmt, entweichen kann, und legst ein Stück Stoff hinein.

Im Prinzip geht es darum, das Gewebe nicht brennen zu lassen. Siehst Du eine Flamme, die aus dem Loch kommt, muss diese sofort erstickt werden. Wenn es qualmt, ist es dagegen gut. Am besten die Dose nicht ins Feuer setzen, sondern in die Glut legen. Schau immer wieder mal hinein, wie es aussieht. Alles sollte schön schwarz sein. Ist es noch nicht verkohlt, drehst Du das Stück

Natürlicher Zunder: ***oben v.l.n.r.:*** **Pappelsamen, Moos, Platanensamen, Rohrkolben, Flechten;** ***unten v.l.n.r.:*** **Disteln, Löwenzahn, Waldrebe, Holzmehl.**

Stoff um und legst die geschlossene Dose wieder in die Glut. Das wiederholst Du, bis alles schwarz ist. Jetzt lässt Du alles abkühlen – fertig ist der Super-Zunder, auch Charcloth genannt.

Die gleiche Herstellungsmethode lässt sich auch auf andere natürliche Materialien übertragen, z.B. morsches, trockenes Holz oder Baumpilze. Die solltest Du vorher allerdings etwas klein schneiden.

Verkohlte Baumwolle (Charcloth) als selbstgemachter Zunder.

DAS ZUNDERNEST

Der Name Zundernest bezeichnet seine Form. Pflanzliche Materialien werden wie ein Nest geformt, dessen Funktion es ist, den Zunder aufzunehmen und in eine Flamme zu verwandeln. Es reicht, eine Vertiefung in die Mitte des Zundernests zu drücken, wo der Zunder mit Glut hineingelegt werden soll.

Gute pflanzliche Materialien sind Schilfgras, Klettenlabkraut, trockene Gräser oder trockener Lindenbast – alles, was wie Stroh oder Heu aussieht. Sind die Materialien zu starr, müssen sie zerrieben werden, bis Du lockere Fasern hast, die Du zu einem Nest formen kannst.

Es bedarf immer einer gewissen Entzündungstemperatur. Diese bekommst Du nur über die Glut. Je feuchter das Zundernest ist, desto mehr Zunderanteil/Glut brauchst Du. Denn je mehr Zunder Du hast, umso mehr Glut kannst Du anpusten und umso heißer wird alles. Dabei trocknen die Materialien im Zundernest besser und können sich so leichter entzünden.

Schilfgras und trockenes Gras als Zundernest bereitgestellt.

__*Tipp:*__ *Umschließe Dein Zundernest beim Anblasen mit kleinen Streifen von Birkenrinde. So verbrennst Du Dir nicht die Finger, und die Rinde brennt gleich mit an.*

DRUCKSTÜCK

Ein Druckstück hat zwei Funktionen: Zum einen kann ich damit Druck von oben auf die Bohrspindel geben, zum anderen halte ich meine Bohrspindel gerade und stabil. Beides sind sehr wichtige Komponenten beim Feuerbohren. Ein Druckstück sollte einigermaßen gut in der Hand liegen und nicht zu dünn sein. Ein gutes Druckstück kann z.B. aus Stein sein. Mit etwas Glück findest Du einen Stein mit einer Vertiefung in der Mitte, in der sich die Bohrspindel gut drehen kann. Hat der Stein auch eine glatte Oberfläche für die Hand, steht einem Bohrversuch nichts im Wege. Der Vorteil bei solchen Druckstücken ist, dass sie sich nicht weiter abnutzen und immer wieder verwendbar sind. Durch die geringe Abnutzung dreht sich die Bohrspindel leichter und schneller, und Du brauchst weniger Energie.

Aus diesem Grund habe ich mir etwas gebaut, was gerade für Anfänger sehr hilfreich ist. Dazu brauchst Du eine Dose und einen dickeren Ast. Bei dieser Variante kannst Du auch trockenes Holz nehmen. Den Ast umschließt Du mit der Hand. Schneide ihn hinter und vor Deiner Hand ab, so dass das Stück die Breite Deiner Faust hat. Mit einem geeigneten Werkzeug wird der Ast dann in zwei gleichgroße Hälften geteilt: Jetzt hast Du zwei Halbschalen, die sehr gut in Deine Hand passen. Auf der geraden Seite der Halbschalen machst Du eine Vertiefung, etwas größer als Deine Bohrspindel und ca. 5–7 mm tief. Schneide mit einer Blechschere ei-

Verschiedene Druckstücke, eingeklebtes Bierdosenblech *(o.r.)* und ausgehöhlter Stein *(u.r.)*.

nen kleinen runden Deckel aus Deiner Dose. Der Deckel wird vom Rand in Richtung Mitte etwas eingeschnitten. Jetzt kannst Du ihn in das Loch einpassen, wozu Du einen kleinen Hammer verwenden kannst. Ich habe meinen Blechdeckel noch mit Heißwachs eingeklebt. So ein Druckstück hält sehr lange und funktioniert sehr gut.

Willst Du das Druckstück draußen herstellen, kannst Du oft den Müll nutzen, der überall herumliegt. Schneide mit einem Messer etwas Blech aus einer Bierdose und kleb das Blech mit Baumharz fest in Dein Holz ein.

https://www.youtube.com/watch?v=Qyj9XlQz__o

Hast Du kein Blech zur Hand, dann tut es auch ein Holzstück nur mit einer Vertiefung, wie oben beschrieben. Deine Bohrspindel sollte sich darin leicht drehen können. Hinweis: Bei dieser Methode ist es wichtig, frisches Holz zu verwenden, weil die Reibungshitze am Druckstück sonst zu stark wird. Um die Reibung zwischen Druckstück und Spindel noch mehr zu verringern, kannst Du alles, was Du findest, in die Vertiefung am Druckstück schmieren, beispielsweise Pflanzenteile, Harz oder Fett. Es ist wichtig, dass am Druckstück so wenig wie möglich Reibung entsteht. Als Druckstück eignen sich alle Harthölzer wie z.B. Buche, Holunder, Eiche, Haselnuss oder Obstbäume wie Kirsche, Pflaume, Apfel, Birne.

DAS FEUERBOHR-HOLZ

Bohrbretter: Bohrbretter sind abgeflachte Hölzer, auf denen die Bohrspindel (Holzbohrer) sich dreht und Abrieb erzeugt. Die Bohrbretter machst Du etwa 2–3 cm dick. Nimm vorzugsweise ein Weichholz, z.B. Linde, Pappel, Weide oder Fichte. Ein Stock oder etwas dickerer Ast wird dazu auf zwei Seiten abgeflacht, so dass es aussieht wie ein kleines Brett. Dadurch verhinderst Du, dass das Holz kippelt, wenn Du Feuer bohrst. Des Weiteren hat das Abflachen den Vorteil, dass Du an die trockenen Schichten des Holzes herankommst. Nur trockenes Holz ist gutes Holz.

Bohrspindel: Die Bohrspindel oder der Bohrer ist ein 15–20 cm langes rundes Holz von etwa 1,5–2 cm Dicke. Der Bohrer ist vorzugsweise aus hartem Holz, z.B. Haselnuss oder Buche. Haselnuss hat den Vorteil, dass sie gerade wächst und Du so draußen einen fast fertigen Bohrer zur Verfügung hast.

Bogen: Um die Spindel schnell und gleichmäßig drehen zu können, wird ein Bogen benutzt. Als Bogen verwende ich einen Ast mit

Links: **Benutzte Bohrbretter mit Kerbe aus Lindenholz und Weide mit verschiedenen Bohrgrößen.**
Rechts: **Bohrspindeln, *v.l.n.r.:* Linde, Haselnuss und Fichte.**

Links: **Bohrbrett mit vorbereiteter Kerbe für den Abrieb.** *Rechts:* **Bohrbrett mit dazugelegtem Zunder sowie Blatt als Transportunterlage.**

Als nächstes sollte dunkles Pulver oder Holzabrieb aus der Vertiefung kommen. Bohrer und Bohrloch passen sich einander an.

Leg vorsichtig den Bogen mit Bohrer und das Druckstück zur Seite. Pass auf den Bogen auf, der steht noch unter Spannung und könnte sonst wegfliegen. Achte drauf, dass Dein Bohrer trocken bleibt. Es sollte jetzt ein schwarzes, gleichmäßiges Loch zu sehen sein.

Als nächstes machst Du mit dem Messer zwei Linien auf das Bohrbrett, so dass vom Brettrand eine Spitze bis in die Mitte des schwarzen Lochs zeigt. Durch das Anbohren kannst Du jetzt genau sehen, wo die Kerbe anzusetzen ist. Dieses Dreieck wird nun ausgeschnitzt. Dabei darf die Kerbe nicht zu groß, aber auch nicht zu klein gemacht werden. Ist sie zu klein, kommt nicht genug Abrieb hinein, ist sie zu groß, rutscht der Bohrer beim Bohren heraus, oder Du bohrst schief nach außen. Die Kerbe sollte bis fast in die Mitte gehen und sauber gearbeitet sein, damit der Abrieb leicht in die Kerbe rutschen kann. Je genauer Du arbeitest, desto besser wird Dein Ergebnis sein. Jetzt sollte ein Dreieck zu sehen sein, das fast bis in die Bohrmitte reicht.

Das Feuerbohren

Nun beginnt der eigentliche Bohrvorgang, und der Zunder kommt ins Spiel. Ich sichere mich gerne gut ab und lege als erstes ein größeres Blatt auf den Boden, wo mein Bohrbrett mit der eingeschnitzten Kerbe liegen soll. Jetzt nimmst Du den Zunder und formst ihn mit den Händen zu einem verfilzten Ball, damit die Glut sofort um sich greifen und wachsen kann. Die Glut braucht Angriffsfläche. Der Ball wird jetzt etwas auseinandergezogen und mit auf das Blatt gelegt, genau unter die eingeschnittene Kerbe. Nach außen kann der Zunder ruhig etwas hochstehen, das verhindert das Wegfließen

Der Bohrvorgang.

des Abriebs. Die Kerbe muss auf jeden Fall freibleiben. Vergewisser Dich, dass Dein Brett gut liegt. Der Bohrer kommt wieder in sein Bohrloch, und Du fängst an zu bohren. Nur diesmal etwas länger, bis genug Abrieb da ist. Achte am Anfang auf eine gleichmäßige Geschwindigkeit. Den Bogen, wie oben beschrieben, schön weit durchziehen und sobald etwas Rauch zu sehen ist, den Druck etwas erhöhen. Wenn sich die Kerbe mit Abrieb füllt, musst Du unbedingt dranbleiben – Du brauchst mindestens einen halben Teelöffel. Je mehr Rauch und Abrieb, desto höher die Geschwindigkeit und der Druck.

Bist Du fertig mit dem Bohren, dann kommt die nächste wichtige Sache. Das Bohrbrett muss absolut still stehen und darf nicht verwackeln. Der Abrieb ist in dieser Phase sehr sensibel, also alle Materialien sorgfältig und mit Ruhe weglegen. Mit einer Hand wird nun das Bohrbrett festgehalten und so vor dem Verwackeln gesichert. Jetzt erst darf der Fuß das Bohrbrett verlassen.

Oben: **Im Abrieb entsteht Glut. Der glühende Abrieb wird vorsichtig mit dem Messer gelöst aus der Kerbe und** ***unten:*** **auf den Zunder übertragen.**

Zunder wird durch gezieltes Pusten zum Glühen gebracht.

Nun gibt es zwei Möglichkeiten, eine Glut entstehen zu lassen: Entweder Du pustest ganz leicht, oder Du nimmst ein Hilfsmittel zum Luftzufächern. Unbedingt aufpassen, dass Du nicht zu stark pustest und alles umherfliegt. Es braucht also etwas Gefühl. Ist die Glut zu sehen, nimmst Du Dein Messer und löst vorsichtig den gesamten Abrieb mit der Glut vom Bohrbrett. Jetzt kannst Du das Bohrbrett wegnehmen, und da liegt Dein Gluthäufchen auf dem Zunder. Wenn Du gut vorbereitet bist, dann liegt griffbereit, aber so, dass es beim Feuerbohren nicht stört, Dein Zundernest.

Mit etwas Geschicklichkeit lässt sich die Glut in den Zunder einpacken und weiter anpusten. Wem das zu unsicher oder zu heiß ist, der kann das ganze Blatt aufheben und den Zunder im Blatt vorsichtig weiter zusammendrücken und anpusten.

Glimmt der Zunder und geht nicht mehr aus, legst Du alles ins Zundernest. Drück es ein wenig zusammen und heb es auf. Jetzt drückst Du die Außenseiten des Zundernests ein wenig nach innen und bläst in die Glut, die gut in der Mitte verstaut ist. Der Zunder darf auf keinen Fall so locker darinsitzen, dass er einfach rausgeblasen wird. Beim Anblasen des Feuers ist darauf zu achten, dass das Zundernest nach vorne und nach oben gehalten wird. Die Glut so lange anblasen, bis sich eine Flamme zeigt.

Brennt Dein Zundernest, dann dreh es vorsichtig hin und her, damit soviel Flamme wie möglich entsteht. Leg es vorsichtig

Der Zunder wird ins vorbereitete Zundernest gelegt und durch Anpusten zur Flamme gebracht.

an den Platz, wo Du Feuer machen willst, und fang an, kleinste Teile Holz (Fichtenreisig) oder schmale Streifen Birkenrinde anzulegen. Die Bohrspindel muss bei jeder Benutzung neu angespitzt werden. Auch das Bohrloch sollte bei jedem Bohrversuch neu gemacht werden. Gerade am Anfang hast Du beim Feuerbohren eine ungewohnte Körperhaltung und Bewegung. Halte durch, Du wirst Dich daran gewöhnen!

Eine für Rechtshänder geeignete Körperhaltung: linker Fuß vorne auf dem Bohrbrett und linkes Handgelenk vorne am linken Schienbein.

FEUERBOHREN ZU ZWEIT

Zu zweit könnt ihr intensiver und kraftsparender Feuer bohren. Eine Person hält den Bogen und das Druckstück mit Spindel, wie oben beschrieben. Die andere hält nur den Bogen. Der Bogen kann etwas länger sein, ca. 70–100 cm.

Das Ganze funktioniert auch ohne Bogen, nur mit einer Schnur: Deren Ende wird einmal um die Hand gewickelt und auf beiden Seiten straff gehalten. Damit der Bohrer nicht aus der Schnur fällt, muss die Schnur immer auf Spannung gehalten werden. Ihr könnt die Schnur auch zwei- oder drei Mal um den Bohrer wickeln. Dabei darf sie sich nicht überschneiden. Die Herausforderung bei dieser Variante ist wieder der gemeinsame Rhythmus. Jeder braucht nur zu ziehen. Habe ich gezogen, muss ich wieder locker lassen, damit der andere ziehen kann. Es darf aber nicht zu locker sein, sonst zieht der andere ins Leere. Spannung behalten und ziehen, Spannung behalten und ziehen.

***Oben:* Feuerbohren zu zweit mit Bogen bzw. *unten:* mit Schnur ohne Bogen.**

Wer die Schnur nicht um die Hand wickeln möchte, kann sich am Ende der Schnur einen kleinen Ast festbinden. So bekommt Ihr eine Art Griff.

DAS FEUERBOHREN MIT EINER DAUMENSCHLAUFE

Bei dieser Variante brauchst Du Dein Bohrbrett, eine Schnur und einen Bohrer. Dieser sollte länger und dünner sein als oben beschrieben. Hier bohre ich gerne mit Haselnuss oder Beifuß auf Linde. Die Bohrspindel sollte ca. 40 cm lang sein und eine Dicke von mindestens 1 cm haben. Unten wird sie stumpf angeschnitten, am oberen Ende machst Du eine Kerbe ins Holz, so dass Du eine Schnur darüberlegen kannst. Die Schnur bekommt zwei Schlaufen, die sich nicht zuziehen, auf jeder Seite eine. Sie müssen groß genug sein, dass Deine Daumen bequem hineinpassen. Die Schnur sollte eine Länge von etwa 40 cm haben. Deine Hände sollten etwa bis in die Mitte der Bohrspindel reichen.

Bei dieser Technik wirst Du sehr schnell merken, wie viel Kraftaufwand es braucht, um die Bohrspindel in Bewegung zu halten. Dein Bohrbrett bereitest Du wie oben beschrieben vor (Vertiefung, Anbohren, Kerbe, Feuerbohren). Dann legst Du die Schnur über die Kerbe am oberen Ende der Bohrspindel und lässt sie auf beiden Seiten gleich lang herunterhängen. Stell die Bohrspindel in die Vertiefung und leg die Daumen in die dafür vorgesehenen Schlaufen. Jetzt reibst Du Deine Hände rechts und links an der Bohrspindel hin und her. Mit den Daumen kannst Du leichten Druck von oben nach unten geben.

Hast Du keinen richtigen Grip, dann spuck in die Hände. Wenn es gar nicht geht, reib Deine Handflächen mit etwas Honig oder Harz ein. Nachteil an dieser Geschichte ist, dass danach alles an Deiner Hand klebenbleibt, also auch der Zunder oder die Glut. Es heißt aufpassen und vorsichtig arbeiten. Wie

Oben: **Fertige Schnur mit Daumenschlaufen.**
Unten: **Bohren mit Daumenschlaufe.**

beim Bogen auch, brauchst Du erst einmal jede Menge Reibung durch Drehbewegung und erst später etwas mehr Druck. Eine kleine Hilfe könnte hier noch sein, etwas Sand oder feinen Dreck ins Bohrloch zu geben. Das erhöht die Reibung am Anfang. Probier es aus. Weiter geht es wie beim Feuerbohren mit dem Bogen.

Vorsicht: *Hier können leicht Blasen an den Händen entstehen!*

DAS FEUERBOHREN MIT DEN HANDFLÄCHEN

Diese Methode, ein Feuer zu bohren, dürfte vielen aus dem Fernsehen oder aus Büchern bekannt sein. Ein dünner Holzstab wird zwischen den Handflächen sehr schnell hin und her gedreht, bis eine Glut entsteht. Diese Methode ist für Anfänger nicht geeignet, weil hier der Kraftaufwand viel zu groß ist und das draußen zu findende Holz nicht die gewünschte Trockenheit besitzt. Am besten bereitest Du zu Hause ein kleines Bohrset vor und nimmst dieses mit auf Tour. Im Herbst, wenn die Pflanzen sich zurückziehen und nicht mehr grün sind, ernte ich zum Beispiel Distelpflanzen und Beifuß. Diese trockne ich über den Winter. So bekomme ich viele Bohrspindeln, mit denen ich Feuer bohren kann. Schneide die gesamte Pflanze ab und entferne alles, was vom Stiel absteht. Diese Bohrer bewahrst Du an einem trockenen Platz auf. Achte darauf, das die Stiele gerade sind. So sammeln sich im Laufe der Zeit immer wieder neue Hölzer an, mit denen Du experimentieren kannst.

Da Dir hier weder Bogen noch Daumenschlaufe zur Verfügung stehen, musst Du die Reibung und den Druck mit Deinen Händen entstehen lassen: Hast Du eine Vertiefung in das Bohrbrett gemacht, setzt Du den Bohrer auf und versetzt ihn mit Deinen Handflächen in Drehung. Weil der Druck nur von oben kommen kann, fängst Du oben an und arbeitest Dich mit den Handflächen nach unten. Hier braucht es etwas Durchhaltevermögen. Und gerade am Anfang sind Blasen an der Hand garantiert.

Wichtig bei dieser Methode ist, dass die Bohrspindel nicht aus dem Loch gehoben wird. Bist Du mit den Händen unten an der Bohrspindel angelangt, dann halte mit einer Hand die Bohrspindel fest und setz die andere Hand wieder nach oben. Jetzt fängst Du wieder an, nach unten zu drehen – so lange bis Du das Loch gut angebohrt hast. Danach machst Du wieder die Kerbe und legst Deinen Zunder zurecht.

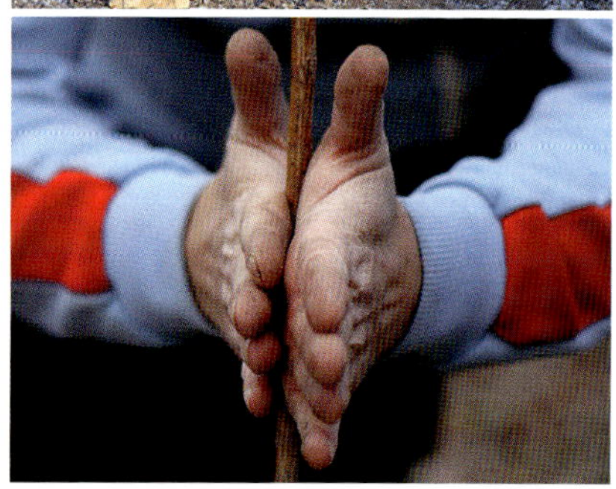

***Oben:* Feuerbohren mit den Handflächen.**
***Unten:* Die Bohrspindel wird durch das schnelle Hin- und Herbewegen der Handflächen in Rotation versetzt.**

Diese Variante geht besser, wenn Ihr zu zweit seid. Einer reibt, bis er unten an der Bohrspindel angekommen ist, und der andere übernimmt oben den Bohrer, immer in Abwechslung von oben nach unten. Dabei immer aufpassen, dass der Bohrer nicht aus dem Bohrloch hüpft: Der, der unten ist, hält den Bohrer so lange, bis der oben ihn sicher übernommen hat, dann erst wird weitergebohrt. Das spart jede Menge Kraft.

Beim Feuerbohren zu zweit löst man sich gegenseitig ab. Ist einer am Boden angekommen, fängt der andere oben wieder an.

DAS FEUERSCHLAGEN MIT EISEN AUF STEIN

Bei dieser Methode geht es darum, durch Zusammenschlagen zweier Gegenstände einen Funken zu erzeugen und ihn auf einen geeigneten Zunder festzusetzen. Dazu brauchst Du ein Eisen und einen Stein. Das Eisen muss hoch kohlenstoffhaltig sein. Je höher der Kohlenstoffanteil im Eisen ist, desto bessere Funken werden entstehen. Das kannst Du an einer Schleifmaschine testen: Wenn Du das Eisen an einen drehenden Schleifstein hältst und er viele Funken macht, ist mit Sicherheit viel Kohlenstoff drin. Sind dagegen nur wenige Funken zu sehen, ist das Eisen für unsere Zwecke ungeeignet. Ich benutze oft alten Werkzeugstahl, z.B. alte Feilen. Neue hochwertige legierte Stähle funktionieren sehr schlecht bis gar nicht. Wenn Du einen Schmied kennst, lass Dir einen Feuerschläger schmieden. Dann hast Du zusammen mit der Zunderdose, wo Dein verkohlter Baumwollzunder drin ist, schon eine gute Ausgangsposition, um draußen ein Feuer zu machen. Der persönliche Feuerschläger sollte auf Deine Handgröße angepasst sein.

Als Stein verwende ich Feuerstein (Flintstein/Silex). Diese Steine findet man häufig im Norden, weil sie mit der Eiszeit aus Skandinavien gekommen sind. Aber auch hier in der Mitte von Deutschland finde ich immer wieder mal einen. Hast Du keinen Feuerstein zur Hand, kannst Du als Alternative auch einen weißen Feldstein nehmen. Such Dir einen Stein mit einer scharfen Kante oder schlag mit einem anderen Stein ein Stück ab, bis Du eine scharfe Kante hast. Leg den Zunder oben auf den Stein, kurz hinter die scharfe Kante, und halte ihn mit dem Daumen fest. In der anderen Hand ist Dein Feuerschläger oder die alte Feile. Halt den Stein mit der scharfen Kante leicht nach unten oder nach vorne gekippt. So kann der Funke, der nach oben will, besser auf den Baumwollzunder fallen. Jetzt ziehst Du das

Obere Reihe v.l.n.r.: **Alte Werkzeugfeile, geschmiedete Schlageisen, Baumwollzunder (Charcloth).**
Untere Reihe v.l.n.r.: **Feldstein/Kiesel, brauner Feuerstein, Feuerstein (Flint/Silex).**

Eisen über die scharfe Kante des Steins. Dabei schlägst Du nicht auf den Stein ein, sondern ziehst mit hoher Geschwindigkeit die ganze Seite des Eisens an der scharfen Kante des Steines entlang.

Hat der Funke sich einmal im Baumwollzunder festgesetzt, kannst Du ihn durch Pusten vergrößern und in Dein vorgefertigtes Zundernest legen. Das Zundernest anblasen und wie weiter oben beschrieben das Feuer entfachen.
Tipp: *Eine weitere Möglichkeit ist es, trockene Birkenrinde zu sammeln und mit einem Messer die feinen Oberschichten abzukratzen oder abzuschaben und in einem anderen Stück Birkenrinde zu sammeln. Nimm ein großes Stück Baumwollzunder und schlag einen Funken rein. Dann nimmst Du den glühenden Zunder und legst ihn auf den abgekratzten Rindenhaufen. Schlag die Birkenrinde, auf der alles liegt, nach oben zusammen; die weiße Außenrinde sollte hier jetzt innen sein. So kannst Du von zwei Seiten reinpusten, bis eine Flamme entsteht.*

Oben: **Abziehen des Schlageisens an der Steinkante.**
Unten: **Festsetzen des Funkens in Baumwollzunder.**

DAS FEUERROLLEN MIT BAUMWOLLE

Noch eine Möglichkeit, ein Feuer zu machen, ist, Baumwolle zu rollen. Baumwolle ist gutes Zundermaterial, das Du in Form von Wattepads, Tampons oder Ohrenstäbchen verwenden kannst. Achte darauf, dass es wirklich 100 % Baumwolle ist. Tampons auf Tour mitzunehmen, ist nie verkehrt, weil Du so immer gut eingepackten, vor Feuchtigkeit geschützten Zunder hast. Kommst Du an einer benutzten Feuerstelle vorbei, nimm etwas weiße Asche und einen kleinen Klumpen Holzkohle mit. Nimm am besten zwei Tampons aus ihrer Verpackung und reiß sie auseinander – so klein wie möglich. Breite die Fetzen zu einer Fläche aus und streu die weiße Asche darauf. Zerreib die Holzkohle und streu sie mit auf die Asche.

Jetzt wickelst Du alles richtig straff zusammen, so dass eine kleine Rolle entsteht, etwa wie eine Zigarette. Leg die Rolle auf einen festen, trockenen, möglichst glatten Untergrund, z.B. einen Betonfußboden, einen dicken Baumstumpf oder einen Tisch. Leg ein nicht mehr als 50 cm langes Brett auf die Rolle und beweg es vor und zurück. Mit Druck von oben auf das Brett und Geschwindigkeit beim Vor- und Zurückbewegen entsteht in

100% Baumwolle: Tampons.

der Rolle so viel Hitze, dass Du innerhalb einer Minute eine Glut hast. Bei zu viel Druck zerreibst Du die Rolle, und es bleibt nichts mehr übrig. Bei zu wenig Druck reicht die Reibung für eine Glut nicht aus. Ist die Rolle klein und schwarz, kannst Du sie aufbrechen. Mit etwas Glück raucht es jetzt. Puste an die Stelle, wo der Rauch aufsteigt, und Du hast eine Glut, die Du weiterverarbeiten kannst und zu einem erfolgreichen Feuer bringst.

Weitere Tipps und mehr über mich und meine Arbeit erfahrt Ihr auf meiner Website. *http://www.natur-instinkte.de/*

Baumwolle und Asche werden unter Druck gerollt, bis Glut entsteht.

LAGER UND UNTERSTÄNDE

WIE FUNKTIONIERT'S?

Um zu verstehen, wie man einen Unterstand am besten baut und benutzt, müssen wir zuerst seine Funktion verstehen. Er sollte so komfortabel sein, dass wir – egal wie die äußeren Bedingungen sind – acht Stunden schlafen können. So muss der Unterstand unserem Körper Schutz vor den wichtigsten Möglichkeiten des Wärmeverlustes bieten und auch als Polster dienen. Dazu sollte er möglichst ansprechend aussehen, und im besten Fall kann man ihn auch noch beheizen oder kühlen.

Machen wir uns zunächst die fünf Möglichkeiten bewusst, wie unser Körper Wärme verliert:

1. ***Konvektion:*** *Wenn Luft oder Wasser am Körper vorbeifließen, entziehen sie ihm Wärme. Daher kann man auch an einem warmen, sonnigen Tag frieren, wenn man einer Brise ausgesetzt ist. Das ist auch der Grund, warum ein Ventilator im Sommer kühlt. Die Wirkung der Konvektion ist so stark, dass die Haut durch die Kälte verletzt werden kann, auch wenn die Temperaturen über dem Gefrierpunkt liegen. Dieser Effekt wird »Windchill«-Effekt genannt. (Beispielsweise bringt bei –5 °C ein Wind von 20 km/h die Temperatur auf –16 °C. Und 20 km/h ist eine leichte Brise!) Konvektion nimmt dem nackten Körper mehr als 2100 Watt Wärme. Ein normaler menschlicher Körper muss fast am Leistungsmaximum arbeiten, nur um 300 Watt zu erzeugen; im Ruhezustand produziert er nur 80 Watt. Jetzt siehst Du, warum es so wichtig ist, Dich vor dem Wind zu schützen. Windschutz ist beim Thema Unterstand der wichtigste Aspekt und ebenso der größte Nutzen, den eine Rettungsdecke bietet. (Auf die richtige Verwendung einer Rettungsdecke komme ich weiter unten noch zu sprechen)*

Windchill bei tiefen Temperaturen und mäßigen Windgeschwindigkeiten

Zustand	**0°C**	**-5°C**	**-10°C**	**-15°C**	**-20°C**
Windgeschwindigkeit	*Vergleichbare Auskühlung wie etwa bei diesen Temperaturen*				
10 km/h	**-6°C**	**-7°C**	**-12°C**	**-19°C**	**-26°C**
20 km/h	**-11°C**	**-16°C**	**-20°C**	**-26°C**	**-32°C**
30 km/h	**-16°C**	**-20°C**	**-27°C**	**-36°C**	**-45°C**
40 km/h	**-18°C**	**-22°C**	**-30°C**	**-38°C**	**-47°C**
50 km/h	**-19°C**	**-24°C**	**-32°C**	**-41°C**	**-49°C**

(Quelle: Johannes Vogel, Outdoor-Survival nur mit dem Messer)

*2. **Konduktion:** Wenn sich ein Gegenstand in direktem Kontakt mit einem anderen Gegenstand befindet, der kälter ist als er selbst, dann gibt er Wärme an den kälteren ab. Deshalb schmerzt es, wenn man im Winter kaltes Metall in den Händen hält, und deshalb bekommst Du kalte Füße, wenn Du im Winter herumstehst. Um diese Art des Abkühlens zu vermeiden, müssen wir zwischen unserem Körper und dem kalten Gegenstand eine Distanz aufbauen. In der Praxis spürst Du diesen Effekt, wenn Du auf einer Matte statt auf dem kalten Boden sitzt oder wenn Du warme Einlegesohlen in Deine Schuhe legst. Wenn wir ein Hochbett bauen oder uns auf andere Weise vom Boden entfernen, dann bekämpfen wir die Auswirkung der Wärmeleitung. Aufgrund der Konduktion ist es auch so wichtig, bei sehr kaltem Wetter Schuhe mit einer dicken Sohle zu tragen oder Dir eine Schicht Zweige unter die Füße zu legen, wenn Du am Feuer sitzt. Direkter Kontakt mit Wasser bewirkt, dass wir 25 Mal schneller Wärme verlieren als im direkten Kontakt mit kalter Luft.*

*3. **Strahlung:** Körper erzeugen Wärme, die sie in Form von Infrarot-Strahlung abgeben. Diese Wärme kann man bei einem Feuer, einer Infrarotlampe oder in der Sauna fühlen. Dies ist auch die Wärme der Sonne. Ein nackter Körper gibt mehr als die Hälfte der erzeugten Wärme durch Strahlung an die Umgebung ab. Die gute Nachricht ist: Diese Art des Wärmeverlusts kannst Du sehr einfach bekämpfen, indem Du gut isolierende Kleidung trägst. Infrarotstrahlung verhält sich ähnlich wie Licht, und ebenso wie Licht kann sie auch reflektiert werden. Davon können wir profitieren, wenn wir eine Rettungsdecke hinter unserem Rücken verwenden, um die Infrarotstrahlung eines Lagerfeuers zu reflektieren. Dies ist besonders wirkungsvoll bei einem Unterstand vom Typ »Gewächshaus«. (Diese Art von Schutz behandle ich weiter unten.)*

*4. **Verdunsten:** Wenn Wasser verdunstet, entzieht es Energie. So funktioniert das Schwitzen, um uns zu kühlen. Das heißt aber auch, dass Schwitzen bei kaltem Wetter gefährlich sein kann: Je mehr Wasser auf unserer Haut verdunstet, desto mehr Wärme verlieren wir. Auch wenn die körperliche Tätigkeit uns im Augenblick warmhält – sobald wir aufhören, uns zu bewegen, wird uns sehr kalt. Schon mal an einem warmen Tag auf einem windigen Gipfel gestanden? Das, was Du fühlst, sind die Wirkungen von Verdunstung und Wärmeleitung. Ein Liter Schweiß, den man innerhalb einer Stunde körperlicher Anstrengung leicht verliert, verbraucht 600 Kalorien; zusätzlich zu den Kalorien, die wir durch den Sport verlieren. Diese Kalorien stehen Dir nachts zum Warmhalten nicht mehr zur Verfügung.*

*5. **Respiration:** Wir verlieren auch Wärme über die Atmung. Egal wie viele warme Kleidungsstücke wir tragen, wir atmen kalte Luft in das Zentrum unseres Körpers: unsere Lungen. Auch wenn diese Art von Wärmeverlust nicht so drastisch ist wie die anderen erwähnten Arten, lohnt sich die Verwendung eines dünnen Schals zum Vorwärmen der Luft, die wir einatmen – besonders nachts.*

Wärmedieb Wasser

Ist Dir aufgefallen, wie oft Wasser erwähnt wurde?

Egal ob Du Wärme durch Konvektion, Konduktion oder Verdunstung verlierst: Der Wärmeverlust wird um das Vielfache gesteigert, wenn Du nass bist! Daher ist feuchtes, windiges Wetter so viel anstrengender für den Körper als trockenes, ruhiges Wetter.

Die meisten Todesfälle aufgrund von Unterkühlung passieren bei +5 bis –5 °C bei nassem, windigem Wetter!

Kalte Luft bewegt sich bergabwärts, daher solltest Du Täler und Seeufer in den Bergen vermeiden. Gipfel und Bergkämme sind dem Wind (Konvektion) sehr ausgesetzt, daher sollten auch diese vermieden werden. Der beste Standort ist 1/3 bergauf.

→ **Sicherheit ist das Wichtigste:** *Prüfe immer, ob nachts von oben, unten oder um Dich herum tote Äste auf Dich fallen können. Mach Dich auch auf die Suche nach offensichtlichen Wasserabläufen und Wildspuren. Nichts kann die Nachtruhe so sehr stören wie eine Herde Wildschweine, die durch das Camp stürmen, weil ihre Autobahn gesperrt wurde.*

→ **Schutz vor Wind und Regen:** *Wähle einen Standort, der viel Schutz vor Wind bietet. Felsen, Wände und natürliche Gegebenheiten im Gelände können hilfreich sein. Halte Ausschau nach einem großen Baum und baue Deinen Unterstand in Windrichtung. Dichte Vegetation kann einen guten Schutz selbst vor starkem Regen und Schnee bieten. Man kann auch direkt in die Zweige einer dichten Kiefer klettern.*

→ **Ressourcen:** *Schau Dich um, ob genug Totholz für das Feuer und Baumaterialien vorhanden sind. Bitte keine lebenden Bäume fällen – dies solltest Du wirklich nur im äußersten Notfall machen! Halte Ausschau nach Blättern auf dem Boden, Kiefernzweigen, Efeu und natürlich einer sicheren Wasserquelle.*

Die Verwendung von Feuer und das Aufwärmen

Denk dran, dass eine Isolierung nur den Wärmeverlust verlangsamen kann. Wenn Du ein Feuer bei Deinem Unterstand betreibst, dann sollte es nur einen guten Schritt vom Eingang entfernt sein.

Der Nachteil eines Feuers ist, dass man es in Gang halten muss. Du solltest erwägen, einige Steine in Feuernähe aufzuwärmen und sie mit in den Unterschlupf zu nehmen, ähnlich wie in einer Sauna oder Schwitzhütte. Diese können bis zu 6 Stunden eine gute, starke Wärme abgeben. Allerdings solltest Du das nur machen, wenn Du die Nacht über »durchheizen« kannst – bist Du durch Kondens feucht, wird es sonst sehr kalt.

Eine im Sturm abgebrochene Baumkrone. Wenn so etwas auf Dich stürzt, sieht es nicht gut aus.

(Quelle: Johannes Vogel, Outdoor-Survival nur mit dem Messer)

Seil und Gummizüge

Für die meisten Unterstände braucht man irgendeine Art von Schnur oder Leine. Ich empfehle, immer fünf mal 2 m einer 4-mm-Leine, 10 m eines 5 mm dicken Seils sowie einige Stückchen dünnere Leine dabei zu haben. Es ist sehr praktisch, ein oder zwei Schlaufen Gummiseil zu haben, damit beispielsweise ein Tarp straff abgespannt werden kann, ohne dass die Aufhängepunkte durch plötzliche Windböen zerrissen werden.

Tarps

Ein Tarp ist der zweitwichtigste Ausrüstungsgegenstand eines Bushcrafters - nach dem Messer. Tarps gibt es in allen möglichen Formen und Größen, Unterschiede gibt es im Material und in der Anzahl und Art der Ösen. Poncho-Tarps werden im Wesentlichen auf die gleiche Weise verwendet. Ich benutze ein Tarp der Größe 3 x 3 Meter, aber ich zeige Dir auch Unterstände, die mit jeder Größe von Tarp gebaut werden können.

→ *Viele Tarp-Unterstände können in Verbindung mit einem kleinen Feuer eingesetzt werden (Flammen nicht höher als Kniehöhe). Aber achte immer darauf, dass das Feuer einen guten Schritt von der Vorderseite der Plane entfernt ist. Geh davon aus, dass alle Tarps brennbar sind.*

→ *Wenn Deine Plane keine Ösen oder Schlaufen an der richtigen Stelle hat – kein Problem! Binde einfach einen kleinen glatten Kiesel in den Stoff, damit das Tarp macht, was Du willst. Ich wende diese Methode bei all meinen Silnylon-Tarps an, weil sie einfach furchtbar schwierig zu nähen sind und ich vorher nie genau weiß, welche Konfiguration ich verwenden werde.*

→ *Du kannst auch Dreibeine statt Stangen mit Abspannleinen und Pfählen verwenden. Das macht mehr Arbeit, aber das Ergebnis ist ein viel sicherer Unterstand.*

→ *Wenn Du Angst hast, dass Stangen herausrutschen könnten, kannst Du diese mit zusätzlichen Stangen sichern oder eine Leine zu einer zweiten Stange zurückführen. Nimm dazu Felsen, Bäume, Baumstämme – alles, was Du finden kannst.*

Besonders wenn es stark stürmt, sind Gummizüge hilfreich beim Errichten eines Lagers.

(Quelle: Johannes Vogel, DMAX Survival-Guide für echte Kerle)

Du brauchst:

- → *Tarp*
- → *Seil, ca. 4 m*
- → *4 Pfosten*
- → *2 Bäume oder Stangen (Wanderstöcke oder Äste).*

Zeitaufwand:
5–10 min.

So gehst Du vor:
Ein Seil zwischen zwei 3–4 m entfernt stehende Bäumen oder Stangen spannen (abhängig von der Größe des Tarps). Spann das Seil etwa auf Taillenhöhe – wenn Du mehr Platz und eine bessere Aussicht willst, kannst Du es etwas höher spannen; wenn Du Dir Sorgen um das Wetter machst und mehr Schutz brauchst, dann niedriger.

Leg das Tarp über das Seil, so dass die Mitte der Plane über dem Seil hängt. Die Ecken abspannen. Fertig!

Tipp: *Die Wände zum besseren Schutz vor der Witterung tiefer bzw. für bessere Aussicht und Belüftung höher abspannen. Steilere Wände verkleinern die Bodenfläche, aber Regen und Schmelzwasser fließen besser ab. Du kannst auch einen Gummi-Zug zum Straffen des Tarps verwenden.*

Lean-to Shelter: klassischer Wind- und Regenschutz mit perfekter Aussicht
Die meisten Leute, die an einen Tarp-Unterstand denken, denken an diesen Schrägdach-Unterschlupf. Dies ist eine sehr einfache und nützliche Konstruktion, wenn man Schutz vor Wind und Sonne benötigt, aber auch viel Kontakt mit der Natur und natürlich eine tolle Aussicht haben will! Funktioniert super mit einem langen, schmalen Feuer. Bau das Feuer einen großen Schritt weit entfernt von der Vorderseite des Tarps. Mit einem Lean-to kannst Du auch einen idealen Windschutz für Deinen Rücken aufbauen. Deine Wanderstöcke und ein Poncho oder eine Rettungsdecke sind alles, was Du dafür brauchst.

Funktion	Eignung
Wetterschutz	*
Grundfläche	***
Platz/Sicht	***
einfacher Aufbau	***
mit einfachen Werkzeugen	***
Verwendung mit Feuer	***

Du brauchst:

- → *Tarp*
- → *Seil, ca. 4 m*
- → *4 Stangen*
- → *2 Bäume oder Stangen (Wanderstöcke oder Äste).*

Zeitaufwand:
5 min.

So gehst Du vor:
Der Aufbau funktioniert genau wie bei einem klassischen A-Frame, nur dass eine Seite offen bleibt: Ein Seil zwischen zwei 3–4 m entfernt stehenden Bäume oder Stangen spannen (abhängig von der Größe des Tarps), maximal in Brusthöhe. Der Winkel sollte etwa 30 Grad betragen. Wenn Du Deine Hand entspannst und der Daumen auf den Boden zeigt, bilden Deine Finger den korrekten Winkel. Experimentiere ruhig ein bisschen!

Tipp: *Bau Dir einen klassischen A-Frame und schlag eine der Wände zurück. So hast Du die gute Belüftung und gute Aussicht eines Lean-to, aber wenn sich das Wetter verschlechtert, kannst Du Dich schnell und einfach schützen. So mache ich's im Gebirge, wenn ich die Sterne genießen, mich aber gleichzeitig vor schnellen und heftigen Wetteränderungen schützen will.*

»Flying V«: das Raumwunder

Das Flying V ist ein sehr solider, einfach aufbaubarer und wetterfester Unterstand, der immer noch einen guten Kontakt zur Natur bietet. Er ist sehr einfach aufzubauen und bietet auch guten Schutz für die Ausrüstung. Wenn Du keinen Fußboden brauchst, können leicht 2 Personen darin Platz finden.

Er bietet Dir Allround-Schutz, weist Regen und Schnee ab und kann auch so aufgebaut werden, dass Du einen geschützten Bodenbereich hast.

Funktion	Eignung
Wetterschutz	***
Grundfläche	**
Platz/Sicht	*
einfacher Aufbau	**
mit einfachen Werkzeugen	***
Verwendung mit Feuer	**

Du brauchst:

→ *Tarp*

→ *Baum oder sonstige Stütze, z.B. Wanderstock oder Zweig*

→ *ein Seil, im Idealfall einen starken, elastischen Gummi-Zug*

→ *3–4 Stangen.*

Zeitaufwand:

5–15 min.

So gehst Du vor:

Befestige die Ecke eines Tarps auf Brusthöhe an einem Baum. Dann befestigst Du die gegenüberliegende Ecke und Seiten. Fertig! Abhängig vom erwarteten Wetter kannst Du das Dach steiler oder flacher gestalten.

Tipp: *Die Öffnung sollte in Richtung eines großen Baums oder eines anderen Windschutzes liegen, um den Witterungsschutz zu optimieren. Oder Du schlägst wie beim klassischen A-Frame eine Wand für eine bessere Aussicht zurück. Wenn kein benutzbarer Baum vorhanden ist, kannst Du ein Dreibein verwenden.*

Variante:

Schlag die Seiten nach innen ein, so dass ein Boden entsteht; dann hast Du ein Biwak-Tarp! Mit Blättern oder anderem Material vollstopfen, und Du kannst reinkriechen und warm bleiben.

Debris Hut: Unterstand aus Waldstreu

Wenn Du in einer Gegend mit vielen Bäumen und Waldstreu auf dem Boden lebst, dann solltest Du lernen und üben, diese Laubhütte zu bauen. Dieser Unterstand bringt Dich durch einen Sturm, auch wenn Du kein Werkzeug, keine Plane, keinen warmen Mantel und kein Feuer hast. Der Bau erfordert jedoch einige Anstrengung. Je kälter es ist, desto dicker muss das Dach sein – für ein vollständig wasserdichtes Dach bei kaltem, windigem Wetter müssen die Wände und das Dach so dick sein wie Dein Arm lang ist. Dies bedeutet, dass Du voraussichtlich ca. 3–4 Stunden Material sammeln musst. Die Debris Hut funktioniert wie ein riesiger wasserdichter Schlafsack.

Unauffällig: Die Debris Hut ist eine echte Dackelgarage.

Funktion	Eignung
Wetterschutz	***
Grundfläche	*
Platz/Sicht	*
einfacher Aufbau	**
mit einfachen Werkzeugen	***
Verwendung mit Feuer	**

Das Wichtigste:

→ *Klein bauen – je weniger Luft Du mit Deiner Körperwärme anwärmen musst, desto wärmer hast Du es.*

→ *Dick auftragen – im Winter muss die Isolierschicht so dick sein, wie Dein Arm lang ist.*

→ *Dicht stopfen – stopf den Unterstand mit Waldstreu voll. Leg Dich hinein, um die Streu zu komprimieren. Dann erneut stopfen. Und nochmal! Es lohnt sich.*

Du brauchst:

→ *Äste*

→ *Blätter/Waldstreu*

→ *Seil (optional)*

→ *Tarp (optional).*

Zeitaufwand:
90 Minuten mit einer Plane oder anderen Abdeckung. 2–4 Stunden, wenn Du ein wasserdichtes Dach brauchst und nur natürliche Materialien zur Verfügung hast.

So gehst Du vor:
Du baust ein Trapper-Bett **(1)** und einen stabilen A-Frame **(2)**. Dann gibst Du viel Waldstreu hinein **(3)**. Schließlich deckst Du den Unterstand mit Streu **(4a)** und, falls vorhanden, einem Tarp **(4b)** ab.

<u>***Tipp:***</u> *Mach diesen Unterstand kleiner, als Du zunächst denkst, und stopfe ihn so richtig voll. Es darf kein freier Raum bleiben. In diesen Unterstand kriechst Du hinein wie in einen Schlafsack.*

Mors Kochanskis Super Shelter: ein arktisches Gewächshaus

Der Super Shelter ist durch Mors Kochanski bekannt geworden und wurde auch vom »Survival-Duo« Dave Canterbury und Cody Lundin in der entsprechenden Discovery-Serie eingesetzt.

Er funktioniert nach dem Gewächshausprinzip: Die Wärme eines Feuers wird in einer Kunststoff-Blase eingefangen. Eine Rettungsdecke an der Rückseite des Unterstands wird benutzt, um die Infrarotstrahlung des Feuers auf den Rücken des Benutzers zu reflektieren. Dies ist ein sehr warmer Unterstand, der sogar allein durch Körperwärme beheizt werden kann. Er ist ideal auch zum Einfangen von Sonnenwärme.

Der Super Shelter ist ein vollständiger Wetter- und Langzeit-Überlebensschutz, der ausreichend Komfort bietet, um bei kaltem Wetter richtig zu schlafen. Die Innentemperaturen steigen schnell, so dass sich eine Person in normaler Kleidung bei Außentemperaturen von –30 °C wohlfühlen kann.

Funktion	Eignung
Wetterschutz	***
Grundfläche	*
Platz/Sicht	*
einfacher Aufbau	**
mit einfachen Werkzeugen	***
Verwendung mit Feuer	***

Du brauchst:

- → *durchsichtige Baufolie/Malerabdeckplane – Größe etwa 4 x 4 m*
- → *Mylar-Rettungsdecke*
- → *Tauwerk, um Struktur zum Anlehnen zu bauen*
- → *optional: hochwertige Rettungsdecke/Tarp – dadurch wird der Aufbau zwar beschleunigt, aber es bedeutet auch mehr Gewicht und Volumen im Rucksack.*

Treibhausgewächs: Auch bei sehr niedrigen Temperaturen wird es Dir darin warm!

Zeitaufwand:
15–45 Minuten; je nachdem, welche Materialien mitgeführt werden.

So gehst Du vor:
Die schnelle Art: Eine Leine zwischen zwei Bäumen stramm spannen. Einen Schrägdach-Unterstand aus einer Plane oder Rettungsdecke bauen. Die Rettungsdecke am hinteren Teil des Unterstands befestigen, damit die Hitze des Feuers reflektiert wird **(1)**. Die Bauplane oben und seitlich darüberlegen. Dabei ist es wichtig, ein Luftloch offen zu lassen **(2)**. Überschüssige Folie vor dem Unterstand zum Verankern mit einem Baumstamm oder Ast belegen. Ein Feuer entzünden, reingehen, verblüfft sein.

Die nicht ganz so schnelle Art: Errichte einen Schrägdach-Unterstand aus Stöcken, Stäben oder anderen natürlichen Materialien oder verwende einen umgestürzten Baum. Dann die Rettungsdecke und die Kunststofffolie darüberlegen.

Verwende ein erhöhtes Trapperbett, um dem konduktiven Wärmeverlust vorzubeugen. Für alles andere ist gesorgt.

1

2

Das Trapper-Bett: der Schlüssel zu Wärme und Komfort

Als wir uns damit beschäftigt haben, wie der Körper auskühlen kann, haben wir gesehen, dass der direkte Kontakt mit einem Gegenstand, der kälter ist als unser Körper, uns Wärme entzieht. Uns wird kalt. Und neben der Kälte ist der Boden auch nicht immer der weichste und bequemste Ort zum Schlafen. Schauen wir uns also das Trapper-Bett einmal näher an. Die luxuriöseste Variante ist das Trapper-Bett mit heißen Steinen. Es wird Dir garantiert gefallen!

Funktion	Eignung
Wetterschutz	***
Grundfläche	*
Platz/Sicht	*
einfacher Aufbau	**
mit einfachen Werkzeugen	***
Verwendung mit Feuer	***

Du brauchst:

→ *2 Stangen, so lang wie Du mit über den Kopf ausgestreckter Hand*
→ *viele Blätter oder kleine Zweige*
→ *15–20 Stöcke, dünner als Dein Handgelenk, aber dicker als Dein Daumen, etwa zwei Finger lang.*

Zeitaufwand:
20 Minuten für das Bett und ca. 1–2 Stunden, damit man wirklich heiße Steine hat.

So gehst Du vor:
Lege die beiden Stangen an einer Seite mit den Enden zusammen und an der anderen etwas weiter als schulterbreit auseinander. Du kannst die Stangen mit Pfählen fixieren oder mit Steinen beschweren, so dass sie nicht auseinanderrollen.

Blätter zwischen die Stangen streuen, mindestens so dick wie von Deinem Hand-

Konstruktion eines Trapperbetts: Idealerweise wird alles noch ordentlich gepolstert.

(Quelle: Johannes Vogel, Outdoor-Survival nur mit dem Messer)

gelenk bis zum Ellenbogen. Verwendest Du Äste oder Zweige, dann achte darauf, dass die dickeren Enden nach außen zeigen, so dass in der Bettmitte eine natürliche Kuhle für Deinen Körper entsteht.

Lege Stöcke über die Stangen, damit Dein Körpergewicht nicht die Blätter zerquetscht.

Jetzt legst Du entlang der Innenseite der Stangen und unter die Blätter heiße Steine, am besten an strategischen Stellen wie den Nieren, dem Hals, den Knien und Füßen. Pass auf, dass die Steine nicht die Blätter in Brand setzen – mach zuerst einen Test vor dem Feuer. Je nachdem, wie kalt es ist und welche Art von Steinen Du verwendest, bleiben die Steine ca. 3–4 Stunden warm.

Und jetzt kannst Du Dich hinlegen und Dich mit Deinem Poncho oder etwas anderem zudecken. Viel Spaß!

Feuer-Bett: langfristige Wärme als Luxus oder Notwendigkeit

Stell Dir vor, es ist kalt, und Du hast keine Campingausrüstung oder warme Kleidung. Du hast ein Feuer, willst aber nicht die ganze Nacht wach bleiben, um es am Brennen zu halten. Warum baust Du Dir nicht ein Feuer-Bett?

Das Prinzip ist einfach: Grabe eine flache Grube und brenne darin ca. 2–3 Stunden lang ein Feuer ab. Mit Erde bedecken. Nun kannst Du auf einem Bett mit Fußbodenheizung schlafen, das bis zum Morgen warm bleibt. Luxus!

Du brauchst aber eine Feuchtigkeitssperre, ansonsten wirst Du durch die Feuchtigkeit im Boden in Form von Dampf selbst feucht werden.

Das Ganze funkioniert ideal an einem Flussufer und auf anderen sandigen Flächen. Leg Dir einige Zweige oder anderes Material unter, um den Komfort zu erhöhen. Auch ein Trapper-Bett ist möglich. Lass einfach Deine Fantasie spielen.

Funktion	Eignung
Wetterschutz	***
Grundfläche	***
Platz/Sicht	***
einfacher Aufbau	**
mit einfachen Werkzeugen	***
Verwendung mit Feuer (heiße Steine)	***

Du kannst auch einfach nur Deine normale Feuerstelle zudecken und Dich oben drauflegen. Hast Du das einmal gemacht, wirst Du es immer wieder tun, wenn es kalt ist.

Du brauchst:

→ *Grabwerkzeug*

→ *Feuer.*

Zeitaufwand:
20–30 Minuten für die Grube,
ca. 2–3 Stunden für das Feuer,
1 Stunde zum Anwärmen des Bodens,
bleibt 5–8 Stunden warm.

So gehst Du vor:
Grab eine Grube, so lang wie die Distanz zwischen Deinen Schultern und den Hüften und 20 cm tief. Die gesamte Feuerstelle sollte etwa so groß wie Dein Rumpf sein. Die Erde um die Grube herum wärmt sich auf, wenn das Feuer brennt. Du kannst handtellergroße Steine an strategisch wichtige Stellen wie Nieren, Hals oder Knie legen.

Entzünde ein Feuer und stelle sicher, dass es über die gesamte Länge der Grube brennt. Lass es ca. 2–3 Stunden brennen. In dieser Zeit kannst Du Dein Essen zubereiten, Dich aufwärmen und die Natur genießen.

Decke dann das Feuer zu und markiere die Kanten der Grube mit in den Boden gerammten Stöcken. Du kannst das Feuer mit der Erde bedecken, die Du beim Ausheben der Grube entnommen hast.

Die Erde muss sich ca. 1 Stunde lang anwärmen; deshalb ist es empfehlenswert, einige brennende Zweige in eine zweite Feuerstelle zu übertragen, damit Du trotzdem warm bleibst.

Woher weißt Du, wie es richtig ist? Wenn der Boden warm ist, bevor 30 Minuten um sind, musst Du wahrscheinlich noch etwas Erde hinzufügen. Wenn er nach 45 Minuten warm ist, ist es perfekt. Wenn der Boden nach einer Stunde noch nicht warm ist, hast Du vielleicht zuviel Erde verwendet.

Hinweis: *Zwei wichtige Dinge sind besonders zu beachten. Du musst unbedingt irgendeine Art von Feuchtigkeitssperre zwischen Dir und der Erde einrichten. Das kann z.B. eine Mylar-Rettungsdecke sein.*

Sei vorsichtig, die Erde wird sehr heiß. Möglicherweise musst Du in der Nacht mehr Erde nachlegen. Ein Luxusproblem, würde ich sagen!

SCHNEE-UNTERSTÄNDE

Sicher werden sich viele von uns daran erinnern, wie sie als Kinder Schneefestungen gebaut haben; und wir alle kennen das Iglu aus Schnee, das die Einwohner der Polarregionen als Schutz verwenden. Lasst uns nun ausprobieren, Unterstände im Schnee zu bauen!

Was Du vielleicht nicht weißt: Schnee ist ein hervorragendes Isolationsmaterial. Zwischen den Schneekristallen ist Luft gefangen und bildet eine Art Daunenjacke, nur mit Schneeflocken statt Federn. Die Temperatur in einem Schnee-Unterstand fällt nie weit unter 0 °C. Wenn draußen –30 °C sind und ein Sturm tobt, dann wirst Du erstaunt sein, wie ruhig und warm es in einem Schnee-Unterstand ist.

Natürlich kannst Du alle üblichen Tarp-Unterstände im Schnee aufbauen. Verwende dazu tief in den Schnee gesteckte Zweige als Anker. Du kannst auch Stock- oder Felsenbündel vergraben und den Schnee darüber festtrampeln. So wird das sehr stabil!

Wenn Du draußen im Schnee schläfst, solltest Du eine zusätzliche geschlossenzellige Isomatte verwenden oder eine dicke Schicht von Ästen aufhäufen. Diese sollte so tief wie die Entfernung von Deiner Hand zum Ellenbogen sein.

Hier siehst Du, was draußen im Winter alles möglich ist:
https://www.youtube.com/watch?v=FhxCBbaF--Q

Nur zur Not: Für das schnelle Biwak (von Joe Vogel)

Baumkoje

(1) Wirklich eine reine Notunterkunft. Eine Baumkoje kann nur das Erfrieren hinauszögern. Als dauerhafte Unterkunft musst Du etwas Geräumigeres mit Heizmöglichkeit bauen. Der Aufbau des Grundgerüsts der Baumkoje ist jedoch in einem Bruchteil der Arbeitszeit geschafft. (2) Das Gerüst der Baumkoje wird mit allem abgedeckt, das den Regen abzuhalten vermag. Das kann Borke, Reisig, Holz oder dichtes Gestrüpp sein. Durch das Anstellen an einen Baum ist die Hütte außerdem durch überhängende Äste und den Stamm geschützt.

Schneehöhle

Eine Schneehöhle im Querschnitt zur Veranschaulichung. (1) In den Schnee wird eine senkrechte Grube von etwa einem Meter Tiefe gegraben. (2) Etwas über dem Boden der Grube wird in die seitliche Wand eine Rinne von etwa Mannslänge eingearbeitet. Dabei kann diese Liegefläche auch länger sein als der Einstieg. (3) Der Boden muss isoliert werden. Der Eingang der Schneehöhle kann mit einem Stück Gewebe abgedeckt werden. Es ist wichtig, dass die Luftzufuhr auch dann noch gewährleistet ist, wenn Du eingeschneit bist. Kältefalle = gestrichelte Linie.

(Quelle: Johannes Vogel, Outdoor-Survival nur mit dem Messer)

ANDERE ARTEN VON UNTERSTÄNDEN

Manchmal nehmen wir nach draußen ein bisschen mehr Ausstattung mit, um den Unterstand stabil und windfest zu machen, ihn leicht aufbauen zu können – oder um einfach mehr Komfort zu haben.

Es gibt sehr gemütliche Unterstände mit einem Gewicht von unter 1 kg, die sicherlich eine Überlegung wert sind. Ich persönlich besitze jede dieser Arten und verwende sie hauptsächlich im Winter, wenn die Tage kurz und die Nächte ziemlich kalt sind.

Hängematte: Luxus in jedem Gelände

Ich verbringe viel Zeit in steilem, bewaldetem Gelände ohne Garantie für eine flache Stelle zum Hinlegen. Dagegen gibt es kein besseres Rezept, als in einer Hängematte zu schlafen. Die leichteste Hängematte, die ich gesehen habe, wiegt nur 270 g! Über die Kunst des Hängematten-Campings sind ganze Bücher geschrieben worden; ich will mich hier auf drei wichtige Tipps beschränken.

1. **Schlafe in der Diagonalen.** *Menschen, die in einer Hängematte schwer schlafen können, versuchen gewöhnlich, der Länge nach darin zu liegen. Aber das funktioniert nicht. Man wird dann krumm wie eine Banane und bekommt Rückenschmerzen. Der Trick ist, die Hängematte ein wenig schlaff hängen zu lassen und diagonal darin zu schlafen, denn so bleibt der Rücken gerade. Ideal auch für alle, die auf dem Bauch schlafen.*

2. **Nimm eine gute Unterlage oder Isomatte als Isolierung.** *Der Wind greift alle Teile der Hängematte an, und sie ist deshalb sehr anfällig für die Auswirkungen der Konvektion. Wenn Du kein gutes Polster verwendest, wirst Du frieren, egal wie warm Dein Schlafsack ist. Du solltest also eine Auflage verwenden. Befestige an Deinem Schlafsack einige winzige Schlaufen und verwende eine leichte, elastische Schnur, um den Schlafsack auf der Unterlage zu halten. Einige Hängematten haben eine Art Fach, in das die Auflage eingeschoben werden kann.*

3. **Verwende bei nassem Wetter ein Tarp und Abtropfbänder.** *Du kannst eine klassische A-Frame-Konstruktion direkt über Deiner Hängematte verwenden, musst jedoch bedenken, dass Wasser den tiefsten Punkt finden und an den Abspannseilen direkt nach unten in Deine Hängematte laufen wird. Daher solltest Du Abtropfbänder oder Karabiner benutzen, um trocken zu bleiben.*

In der Hängematte wird schräg geschlafen. So bleibt der Rücken gerade, und Du liegst bequem.

(Quelle: Johannes Vogel, DMAX Survival-Guide für echte Kerle)

Eine Hängematte aufhängen (von Joe Vogel)

Befestigung

In den Tropen schläft man üblicherweise in Hängematten. Du kannst Dir auch ein Tropen-Schlafsystem zusammenstellen. Dazu benötigst Du eine leichte Hängematte, ein Moskitonetz gegen die Mücken sowie ein Tarp gegen den Regen. Zuerst suchst Du Dir geeignete Bäume. Diese sollten nicht so dick sein (1), dass Du das Seil nicht drumherumschlingen kannst, aber auch nicht so dünn, dass sie sich durchbiegen – die Kraft, die sie aushalten müssen, ist ziemlich groß.

Regen- und Moskitoschutz

(2) Zuerst wird das Tarp aufgehängt. Du solltest es etwa einen Meter höher als die Hängematte hängen. Wenn möglich, wird es an mindestens 4 Punkten aufgespannt. Lässt man es herunterhängen, ist man zwar gegen Regen geschützt, das Schlafklima wird dann aber unerträglich. (3) Nun kann die Hängematte so angebracht werden, dass das Moskitonetz noch ordentlich aufgespannt werden kann. (4) Du brauchst meist etwa einen halben Meter »Luft« über und mindestens einen Meter unter der Hängematte. Die Hängematte sollte nicht zu stramm gespannt werden.

(Quelle: Johannes Vogel, DMAX Survival-Guide für echte Kerle)

Eine Hängematte improvisieren (von Joe Vogel)

Konstruktion

Hast Du keine Hängematte dabei und möchtest trotzdem nicht auf feuchtem Boden übernachten, kannst Du aus Deinem Poncho und etwas Paracord eine improvisieren. (1) Hierzu spannst Du mit zwei Mastwürfen und einem Kreuzknoten ein Seil doppelt zwischen zwei Bäumen. (2) Nun schnitzt Du Dir zwei Äste so, dass sie zwischen die Seile gespannt werden können. (3) Wie bei einer improvisierten Trage kann nun der Poncho (wenn Du Dich vorsichtig hineinlegst und nicht all zu schwer bist, auch die Rettungsdecke) um die Seile gewickelt werden, so dass er sich beim Hineinlegen selbst festklemmt.

Jetzt hast Du zwar eine Liegefläche, aber noch kein Dach. Aber auch da gibt es einen simplen Trick, wie Du Dich regenfest einrichten kannst: Je nach Breite der Hängematte und Größe des Ponchos hast Du nämlich ggf. noch genügend Stoff übrig, so dass Du eine weitere Umwicklung machen kannst, um Dich abzudecken und gegen Regen zu schützen.

(Quelle: Johannes Vogel, DMAX Survival-Guide für echte Kerle)

In die Hängematte steigen (von Joe Vogel)

Aufspannen

Wer noch nicht häufig in einer Hängematte lag, macht beim Einstieg oft Fehler, die mit einem Rückwärtssalto und der Landung im Schlamm enden. Öffne ggf. das Moskitonetz am oberen Drittel ein wenig. Wenn vorhanden, wird der Schlafsack auf ganzer Länge aufgezippt und so ausgebreitet, dass er seitlich über die Hängematte hinunterhängt.

Einsteigen

(1) Nun stellst Du Dich neben die Hängematte und belastest sie nur mit Deinem halben Hinterteil. Alles wird ein wenig nachgeben.
(2) Dann wird das der Schlafstätte nächste Bein vorsichtig angehoben und gerade in die Matte gelegt. Mit einem Bein bist Du jedoch noch fest auf dem Boden und kannst Dich halten, falls die Hängematte kippt. Nun legst Du Dich vorsichtig mit dem Oberkörper hinein.
(3) Achte darauf, dass die Matte nicht mehr schwingt, bevor Du das noch auf dem Boden stehende Bein anziehst und Dich endgültig hinlegst.

(Quelle: Johannes Vogel, DMAX Survival-Guide für echte Kerle)

Lavvu: das geheizte nordische Hotel

Es gibt im Winter nichts Besseres als einen beheizten Lavvu-Unterstand. Deine Kleidung kann trocknen, Du kannst Dich aufwärmen und Dich bewegen, ganz ohne schwere Ausrüstung. Du kannst so viel kochen und Wasser bereiten, wie Du Lust hast. Fast wie ein Wohnzimmer.

Das Lavvu, ein Tipi-ähnlicher Kegel, hat in Skandinavien eine lange Tradition als Unterstand fürraueste Witterungsverhältnisse. Lavvus gibt es in Größen für 2 bis 20 Personen und in unterschiedlichem Gewebe, z.B. schwere Leinwand oder Silnylon. Die Kegelform und die verstellbare Öffnung an der Spitze machen das Lavvu ideal für den Einsatz mit einem Zelt-Kocher und Schornstein; in den größeren Lavvus aus Leinwand kann sogar eine Feuerkammer verwendet werden.

Probier aus, ob es Dir gefällt. Der größte Nachteil ist, dass man keine Aussicht hat.

Funktion	Eignung
Wetterschutz	***
Grundfläche	***
Platz/Sicht	*
einfacher Aufbau	**
mit einfachen Werkzeugen	***
Verwendung mit Feuer	**

Ein gutes Lavvu kannst Du an der Spitze für einen Rauchabzug öffnen.

(Quelle: Joe Vogel)

Loue: ultraleichte Förster-Festung

Das Loue ist ein traditioneller finnischer Unterstand für Forstleute. Es handelt sich um einen Dreiviertel-Kegel, der mit einem langgezogenen Feuer verwendet wird.

Der Bau ist einfach und kann geschlossen werden, um vollständigen Schutz vor einem Sturm zu gewähren. Ein Gewicht von weniger als 700 g für einen Unterstand für 3 Personen ist wirklich nicht schlecht. Diesen Unterstand solltest Du mit dem Rücken zum Wind aufbauen. Dann hast Du eine extrem warme und gemütliche Unterkunft, die warm genug ist, um Socken zu trocknen – mit toller Aussicht!

Funktion	Eignung
Wetterschutz	**
Grundfläche	*
Platz/Sicht	**
einfacher Aufbau	**
mit einfachen Werkzeugen	***
Verwendung mit Feuer	**

Auf ihrem YouTube-Kanal kannst Du die Autorin in Action erleben:
https://www.youtube.com/user/susannewilliams

Ein Loue (hier das Vihe Loue 1) schützt Dich von drei Seiten. *(Quelle: Wildward)*

Goldene Shelter Regeln

Du solltest wirklich nie in kaltem, nassem und windigem Wetter oder gar im Schnee ohne Unterstand sein.

- → ***zuerst*** *Unterstand*
- → ***dann*** *Feuer*
- → ***dann*** *Wasser*
- → ***dann*** *Essen.*

Man kann in weniger als drei Stunden sterben, wenn man nass ist und sich in kalter, windiger Umgebung befindet. Man stirbt schneller an Auskühlung, als dass man verdurstet oder verhungert. Daran solltest Du immer denken! Ein Unterstand hat höchste Priorität. Überlass nichts dem Zufall und übe!

ARBEITEN MIT DEM MESSER

Der US-amerikanische Messerhersteller Spyderco legte Anfang der 1990er Jahre einen Katalog auf, der inzwischen heiß gehandelt wird. Auf seinem grafisch gestalteten Cover sind Raubtiere wie Tiger, Hai und Grizzly zu sehen, aber auch Delfine, ein Hirsch, eine Biene und ein Reiher. Dazu ist der Slogan »All God's Critters Have Knives. Think about it.« abgedruckt, was im übertragenen Sinne bedeutet: »Alle wilden Geschöpfe haben Messer. Denk mal darüber nach.«

Wir Menschen sind allerdings keine wilden Tiere mehr. Unsere Zähne taugen nicht zum Durchbeißen eines Holzstamms oder zum Zermalmen von Knochen. Und unsere Fingernägel sind nur schlecht zum Graben von Löchern in hartem Boden geeignet und zerfetzen auch kein Fell. Ohne Werkzeuge sind wir nahezu wehrlos – sogar im Vergleich zu heimischen Tierarten wie einer Wildkatze oder einem Dachs. Doch dafür beherrschen wir den Umgang mit Werkzeugen. Und das wichtigste Werkzeug der bisherigen Menschheitsgeschichte ist das Messer. Da sind sich die meisten Anthropologen und Kulturwissenschaftler einig. Mit der ersten, vor rund 3,4 Millionen Jahren scharfkantig zugeschlagenen Feuersteinknolle änderten sich für die damaligen Menschen die Möglichkeiten der Nahrungsbeschaffung, die Essgewohnheiten und in der Folge auch das Zusammenleben grundlegend.

Mit dem Messer und seinen scharfen »Nachkommen« wie Beil, Säge und Feile schufen die Menschen weitere Werkzeuge und gestalteten Lebensumwelten, die ihnen Sicherheit gaben und sie in ihrer Entwicklung voranbrachten.

Anders als wilde Tiere benötigen wir Menschen Hilfsmittel, um in der Natur (über-)leben zu können.

AUFGABEN EINES BUSHCRAFTMESSERS

Vieles lässt sich in der Natur improvisieren, doch ohne Messer wird es schwierig. Deshalb ist das Messer für die meisten Bushcrafter das wichtigste Werkzeug. Eine scharfe, belastbare Klinge und das Wissen, was man damit machen kann, sind der Schlüssel zum guten Leben in der Natur – und unter Umständen sogar zum Überleben.

Eine scharfe Klinge ist Messer und Gabel, und wer keinen Löffel hat, schnitzt sich einen. Mit dem Messer nimmst Du geangelte Fische aus, bereitest das Essen zu, spitzt

Auch ein kleines Messer kann große Dinge leisten. Hier das Eldris von Morakniv aus Schweden, das im Set mit einem guten Mischmetall-Feuerstab geliefert wird.

Grillspieße, Grabstöcke und Tarpheringe an, formst Topfaufhängungen und verwandelst starke Äste in Wanderstöcke. Wo mit Reepschnüren, Schlingen und Seilen gearbeitet wird, gibt es oft etwas zu schneiden – und das mit möglichst sauberen Schnittkanten. Mit der Spitze des Messers lassen sich Dornen und Spreißel aus der Haut entfernen.

Wenn Du Dich verläufst oder von einem Unwetter überrascht wirst, kann ein Messer zum rettenden Helfer werden, mit dem Du Feuerholz, Feathersticks und Zunder vorbereitest und Funken schlägst (siehe Kapitel »Feuer«). Auch für den Bau einer Notunterkunft kann es entscheidend sein (siehe Kapitel »Lager und Unterstände«).

Outdoorguides berichten immer wieder von Situationen, in denen sich Bergsportler mit ihren Haaren oder der Kleidung in Abseilachtern verfangen hatten und nur durch Schnitte schnell aus ihrer Notlage befreit werden konnten. Einer der spektakulärsten Messereinsätze im Bergsport ging mit einer abgetrennten Hand und dem gewonnenen Leben aus. Aron Ralston hatte nach einem Unfall seinen Arm unter einem Felsblock eingeklemmt und hing rettungslos fest. Nach fünf Tagen und Nächten gelang es ihm, mit seinem billigen und stumpfen Taschenmesser die Hand von seinem gebrochenen Unterarm zu trennen. Auch die Extrembergsteigerin Gerlinde Kaltenbrunner verdankt ihr Leben vermutlich dem kleinen scharfen Messer, das sie von ihrem Mann geschenkt bekommen hatte und an ihrem Klettergurt trug, als ihr Zelt am Dhaulagiri den Berg hinabgerissen wurde. Mithilfe des Messers konnte sie sich aus dem unter Schnee begrabenen Zelt befreien.

GEEIGNETE BUSHCRAFT-MESSER

Dafür, wie das perfekte Messer für all diese Aufgaben aussieht, gibt es keine Patentlösung. Kaum eine Ausrüstungsfrage wird leidenschaftlicher diskutiert. Hier zumindest ein paar Anregungen.

Jagdmesser

»Ein gutes Jagdmesser ist ein gutes Outdoormesser!« Dieses Zitat stammt von dem erfahrenen Jäger Heiner Schmidbauer, der seit vielen Jahren Mitglied der Deutschen Messermacher Gilde ist. Begründet hat er seine Aussage auch. Denn im Revier sind Jäger, Förster oder Jagdaufseher mit vielfältigen Aufgaben konfrontiert. Dazu gehört natürlich das Ausnehmen des erlegten Wilds: Nur wenn der Jagdbeute möglichst rasch die Organe und der Darm entnommen werden, kühlt der Körper schnell genug ab, um das Fleisch hygienisch zu halten. Manchmal, wenn der Einsatz der Schusswaffe aus Sicherheitsgründen nicht möglich ist, werden Jagdmesser auch zum Töten von schwer verletztem oder angefahrenem Wild benutzt. Doch genauso wichtig sind all die anderen Arbeiten im Revier: das Auslichten von Gestrüpp rund um den Hochsitz, das Zurechtschneiden eines Wanderstocks, das Kürzen von Seilen oder das Anspitzen einer Holzstange für den Salzleckstein.

Gemeint sind mit der Aussage übrigens nicht die speziellen Jagdmesser wie Skinner-Messer, Auswaid-Messer, Waidblatt oder Saufeder, sondern Messer, wie sie auch Heiner Schmidbauer fertigt: feststehende Messer, die auch bei längeren oder schweren Arbeiten einen komfortablen Griff erlauben und schlanke Klingen in praktikabler Länge haben. Wichtig ist die Qualität des Stahls und eine schneideffiziente Klingengeometrie.

Skandinavische Messer

Inspiration bietet auch ein Blick nach Skandinavien. Die nördlichen Länder haben eine lange Messerkultur, die bis heute bewahrt wurde. Trotz regionaler Unterschiede ähneln sich die traditionellen Messer der Schweden, Norweger und Finnen in vielen Punkten. Die Klingen sind relativ schlank. Ihre Spitzen liegen auf der Höhe des gerade verlaufenden Rückens oder sind leicht abgesenkt. Der Verlauf der Schneide wird erst zur Spitze hin bauchig.

Der typische Schliff dieser nordischen Messer ist so prägnant, dass sich dafür inzwischen auch bei uns der Begriff »scandi grind« oder »Skandischliff« eingebürgert hat: Ab dem Klingenrücken behält die Klinge über einen gewissen Teil ihrer Höhe – oft sind es bis zu zwei Drittel – ihre volle Stärke. Erst dann läuft sie in gleichbleibendem Winkel v-förmig zur Schneidkante zusammen. Dadurch entstehen sehr feine Schneidenwinkel, was sich beim Schnitzen positiv bemerkbar macht.

Genauso typisch ist die Steckangel-Konstruktion (»hidden tang«): Die oft nicht ganz

Ein gutes Jagdmesser (hier ein Custom von Heiner Schmidbauer) ist ein gutes Outdoormesser.

Die in den skandinavischen Ländern teils seit Jahrhunderten benutzten Messertypen sind auch bei uns sehr beliebt. Hier Modelle von Ahto, Mora und Iisakki Järvenpää.

Vor- und Nachteile der Skandimesser

Der skandinavische Schliff (oft als »Skandi« abgekürzt) zeichnet sich dadurch aus, dass die Klingenflanken in gleichbleibendem Winkel zur Schneidkante zusammenlaufen. Ein Messer mit dieser Geometrie legt man zum fachgerechten Nachschärfen mit den Anschliffseiten flach auf den Schleifstein auf.

Diese Methode ist einfach. Besonders schnell geht es so jedoch nicht, da über die gesamte Fase, die ja hier recht breit ist, Material abgetragen werden muss. Eine nur Bruchteile von Millimetern breite Schneidfase wie an einem Opinel-Messer mit regulärem Flachschliff hat man schneller geschärft als eine 8-Millimeter-Fase an einem Mora-Messer.

Wer sich unterwegs die Arbeit erleichtern will, kann die Skandiklinge etwas stumpfwinkliger anlegen und damit eine kleine Sekundärfase anschleifen. Das macht die Schneidkante stabiler, nimmt ihr aber auch etwas von ihrer Schneidfähigkeit. Zu Hause sollte man dann wieder den feineren Winkel anlegen.

Mit spitzwinkligen Schneidkanten, wie sie typisch für den Skandischliff sind, schnitzt man außerordentlich gut. Allerdings muss die Klinge dafür aus einem Stahl bestehen, der hohe Belastungen verträgt und nicht allzu leicht ausbricht oder sich umlegt: Hier sind nicht rostfreie, feinkörnige Werkzeugstähle oder moderat legierte »Rostfreie« mit ausreichender Härte im Vorteil.

Da die Klingenstärke von der Schneide ausgehend sehr schnell zunimmt, können sich Skandiklingen in manchem Schneidgut verkeilen und sind daher nicht für alle Schneidaufgaben die erste Wahl.

bis zum Griffende reichende Angel des Messers verjüngt sich hinter der Klinge deutlich und wird in einer passgenauen Bohrung des Griffs verklebt. Reicht die Rundangel durch den gesamten Griff hindurch, wird sie am Griffende mit einer Abschlussplatte vernietet oder verschraubt.

Einen Abrutschschutz findet man selten an den Griffen von Skandimessern, und in der Scheide sitzen die Messer typischerweise sehr tief. Griff und Scheide bestehen üblicherweise aus regional vorkommenden Materialien wie Birkenholz oder -rinde, Rentierhorn und Leder.

Alles an diesem nordischen Messerdesign hat einen Zweck: Die schmale Klinge ist wendig. Der Skandischliff führt zu einer hoch schneidfähigen Schneide, die leicht ins Holz eindringt. Der gleichbleibend starke obere Teil der Klinge sorgt für gute Stabilität. Auf den geraden Rücken kann man mit der zweiten Hand kontrolliert Druck ausüben. Natürliche Griffmaterialien fühlen sich auch bei Kälte angenehm an. Der Verzicht auf einen Handschutz erleichtert es, das Messer direkt an der Klinge zu greifen – eine Technik, die besonders bei feinen Schnitten eingesetzt wird.

Zu den bekanntesten Skandimesser-Nutzern gehören die bekannten Survival- und Bushcraftexperten Ray Mears und Cody Lundin oder Outdoorguides wie der Schwede Johan Skullman.

Klappmesser

Feststehende Messer sind belastbarer und pflegeleichter als Klappmesser. Deshalb werden sie allgemein auch als Bushcraftmesser empfohlen. »Man« will sein Messer ja notfalls auch als Steighilfe oder zum Aufstemmen einer Tür benutzen …

Doch wer mit Sachverstand an die Sache rangeht, kommt auch mit einem guten Klappmesser sehr weit und durch fast alle Situationen, die einen in der Natur erwarten können. Bestes Beispiel dafür ist der Schweizer Messerpädagoge Felix Immler, der mit seinem multifunktionalen Victorinox-Taschenmesser vermutlich auch ein Blockhaus bauen könnte.

Wenn es ein Klappmesser sein soll – und dafür können gesetzliche Reglementierungen (§ 42a WaffG) sprechen oder einfach nur die besonders sichere und komfortable Mitführbarkeit – sind Messer mit arretierbarer Klinge empfehlenswert. Denn was man ab-

Solide Klappmesser mit feststellbaren Klingen sind besonders leicht und sicher mitzuführen.

seits der Zivilisation sicher nicht brauchen kann, ist eine Klinge, die versehentlich einschnappt und dabei die noch wertvolleren Werkzeuge des Menschen, nämlich seine Finger und Hände, verletzt.

Denkbar wären Klassiker wie ein Opinel oder ein Buck 110. Die großen Modelle des Schweizer Herstellers Victorinox sind definitiv eine Empfehlung wert. Sie verfügen über stabil vernietete Klingen, die herausgeklappt festgestellt werden. Wähle ein Modell, das zusätzlich zur Klinge noch eine Säge hat. Diese sind ebenfalls von bekannt hoher Qualität und machen dickes Holz schneller zu Kleinholz als die meisten Messer. Auch eine Ahle kann für Reparatur- und Bastelarbeiten sinnvoll sein. Und wer den Kapselheber zu Hause anschärft, hat gleich noch ein Stemmeisen an Bord.

DIE GRUNDLAGEN DER SCHÄRFE UND DES SCHNEIDENS

Der schwedische Schwertschmied Peter Johnsson, ein weltweit anerkannter Spezialist für authentische Schwertrekonstruktionen, hat den Begriff »Sword Like Object« (SLO) geprägt. Darunter versteht er einen Gegenstand, der zwar wie ein Schwert aussieht und von vielen für ein solches gehalten wird, jedoch der echten Funktionalität eines Schwerts nicht gerecht wird. Und so etwas gibt es auch bei Messern, sogar bei hochpreisigen: Sie sehen aus wie Messer, schneiden aber schlecht. Die folgende kurze theoretische Einführung hilft Dir zu verstehen, welche Parameter ein Messer zu einem guten Messer machen.

Die Schneide

Wie gut man etwas schneidet, wird zunächst vom untersten Teil der Klinge bestimmt: der Schneide. Die Stärke der Schneidkante bestimmt maßgeblich die Kraft, die man fürs Trennen der Molekülverbindungen des Schneidguts benötigt.

Je dünner die Schneidkante ist, desto konzentrierter der Druck aufs Schneidgut und desto höher die Schärfe. Die Stärke der Schneidkante kann wenige Tausendstel Millimeter betragen (bei einer hochwertigen Rasierklinge sind es sogar nur 0,0005 Millimeter). Bei einer Klinge, die härtere Materialien schneiden soll, muss die Schneidkante allerdings dicker sein. Sonst würde sie allzu leicht beschädigt werden.

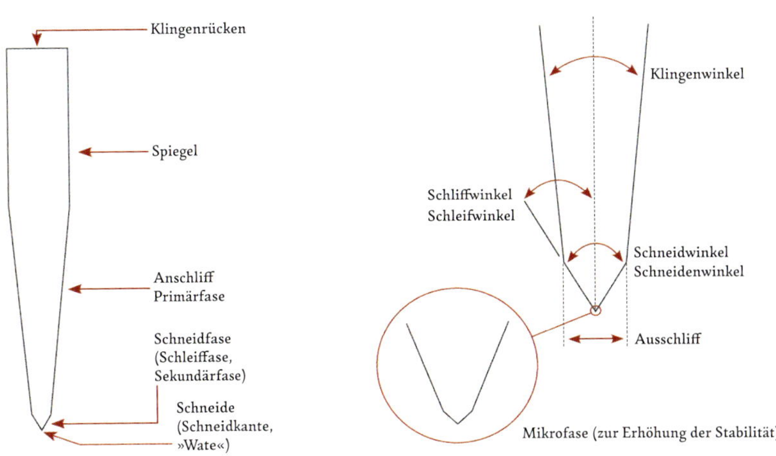

Die Geometrie der Messerklinge

Schneidfase und Schneidenwinkel

Der von der Schneidkante aus v-förmig auseinanderlaufende Bereich wird Schneidfase genannt. Die Schneidfase bei Klingen mit Sekundärfase ist oft nur 0,5 bis zwei Millimeter breit. Bei Flachschliffklingen ohne Sekundärfase wie den typischen Skandimessern sind sechs bis zehn Millimeter Breite typisch. Der Winkel, in dem die Fasen-Flanken zueinander stehen (der sogenannte Schneidenwinkel), beeinflusst die Stabilität der Schneidkante und bestimmt maßgeblich, mit welcher Leichtigkeit die Klinge einschneidet.

Die Parameter Stabilität und Schneidfreudigkeit sind allerdings leider gegenläufig. Ein derber Schneidenwinkel führt zu einer stabileren Schneide als ein feinerer Schneidenwinkel. Mit einem feineren Schneidenwinkel schneidet man wiederum besser als mit einem derben. Messer, mit denen man auch mal grob zur Sache geht und die besonders harte Materialien schneiden müssen, haben typischerweise einen Schneidenwinkel zwischen 35 und 45 Grad. Bei Koch-, Schnitz- oder Skandimessern sieht man häufig Schneidenwinkel zwischen 20 und 30 Grad.

Ausschliff

Die Stärke der Klinge am Übergang der Schneidfase zum Klingengrundschliff wird umgangssprachlich Ausschliff genannt oder auch als »Stärke hinter der Wate« bezeichnet. Wie dick die Klinge an diesem Übergang ist, hat ebenfalls Einfluss auf die Schneidfähigkeit. Die Kombination aus feinem Schneidenwinkel und geringer Ausschliffstärke ist üblicherweise ein Garant für eine exzellente Schneidleistung. Die Kombination aus großem Schneidenwinkel und hoher Ausschliffstärke jedoch sorgt bei Menschen, die ihr Messer nicht nur ansehen, sondern auch schneidend nutzen wollen, regelmäßig für Ärger.

Dünn vs. dick

Eine im Querschnitt, also vom Klingenrücken bis zur Schneidkante, sehr dünne Klinge durchtrennt viele Materialien leichter als eine grundsätzlich ebenso scharfe, aber deutlich stärkere Klinge. Erstere gleitet leicht durch das Schnittgut hindurch, während die andere stärker reibt, sich verkeilt und daher mehr Kraftaufwand erfordert.

Allerdings hat eine Klinge mit sechs Millimeter starkem Rücken enorme Stabilitätsreserven und lässt sich zur Not auch als Brechstange verwenden. Mit einer Zwei-Millimeter-Klinge sollte man das lieber nicht versuchen. Die Balance zwischen Schneidfähigkeit und Stabilität ist ein Kompromiss, den jeder für sich selbst bestimmen muss.

Links: **Am Übergang der Primär- zur Sekundärfase sollte die Klinge nicht zu dick sein.**
Rechts: **Die Klingenstärke beeinflusst die Stabilität und Schneideffizienz.**

Schliffarten

Wenn sich die Klinge vom Rücken oder einer tiefer gesetzten Kante aus v-förmig verjüngt, spricht man von einem **Flachschliff**. Der typische Flachschliff ist zweiteilig aufgebaut. Als Primärfase bezeichnet man den v-förmigen Grundanschliff. Dieser geht dann im Schneidenbereich in die stumpfwinkliger abgesetzte Sekundärfase über. Bei einem Flachschliff auf Null läuft die Primärfase ohne Sekundärfase bis in die Schneidkante hinein. Diesen Flachschliff kennt man von vielen Skandimessern. Der Flachschliff bietet einen guten Kompromiss aus Stabilität und Schneidfähigkeit. Daher ist er sehr beliebt. Er kann für eine hohe Schneidleistung fein ausgeprägt sein oder für eine höhere Belastung stabil angelegt werden.

Bei einem **Hohlschliff** sind die Klingenflanken nach innen gewölbt. Das erreicht man, indem man zum Schleifen runde Schleifsteine nutzt. Je größer der Radius der verwendeten Schleifsteine ist, desto moderater wird der Hohlschliff. Auch Hohlschliffklingen haben zumeist eine flach geschliffene Sekundärfase. Eine gut gemachte Hohlschliffklinge wird vom Ausschliff ausgehend nur langsam dicker und dringt daher zunächst sehr gut ein. Das ist auch für das Nachschleifen der Klinge vorteilhaft. Eine starke Aushöhlung kann die Klinge jedoch schwächen. Und irgendwann wird die Klinge abrupt stärker und verkeilt sich dadurch unter Umständen leichter.

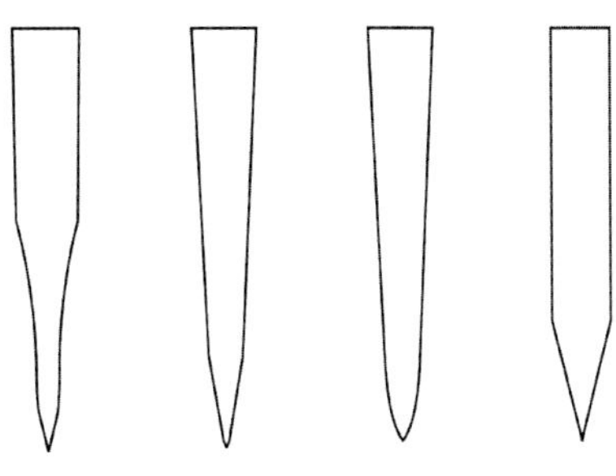

Schliffarten: Hohlschliff, Flachschliff, balliger Anschliff und Skandischliff *(v.l.n.r.)*.

Beim **balligen Schliff** sind die Klingenflanken ähnlich einem Apfelkern nach außen gewölbt. Die Klingenflanken laufen bogenförmig zusammen und bilden dort, wo sie zusammentreffen, die Schneidkante aus. Es gibt ausgeprägte ballige Schliffe (zum Beispiel bei Spaltäxten) und moderate ballige Schliffe. Oft ist auch nur die Schneidfase ballig geformt. Durch die Bogenform liegt der ballige Schliff nur punktuell am Schneidgut an, was vorteilhaft sein kann. Viele Nutzer scheuen sich jedoch vor dem Nachschärfen balliger Geometrien. Ich zeige jedoch später, wie das relativ einfach geht.

Stahl

Damit ein Messer ein gutes Messer ist, muss nicht nur seine Form stimmen. Es benötigt auch eine gute Grundlage – und das ist der Stahl. Grundsätzlich bestimmen die prozentualen Beimengungen von Kohlenstoff (**C**; wichtigster Bestandteil), Chrom (**Cr**) und weiteren Legierungselementen wie Vanadium (**V**) oder Wolfram (**W**) sowie die Wärmebehandlung (Härten und Anlassen) die Eigenschaften des Stahls.

Das Thema Messerstahl ist komplex, füllt ganze Fachbücher und wird teils kontrovers diskutiert. Hier findest Du eine Einschätzung, die auf theoretischem Wissen und jahrelanger praktischer Erfahrung beruht und Dir hoffentlich bei der Beurteilung des Messerstahls hilft.

Der beste Messerstahl ist so hart, dass er sich nicht verbiegt. Er ist so zäh, dass er niemals bricht. Er ist so verschleißfest, dass er sich nicht abnutzt und immer scharf bleibt. Er rostet niemals. Da gibt es nur ein Problem: Diesen besten Messerstahl gibt es nicht.

Denn alles auf einmal kann man nicht haben, da einige Parameter in einem Zielkonflikt zueinander stehen: Klingen aus besonders harten und verschleißfesten Stählen schneiden besonders ausdauernd, sind aber nicht allzu zäh und daher bei unsachgemäßem Einsatz bruchgefährdet. Stähle mit besonders feinem Gefüge sind in der Regel mechanisch hoch belastbar und nehmen feine Schneidenwinkel und eine hohe Schärfe an – sie können jedoch rosten und sind nicht so verschleißfest. Doch keine Sorge! Unter den gut 200 für Messerklingen eingesetzten Stahllegierungen gibt es viele, die ihren Job gut erledigen. Hier einige typische Bushcraftmesser-Stähle in der Kurzbeurteilung:

→ ***1.4034, 1.4110, 1.4116, 420HC, 8Cr13MoV, 12C27, 14C28N, AUS-8, VG-10:*** *Die aufgeführten Stähle sind herkömmlich erschmolzen und allesamt gut rostbeständig. Dafür ist ein Chromanteil von mindestens zwölf Prozent verantwortlich. Der Kohlenstoffanteil (C) variiert zwischen 0,45 und 1,05 Prozent. Je höher der C-Anteil ist, desto höhere Härten können erreicht werden. Hier sind es zwischen 55 und 61 HRC. Alle genannten Stähle nehmen eine gute Schärfe an und sind für schneidende Aufgaben gut geeignet. Sie sind bei Schneidenwinkeln zwischen 30 und 40 Grad gut nutzbar und mit herkömmlichen Mitteln gut schärfbar.*

→ ***CPM-154, CPM-S30V, S35VN, RWL-34:*** *Diese Stähle sind allesamt rostbeständig und werden pulvermetallurgisch erzeugt. Ihr gemeinsames Kennzeichen ist eine hohe Härte und Verschleißfestigkeit. Der C-Anteil beträgt zwischen 1,05 und 1,45 Prozent. Sie werden meist mit Härten zwischen 58 und 61 HRC eingesetzt. Für schneidende Aufgaben sind sie gut geeignet. Der Schneidenwinkel sollte dabei zwischen 35 und 45 Grad betragen. Zum Schärfen ist – eben aufgrund der hohen Verschleißfestigkeit – ein höherer Aufwand nötig.*

→ ***C60, L6, 1075, 75Cr1, 1095, O1, A2, SK-5, 80 CrV2:*** *Diese sogenannten Kohlenstoffstähle sind allesamt nicht rostbeständig. Ursache dafür ist ein zu geringer oder teils gar nicht vorhandener Chromanteil. Der Kohlenstoffanteil beträgt zwischen 0,6 und 1,05 Prozent. Die durch die Wärmebehandlung angestrebten Härten liegen zwischen 57 und 61 HRC. Typisch für diese Stähle ist die Feinkörnigkeit ihres Stahlgefüges. Dadurch sind sie besonders einfach zu schärfen, fein ausschleifbar und entsprechend scharf. Kohlenstoffstähle wie diese werden oft mit feinen Schneidenwinkeln zwischen 20 und 35 Grad eingesetzt. Die vom C-Gehalt her moderateren Legierungen wie C60 sind sehr belastbar und auch für Haumesser verwendbar.*

Nicht rostfreie Messer haben Vorteile, müssen aber vor Korrosion geschützt werden.

Härte

Eine weich belassene Klinge gibt bei zu großer Belastung nach und verbiegt sich dauerhaft. Brechen tut sie aber nicht. Eine hoch gehärtete Klinge widersteht einer höheren Belastung, bricht aber irgendwann. Vor allem schockartige Belastungen, wie sie beim Hacken auftreten, und seitliches Verkanten führen bei hoch gehärteten und auch grobkörnigen Klingen zu Ausbrüchen an der Schneide. Eine hohe Härte wirkt sich allerdings positiv auf die Standzeit der Schneide aus, also darauf, wie lange die Klinge ihre brauchbare Schärfe behält.

Wie hart eine Klinge ist, erkennt man an der HRC-Angabe (Hardness Rockwell C = Härte nach der Rockwell-Skala C). Bei Messerklingen findet man Werte zwischen 52 und 65 HRC. Für ein vielseitig nutzbares Outdoormesser sollten es, abhängig vom Potenzial des Stahls, zwischen 55 und 60 HRC sein. Zur Ermittlung des HRC-Werts wird ein speziell geformter Diamantkegel unter vorgegebenem Druck in den Stahl gepresst. Je geringer die Eindringtiefe des Diamantkegels ist, desto härter ist der Stahl.

Sicherheitsregeln im Umgang mit dem Messer

- *Mit einer offenen – scharfen und spitzen – Klinge läuft man nicht herum (gilt auch für Sägen und Beile). Zu schnell stolpert man oder bleibt irgendwo hängen.*
- *Messer und andere gefährliche Werkzeuge werden so abgelegt, dass man nicht versehentlich hineintritt.*
- *Nach einem spitzen oder scharfen Gegenstand greift man nicht, wenn er herunterfällt.*
- *Ein individuell angepasstes Erste-Hilfe-Set gehört immer ins Gepäck.*

ARBEITSTECHNIKEN

Beim Bushcraften wird das Messer vor allem zum Bearbeiten von Holz eingesetzt. Und schnitzen kann doch schließlich jeder. Oder? Tatsächlich gibt es einige Tricks, mit denen »jeder« noch besser schnitzen kann. In den folgenden Abbildungen zeige ich Dir grundlegende Holzbearbeitungstechniken mit dem Messer.

Messer sicher überreichen

Normalerweise übergibt man ein Messer mit eingeklappter Klinge oder in der Scheide. Es geht aber auch so: Kündige die Übergabe verbal an. Schwenke aus dem sogenannten Hammergriff den Griff nach vorne.

Es darf zugegriffen werden.

Schnelles Abschneiden eines Asts oder jungen Baums

Biege den Ast, soweit es geht. Setz Deine Klinge dann an der Außenwölbung des gebogenen Asts an und schneide schräg und tief ein. Durch die Faserspannung reichen oft wenige Schnitte.

Richtiges Schnitzen im Stehen und im Sitzen

Im Stehen verankert man das Schnittgut am Oberschenkel: bei Rechtshändern mit der linken Hand am rechten Oberschenkel. Die Schnitzbewegung führt vom Körper weg. In Reichweite der Klinge sollte sich niemand befinden.

Schnelles Abschneiden eines Asts oder jungen Baums.

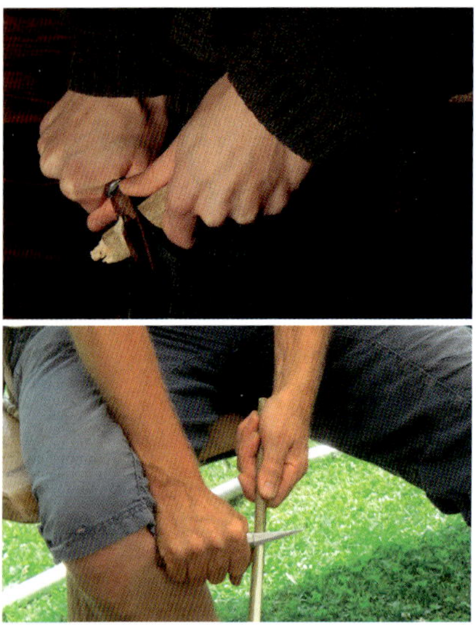

Richtiges Schnitzen im Stehen und im Sitzen.

Powercut.

In der Hocke oder im Sitzen schnitzt man am sichersten, wenn man die Unterarme auf den Oberschenkeln auflegt. Die gesamte Schnitz-Prozedur findet vor dem Körper statt.

Powercut: kraftvolles Schnitzen

Bei der Powercut-Technik kommt die Kraft aus den starken Schultern. Greif das Messer wie einen Hammer, wobei die Schneide aber nicht nach vorne schaut, sondern zu Dir.

Verankere die Hand, die den Ast hält, und das Griffende des Messers am Brustkorb, leg die Schneide am Ast an und zieh Deine Schultern kräftig nach hinten. Die Späne werden nur so durch die Gegend fliegen.

Kontrolliertes Schnitzen

Die eiserne Regel lautet ja eigentlich: In Richtung der Schnitzbewegung liegt kein Körperteil. Bei Feinarbeiten ist es aber manchmal einfacher, zum Körper hin zu schnitzen.

Halte den Zeigefinger dennoch außerhalb der direkten Klingenbewegung. Der Daumen gibt kontrolliert Druck. Mit einer scharfen Klinge arbeitet es sich sicherer, da nicht so viel Kraft aufgebracht werden muss.

Kurzgreifen des Messers

Erfahrene Schnitzer fassen ihre Messer für Feinarbeiten gelegentlich direkt an der Klinge. Diese sollte daher eine gewisse Breite haben. Der Griff muss fest sitzen.

Hier wird der anzupassende Stock mit der linken Hand so gegen den Rumpf gepresst, dass er nicht verrutscht. Mit dem kurz gegriffenen Messer lassen sich Späne behutsam und kontrolliert abnehmen.

Eine stabile Spitze schnitzen

Forme das Ende des Stabs mit Powercuts oder herkömmlichen Schnitzbewegungen vierkantig an. Fase anschließend die Kanten an. Die so entstandene Spitze ist sehr widerstandsfähig und kann zum Beispiel für Zeltheringe benutzt werden.

Kontrolliertes Schnitzen.

Schnitzen einer Sollbruchstelle

Man kann einen Ast quer zum Faserverlauf durchtrennen, indem man die im rechten Winkel aufgesetzte Klinge mittels Knüppel-Schlägen auf den Klingenrücken ins Holz treibt (englisch »truncating«).

Materialschonender und nicht so laut ist folgende Methode: Bringe rundum einen möglichst tiefen Einschnitt an. In frisches Holz lässt sich die Schneide gut mit dem Daumen drücken. Dann setzt Du etwas weiter vorne an und schnitzt schräg und tief bis zum Stopperschnitt. Je nach Dicke des Asts muss man manchmal nacharbeiten. Mit wenig Kraft lässt sich der Stock nun an dieser Sollbruchstelle brechen.

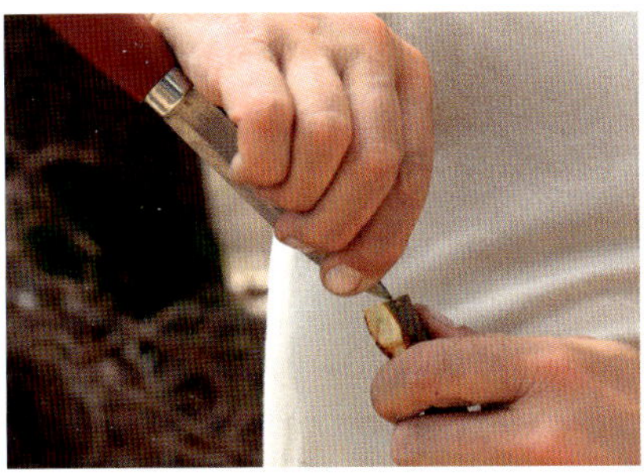

Kurzgreifen des Messers.

Sollbruchstelle.

Eine stabile Spitze schnitzen.

Spalten von Ästen und Stammabschnitten

Es scheint, dass »Batoning« zu den Pflichtveranstaltungen beim Bushcraften und bei jedem Bushcraftmesser-Test gehört. Dabei wird die Klinge durch Schläge mit einem Ast auf den Klingenrücken entlang der Faserrichtung durchs Holz getrieben. Eine schnelle, aber nicht besonders messerschonende Methode.

Eleganter geht es so. Schnitze harte Äste keilförmig an. Je nach Stärke und Länge des zu spaltenden Stamms muss man mehrere Keile, teilweise auch mit unterschiedlichen Durchmessern, verwenden.

Setz Dein Messer an und schaff durch Schläge auf den Klingenrücken einen ersten Zugang für die Keile. Treibe nun die Keile tief ins Holz, bis der Holzblock entlang des Faserverlaufs aufspaltet.

Kreuzweises Verbinden von Rundhölzern

Schneide ein tiefes X in jeden Ast (fast bis zur Mitte) und heble dann den seitlichen Teil heraus. Sind die Äste gleichförmig eingeschnitten, verkeilen sie sich förmlich ineinander.

Diese ohnehin schon gute Verbindung kannst Du nun durch ein Seil oder einen Draht sichern. Auf diese Weise lässt sich ein stabiles Tragegestell improvisieren.

Spalten von Ästen und Stammabschnitten.

Kreuzweises Verbinden von Rundhölzern.

Lochen.

Haken.

Holzlocken.

Schnitzen mit dem Haken- oder Löffelmesser.

Lochen eines Asts

Klapp die Ahle Deines Schweizer Taschenwerkzeugs aus und bohr ein Loch.

Wer keine Ahle hat, macht es so: Flache den Ast etwas ab und schneide ihn mit zwei parallelen Schnitten quer zum Faserverlauf ein. Das Holz dazwischen lässt sich ganz leicht mit der Spitze herausbrechen.

Auf gleiche Weise gehst Du auf der anderen Astseite vor. Wer ein Messer mit besonders feiner Spitze benutzt, sollte behutsam vorgehen.

Schnitzen eines Hakens

Ein Haken kann als Aufhängung für einen Topf oder zur Fertigung einer Speerschleuder notwendig sein. Schneide dazu den Ast x-förmig bis ungefähr bis zur Mitte ein.

Schneide mit kontrollierten, schräg angesetzten Schnitten von unten her das Holz bis zur Gabelung, dem »V«, ein. Die so entstandene v-förmige Kerbe muss nun noch etwas hinterschnitten und ausgehöhlt werden. Fertig ist ein praktischer Haken.

Schnitzen von Holzlocken (als Anzündhilfe)

Das Innere von Totholz ist oft auch bei feuchter Witterung trocken. Spalte den Ast und schnitz daraus einen sogenannten Featherstick (siehe auch Kapitel »Feuer«). Besonders einfach geht das, wenn Du den Stock am Boden aufsetzt und die Klinge mit gestrecktem Arm und festem Handgelenk ansetzt.

Der Druck auf die Schneide kommt nicht über das Ellenbogengelenk, sondern resultiert aus einer kompletten Gewichtsverlagerung auf den gestreckten Arm. Das funktioniert auch bei hartem Holz.

Schnitzen mit dem Haken- oder Löffelmesser

Die im Englischen »Crook Knife« genannten Messer eignen sich besonders gut zum Aushöhlen. Fixiere das Werkstück zwischen den Schenkeln und arbeite mit Bewegungen in Richtung Körper.

SCHÄRFEN VON MESSERN

Selbst eine Klinge aus dem besten Stahl verliert irgendwann ihre Schärfe. Grund dafür ist die feine Schneide, die nicht unendlich belastbar ist: Sie nutzt sich durch abrasive Bestandteile im Schneidgut ab, bricht an besonders belasteten Stellen aus, legt sich um oder wird von Rost angenagt. In der Folge wandert die einst spitzwinklige Kante immer weiter nach oben und wird breiter und breiter. Und breit ist das Gegenteil von scharf. Denn je breiter die Schneidkante ist, desto mehr Kraft muss man aufwenden, um die Molekülverbindungen des Schneidguts voneinander zu trennen.

Spätestens wenn beim Schneiden ein erhöhter Kraftaufwand spürbar wird, ist es Zeit, die Klinge zu schärfen. Durch Materialabnahme muss die Schneidkante neu geformt werden. Dazu braucht man ein Schärfmedium, das härter sein (oder härtere Bestandteile besitzen) muss als die härtesten Bestandteile im Klingenstahl und zusätzlich eine gewisse Rauigkeit (die sogenannte Körnung) aufweist. Grobkörnige Schleifmittel nehmen schnell und relativ unkontrolliert Material ab. Besonders feine Schleifmittel nehmen kaum noch Material ab und führen eher zu einer Politur.

Bevor es gleich an die Schleiftechniken geht: Nur keine Angst vorm Schärfen! Und lass Dich nicht kirre machen – beim Schärfen führen viele Wege zum Ziel.

Übe zunächst mit einem einfachen Messer wie einem Opinel. So findest Du Deinen persönlichen Einstieg ins Thema, und Deine Bewegungen verfestigen sich motorisch. Wenn das Messer danach deutlich besser schneidet als zuvor, hast Du gewonnen. Alles andere ist höhere Kunst.

Schärfen mit dem Schleifstein

Egal ob man einen japanischen Wasserstein, einen Belgischen Brocken, einen Keramikstein oder einen Schleifstein mit diamantbeschichteter Oberfläche benutzt – die Schleifbewegungen sind im Grunde dieselben: Richte den Schleifstein so aus, dass Du bequem darauf arbeiten kannst. Eine Hand umfasst den Messergriff, die andere wird zur Stabilisierung und Führung auf die Klinge gelegt. Leg die Klinge auf den Schleifstein und heb den Klingenrücken zum Nachschärfen des bestehenden Schneidenwinkels so weit an, bis die Schneide in den Stein beißt. Senk den Rücken wieder ein kleines Stück und schieb die Klinge nach vorne. Ob das in gerader Linie, abschnittsweise oder in einer umfassenden Scheibenwischerbewegung erfolgt, ist Geschmacks- und Übungssache und hängt auch von der Form der Klinge und der Breite des Schleifsteins ab.

Wer sich unsicher wegen des einzuhaltenden Winkels ist, kann die Schneidfase mit einem Permanentmarker markieren. Stimmt der Anstellwinkel, wird die Markierung während des Schleifens komplett entfernt. Eine gute Hilfe für den Einstieg sind auch aus Holz oder alten Kreditkarten gefertigte Winkelkeile, mit denen Du zwischendurch immer wieder Deinen Anstellwinkel überprüfen kannst.

Alternativ dazu kann man den Abstand, den die Mittelachse des Messerrückens vom Schleifstein haben sollte, mit folgender Formel berechnen: Die Breite der Klinge wird geteilt durch 3, 4, 5 oder 6. Das Ergebnis entspricht der Distanz zwischen dem Schleifstein und der Messerrückenachse für die Schleifwinkel 20, 15, 12 oder 10 Grad. Wenn der Anstellwinkel grundlegend passt, werden sich kaum zu vermeidende Verwackler nicht spürbar auswirken. Nur keine Hemmungen!

Geschliffen wird abwechselnd die eine, dann wieder die andere Seite. Fünf bis 30 Züge auf der einen Seite, fünf bis 30 Züge auf der anderen Seite ergeben einen gleichmäßigen Materialabtrag an beiden Seiten der Schneidfase und sorgen für einen guten Rhythmus. Hier muss aber jeder selbst herausfinden, welche Sequenzen für ihn am besten »laufen« und gute Ergebnisse bringen.

Schleife zunächst auf einem ausreichend groben Stein so lange, bis die Klinge wieder spürbar scharf ist. Das erkennst Du daran, dass sich Papier wieder schneiden lässt oder sich die Klinge festbeißt, wenn sie schräg auf dem Daumennagel oder den Haaren des Hinterkopfs aufgesetzt wird. Wechsle erst dann zu einem Stein mit feinerer Körnung. Sonst dauert das Schärfen nur unnötig lange oder wird gar nichts. Rund 80 Prozent der Schärfarbeit werden mit dem groben Stein gemacht. Das Glätten der Schneide und das Entfernen des Grats ist dann die Aufgabe von Schleifsteinen mit einer feineren Körnung.

Achtung: *Die Körnungsangaben für europäische und japanische Schleifsteine sowie Schleifpapier entsprechen sich nicht! Umrechnungstabellen finden sich im Internet unter Suchbegriffen wie »Schleifmittel Korngrößen« oder »FEPA & JIS«.*

Folgende Tipps gelten für japanische Wassersteine: Eine beschädigte Schneide oder eine Schneide, deren Winkel grundlegend verändert werden soll, schärft man zunächst mit Schruppsteinen, deren Körnung zwischen J60 bis J800 liegt. Alternativ sind dazu auch Sensenwetzsteine aus dem Baumarkt brauchbar. Abgestumpfte, aber in-

Beim Schärfen auf dem Bankstein wird die Klinge im Schleifwinkel angesetzt und nach vorne geschoben. Um der Wölbung der Schneide zu folgen, zieht man den Griff entsprechend zurück.

So schärft man die andere Klingenseite. Alternativ kann man die Klinge auch – ohne Griffwechsel – am entfernten Schleifsteinende aufsetzen und zu sich ziehen.

takte Schneiden lassen sich mit Körnungen um die J800 bis J2000 auf eine gute Gebrauchsschärfe bringen. Wer es feiner mag, nutzt Körnungen von J3000 an aufwärts. Beliebte Kombisteine haben Körnungen von 1000/3000 oder 1000/6000. Schleif-Freaks und Liebhaber allerfeinster Schneiden krönen ihre Arbeit mit dem Abziehen auf Leder.

Mein persönliches Schärfe-Kriterium: Schneidet das Messer Zeitungspapier auf Druck rupffrei, ist die Klinge scharf genug.

Schärfen von balligen Schneiden

Um ballig angelegte Schneiden zu schärfen, gibt es einen guten Trick: die Mousepad-Methode. Anstelle eines Schleifsteins benutzt man Nassschleifpapier, das man auf eine weiche, nachgiebige Unterlage klebt. Mousepads oder Moosgummipads sind dafür sehr gut geeignet.

Zum Schärfen führt man die Klinge mit dem Rücken (und nicht mit der Schneide) voran übers Papier. Wähle einen zum Schneidenwinkel passenden Anstellwinkel (eher etwas niedriger) und arbeite ohne Druck. Das Eigengewicht der Klinge reicht aus. Denn durch den weichen Untergrund passt sich das Schleifpapier auch bei geringem Anpressdruck an die vorhandene Bogenform der Schneide an und formt diese nach. Zu viel Druck würde die Schneide verrunden.

Wellenschliff schärfen

Bei typischen Outdooraufgaben schneiden Messer mit gut geschärften glatten Schneiden deutlich besser ab als Messer mit Wellenschliff. Gerade beim Schnitzen braucht kein Mensch einen Wellenschliff. Selbst Seile lassen sich mit einer glatten Klinge oft einfacher und sauberer kappen.

Wenn man an Einsatz- und Rettungsmessern dennoch häufig Wellenschliffbereiche vorfindet, hat das vor allem einen Grund: Die Abfolge von konkav geformten Schneidflächen und kantig-scharf hervorstehenden »Wellenkämmen« reißt sich auch dann noch durchs Schneidgut, wenn eine glatte Schneide abgestumpft wäre und nichts mehr ausrichten würde.

Wellenschliffe lassen sich – Welle für Welle – nachschärfen. Dazu benötigst Du gerundete Schärfmittel, deren Durchmesser zum Wellenschliff passt (Tipp: Schleifpapier auf Holzstäben). Manchmal reicht es, die dem Wellenschliff gegenüberliegende Klingenseite abzuziehen.

Improvisiertes Schärfen

Wer einen längeren Wildnisaufenthalt plant, denkt sicher daran, einen transportablen Schärfstein mitzunehmen. Das können kleine, flache Schleifsteine sein, wie sie unter anderem von Spyderco (etwa Pocket Stone 303MF, keramisch gebunden) oder Wästikivi

Auf einer nachgiebigen Unterlage lassen sich ballige Klingen leicht nachschärfen.

Zum Nachschärfen eines Wellenschliffs benötigt man Schleifmittel mit rundem Profil.

(ein finnischer Naturstein) hergestellt werden. Ein paar zurechtgeschnittene Rechtecke Nassschleifpapier im Geldbeutel in 400er- bis 1200er-Körnung, eventuell schon auf eine alte Kreditkarte aufgeklebt, spürt man noch nicht mal. Was man auf jeden Fall vor einer längeren Tour machen sollte, ist, seine Schneidwerkzeuge in einen Topzustand zu bringen: sie zu schärfen und eventuell auch die Klingengeometrie zu optimieren.

Doch auch wenn es einen mal unvorbereitet erwischt, gibt es Möglichkeiten, sein Messer scharf zu halten oder wieder scharf zu bekommen. Selbst mit Haushaltsmitteln oder Fundstücken lassen sich Klingen schärfen. So ist es kein Märchen, dass Messer früher am unteren Tellerrand unglasierter **Porzellanteller** abgezogen wurden. Denn Porzellan enthält unter anderem Quarze mit Schleifwirkung. Zu empfehlen ist das jedoch nur im Notfall. Und besonders verschleißfeste Stähle lachen sich über eine Untertassen-Behandlung eher schlapp.

Die in **Zahnpasta** enthaltenen Putzkörper bestehen aus Silikatverbindungen, Schlämmkreide oder auch Marmorpulver. Letztendlich enthalten diese Stoffe allesamt Mineralien, die zwar deutlich weicher als Diamant, aber dennoch zum Schärfen von Stahl geeignet sind. Am besten reibt man die Zahnpasta in einen Ledergürtel hinein und legt diesen auf eine plane Unterlage oder zieht ihn stramm. Dann zieht man die Klinge mit dem Rücken voran im passenden Schärfwinkel übers Leder. Der erzeugte Abrieb ist allerdings sehr gering. Um bei einer noch scharfen Klinge den Verschleiß zu verzögern oder die Schneide etwas nachzubessern, ist die Methode geeignet. Für mehr aber auch nicht.

Kartonpappe besteht aus pflanzlichen Faserstoffen und zu einem gar nicht mal kleinen Teil aus Mineralien wie Kaolin und Kalziumkarbonat sowie Sand und unter Umständen mineralischen Oberflächenveredelungen und Titandioxid. Darum stumpfen Messer beim Schneiden von Karton auch so schnell ab. Doch was ein Messer stumpf machen kann, könnte doch auch zum Schärfen geeignet sein? Es gibt bekannte Messermacher, die ihre Klingen für den feinsten Schliff zuletzt auf nassem

Ein kompakter Schleifstein oder ein paar vorab zurechtgeschnittene Bögen Nassschleifpapier erleichtern das Scharfhalten der Messer auf Tour. Sonst muss man eben improvisieren.

Zeitungspapier abziehen. Zum behelfsmäßigen Abziehen ist Pappe dank der harten Einschlüsse geeignet.

Sehr gute Ergebnisse bei fast allen Stählen lassen sich mit **wasserbeständigem Schleifpapier oder Schleifleinen** erzielen. Denn der Trägerstoff des Schleifpapiers ist üblicherweise mit harten Siliziumkarbid-Partikeln beklebt. Als plane Auflagefläche für das Papier eignet sich eine Glasplatte, die man mit Wasser befeuchtet. Das Schleifpapier saugt sich darauf förmlich fest. Man kann das Schleifpapier aber auch über ein Buch oder einen abgeflachten Ast spannen oder behelfsmäßig auf dem Oberschenkel fixieren.

Achtung: *Nutzt man Schleipapier zum Schärfen, führt man die Klinge mit dem Rücken voraus übers Papier. Würde man wie auf einem Schleifstein die Schneide voranführen, würde man ins Papier schneiden.*

Die Stängel von **Schachtelhalm** enthalten harte Kieselsäuren und können ebenfalls zum behelfsmäßigen Schärfen benutzt werden. Lege möglichst lange Stängel nebeneinander auf eine ebene Unterfläche, drück die Oberfläche der Stängel platt und zieh Dein Messer wie auf Schleifpapier ab. Das funktioniert bei leicht zu schleifenden Stählen erstaunlich gut.

Das vielleicht am häufigsten angeführte Hilfsmittel für das improvisierte Schärfen von Klingen abseits der Zivilisation sind **Flusskiesel und Sandsteine**. Die bestehen oft aus harten Quarzkörnern. Wichtig ist, dass die Steine möglichst plan sind. Getestet wurde diese Methode mit Klingen aus einfachem C60-Stahl (nicht rostfrei), aus verschleißfesterem 14C28N-Stahl und dem besonders verschleißfesten CPM-S30V.

Alle Klingen wurden zuvor so abgestumpft, dass sie über den Daumennagel rutschten und Papier nicht mehr einschnitten. Mit dem befeuchteten Stein in der einen und dem Messer in der anderen Hand wurde jede Klinge in kreisenden und schiebenden Bewegungen und Schärfwinkeln von rund 20 bis 25 Grad von beiden Seiten jeweils ein bis drei Minuten lang über den Stein geführt. Ergebnis: Der Stahlabrieb war auf dem Stein deutlich erkennbar, und die Klingen hatten spürbar an Biss gewonnen. Ein Sisalseil, gefaltetes dickes Papier, feines Papier und Holz ließen sich mit den zwar sehr rauen, aber scharfen Schneiden wieder gut schneiden. Also, keine Panik: Auch mit einem recht verschlissenen Messer steht man nicht zwangsläufig stumpf in der Wildnis rum.

Nassschleifpapier enthält harte Siliziumkarbid-Partikel.

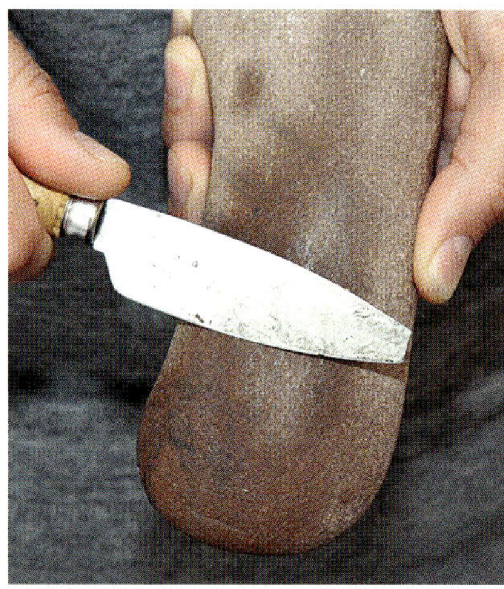

Flache Steine mit harten Mineraleinschlüssen eignen sich zum improvisierten Schärfen.

Messer gehören zu den essenziellen Hilfsmitteln draußen. Und was einem wichtig ist, sollte man gut behandeln.

Ein bisschen Pflege muss sein

Ein gutes Werkzeug sollte man gut behandeln – ein unter Umständen lebensnotwendiges sowieso. Bei Messern ist das im Grunde nicht schwer. Hier ein paar Tipps:

1. *Die Schärfe Deines Messers lässt sich deutlich länger erhalten, wenn Du darauf achtest, auf welchem Untergrund Du schneidest. Porzellan und Steine sind wahre Schneidenkiller.*
2. *Steck Dein Messer nicht zum Spaß in den Sand oder die Erde.*
3. *Warte mit dem Abziehen oder Nachschärfen nicht, bis die Schärfe ganz dahin ist.*
4. *Auch rostbeständige Stähle können Rost ansetzen, bei niedrig-legierten Kohlenstoffstählen kann es richtig schnell gehen.*
5. *Reinige und trockne Dein Messer nach jedem Gebrauch ab. Blut beispielsweise ist extrem aggressiv.*
6. *Versorge Dein Messer, wenn es geht, nicht in einer feuchten Scheide.*
7. *Etwas Schmalz oder Öl schützt die Klinge. Unterwegs kannst Du die Klinge ein paar Mal vorsichtig durch die Haare führen und erhältst so auch einen schützenden Fettfilm.*
8. *Versenkt man Kohlenstoffstahlklingen für ein paar Stunden in starkem Kaffee, kann sich eine zumindest etwas schützende Patina entwickeln.*
9. *Holzgriffe können gepflegt und gegen »Wassereintritt« geschützt werden, wenn man sie gelegentlich für eine halbe Stunde in erhitztes Leinöl taucht.*
10. *Leg Dein Messer nicht zu nahe am Feuer ab und tritt nicht drauf.*
11. *Vermeide schockartige Belastungen Deines Messers – es gibt Alternativen zum Batoning.*
12. *Wenn Du beim Schnitzen auf harte Knoten im Holz stößt, dann heble diese nicht raus, sondern schnitz die harten Stellen raus. Deine Messerschneide dankt es Dir.*

KNOTEN

Wenn wir Zeit im Freien verbringen, merken wir sehr schnell, dass wir immer wieder Dinge befestigen bzw. zusammenbinden müssen. Vielleicht wollen wir eine Schaufel an unserem Rucksack festmachen, einen Unterstand bauen oder ein paar Bäume aus dem Wald ziehen. Wir müssen sicherheitshalber unsere Tiere anbinden oder wollen uns einen bequemen Sessel bauen. Für all diese Aufgaben brauchen wir zwei Dinge – ein Seil und Knoten. Hier stelle ich einige meiner Lieblingsknoten vor.

WARUM BRAUCHEN WIR KNOTEN?

Knoten sind unglaublich vielseitig, und es gibt Hunderte verschiedener Knoten, Schläge und Variationen zu lernen. Die gute Nachricht ist: Wir müssen nicht alle Knoten lernen; wichtig ist, dass wir uns über den jeweiligen Verwendungszweck klarwerden und ein Verfahren entwickeln, Knoten für bestimmte Situationen auszuwählen.

Bei der Auswahl des geeigneten Knotens müssen wir zwei Fragen berücksichtigen:

→ *Welche Funktion muss der Knoten erfüllen?*

→ *Was ist in der Situation, in der ich mich befinde, außerdem noch wichtig?*

Die Funktionen eines Knotens können sein:

→ *zwei Seile verbinden*

→ *ein Seil an einem Ring befestigen*

→ *ein Seil an einem Stock befestigen*

→ *eine Schlinge machen*

→ *ein Seil kontrolliert auslaufen lassen*

→ *Spannung auf ein anderes Seil aufbringen*

→ *ein Stopperknoten am Ende eines Seils.*

Neben der Funktion des Knotens gibt es noch weitere Faktoren, die wir bei der Knotenwahl beachten müssen (*s. Tabelle rechts*).

ARTEN VON KNOTEN

Schauen wir uns jetzt mal die Knoten selbst näher an:

Achterknoten

Wenn Du nur einen Knoten lernen willst, dann diesen! Der Achterknoten ist in der freien Natur der allernützlichste Knoten. Er ist leicht zu binden, auch mit einer Hand. Er ist vielseitig anwendbar. Er ist absolut zuverlässig. Beim Klettern wird er verwendet, um das Seil am Kletterharness zu befestigen. Du kannst sicher sein, dass dieser Knoten hält.

Der »Achter«: ein besonders sicherer Knoten.

Wichtige Faktoren bei der Auswahl eines geeigneten Knotens

Faktor	Warum ist das wichtig?
einfach	Sind Knoten einfach und leicht zu erlernen, dann erinnern wir uns besser daran, wenn es darauf ankommt.
sicher	Natürlich sollte ein Knoten halten. Aber manchmal kann Sicherheit kann auch etwas anderes bedeuten: In einigen Situationen, z.B. beim Anbinden eines Tiers, das in Panik geraten könnte, ist es noch wichtiger, dass der Knoten leicht zu lösen ist. Wir müssen uns also immer wieder klarmachen, was Sicherheit in der jeweiligen Situation bedeutet.
viele Anwendungen	Einige Knoten (wie der Achterknoten) sind so vielseitig einsetzbar, dass wir mit diesen fast alles machen könnten. Sie bilden den Kern meiner Knotenauswahl.
bester Knoten für einen bestimmten Verwendungszweck	Manchmal gibt es nur einen einzigen Knoten für die jeweilige Anwendung. Wenn das der Fall ist, dann lohnt es sich, diesen Spezialknoten zu erlernen.
leicht erkennbar, ob korrekt gebunden	Wenn wir müde sind oder uns kalt ist, neigen wir eher dazu, Fehler zu machen. Dann ist es besonders gut, wenn man sehr deutlich erkennen kann, ob ein Knoten richtig gebunden wurde oder nicht.
einfach zu lösen	Wenn auf Knoten viel Last liegt, dann sind einige nur sehr schwer wieder zu lösen. Mit kalten Händen kann dies zum echten Problem werden. Deshalb muss man oft einen Kompromiss finden zwischen Knoten, die sehr sicher halten, und solchen, die einfach zu lösen sind. Überleg Dir jeweils genau, was Dir wichtiger ist.
adjustierbar	Wenn Seile nass werden, dehnen sie sich und müssen adjustiert werden. Oft müssen wir auch Knoten adjustieren, wenn wir kompliziertere Strukturen wie Unterstände aus Planen bauen oder eine Hängematte aufhängen. Mir gefallen besonders Knoten, die unter Last verstellt werden können.
mit einer Hand zu binden	Stell Dir vor, dass Du ein Pferd, ein Boot oder auch nur zwei Stöcke, die Du verbinden willst, hältst. Praktisch, wenn man den Knoten dann mit einer Hand binden kann!

Anwendungen	Eignung
zwei Seile verbinden	***
ein Seil an einem Ring befestigen	***
ein Seil an einem Stock befestigen	**
eine Schlinge machen	***
ein Seil kontrolliert auslaufen lassen	X
Spannung auf ein anderes Seil aufbringen	X
ein Stopperknoten am Ende eines Seils	***

Faktor	Eignung
einfach	***
sicher	***
viele Anwendungen	***
bester Knoten für einen bestimmten Verwendungszweck (hier: sicher an ein Kletterseil zu binden)	***
leicht erkennbar, ob korrekt gebunden	***
einfach zu lösen	**
adjustierbar	*
mit einer Hand zu binden	**

Wie binden?

(1) Das Seil wird zu einem Auge gelegt. **(2)** Das »kurze« Seilende wird einmal hinter das »lange« geführt. **(3)** Jetzt kann das Seilende von oben in das Auge gefädelt werden.

Varianten

Der Achterknoten ist der vielseitigste Knoten im Freien, er kann auf viele verschiedene Arten gebunden werden. In der *Abbildung unten* siehst Du einige Varianten. Der Achter lässt sich z.B. auch mit einem Doppelstrang legen **(1,2)**, um beispielsweise einen Klettergurt zu improvisieren **(3)**. Macht man erst einen »einfachen« Achter, führt das Seil durch eine Öse und legt es zurück, kann man ihn zum Einschlaufen in den Klettergurt verwenden **(4,5)**.

Nachteile

Manchmal ist der Achterknoten schwierig zu lösen, wenn viel Last darauf lag. Er kann leicht gelöst werden, wenn man ein Band, einen Stab oder einen Knebel im Knoten platziert.

__Tipp:__ Übe, den Achterknoten mit nur einer Hand zu binden. Dies ist der rettende Knoten, wenn Du mit einem Seil geborgen werden musst.

Oben: **Standard-Achterknoten, *unten:* Varianten.**

Halber Schlag

Das ist ein vielseitiger Verbinder, den man mit einer Hand binden kann. Wenn Du ein Seil an einem Ring oder Stock befestigen willst, dann ist der Halbe Schlag wichtig. Er ist schnell und einfach unter Spannung mit einer Hand zu binden und bildet die Grundlage für allerlei nützliche Knoten. Belegt mit einem Slipstek wird er verwendet, um Pferde so an einem Ring zu befestigen, dass der Knoten unter Spannung sehr leicht gelöst werden kann, wenn das Pferd in Panik gerät. Bedenke also, dass der Knoten ganz leicht gelöst werden kann, und belege daher das Ende.

Anwendungen	Eignung
zwei Seile verbinden	*
ein Seil an einem Ring befestigen	***
ein Seil an einem Stock befestigen	***
eine Schlinge machen	*
ein Seil kontrolliert auslaufen lassen	X
Spannung auf ein anderes Seil aufbringen	X
ein Stopperknoten am Ende eines Seils	X

Faktor	Eignung
einfach	***
sicher	**
viele Anwendungen	***
bester Knoten für einen bestimmten Verwendungszweck	*
leicht erkennbar, ob korrekt gebunden	**
einfach zu lösen (hier: falls mit einem Slipstek verwendet)	***
adjustierbar	**
mit einer Hand zu binden	***

Sicherheitshinweis:

Verwende diesen Knoten niemals, um Lasten über Deinen Kopf zu heben oder Dich selbst an einem Seil zu sichern!

Wie binden?

Leg ein Auge **(1)** und mach einen einfachen »Schlupf«. **(2)** Winde jetzt das Seil in derselben Richtung nochmal um »sich selbst«. **(3)** Fertig sind zwei Halbschläge.

Varianten

Unten siehst Du einen tollen Knoten für ein langes Seil. Man macht einen einfachen Törn und führt ihn um den Anker. Mit einem Slipstek befestigen oder mit einem kleinen Knebel belegen *(s. Abbildung unten)*.

Weitere Varianten: Einfacher Törn mit zwei Halben Schlägen bzw. Halber Schlag auf einem Slipstek mit verschiedenen Methoden zum Sichern des Endes *(s. Abbildungen auf der nächsten Seite)*.

Unten: **toller Knoten für ein langes Seil.**

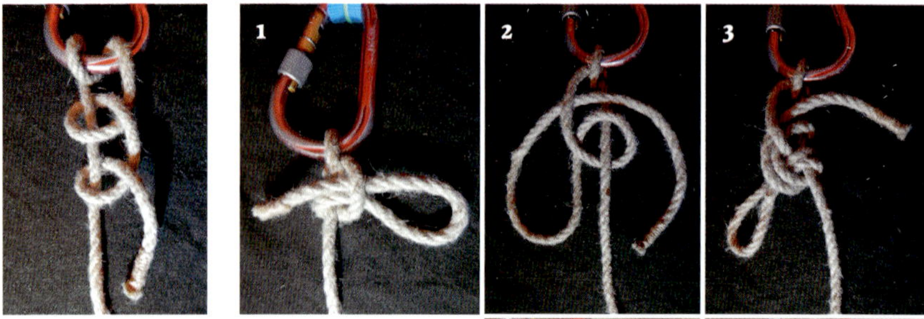

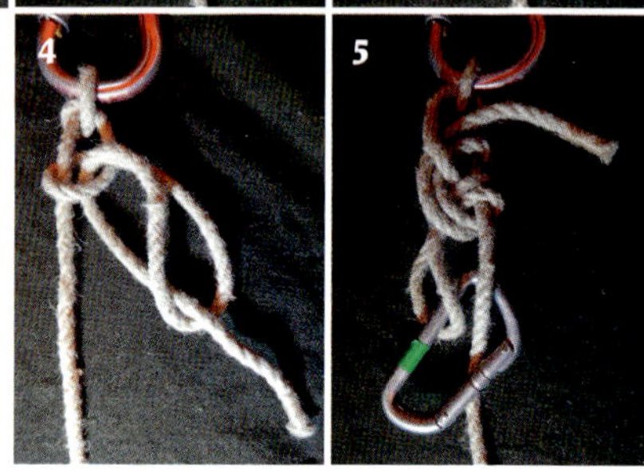

Oben: Einfacher Törn mit zwei Halben Schlägen, *rechts:* Halber Schlag auf einem Slipstek mit verschiedenen Methoden zum Sichern des Endes. (1) Einen Slipstek kannst Du einfach lösen, wenn Du am kurzen Ende des Seils ziehst. (2) Er wird geknüpft, indem Du einen zweiten und (3) dritten Halbschlag mit doppelter Leine knotest. Gegen das unbeabsichtigte Lösen kannst Du das »kurze« Ende hindurchfädeln oder einen Clip einhängen.

Webeleinstek

Dieser Knoten bietet adjustierbare Sicherheit. Den Webeleinstek wählst Du dann, wenn Du ein Seil befestigst und noch in der Lage sein musst, es zu verstellen. Beim Klettern wird er verwendet, um das Seil mit dem Hauptanker zu verbinden, der den Bergsteiger am Berg hält. In dieser Situation ist es wichtig, dass die Verbindung sicher ist und dass Du die Länge anpassen kannst, ohne den Knoten lösen zu müssen.

Es ist der wichtigste Knoten zum Verbinden von zwei Stangen beim Aufbau von Stativen und Unterständen.

Nachteile

- *Es ist ein bisschen verwirrend, bis man ihn »raushat« – dann ist er aber superschnell und leicht zu binden.*
- *Kann seitlich unter wechselnden Belastungen verrutschen – lieber den Konstriktorknoten verwenden.*
- *Es ist schwierig, ihn nach schwerer Belastung zu lösen.*

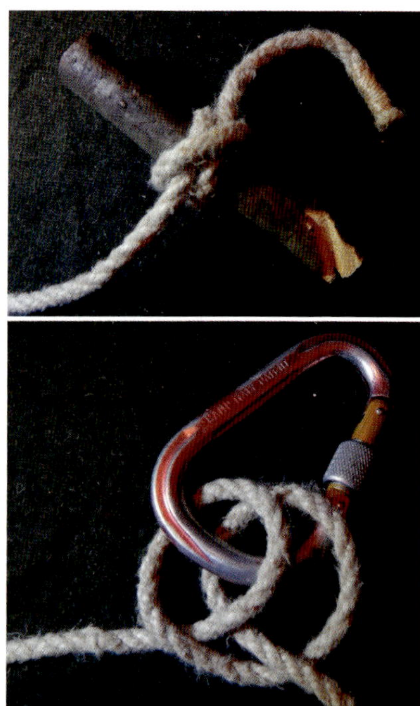

Webeleinstek.

Anwendungen	Eignung
zwei Seile verbinden	X
ein Seil an einem Ring befestigen	***
ein Seil an einem Stock befestigen	***
eine Schlinge machen	X
ein Seil kontrolliert auslaufen lassen	X
Spannung auf ein anderes Seil aufbringen	X
ein Stopperknoten am Ende eines Seils	X

Faktor	Eignung
einfach	**
sicher	***
viele Anwendungen	***
bester Knoten für einen bestimmten Verwendungszweck (hier: Seil an Ring oder Stange sichern)	***
leicht erkennbar, ob korrekt gebunden	**
einfach zu lösen	*
adjustierbar	***
mit einer Hand zu binden	***

Wie binden?

Der Webeleinstek kann auf zwei Arten gebunden werden. Zwei Augen – gelegt bzw. gestochen – allgemeine Art (*siehe Abbildung*). **(1)** Du legst zwei Spiralen nebeneinander. **(2)** die vordere wird hinter die andere gelegt. **(3)** Nun kann der Webeleinstek eingehängt werden.

Variante

Der **Konstriktorknoten** wird am häufigsten verwendet, um Stangen beim Bauen eines Unterstandes zu verbinden. Er zieht sich unter Belastung zu und ist dann meist nicht mehr zu lösen. Nur zu verwenden, wenn das Seil wirklich nicht verrutschen darf und man bereit ist, sein Seil zu opfern (*siehe Abbildung unten rechts*).

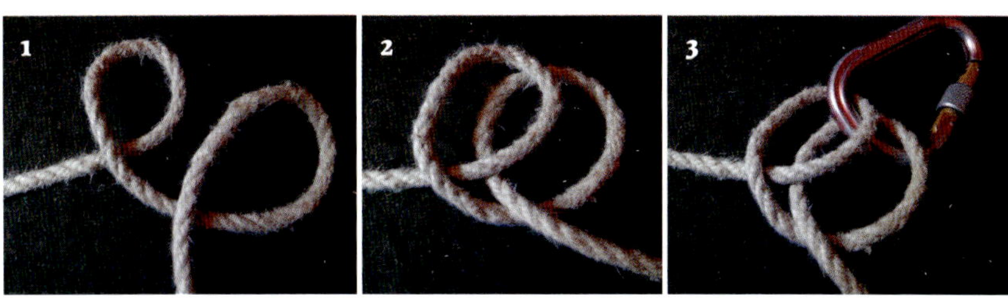

Oben: **Webeleinstek, gelegt,** ***unten:*** **Webeleinstek gestochen,** ***rechts:*** **Konstriktorknoten.**

Halbmastwurf

Der Halbmastwurf (HMS, englisch Munter Hitch genannt) ist ein Bremsknoten. Er wurde von einem Bergsteiger namens Werner Munter in den 1980er Jahren bekannt gemacht. Er dient zum dynamischen Sichern und Abseilen.

Der Halbmastwurf ist unter Belastung und auch nach schwerer Last ganz einfach wieder zu lösen. Dadurch ist er ideal, wenn man das Seil kontrolliert auslaufen lassen oder ein Seil an einem festen Gegenstand befestigen und es kontrolliert lösen möchte. Dies ist der einzige Knoten, den man zum Absenken einer Last an einem Seil verwenden kann. Lerne, diesen Knoten unter Last zu binden, und lerne, ihn mit einer Hand zu binden. Dies ist der Knoten, der Deinem Kameraden aus der Patsche hilft, wenn Du ihn retten oder am Seil sichern musst.

Anwendungen	Eignung
zwei Seile verbinden	X
ein Seil an einem Ring befestigen	X
ein Seil an einem Stock befestigen	X
eine Schlinge machen	X
ein Seil kontrolliert auslaufen lassen	***
Spannung auf ein anderes Seil aufbringen	X
ein Stopperknoten am Ende eines Seils	X

Faktor	Eignung
einfach	***
sicher	**
viele Anwendungen	*
bester Knoten für einen bestimmten Verwendungszweck (hier: Seil unter Belastung auslassen)	***
leicht erkennbar, ob korrekt gebunden	***
einfach zu lösen	***
adjustierbar	***
mit einer Hand zu binden	***

Sicherheitshinweis

Wenn Du in Eile den Halbmastwurf nicht ganz korrekt knotest, dann wird die Last nicht getragen, und Du verbrennst Dir Deine Hand (im besten Fall!). Beim Knoten also stets eine Sichtprüfung vornehmen!

Wie binden?

(1) Du legst ein Auge durch den Karabiner, **(2)** das kurze Ende wird nun hinter den Clip geführt und **(3)** hindurchgefädelt.

Varianten

HMS mit Stopper: Wenn Du die Last aus irgendeinem Grund anhalten musst, kannst Du einfach einen Stopper-Knoten wie den Halben Schlag machen *(s. Abbildungen auf der nächsten Seite)*.

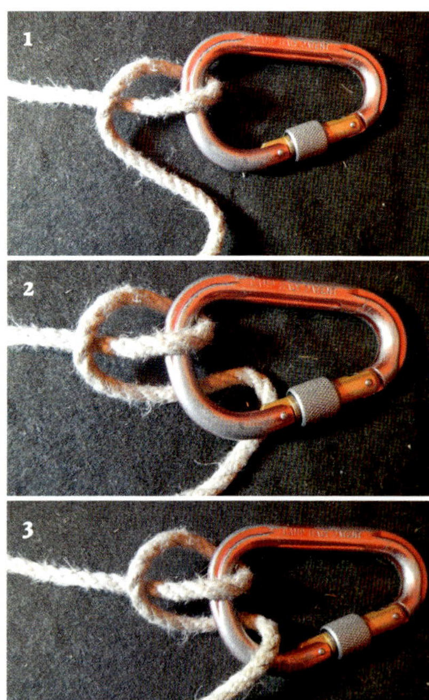

Halbmastwurf-Variante mit Stopper: (1) Auf den HMS wird ein Slipstek (Halbschlag aus Schlaufe) gelegt (2) und stramm gezogen. (3) Das Ende wird mit einem Karabiner am langen Ende gesichert.

Hängematten-Knoten

Jeder, der in einer Hängematte schläft, kennt das Problem, wie er seine Hängematte sichern, die Leinen unproblematisch anpassen und den Knoten am nächsten Morgen immer noch lösen kann. Dieser Knoten ist die Antwort – einen anderen brauchst Du nicht. Diese Mischung aus Mastwurf und Halbmastwurf hat auch viele andere Anwendungszwecke.

Warnung: *Du wirst Dich bestimmt ärgern, dass Du nicht selbst darauf gekommen bist!*

Anwendungen	Eignung
zwei Seile verbinden	X
ein Seil an einem Ring befestigen	***
ein Seil an einem Stock befestigen	***
eine Schlinge machen	***
ein Seil kontrolliert auslaufen lassen	X
Spannung auf ein anderes Seil aufbringen	X
ein Stopperknoten am Ende eines Seils	X

Faktor	Eignung
einfach	***
sicher	***
viele Anwendungen	***
bester Knoten für einen bestimmten Verwendungszweck (hier: Aufhängen einer Hängematte oder Plane)	***
leicht erkennbar, ob korrekt gebunden	***
einfach zu lösen	***
adjustierbar	***
mit einer Hand zu binden	**

Wie binden?

(1) Du beginnst wie beim HMS, legst aber dann **(2)** das kurze Ende doppelt zurück in die Öse **(3)** und ziehst fest.

Varianten
Du kannst wie gewohnt den Hängematten-Knoten binden.

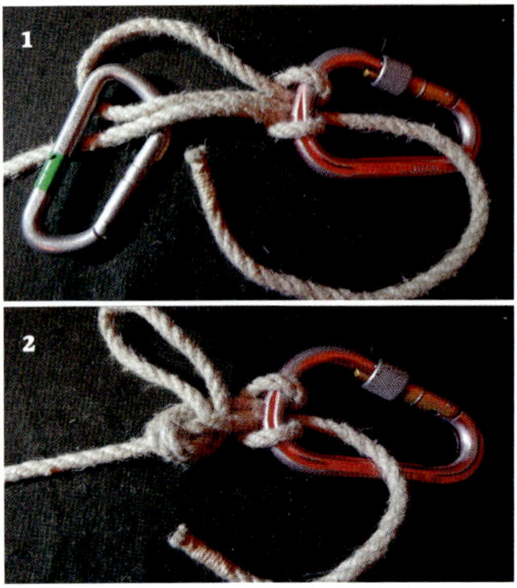

Hängematten-Knoten, Variante.

Anwendungen	Eignung
zwei Seile verbinden	X
ein Seil an einem Ring befestigen	X
ein Seil an einem Stock befestigen	X
eine Schlinge machen	X
ein Seil kontrolliert auslaufen lassen	X
Spannung auf ein anderes Seil aufbringen	***
ein Stopperknoten am Ende eines Seils	X

Faktor	Eignung
einfach	**
sicher	***
viele Anwendungen	*
bester Knoten für einen bestimmten Verwendungszweck (hier: auf ein Seil Spannung aufbringen)	***
leicht erkennbar, ob korrekt gebunden	***
einfach zu lösen	***
adjustierbar	***
mit einer Hand zu binden	X

Prusikknoten

Der Prusikknoten (auch Anker plus 1 genannt) ist ein Klemmknoten. Er ermöglicht uns, Spannung auf ein Seil aufzubringen. Wir wickeln ein kleines Seil mehrmals um das Hauptseil. Der Knoten greift das Seil wie eine Klammer. Je schwerer die Last, desto enger der Griff. Kletterer und Baumpfleger benutzen diesen Knoten, um an einem Seil hochzuklettern. Du kannst sicher sein, dass er bombenfest ist. Beim Bushcraften nutzen wir ihn hauptsächlich, um eine Plane zu straffen. Es ist im Grunde ein Ankerstich mit einer zusätzlichen Schlaufe.

Wie binden?
Du legst eine geknotete Schlaufe hinter das Seil **(1)** und ziehst die Enden mehrfach in sich **(2, 3)** zurück.

Varianten
Um noch mehr Festigkeit zu bekommen, kann man noch eine dritte Schlaufe hinzufügen *(siehe Abb.)*.

Oben: **Standard-Prusik,** ***unten:*** **mit dritter Schlaufe.**

Zimmermannsknoten

Dieser Knoten dient dem (Hoch-)Ziehen von Hölzern. Als Bushcrafter verbringen wir viel Zeit damit, Hölzer aus dem Wald zu ziehen. Da ist der Zimmermannsknoten gut geeignet: Er ist sehr schnell und einfach zu knüpfen, auch mit dicken Handschuhen oder Fäustlingen. Er rutscht leicht ab, wenn die Last entfernt wird, ist schnell und sehr stark.

Du kannst diesen Knoten mit jeder Art von Tauwerk knüpfen, auch Reben, Metalldraht oder dickes Stahlseil sind möglich. Dadurch ist dieser Knoten sehr nützlich zum Befestigen, wenn Du kein richtiges Seil zur Hand hast.

Anwendungen	Eignung
zwei Seile verbinden	X
ein Seil an einem Ring befestigen	*
ein Seil an einem Stock befestigen	***
eine Schlinge machen	X
ein Seil kontrolliert auslaufen lassen	X
Spannung auf ein anderes Seil aufbringen	X
ein Stopperknoten am Ende eines Seils	X

Faktor	Eignung
einfach	***
sicher	**
viele Anwendungen	***
bester Knoten für einen bestimmten Verwendungszweck (hier: Ziehen von Baumstämmen)	***
leicht erkennbar, ob korrekt gebunden	***
einfach zu lösen (hier: besonders nach einer schweren Last)	***
adjustierbar	**
mit einer Hand zu binden	**

Zimmermannsknoten

Sicherheitshinweis:

Dieser Knoten ist darauf ausgelegt, dass er ganz leicht abrutscht, wenn die Belastung nachlässt – sei also unbedingt darauf vorbereitet. Der Knoten zieht sich unter Spannung zusammen, daher sollte er nicht verwendet werden, um eine Person zu sichern.

Wie binden?

Du sicherst das »kurze« Ende am »langen« durch Zurückschlagen und mehrfaches Verwinden.

Varianten

Ein zusätzlicher Halber Schlag sorgt für noch bessere Zugkraft *(siehe Abb. unten)*.

Oben: **Zimmermannsknoten,** ***unten:*** **Variante**

Fuhrmannsknoten

Dies ist ein Knoten für Schwerlasten: Wenn wir etwas mit einem Seil fixieren möchten, müssen wir manchmal eine Menge zusätzliche Spannung aufbringen. Zum Beispiel, wenn wir ein Kanu auf dem Auto festbinden wollen.

Dies ist genau der richtige Knoten dafür: Er funktioniert wie ein einfacher Flaschenzug, so dass Du viel mehr Zug auf das Seil aufbringen kannst, als Du es allein mit Deinen Händen schaffen würdest. Außerdem kannst Du den Knoten so auch mit viel Spannung knüpfen, und er ist sehr einfach wieder zu lösen.

Anwendungen	Eignung
zwei Seile verbinden	**
ein Seil an einem Ring befestigen	***
ein Seil an einem Stock befestigen	***
eine Schlinge machen	X
ein Seil kontrolliert auslaufen lassen	*
Spannung auf ein anderes Seil aufbringen	***
ein Stopperknoten am Ende eines Seils	X

Faktor	Eignung
einfach	*
sicher	***
viele Anwendungen	***
bester Knoten für einen bestimmten Verwendungszweck (hier: auf ein Seil eine starke Spannung aufbringen)	***
leicht erkennbar, ob korrekt gebunden	***
einfach zu lösen (hier: besonders nach einer schweren Last)	***
adjustierbar	***
mit einer Hand zu binden	*

Fuhrmannsknoten.

Sicherheitshinweis:
Sei vorsichtig! Dieser Knoten bringt auf ein Seil VIEL Spannung auf. Ich habe sogar einmal eine Beule in mein Boot gemacht, als ich es mit diesem Knoten auf meinem Gepäckträger befestigt habe.

Wie binden?

(1) Das Seil an einem Anker mit einer Schlaufe befestigen. **(2)** Den Flaschenzug mit einem Slipstek vorbereiten. **(3)** Flaschenzug erstellen und festziehen. **(4)** Last anbinden.

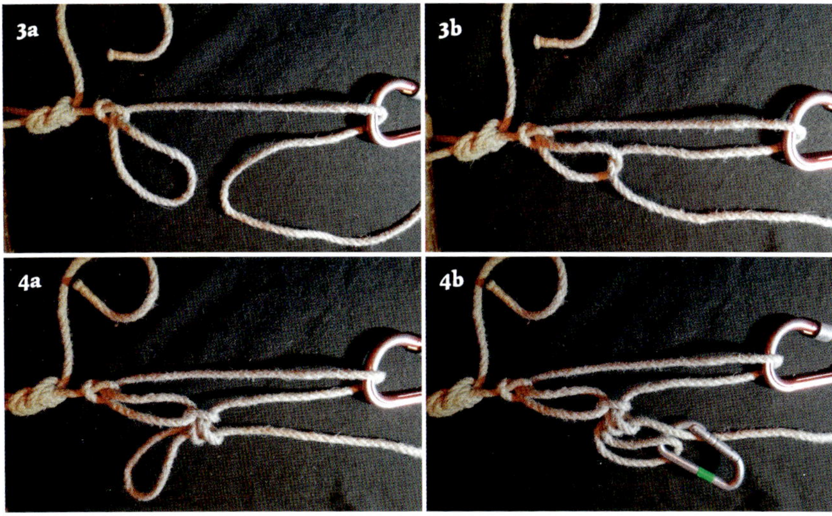

Varianten

Durch Schlaufen kannst Du die Zugkraft dieses Knotens steigern – aber vergiss nicht, dass sich dadurch auch die Reibung erhöht. Dies kannst Du durch die Verwendung eines starken Karabiners beheben (Das Seil erzeugt genügend Spannung, um minderwertige Karabiner zu zerstören).

Knoten können viele Arbeiten wie das Sichern von Lasten, den Lagerbau oder das Sammeln von Brennholz stark vereinfachen.

(Quelle: Joe Vogel/Patricia Braun)

LEDERARBEITEN

WAS, WIE, WOZU?

Leder ist das älteste Textil, das die Menschheit kennt. Bereits vor ca. 800.000 Jahren erkannten unsere steinzeitlichen Vorfahren, dass Produkte aus Tierhäuten sich für sehr viele nützliche Dinge eignen, wodurch der Alltag leichter zu bestreiten war. Aber was ist Leder eigentlich, wie entsteht es, und welchen Einfluss hatte es auf die Geschichte der Menschen? Um Leder herstellen zu können, benötigt man Tierhaut, die von Säugetieren, Reptilien oder auch von Fischen stammen kann. Damit Tierhaut zu Leder wird, muss man sie erst entfleischen und enthaaren, um sie durchs Gerben haltbar machen zu können.

In der langen Geschichte des Leders haben sich viele verschiedene Gerbtechniken entwickelt. Die aus der Steinzeit stammende älteste Methode ist die Hirngerbung, die bis heute von nordamerikanischen Indianern, dem Volk der Zulu in Afrika, in Teilen Asiens sowie von den Sami in Skandinavien praktiziert wird. Dabei handelt es sich um eine Fettgerbung, wie auch bei der Sämischen Gerbung, die allerdings mit Tran statt mit Hirn durchgeführt wird. Bereits ca. 3000 v. Chr. entstanden in Ägypten gleich zwei Gerbmethoden: die Alaungerbung als erste mineralische Gerbung (diese wird auch Weißgerbung genannt, da das Leder besonders hell wird) sowie die erste pflanzliche Gerbung mit aus Arabien importierten Akazienschoten. Erst 1858 wurde von Prof. Friedrich Knapp aus Leipzig die Chromgerbung erfunden, die heute bei 98 % der weltweiten Lederproduktion angewandt wird. Es gibt auch Gerbtechniken, bei denen verschieden Arten kombiniert werden.

Wie kann man nun erkennen, welches Leder wie gegerbt wurde und wofür es sich es am besten eignet? Dazu musst Du wissen, dass Leder entweder gar nicht, nur oberflächlich oder durch und durch gefärbt sein kann, was die Identifikation der verwendeten Gerbmethode erschwert.

Chromgegerbtes Leder hat ungefärbt eine graue Grundfarbe, die man oft an der Schnittkante oder an bereits abgenutzten Lederwaren erkennen kann. Sie kann je nach Zusammensetzung der Gerbbrühe auch graugrün, graublau oder graugelb sein. Dieses Leder eignet sich für nahezu alle Ausrüstungsgegenstände wie Beutel, Gürtel oder Kleidungsteile, da es sich unter Einfluss von Nässe und Wärme kaum ungewollt verformt.

Wenn Du aber zum Beispiel eine Messerscheide anfertigen möchtest, die passgenau auf das Messer angeformt ist, eignet sich dazu pflanzlich gegerbtes Leder viel besser, da dieses Leder in nassem Zustand nahezu jeder Form angepasst werden kann. Dieses Leder erkennt man an einer hellbraunen Färbung, die von den natürlichen pflanzlichen Gerbstoffen, wie z.B. von der Eiche, stammt. Ich persönlich bevorzuge pflanzlich gegerbtes Leder wegen seiner Naturbelassenheit. Es wird auch als vegetabiles Leder oder Bio-Leder bezeichnet.

Achte für jedes Vorhaben auf die richtige Stärke des Leders: für Beutel und Taschen sind Stärken zwischen 1 und 3 mm gut geeignet, für Messerscheiden oder Holster zwischen 2 und 3,5 mm und für Gürtel und Trageriemen zwischen 3 und 4,5 mm. Es kommt immer auch darauf an, wie fest das Leder ist. Dabei können dünne Leder hart sein, aber auch dicke weich – das hängt davon ab, wie lange bestimmte Arbeitsschritte beim Gerben durchgeführt werden. Außerdem kann die Stärke von Leder über die gesamte Fläche leicht abweichen.

Hinweis: *Dünnere Leder, die sogenannten Oberleder, werden traditionell nach Quadratfuß (sqft) oder auch nach Quadratmeter (m^2) berechnet. Bei dickeren und festeren Ledern wie Bodenleder oder Blankleder berechnet sich der Preis nach Gewicht (kg).*

Wer sich Leder für diverse Projekte kaufen möchte, kann zum Beispiel bei einem Schuster seines Vertrauens oder in einem Lederfachgeschäft nachfragen. Es gibt auch viele Onlineshops – allerdings ist es vorteilhaft, wenn man das Leder vor dem Kauf in die Hand nehmen kann, um zu testen, wie fest es ist und ob es den eigenen Vorstellungen entspricht.

Was macht nun Leder zu einem geeigneten Textil für Bushcrafter? Zum Ersten spricht die lange Tradition der Materialwahl von der Steinzeit über die Trapper und Waldläufer dafür, außerdem ist es ein Naturprodukt und kann sehr strapazierfähig sein. Aus Leder lassen sich eine Vielzahl von Ausrüstungsgegenständen herstellen, die nützlich für den Bushcrafter-Alltag sind: Taschen, Beutel, Messerscheiden, Gürtel, Holster, Teile der Bekleidung und vieles mehr.

GERBEN

Wasserwerkstatt

Um in alter Trappermanier ein Leder oder Fell zu gerben, brauchst Du zuerst eine frisch abgezogene Tierhaut. Diese kannst Du in der Regel kostenlos von Jägern bekommen, da die Tierhäute normalerweise entsorgt werden. Wenn Du nicht direkt beginnen kannst, die Tierhaut zu bearbeiten, kannst Du sie auch in einen Beutel geben und einfrieren, oder Du gibst auf die Fleischseite mehrere Handvoll Salz. Dazu kannst Du gewöhnliches Streusalz verwenden. Auf der ganzen Fläche sollte sich eine dünne Schicht Salz befinden, auch in den Läufen. Falte es zusammen, gib das gesalzene Fell in einen Müllbeutel und häng diesen auf. Über ein kleines Loch, das Du in die Tüte gestochen hast, kann das Wasser, welches dem Fell durch das Salz entzogen wird, abtropfen. Wenn das Wasser nach ein paar Tagen abgetropft ist, legst Du die Tüte mit dem Fell in einen Eimer mit Deckel und bewahrst sie an einem möglichst kühlen, dunklen und trockenen Ort auf.

Verschiedene Lederarten *(v.o.)*: chromgegerbt & oberflächlich gefärbt, chromgegerbt & durchgefäbt, pflanzlich gegerbt & oberflächlich gefärbt, pflanzlich gegerbt & ungefärbt.

Um ein Leder oder Fell mit Hirn zu gerben, eignet sich die warme Jahreszeit besser, da das werdende Leder immer wieder trocknen muss. Die genaue Vorgehensweise wurde in der Vergangenheit je nach Klimazone und Wasserressourcen abgewandelt. Die folgende Erklärung setzt voraus, dass warme Temperaturen herrschen und ausreichend Wasser vorhanden ist. Dann kann man auch in einem Bushcraftcamp ein Fell oder Leder in wenigen Tagen gerben.

Für die Herstellung von Leder benötigt man nur einen Teil der Tierhaut: die mittlere Schicht oder Lederhaut (lat. Corium). Um diese zu erhalten, müssen die Haare und die Oberhaut (lat. Epidermis) sowie die Unterhaut (lat. Subcutis, engl. Membrane) entfernt werden, was man als Enthaaren und Entfleischen bezeichnet. Die Lederhaut besteht aus zwei Schichten, der Retikular- und der Papillarschicht. Die Retikularschicht (das bedeutet »netzartig«) wird auch als Fleisch- oder Aasseite bezeichnet. Die Papillarschicht (engl. *Grain*), die auch Narbenschicht genannt wird, bildet die glatte Oberfläche, den Narben. Bleibt der Narben unversehrt, hast Du Glattleder, wenn Du ihn leicht anraust, erhältst Du Nubukleder. Der Narben stabilisiert die Faserstruktur und sorgt somit für ein strapazierfähiges Leder. Entfernst Du den Narben komplett, bekommst Du Veloursleder. So haben es meist die nordamerikanischen Indianer gemacht, dies ergab die typische Rauleder-Optik. Da Häute von nicht domestizierten Tieren ein festeres Bindegewebe haben, ist auch das Veloursleder daraus sehr strapazierfähig. Wenn Du statt Leder ein Fell herstellen möchtest, musst Du lediglich die Unterhaut entfernen, die Oberhaut bleibt mit den Haaren bestehen.

Bevor es ans Gerben geht, sollte die Haut aufgetaut oder gründlich vom Salz befreit sein, indem das Salz zuerst abgestreift wird, um die Haut danach mehrmals mit Wasser zu spülen. Wenn Du ein Fell gerben möchtest, kannst Du jetzt direkt die Haut entfleischen. Wenn Du aber ein Leder herstellen möchtest, braucht es noch einen weiteren Schritt. Damit sich die Haare aus der Haut lösen, wird sie geäschert. Dazu füllst Du eine Wanne mit Wasser und gibst ein paar Handvoll feine Asche dazu, so dass Du eine gesättigte Lösung erhältst. Da Du in einem Bushcraftcamp in der Regel keine Wanne zur Hand hast, kannst Du auch eine Grube graben und diese mit einer wasserdichten Plane auslegen.

Hinweis: *Wenn Du ein frisches rohes Ei in die Lösung legst und es oben schwimmt, ist ausreichend Asche zugesetzt.*

Leg nun die Haut in die Äscherlösung und beschwere sie mit sauberen Steinen, so dass sie komplett unter Wasser ist. Je nach den herrschenden Temperaturen kann dieser Vorgang zwei Tage oder auch eine Woche dauern. Du solltest auf jeden Fall täglich überprüfen, ob sich die Haare bereits lösen, wenn man daran zieht. Wenn die Haare sich ohne spürbaren Widerstand lösen lassen, wird das Fell aus der Äscherlösung herausgenommen.

Gerberbaum.

Achtung: *Bis die Haut von Haaren und Fett befreit ist, solltest Du Schutzhandschuhe tragen, da die Haut durch Bakterien hoch infektiös ist.*

Es wird empfohlen, die Haut vor dem Weiterbearbeiten gründlich mit Wasser zu spülen. Wenn vorhanden, kann man dies auch mit einer leichten Essiglösung machen.

Wichtige Werkzeuge zur Lederbearbeitung *(v.o)*: Ziehmesser, scharfes Arbeitsmesser, Leuku.

Das neutralisiert die Äscherlösung und sorgt für ein weicheres Leder. Wenn Du zu lange äscherst, löst sich zu viel Gelatine aus der Haut, wodurch sie unbrauchbar wird. Alternativ zum Äschern kann man die Haut auch nur in Wasser einlegen. Bei dieser Methode kann es aber 2–3 Wochen dauern, bis sich die Haare lösen, da sich erst Fäulnisbakterien bilden müssen, die für den Porenaufschluss sorgen. Das Äschern (und auch das Wässern) kann durch die hohe Konzentration von Bakterien sehr geruchsintensiv sein. Um die Haut von den restlichen Haaren und Fett zu befreien, ist es sinnvoll, sich einen Gerberbaum zu bauen, denn damit wird die Arbeit sehr erleichtert.

Zum Abschaben der Unterhaut und Haare bietet sich der Rücken eines Ziehmessers an, aber auch jedes andere Werkzeug aus Metall mit einer 90-Grad-Kante, z.B. der Rücken eines großen Messers. Auch Werkzeuge aus Knochen oder Stein kannst Du dafür verwenden.

Schneide die Läufe auf der Innenseite auf, damit Du sie flach auflegen kannst. Um die Haut nun zu entfleischen, legst Du sie mit den Haaren nach unten auf den Gerberbaum und presst Deinen Bauch dagegen, um die Haut zu fixieren. Durch das Anpressen können Abdrücke entstehen, die später wieder restlos verschwinden. Achte darauf, dass die Haut nach unten immer faltenfrei glatt gezogen ist, ansonsten kannst Du Dir schnell Löcher in die Haut reißen. Setz Dein Schabewerkzeug in einem Winkel von ca. 20 bis 30 Grad an und drück die Unterhaut in kleinen und geraden Bewegungen nach unten weg. An hartnäckigen Stellen kannst Du auch, mit viel Gespür, die Klingenschneide verwenden. Die Unterhaut ist ein labberiges, mit Fett durchzogenes Gewebe, das an der Lederhaut endet. Die Lederhaut erkennst Du an einer glatten weißen Oberfläche wie auch an der festen Struktur. Arbeite Dich von der Mitte der Haut nach außen durch und dreh sie immer wieder weiter. Falls noch einige Sehnenbändchen verbleiben, die nicht

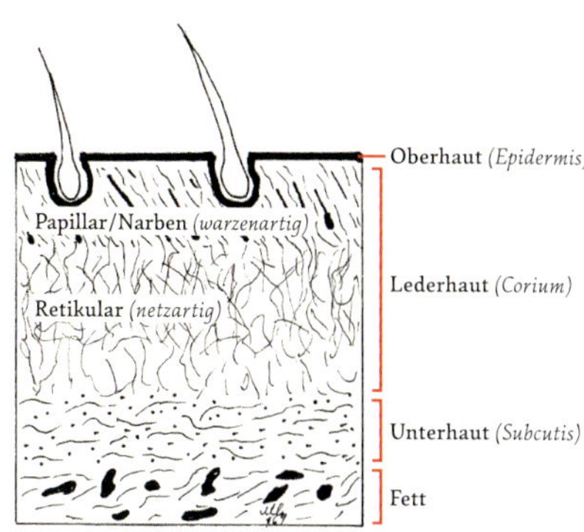

Querschnitt durch die Haut eines Säugetiers.

Getrocknete Rohhaut, hirngegerbtes Leder, Fell *(v.l.)*.

weggehen wollen, ist das kein Problem. Diese verschwinden in einem späteren Arbeitsgang.

Um die Haare zu entfernen, drehst Du die Haut um. Versuche, so viel Haare wie möglich per Hand abzuzupfen, bevor Du mit dem Abschaben beginnst. Das Abschaben der Haare ist ähnlich wie bei der Unterhaut, jedoch kann es sein, dass Du die Haut öfter drehen musst, um die Haare von verschiedenen Seiten anzugehen, wenn sie sich nicht lösen wollen. Zusammen mit den Haaren löst sich in der Regel auch die Oberhaut – diese ist sehr dünn und muss wie die Unterhaut entfernt werden. Auf der Narbenseite kannst Du dann kleine Poren erkennen, in denen die Haare waren. An manchen Stellen sitzen die Haare fester, dort kann man mit der Klingenschneide die Haare regelrecht abrasieren. Wenn Du nun die Haut von Haaren und Fett befreit hast, spüle die soeben hergestellte Rohhaut mit Wasser durch. An dieser Stelle kannst Du, wenn nötig, eine Pause einlegen, indem Du sie z.B. auf einer Platte glattziehst und in der Sonne trocknest. Die getrocknete Rohhaut kannst Du bei trockenen Bedingungen nahezu ewig lagern.

Die Rohhaut wird auch Blöße genannt, da die Haut nackt und bloßgestellt ist. Aus dünn geschabten Blößen von Ziegen und Schafen wurde das erste Pergament hergestellt, ein Vorgänger des Papiers. Bereits aus Rohhaut kann man z.B. Schnüre, Kisten, Messerscheiden, Trommelfelle, Fenster, Schilder und vieles mehr herstellen.

Als Gerbstoff verwenden wir im Idealfall das Hirn des erlegten Tieres wie auch dessen Unterhautfett, Leber und optional dessen Knochenmark. Die Organe müssen jedoch nicht von demselben Tier stammen, von dem Du die Haut hast, entscheidend ist die Gesamtmasse. Alternativ kann man auch Schweinehirn bei einem Metzger mit eigener Schlachtung kaufen. Die Leber sorgt dafür, dass das Leder weicher wird, und das Knochenmark sorgt für eine hellere Farbe. Wenn Du nur mit Knochenmark gerbst, erhältst Du fast weißes Leder. Für eine Rehdecke benötigt man ca. 800 g Hirn oder eine Mischung aus den oben genannten Organen.

Hirn

Bevor Du das Hirn zum Gerben verwenden kannst, musst Du es noch vorbereiten. Achte darauf, dass die Hirnhaut entfernt ist und im Hirn keine Knochensplitter sind, da diese später das Leder verletzen können. Zerschneide und zerdrücke das Hirn so fein als möglich, so dass Du einen glibberigen Brei bekommst. Wenn Du das Hirn bereits zuhause mixt oder fein wolfst, lässt es sich später noch besser einarbeiten. Koche unter ständigem Rühren 800 g rosaroten Hirnbrei mit ca. 1 Liter Wasser so lange, bis die Hirnsuppe weiß wird. Sie soll danach eine schlotzige Substanz haben. Wenn sie zu fest sein sollte, gib einfach noch etwas Wasser dazu. Ein Schuss Essigessenz rundet die Hirnsuppe ab und sorgt für ein weicheres Leder. Manch einen erinnert der Geruch dabei an gekochte

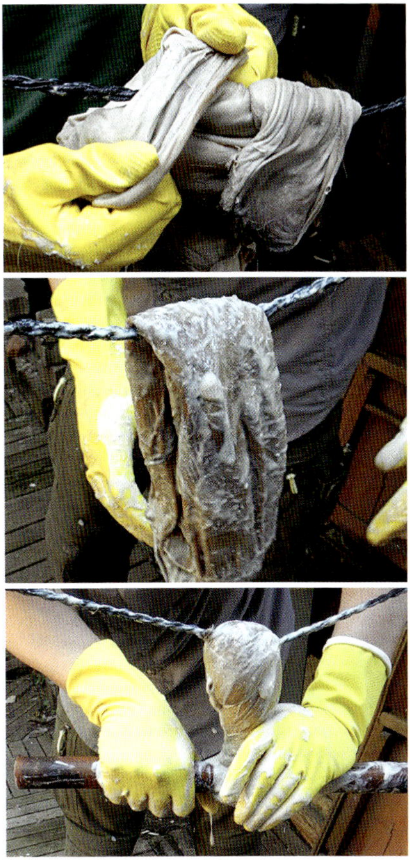

Hirn einarbeiten (drehen).

Stollen des Leders.

Eier. (Der Hirnbrei kann übrigens auch mit Eigelb gestreckt werden, das verleiht dem Leder einen leichten Gelbstich.) Wenn die Hirnsuppe nur noch handwarm ist, kannst Du eine frische oder eine getrocknete Rohhaut hineinlegen. Getrocknete Rohhäute saugen die Hirnsuppe regelrecht auf, wohingegen bei frischen Rohhäuten erst das Wasser in den Fasern verdrängt werden muss. Wenn die Hirnmasse zu stark abgekühlt ist, solltest Du sie aufwärmen, da sich durch die Wärme die Poren öffnen und das Fett leicht einzuarbeiten ist.

Wenn die Rohhaut ca. 20 Min. in der Hirnsuppe gelegen hat, wird die Haut ausgedreht. Dazu spannst Du so stramm wie möglich ein dünnes Seil oder verdrillte Schnüre z.B. zwischen zwei Bäumen. Der Abstand sollte nicht zu lang sein, da es sonst zu stark nachgibt. Du legst die Haut mit ca. einem Viertel der Länge über das Seil.

Den Rest schlägst Du so um das Seil, dass auf jeder Seite zwei Lagen Haut hängen und sich eine Röhre bildet. Die äußeren Enden der Röhre schlägst Du wie einen Hemdärmel ein, so dass sich beide Enden in der Mitte treffen. Jetzt steckst Du einen Ast durch den entstandenen Ring und wringst die Haut aus. Diesen Arbeitsschritt könnt Ihr auch zu zweit mittels zwei Ästen durchführen. Fang dabei die abtropfende Hirnmasse in einem Behälter auf. Dieser Vorgang wird mindestens fünfmal wiederholt, bis die gesamte Hirnmasse eingearbeitet ist. Zwischendurch kannst Du die Haut auch zum Trocknen aufhängen und sie in alle Richtungen dehnen, so dass sich die Poren öffnen und aufnahmefähiger werden. Besonders an dicken Stellen der Haut wie Hals, Rückenkamm und Hüfte ist es ratsam, zusätzlich die Hirnmasse liegend mit einem Stein einzuarbeiten. Wenn Du das Leder gegen das Licht hältst, sollen keine halbtransparenten Stellen mehr zu erkennen sein. Je blickdichter das Leder wird, desto mehr Fett hat sich bereits angelagert.

Wenn Du die gesamte Masse verarbeitet hast und das Leder getrocknet ist, muss es gedehnt werden. Dazu gibt es verschiedene Techniken. Das sogenannte »Stollen« funktioniert so, dass Du das Leder über eine möglichst dünne und abgerundete Kante ziehst.

Dazu kannst Du z.B. ein Paddel vom Boot verwenden, oder Du ziehst es über Dein Knie. Beim Stollen werden die Fasern gedehnt, was man an der weißen Verfärbung erkennen kann. Dadurch wird das Leder auch weicher und geschmeidiger. Beim »Seilen« ziehst Du das Leder über ein gespanntes Seil hin und her, wobei vom Entfleischen stehengebliebene feine Fasern und Adern verschwinden. Der Rand des Leders, wie der Halsbereich, wird oft nicht ganz so weich, da dort meist nicht so viel Fett eingedrungen ist.

Räuchern

Wenn Du so weit gekommen bist, hältst Du ein fettgares Leder in Deinen Händen. In diesem Zustand kann das Fett z.B. durch Regen oder Schweiß ausgewaschen werden. Um die Gerbung zu fixieren, musst Du das Leder noch kalt räuchern. Das Formaldehyd im Rauch lagert sich auf dem Leder ab und wirkt wie eine Imprägnierung. Dies kannst Du auf verschiedenen Wegen erreichen. Am besten hängst Du Dein Leder in ein Dreibein und umwickelst es mit einer Plane. Dadurch wird der Rauch eingefangen und kann länger auf das Leder wirken. Das Aktivräuchern benötigt zwar weniger Vorbereitung, dafür musst Du ständig anwesend sein: Aus einem daneben liegenden Feuer entnimmst Du ein stark rauchendes (nicht brennendes!) Stück Holz und hältst es unter das Leder. Wenn das Holz nicht mehr raucht, nimmst Du das nächste Stück und fährst fort, so lange bis das Leder eine leicht goldgelbe Farbe angenommen hat, so wie man es von geräuchertem Fisch kennt. ***Achtung:*** *Der Rauch sollte auf Höhe des Leders nur handwarm sein, sonst kann es verbrennen.*

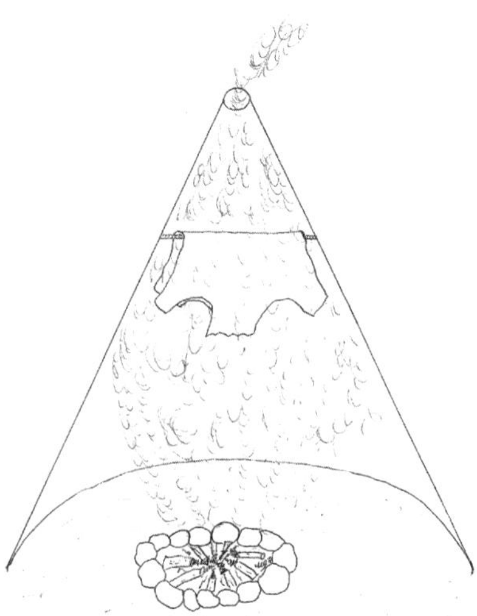

Das Leder wird unter einer Plane geräuchert.

Du kannst den Rauch auch in einem Grubenfeuer mit einem Rauchabzug, z.B. mit einem alten Ofenrohr, erzeugen. Durch das Rohr leitest Du den Rauch dann in die Räucherkammer. Diese sollte oben etwas geöffnet sein und im Wind liegen, so dass ein Kamineffekt entsteht und der Rauch hindurchgezogen werden kann. Auch mit einem Feuer in einem Tipi kannst Du Dein Leder räuchern. Egal wie Du räucherst, Du musst das Leder immer wieder drehen, damit der Rauch überall hingelangt. Nachdem Du das Leder fertig geräuchert hast, dehne es erneut auf. Wenn Dein Leder immer noch an einigen Stellen nicht blickdicht ist, kannst Du erneut Hirn einarbeiten und räuchern. Nach starkem Gebrauch empfiehlt es sich sogar, das Leder auf diese Art zu pflegen. Besonders guten Rauch kannst Du mit der Rinde von Nadelhölzern erzeugen. Wenn Du das Leder zu Kleidung verarbeiten möchtest, wasch es mit Wasser und etwas Kernseife, da das Formaldehyd Hautreizungen verursachen kann. Wenn Dich der Rauchgeruch stört, lüfte gründlich an der frischen Luft.

Fell

Wenn Du kein Leder, sondern ein Fell gerben möchtest, musst Du etwas anders vorgehen. Die Haut wird weder geäschert noch gewässert, sondern nur gut mit lauwarmem Wasser und etwas Kernseife gewaschen. So löst sich der Dreck aus den Haaren, besonders bei wolligen Haaren. Bei Schaf oder Lamm kann eine alte Haarbürste sehr hilfreich sein, damit lassen sich Pflanzenreste und Verfilzungen im Haar entfernen. Nachdem Du auf dem Gerberbaum die Unterhaut entfernt hast, ist es ratsam, das Fell aufzuspannen. Du kannst es bei trockenem Untergrund mit Holzpflöcken auf den Boden oder mit Schnur in einen Rahmen spannen. Egal wie und wo Du Tierhäute spannst, sollten sie immer feucht bis nass sein, da sie sonst schnell reißen können. Zuvor solltest Du alle Löcher in der Haut zunähen, da diese gedehnt werden oder sogar weiter einreißen können. Wenn Du das Fell auf dem Boden gespannt hast, massierst Du mit Hilfe eines großen Kieselsteins die Hirnmasse peu à peu in die Haut ein. Durch das Einmassieren dehnt sich die Haut und muss immer wieder nachgespannt werden. Nachdem Du die gesamte Masse eingearbeitet hast, kannst Du das Fell dehnen und räuchern, wie beim Leder beschrieben.

Wenn Du das Fell in einen Rahmen spannst, kannst Du Dir beim Dehnen von der Schwerkraft helfen lassen. Achte darauf, dass der Rahmen groß genug ist, da das Fell durchs Dehnen noch größer wird.

Zunächst stichst Du am Rand mit einem spitzen Messer Löcher ein. Diese sollten etwa 1,5 cm Abstand zum Rand haben und parallel dazu liegen. Mach die Schlitze nur so lang, dass Deine Schnur durchpasst. Der Abstand zwischen den Löchern sollte 15–20 cm betragen. Je gerader die Kante verläuft, desto größer können die Abstände sein. Bei engeren Kurven, wie zwischen Hals und Vorderläufen, kannst Du den Abstand auch verringern. Jetzt fädelst Du die Schnüre in die Löcher ein. Pro Biegung im Fell empfiehlt es sich, jeweils eine separate Schnur zu verwenden, damit sich die Spannungskraft besser auf das Fell verteilen kann. Die Enden dieser Schnur werden am Rahmen befestigt. Durch die entstandenen Schnurschlaufen zwischen den Löchern in der Haut wird mit einer weiteren Schnur das Fell nach außen in Richtung Rahmen gespannt. Dies ermöglicht ein leichteres

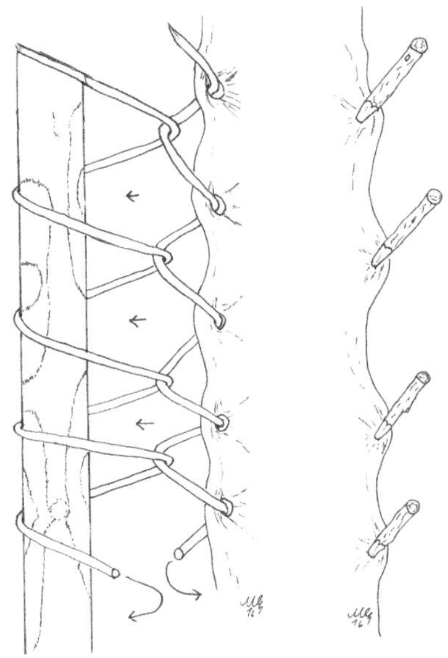

Spanntechnik: Schnur, Pflöcke.

Nachspannen, als wenn die Spannschnur direkt durch das Leder läuft. Dabei wird nur die Schnur, die um den Rahmen läuft, nachgespannt; die Schnur, die durch die Haut gefädelt ist, nur dann, wenn die Schlaufen zu groß sein sollten. Achte darauf, dass das Fell möglichst mittig im Rahmen liegt.

Bock den Rahmen nun an den Ecken auf, so dass das Fell in der Luft hängt. Gib eine Portion Hirnmasse darauf und massiere diese restlos mit einem Stein ein. Nun kannst Du das Fell langsam mit Steinen beschweren, damit es gedehnt wird. Eine Tierhaut hält mehr aus, als Du denkst. Das Fell kannst Du wenige Minuten bis zu mehreren Tagen in dieser Stellung halten. Nachdem Du die Steine runtergenommen hast, hängt die Haut nach unten durch. Spanne nun über die Schnüre die Haut nach, so dass sie wieder straff und waagerecht im Rahmen hängt. Wenn sie zu trocken sein sollte, feuchte sie erst an, damit sie nicht reißt. Das wiederholst Du so lange, bis die Hirnmasse aufgebraucht ist. Danach kannst Du das Fell noch zusätzlich dehnen und räuchern. Wenn Du das

Gerben auf mehrere Tage streckst, stell die restliche Hirnmasse kühl, da sie sonst ranzig werden kann. Wenn Du besonders große Häute hast, wie z.B. von einem Rothirsch, kannst Du auch Leder im Rahmen gerben. Massiere hierbei abwechselnd das Hirn von beiden Seiten ein. Du kannst natürlich Leder und Felle auch im Rahmen räuchern. Dazu stellst Du Deinen Rahmen neben ein Feuer, das Du z.B. mit Rinde von Nadelhölzern zum Qualmen bringst. Achte darauf, dass der Rauch, der am Rahmen ankommt, nicht zu heiß ist.

LEDERRIEMEN SCHNEIDEN

Um Leder zu schneiden, brauchst Du vor allem eine scharfe Klinge. Es ist wichtig, dass das Messer Dir gut in der Hand liegt und dass die Klinge nicht zu dick ist. Gerade Streifen von einem Leder zu schneiden, ist recht einfach, vor allem mit Hilfe eines Lineals, aber manchmal reicht die entstehende Länge für das gewünschte Projekt nicht aus.

Um die größtmögliche Länge zu erhalten, musst Du das Leder spiralförmig von innen heraus schneiden. Diese Technik wurde schon von verschiedenen Autoren in Outdoor- und Survivalbüchern beschrieben. Nur die wenigsten haben es allerdings geschafft, nach diesen Beschreibungen erfolgreich Riemen zu schneiden. Aus meiner jahrelangen praktischen Erfahrung mit Profi-Lederwerkzeugen habe ich die Funktion eines Riemenschneiders so adaptiert, dass auch ein Outdoor-Einsatz möglich ist. Der Trick dabei ist, das Leder in die richtige Richtung zu leiten. Dafür sollte es nicht zu weich und zu dünn sein, da es dann schwerer zu kontrollieren ist; das Leder neigt bei dieser Technik dazu, sich nach oben und zur Seite zu drücken. Das kannst Du verhindern, indem Du eine kleine Führung schnitzt, die das Leder in seine Schranken weist. Dies musst Du je nach Leder und gewünschter Riemenbreite anpassen. Dein kleines Hilfsmittel gibt die Breite zur Klinge und die Höhe vor, so hat das Leder kaum Platz, auszuweichen.

Lederriemen mit einer Klinge zum Band schneiden.

Du schneidest zuerst mittig ein Loch mit ca. 3 cm Durchmesser in das Leder. Nimm die Narbenseite nach unten, so gleitet das Leder später besser. Jetzt schneidest Du, für Rechtshänder in Uhrzeigersinn, den Anfang vor, ca. um den halben Umfang. Er sollte etwas dünner sein als die spätere Riemenbreite. Lege erst das Leder über Dein Führungshölzchen, bevor Du das Messer danebensetzt. Fädle den vorgeschnittenen Anfang durch den entstandenen Tunnel, zwischen Messer und Hölzchen. Da das Messer instabil sein kann, weil es nur mit der Spitze im Holz steckt, kannst Du z.B. Dein Kinn auf den Messergriff legen, um es so zu stabilisieren. Jetzt kannst Du mit einer Hand langsam an der Riemenspitze ziehen und drehst mit der anderen Hand den Rest des Leders mit. Taste Dich langsam heran, und versuche, ein Gefühl fürs Leder zu bekommen. Falls Du abrutschst und den Riemen abschneidest, kannst Du wieder neu ansetzen. Das machst Du so lange, bis Du an den Rand Deines Leders kommst oder der Riemen Dir lang genug erscheint.

Lederriemen können je nach Stärke und Breite für unterschiedliche Verwendungszwecke eingesetzt werden. Du kannst sie zum Vernähen von Beuteln und Taschen, aber auch als Schnur-Ersatz im Camp benutzen.

Klassische Lederbeutel: Ein nahtloser Lederbeutel *(links)* und ein genähter.

Wenn z.B. eine Verbindung eines Dreibeins dauerhaft halten muss, eignen sich Riemen aus Rohhaut besonders gut, da diese sich in nassem Zustand anschmiegen und trocken fest werden.

https://youtu.be/4zNvikSl_bw

NÄHTECHNIKEN

Möchtest Du Leder nähen, ist es sinnvoll, Dir Ledernadeln (dreikantige Spitze) und Sattlernadeln (stumpfe Spitze) sowie eine Stechahle zum Vorstechen zuzulegen. Dünnere Leder kannst Du meist mit Ledernadeln ohne Vorstechen nähen, da die dreikantige Spitze direkt durchs Leder schneidet. Bei dickerem Leder musst Du mit der Ahle Löcher vorstechen, um dann mit den Sattlernadeln nähen zu können. Du kannst auch mehrere Leder mit dünnen Riemen vernähen, wenn Du vorab mit Lochzange oder Locheisen Löcher entlang der Kante anbringst. Eine detaillierte Anleitung zu verschiedenen Nähtechniken findest Du im Video.

https://youtu.be/CPykoP-5fWQ

PROJEKTE AUS LEDER

Runder Lederbeutel

So kannst Du Dir ganz einfach, ohne zu nähen, selbst einen Lederbeutel herstellen. Du benötigst dazu nur ein scharfes Messer und eine Lochzange als Werkzeug. Überleg Dir, was alles in den Beutel reinpassen soll, um abzuschätzen, wie groß er werden muss. Zur besseren Vorstellung kannst Du alle Gegenstände, die reinpassen sollen, auf ein Blatt Zeitungspapier legen und es darumknüllen. So kannst Du etwa abschätzen, wie viel Flä-

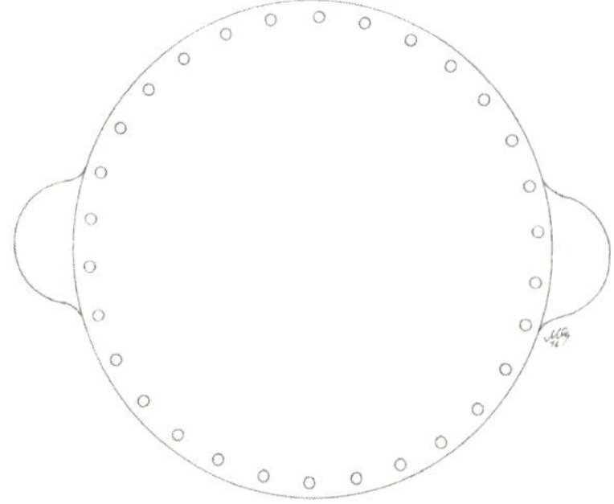

Schablone für den runden Lederbeutel.

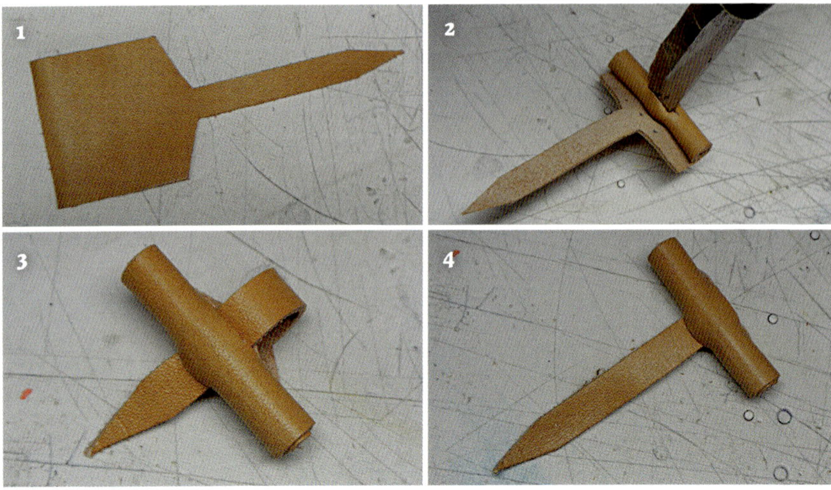

Lederknopf: (1) Die Grundform für den Knopf wird geschnitten. (2) Der breite Lappen wird eng gerollt und mit einem durchgehenden Schnitt versehen. (3) Die schmale Zunge wird hindurch gefädelt. (4) Schon ist der Knopf fertig.

che der Beutel haben muss. Als Hilfsmittel zum Aufzeichnen eignen sich Eimer oder Teller, die Du im Haushalt findest.

Nachdem Du einen Kreis mit dem gewünschten Umfang auf dem Leder aufgezeichnet hast, zeichne noch zwei gegenüberliegende Laschen dazu. An diesen lässt sich der Beutel später besser aufziehen. Nachdem Du den Beutel ausgeschnitten hast, musst Du am Rand entlang Löcher für die Schnur machen. Nun brauchst Du noch zwei Schnüre, die etwas länger sind als der Kreisumfang. Diese werden so eingefädelt, dass sie an einer Lasche beginnen, herumführen und ein Loch neben dem Anfang enden. An jeder Lasche sollten zwei Schnurenden herausschauen.

Wenn beide Schnüre so eingefädelt sind, kann der Beutel sauber von beiden Seiten zugezogen und an den Laschen wieder leicht geöffnet werden. So einfach ist es, sich selbst einen Lederbeutel zu machen, wo z.B. Dein Feuer-Kit oder Zunder seinen Platz finden kann.

Lederknopf

Um einen Knopf aus Leder herzustellen, eignen sich kleine Abschnitte, die sonst oft keine Verwendung mehr finden. Du benötigst dafür nur ein spitzes und scharfes Messer. Dazu schneidest Du das Leder so zu, dass es der Form eines Pfannenwenders ähnelt. Der breitere Teil wird fest eingerollt bis zum Beginn des schmalen Abschnitts. Dann stichst Du mit dem Messer so durch die Lederrolle, dass Du den schmalen Streifen durchfädeln kannst.

Du kannst auch zuvor ein Stück Draht durch die Spitze ziehen, das als Nadel fungiert. Nun musst Du den Knopf nur noch mit dem abstehenden Stück annähen, fertig!

https://youtu.be/Y9e8GCKQiGA

Genähter Lederbeutel

Um Dir eine schöne Bushcraft-Gürteltasche zu machen, benötigst Du einige Werkzeuge und zwei verschiedene Leder. Als Material für den Beutel selbst verwendest Du ein wei-

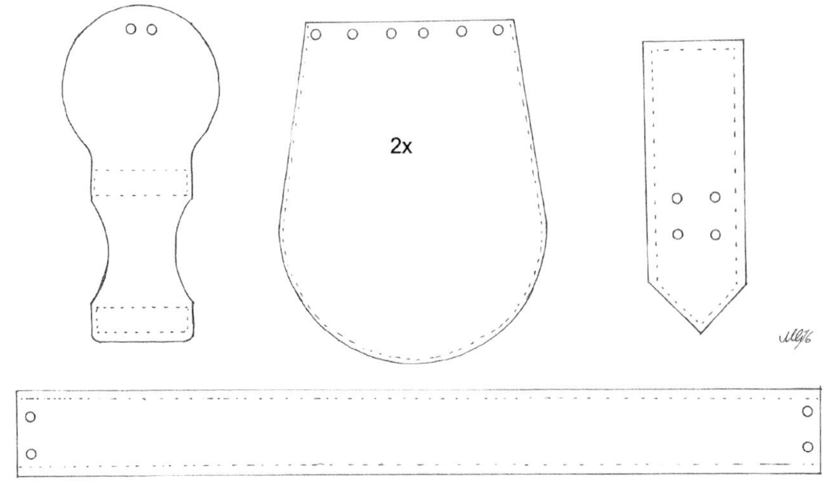

Schablonen für den genähten Lederbeutel.

ches Leder mit ca. 1–2 mm Stärke. Für den Aufsatz, an der Front und für den Deckel sollte das Leder fester sein und eine Stärke von ca. 2–2,5 mm haben. An Werkzeugen benötigst Du ein scharfes Messer, Lochzange, Nadel und Faden sowie eine Stechahle, um die Löcher vorzustechen. Den gezeigten Beutel kannst Du in beliebiger Größe und in abgewandelter Form herstellen. Achte aber darauf, dass der Umfang der Öffnung so groß ist, das Du noch hineingreifen kannst. Sollte Dein Beutel eher kleiner ausfallen, empfehle ich Dir, den Deckel und den Aufsatz an der Front erst aufzunähen, bevor Du den eigentlichen Beutel zusammennähst. Bei größeren Modellen kommst Du leichter in den Beutel um zu nähen.

Der Hauptteil des Beutels sollte an der Oberkante mindestens handbreit sein, damit Du später bequem in den Beutel greifen kannst. Diesen Teil benötigst Du zweimal.

Mit der Breite des langen Streifens kannst Du die Weite Deines Beutels regulieren. Achte darauf, dass er lang genug ist, damit er um den Hauptteil herumreicht. Wenn Du den Frontteil vorbereitet hast, fädle bereits vor dem Nähen Deine Schnur durch die Löcher; daraus wird später der Verschluss. Am Deckel befindet sich auch die Gürtelschlaufe, die Du auf Deine persönlichen Bedürfnisse anpassen solltest. Wenn Du diese später annähst, achte darauf, dass die oberste Naht an der Gürtelschlaufe etwas Abstand zur Oberkante des Beutels hat, da dort der Kordelzug vorbeiläuft. Auf S. 159 siehst Du einen fertigen Beutel. Vor dem Nähen solltest Du alle Löcher für die Naht vorgestochen haben. Ich würde erst die festen Teile aufnähen und dann den langen Streifen mit den Hauptteilen vernähen. Du kannst auch außen eine schöne Ziernaht setzen oder den Beutel mit einem Lederband vernähen. Wenn Du Deinen Beutel vernäht und auf die richtige Seite gedreht hast, fädle einen selbstgeschnittenen Lederriemen oder eine Schnur ein, um den Beutel zuzuziehen. Am Deckel befestigst Du noch einen Knebel aus Horn, Holz oder einen Lederknopf, um ihn so zu verschließen.

https://youtu.be/V2oMF9kKSGY

SPURENSUCHEN & FÄHRTENLESEN

Zu Beginn eine Bitte:

- *Bei der Spurensuche und beim Fährtenlesen bring keine Hektik mit! Darauf werden Tiere sofort reagieren und Reißaus nehmen.*
- *Außerdem kann es für Dich schwer sein, wahrnehmungsfähig zu sein. Du musst alle Sinne nutzen und solltest auf jeden Fall die ersten beiden Übungen aus dem Kapitel »Aufmerksamkeit & Naturwahrnehmung« schon mal gemacht haben.*
- *Versuche darüber hinaus, die Tiere vor allem im Winter nicht unnötig zu stören – uns würde es schließlich auch nicht gefallen, wenn plötzlich Mountainbiker bei uns durchs Bad fahren.*
- *Respektiere die Natur und unterschätze sie nicht.*
- *Und: Mach Dir bei den Übungen Knie und Finger dreckig, sonst ist was falsch gelaufen.*

GENAUER HINSCHAUEN

Sei es für das Beobachten von Wildtieren, bei der Jagd oder um beim Bushcrafttraining zu wissen, wer einen nachts so alles besucht hat: Das Spurensuchen und Fährtenlesen eröffnet eine weitere Ebene des Wahrnehmens und Erfahrens unserer Umgebung. Dabei hat sich das menschliche Gehirn über einen langen Zeitraum als Jäger und Sammler in der Natur sehr erfolgreich darauf spezialisiert, mit den eigenen Sinnen Muster zu erkennen und zu kategorisieren. Das passiert meist unbewusst und sehr schnell. So ist es zum Beispiel beim Lesen. Versuch einmal, auf die Überschrift des nächsten Abschnitts zu schauen, diese scharf im Fokus wahrzunehmen und dabei NICHT zu lesen. Es ist praktisch unmöglich (vorausgesetzt, Du kannst lesen, was das Lesen dieser Zeile ja impliziert). Diese Muster und ihre Bedeutung im Kontext musstest Du aber zuerst lernen – mit viel Übung. Und heute ist es Dir möglich, selbst wenn die Buchstaben auf dem Kopf stehen, gespiegelt sind oder gewisse Teile fehlen, den Sinn daraus zu erschließen.

Fast genauso ist es auch bei den Spuren. Allerdings können wir hier alle Sinne mit einbeziehen und uns so einen noch detaillierteren Eindruck verschaffen, was unser Lernen und später das Abrufen der Informationen erleichtert. Du musst beginnen, wie Sherlock Holmes im Wald deduktiv das Geschehene herzuleiten, und Dich auch mal mit einer dicken Lupe in den Matsch knien. Es geht darum, zu entdecken und zu lesen, was passiert ist, um so anhand der Spuren den Fährten der Protagonisten zu folgen. Die Einzelspuren stellen hier quasi das Alphabet dar und die Fährte als Aneinanderreihung von Spuren Worte und Sätze, die den persönlichen Weg und die Geschichte des Hauptdarstellers erzählen. Manche von diesen hinterlassen dabei mehr Spuren, andere weniger. Versuche, Dir selbst einmal der Spuren, die Du täglich zurücklässt, bewusst zu werden.

Darüber hinaus kann man sich viele Einzeleindrücke und Spezialwissen aneignen, die es erlauben, auch feinste Abweichungen zu unterscheiden, so wie Meister Sherlock zum Beispiel lernte, Zigarrenasche zu unterscheiden. Das kann aber sehr zeitaufwändig sein. Auch wenn Detailverliebtheit gerade beim

Spurensuchen und Fährtenlesen eine wichtige Rolle spielt, sollte man es zu Beginn damit nicht übertreiben. Ich will hier für die Anfänger erst einmal einen Überblick schaffen und die allgemeinen Prinzipien erklären. So kann man mit ein wenig Übung auch als heutiger Zivilisationsmensch schnell erstaunliche Unterschiede wahrzunehmen lernen, wenn man nur genauer hinschaut und genügend Neugier und Geduld mitbringt. Allerdings ist Vorsicht vor voreiligen Schlüssen geboten. Klar ist es möglich, Lücken durch Interpretation aus dem Kontext zu schließen. Versuch Dir dabei aber stets dessen bewusst zu sein, was Du wirklich weißt und wahrnimmst und was Du lediglich vermutest – und vor allem was der Unterschied ist. Außerdem neigt unser Gehirn dazu, »zu viel zu sehen«. So können wir wenige locker aufgestellte Holzscheite schnell als Muster oder Figur wahrnehmen. Dazu kann es passieren, dass bei »zu starkem Hinschauen« und fehlenden Veränderungen ähnlich wie beim Meditieren plötzlich Muster erscheinen, die eigentlich nicht wirklich da sind. Zusätzlich muss man den sogenannten Hyperfokus vermeiden, also darf nicht durch eine einzelne Spur gefangen die periphere Wahrnehmung der Umgebung zu sehr vernachlässigen.

BUCHSTABIEREN LERNEN

Langsam sollte klar werden, dass alles um uns herum in irgendeiner Art und Weise eine Spur darstellt. Sei es, dass etwas, was schon vorhanden ist, manipuliert wird oder dass etwas anderes zurückgelassen wird. Dies kann beispielsweise durch Tiere oder Menschen geschehen, die mit einem Fuß in den Matsch treten. Die Fichte als Pflanze kann einen bleibenden Eindruck durch die abgeworfenen Zapfen auf dem Boden oder auf dem Autodach hinterlassen. Aber auch das Wetter hinterlässt Spuren, sei es die Sonne, der Wind oder der Regen. Es ist wichtig, sich dieser Gesamtheit und der Unterschiede bewusst zu werden.

Grundsätzlich sind Arten von Tierspuren, was auch menschliche miteinbezieht, Manipulationen, also Veränderungen des Vorhandenen, oder Hinterlassenschaften. Zu den Veränderungen gehören Trittsiegel oder Fußabdruck, abhängig von Länge und Breite des Fußes, dem Gewicht und der Geschwindigkeit. Sie dienen als Bindeglieder zwischen den anderen Spuren. Dazu kommen abgebrochene Äste, unterschiedlichste Liegeplätze wie bei Reh oder Hase oder Bauten wie bei Fuchs oder Eichhörnchen. Aber auch

Rehschädel mit Fraßspuren der Maus.

Schabestellen der Schweine an Bäumen oder allgemein fehlendes Moos auf Wildwechseln zeigen Orte und Wege an. Fraßspuren an Teilen von Pflanzen oder Tierkadavern kann man – ähnlich wie unseren Abfall – ebenfalls häufig draußen finden, und sie lassen viele Rückschlüsse auf das Verhalten zu. Hinterlassen werden von Tieren meist Ausscheidungen wie Kot, auch Losung genannt, oder sogenanntes Gewölle von Vögeln, also ausgewürgte unverdauliche Futterreste. Darüber hinaus können auch Haare, Federn oder Blut zu finden sein. Realistisch betrachtet, ist die letzte Spur, die man hinterlässt, der leblose Körper. So sind im Wald Knochen, Schädel oder Fell zu finden, was immer im Kontext gesehen werden muss, denn oft sind hier auch wieder Fraßspuren oder andere Spuren daran zu finden.

Übung 1: Das Revier
Kläre mit einem Rechen (o.ä., Dir fällt da als Bushcrafter schon was ein) einen etwa 3 x 3 m großen Bereich nach Möglichkeit auf einem Wildwechsel in der Nähe Deines Platzes aus Übung 1 des Kapitels »Aufmerksamkeit & Naturwahrnehmung«. Der Bereich um diesen Platz wird nun Dein Revier. Eine weitere Stelle kann auch in Deinem Garten sein. Beobachte regelmäßig, ob Du Spuren von den am Ende des Kapitels beschriebenen Tieren oder deren Verwandten findest, und präge sie Dir ein.

DIE FÄHRTE AUFNEHMEN

Das Erkennen von Trittsiegeln beziehungsweise Fußspuren und daraus entstandenen Gangmustern lässt sich auf leicht feuchtem Sand besonders gut üben. »Sand« kann hier allerdings sehr unterschiedliche Dinge bezeichnen, von Lehm bis hin zu Pflanzerde. Es bieten sich in der freien Wildbahn frisch gepflügte Äcker an, wo Du auch als Anfänger lange Fährten verfolgen kannst. Aufgewühlte Wiesen sind selbst schon ein Anzeichen von Wildaktivität und bieten darüber hinaus einen guten Grund, um Fußspuren zu suchen. Auch besonders nasse Stellen von Suhlen über Wasserlöcher bis hin zum Strand sind gute Anfangspunkte, um erste »Buchstaben« zu lernen oder sogar eine einzelne Fährte aufzunehmen. An die Wasserstelle kommen sie alle: Wildschweine, Rehe, Füchse, Dachse, Marder, Ratten, Mäuse und auch viele Vögel. So ist es auch gerade nach einem Regenschauer reizvoll, sich auf die Suche nach frischen Spuren zu machen.

Trittsiegel sollten dabei zwischen dem Auge und der Lichtquelle liegen, da so Schatten und Kanten besser erkannt werden. Darüber hinaus ist Schnee natürlich zum Erlernen der Basismuster oder zum Folgen einer Fährte über eine längere Strecke besonders gut geeignet. Hierbei sollte man allerdings beachten, dass die Helligkeit auf Dauer eine große Belastung für die Augen bedeutet und man diese also dabei schützen muss.

Wenn hier jetzt die Grundlagen gelegt sind, geht es weiter zu den Übergängen in Wiese und Wald. Hier geht es darum, die vorher geprägten Muster auf sich deutlich unterscheidendem Untergrund wie Gras, Laub, Moos wiederzuerkennen, was am besten funktioniert, wenn man vorher viel geübt hat. Dazu kommt die Vegetation, die uns durch abgebrochene Halme, Äste oder Bruchkanten in Blättern weitere Schlüssel liefert.

Du musst nun diese Prinzipien verinnerlichen, stetig Deine Wahrnehmung und Dein Gehirn mit diesen »Eindrücken« prägen und darüber hinaus das Verhalten der Tiere antizipieren. Ein grundsätzliches erstes ABC und eine Checkliste der ersten Schritte gibt's am Ende des Kapitels. Besorg Dir darüber hinaus allgemein Informationen über das jeweilige Biotop und seine Bewohner. Geh dabei interdisziplinär vor, bedien Dich also bei Survival, Bushcraft, Naturfotografen, Jägern und allem, was Dir sonst noch einfällt. Jetzt besorgst Du Dir spezielle Infos zu dem, was da gerade bei Dir so kreucht und fleucht.

GANGARTEN UND VERHALTEN

Um nun das Entstehen von Einzelspuren und deren Interpretation in einen Kontext zu bringen, muss man sich gewisse Ordnungen in Wald und Wiese vor der Haustür bewusst machen. Diese werden von verschiedensten Tieren bewohnt, von Jägern und Gejagten, bei Tag und bei Nacht, in der Luft, auf und unter der Erde. Hier spielt die Nahrungskette eine große Rolle, denn viele Jäger sind auch selbst Gejagte. Allgemein benötigen aber alle Lebewesen einen Schutz vor Witterung oder einen Schlafplatz, haben Vorlieben bei der Wasser- und Nahrungsaufnahme und betreiben in irgendeiner Form Hygiene - salopp gesagt: Nach dem Aufstehen wird sich gestreckt, dann ab ins Bad und Frühstück. Hierbei wird meist der Weg des geringsten Widerstands genommen, einfach um Energie zu sparen. Dadurch bilden sich Pfade oder Wildwechsel, die bei genauem Hinschauen im Wald leicht zu identifizieren sind. Wenn Du diesen Wechseln einmal folgst, wirst Du wahrscheinlich leicht zu Liegeplätzen, einem Bau, einem Wasserloch oder einer Suhle finden.

Allgemein resultieren die Gangarten, die man aus einer Reihe von Trittsiegeln besonders auf Sand oder Schnee ablesen kann, aus dem Verhalten der Tiere in ihrem Biotop. Es sei dabei allgemein in energiesparend oder harmonisch, unsicher oder vorsichtig, flüchtend, stöbernd oder pirschend und hetzend oder jagend unterschieden. Dazu haben die Jahreszeiten und das Wetter einen klaren Einfluss auf das Verhalten und die üblichen Gewohnheiten.

Übung 2: Auf die Knie

Hebe eine etwa 10 m lange Sandbox aus und geh 10 Schritte darin, schick Deinen Hund, Katze oder Maus hindurch. Markiere nun jedes einzelne Trittsiegel am Ende mit einem kleinen Stäbchen. Beginne, Breite und Länge des Einzelabdrucks, aber auch andere Merkmale wie die Länge eines Schrittes, linker und rechter Fuß zu erfassen. Jetzt laufe, pirsche und so weiter darin und vergleiche die entstandenen Muster - am besten auf den Knien mit der Nase am Boden.

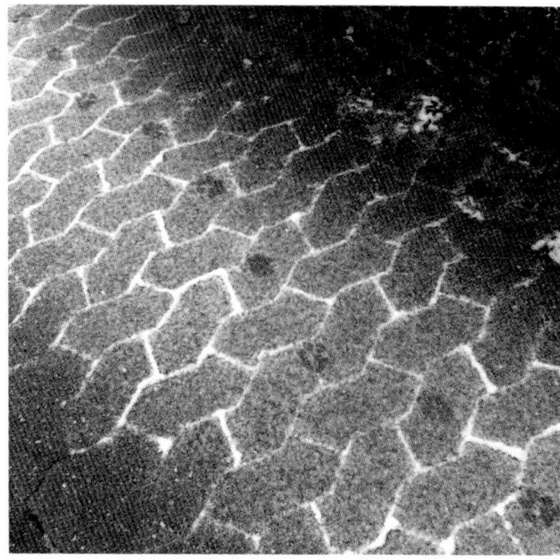

Gangart: Hundespuren im Schnee auf Asphalt.

BASELINE

Die Tiere nennen nun mal »Draußen« ihr Zuhause und müssen, um dort zu bestehen, mit allen Sinnen aufmerksam sein. Normalerweise kennen sie diesen Bereich aber auch ihr Leben lang und reagieren schon auf kleine Veränderungen. Wir müssen auch hier wieder erkennen, dass wir ein Teil davon sind, ununterbrochen mit unserer Umgebung interagieren und verschiedenste, wahrnehmbare Spuren hinterlassen. Darum sollte man sich beim Erlernen von Spurensuche und Fährtenlesen bemühen, ein sogenanntes Grundmuster oder eine »Baseline« zu etablieren. Damit ist gemeint, dass im Gehirn ein grundsätzlicher Eindruck der Umgebung geprägt ist und die daraus resultierenden Zusammenhänge berücksichtigt werden.

Dies kannst Du zum Beispiel über die Übungen aus dem Kapitel »Aufmerksamkeit & Naturwahrnehmung« erreichen und dann auf Wildwechsel und markante Punkte übertragen: Wie sehen diese Orte normalerweise aus? Was ist bei welchem Wind und Wetter der grundsätzlich vorherrschende Geruch, und welche Geräusche sind zu hören? Welche Orte fangen die Aufmerksamkeit, und was wird leicht »übersehen«? Sollten hier nun Veränderungen auftreten, handelt es sich um Spuren, denen man auf den Grund gehen kann – so wie man zu Hause vielleicht bemerkt, wenn die Fernbedienung nicht mehr auf »ihrem Platz« ist. Hierbei hilft das Dokumentieren von Einzelspuren, sei es das Markieren von Trittsiegeln zum Beispiel mit kleinen Fähnchen oder das Fotografieren und Zeichnen. Alles prägt und schärft die Wahrnehmung weiter und lässt so später leichter Strukturen erkennen. Erfahrung und Erfahren sind entscheidend.

Übung 3: Alle Sinne

Wenn Du die Übungen 1 und 2 aus diesem Kapitel machst, setz dabei alle Sinne ein. Versuche bei Spaziergängen oder beim Sitzen auf Parkbänken, Dein Umfeld mit allen Sinnen zu erfahren und Veränderungen ruhig aufzunehmen. Welcher Geruch herrscht an einem Wildwechsel oder an einer Suhle? Hör auf die Vögel und beobachte ihr Verhalten, wenn zum Beispiel eine Katze in der Umgebung ist.

INTERPRETATIONSSACHE

Um mit dieser Flut an Informationen, die man wahrnehmen kann, nun besser umzugehen und diese besser unterscheiden zu lernen, ist es nötig, die richtigen W-Fragen in der richtigen Reihenfolge und im Kontext, also draußen in der Natur, zu stellen.

Beginnen sollte man mit den einfachen Fragen, die meist sehr direkt aus einer Spur ablesbar sind:

Wer *hat die Spur erzeugt? Hier geht es vorerst nur um die Bestimmung der Art des Erzeugers, also beispielsweise ob ein Blatt gerade vom Baum herabgefallen ist oder vom Wind oder einem Tier gedreht wurde.*

Wohin *ist die Spur ausgerichtet, oder woher kommt sie? Eine Spur kommt selten allein und hat bei Tieren meist einen Vorgänger und einen Nachfolger. So kann man um die Eiche viele Eichblätter finden, die sich gleichmäßig im Wind bewegen. Tierspuren dagegen verlaufen in einer Linie, die aber durchaus Ecken und Kanten hat, wo vielleicht beim Stöbern Laub zerwühlt wurde oder einfach bedingt durch Terrain oder Hindernisse Richtungswechsel stattfanden.*

Bei den weiteren Fragen werden nun Einzelspuren miteinander verglichen und in Beziehung zueinander gebracht, was Rückschlüsse auf das Verhalten ermöglicht, im Gesamtkontext allerdings schwerer wird:

Was *ist geschehen beziehungsweise wurde getan? Es muss also das Wer und Wohin mit der Umgebung in Bezug gebracht werden. Beispielsweise sind Fraßspuren von Wildschweinen und deren Trittsiegel oft unter Eichen zu finden, da dort eben viel bevorzugte Nahrung vorhanden ist. Außerdem werden Wildschweinspuren zum Baum hin und wieder weg führen.*

Wie viele *Protagonisten waren hier? Hier geht es darum, den Einzelgänger von der Gruppe zu trennen oder das Aufeinandertreffen zweier Arten zu erkennen, wobei viele Details wie zum Beispiel Länge und Breite von Einzelabdrücken unterschieden werden müssen.*

Wie *wurde sich dabei verhalten? Nun sucht man nach Veränderungen im Rhythmus des Verhaltens eines Tieres, zum Beispiel wie sich die Schrittlänge oder Richtung verändern oder eben gleich bleiben.*

Ab jetzt werden die Fragen deutlich schwerer und sind nur mit einer guten Wahrnehmung und Kenntnis des Biotops klar zu beantworten. Es muss deutlich getrennt werden, was Vermutung und was Wissen darstellt:

Wann *wurde die Spur hinterlassen? Spuren altern in unterschiedlichster Art und Weise. Dabei spielt das Wetter, besonders Regen und die Sonneneinstrahlung, eine große Rolle. So kann es Orte geben, wo für wenige Meter eine alte Spur wie frisch entstanden erscheint, da die Stelle vor Wetter geschützt ist. Die Feuchtigkeit von Sand oder Lehm ist entscheidend für die Haltbarkeit eines Trittsiegels, was man am Meer sehr leicht beobachten kann. So sollte das Alter einer Spur zwingend immer im Kontext des Alters der Fährte, zu der sie gehört, gesehen werden. Zu einer klaren Bestimmung gehört hier viel Übung und Erfahrung.*

Warum *ist diese Spur entstanden, warum wurde sich so verhalten oder welche Geschichte wird erzählt? Dabei geht es nicht mehr darum, eine Einzelspur in einen Kontext zu bringen, sondern darum, den Kontext der Einzelspuren zu erschließen. Nachdem man sich mit allen Einzelfragen ein Bild geschaffen hat, gilt es jetzt, die Puzzleteile zusammenzufügen, um das Gesamtbild und die Einzelwege der Protagonisten zu erfassen.*

Wer genau *war es? Eine exakte Dokumentation wird bei der Königsdisziplin »Bestimmung einzelner Individuen anhand ihrer Spuren« sehr wichtig, um Verwechslungen so gut wie möglich auszuschließen. Verschiedenste Merkmale wie die Länge und Breite von Trittsiegeln, die Länge von Schritten sowie Gangarten auf verschiedenen Untergründen, Verhalten und Vorlieben bei Schlaf, Wasser- und Nahrungsaufnahme oder Hygiene müssen miteinbezogen werden und bekannt sein. Des Weiteren müssen äußere Einflüsse und das Biotop berücksichtigt und dokumentiert werden.*

Übung 4: Fährtenstock, Alter

Finde zu Beginn auf Sand eine möglichst frische Spur und die dazugehörende Fährte in der freien Wildbahn. Führe Übung 2 damit durch. Versuche, 100 Einzeltritte in Folge zu erkennen und zu markieren. Ein sogenannter Fährtenstock kann Dir dabei helfen, einem einzelnen Tier treuzubleiben.

Dazu markiere mit einem Messer an einem etwa 1,5 m langen Stock Breite und Länge der Tritte, die Länge der Schritte von gleichem zu gleichem Fuß, die Breite der Spur und was Dir sonst noch einfällt, so dass Du es auch danach noch unterscheiden kannst.

Besuche diese Stelle mit der markierten Fährte nun regelmäßig und beobachte, wie sich die Abdrücke mit der Zeit verändern. Lege weitere Fährtenplätze auf verschiedenem Untergrund an.

Strohhalme als Markierungen von Trittsiegeln und Gang.

VISUALISIEREN UND UMSCHAU HALTEN

Wenn Du die Tiere in Deinem Revier studierst, darfst Du nicht nur Bücher anschauen oder nach Spuren auf dem Boden oder an Bäumen Ausschau halten. Geh dazu auch mal in den Tierpark oder schau Dir Tierdokumentationen an, um ein Gefühl für die Bewegungen eines Tieres in seinem Umfeld zu erhalten. Wenn Du jetzt wieder draußen vor Deiner Haustür umherstreifst und Spuren suchst, stell Dir vor, wie das Reh oder der Hase vom Acker oder der Wiese ins dichte Gebüsch wechseln oder die Wildsau den Boden umgräbt. An Liegeplätzen versuch Dir vorzustellen, wie das Tier gelegen hat oder wie es aufgestanden ist. Daraus wird sich vor Deinem geistigen Auge die Spur regelrecht manifestieren, und Du kannst schnell einzelne Bestandteile wie Fußabdrücke oder Haare erkennen oder beispielsweise nach Sprüngen über Hindernisse die Spur wieder aufnehmen.

Übung 5: Du bist der Hase!

An den Orten aus Übung 4 musst Du jetzt visualisieren, das heißt, die Tiere, deren Spuren Du markiert hast, vor Deinem geistigen Auge dort entlanglaufen sehen. Lass Dir etwas Zeit dafür. Geh im nächsten Schritt auf alle Viere und personifiziere das Tier, das heißt, ahme das Verhalten nach, welches Du aus der Fährte liest. Versuch dabei, zum Beispiel wie ein Hase, Dachs, Hund, Katze oder wer auch immer zu fühlen, nicht zu denken. Beachte, was Du vielleicht im Tierpark gesehen hast. Halte Umschau und sei wachsam (Vielleicht will Dich jemand fressen!), aber hab auch Spaß dabei – ist ein gutes Training.

SPEICHERN

Dazu musst Du erleben, wie es ist, mit den Augen eines Kindes zu sehen, Deine natürliche Neugier wiederentdecken und geprägte Scheu ablegen. Dies kann man nicht erzwingen oder lernen, sondern man muss in gewisser Weise einfach mal loslassen. Eine Faszination für das Geschehen und Fantasie gehören auch dazu. So wie Du vielleicht gern Bücher liest, kannst Du der Geschichte einer Spur im Wald folgen. Du kannst entdecken, was davor oder danach passierte. Die Lücken musst Du selbst füllen und zwischen Wahrnehmung und Vermutung unterscheiden. Die Gesamtheit der Informationen kann so besser »abgespeichert« und später wieder abgerufen werden.

Blut und Federn!

Früh an einem Herbstmorgen, nachdem es in der Nacht noch geregnet hatte, finde ich eine frische Rehspur auf einer Wiese, auf der noch leichter Nebel steht. Dort hat ein einzelnes Tier das Gras mit dem frischen Regen genossen und führt mich jetzt ins Unterholz. Die Vögel scheinen mir unruhig. Gerade will ich mir einen Fährtenstock schneiden, als plötzlich der Eichelhäher warnt und darauf sofort wildes Geschrei in meiner Nähe zu hören ist. Es dauert einen Moment, dann folgt Stille, kein Gezwitscher. Ich verharre einen Moment und gehe meine Sinne durch und glaube, leises Rascheln zu hören. Langsam bewege ich mich in Richtung des verstummten Geschreis. Hinter einer Kuppe am Wasserloch liegen ein paar Federn. Nach kurzer Suche finde ich dazu aufgewühltes Laub und Matsch, wo diese nicht hingehören, dazu Blut und etwas weiter entfernt Bissspuren an weiteren Federn. Langsam glaube ich, eine Schleifspur im Laub zu erkennen. Aber wer lässt sich schon gern beim Essen stören? Daher folge ich ihr nicht weiter, sondern gehe vorsichtig, ohne selbst zu viel zu zerwühlen, zurück zur Wasserstelle. In einem Meter Umkreis um die ersten Federn finde ich wenig außer Chaos, doch etwa zwei Meter entfernt hinter einem Farn: Spuren im Lehm, nebeneinander und tief. Für einen kleinen Hundeartigen ging es wohl auf zum Sprung. Auf einem bemoosten Baumstamm kann ich seinen Weg weiter zurückverfolgen, wie er sich zuerst anpirschte. Davor blieb er kurz stehen. Die Spur führt ab hier im harmonischen Trab weiter zurück bis zu einer Stelle, wo Laub aufgewühlt ist. Bei genauerem Hinsehen finde ich frische Fraßspuren vom Eichhörnchen, das über mir im Baum schimpft. Es wird wohl zum zweiten Mal beim Essen gestört. Aber für Reineke gab es heute wohl kein Eichhörnchen. Die Spur ist wieder weg. Im Umkreis von einem Meter finde ich nichts. Bei etwas mehr als drei Metern hinter einem kleinen Busch geht's weiter. Weit gesprungen, aber eben verfehlt. Die Spuren sind wieder sehr kurz, langsam, und davor wurde ruhig geschlendert. Dann liegt ein kleiner Haufen Kot auf einem Baumstumpf – Vorsicht vor dem Fuchsbandwurm! Dahinter kann ich der Fährte weiter folgen. Im sandigen Boden finde ich deutliche Spuren, die aber vom Gang her wesentlich unpräziser sind als die bisher entdeckten. War da etwa jemand noch verschlafen? Die Fährte beginnt zu verschwinden. Die Spuren sind vom Regen in der Nacht verwaschen und führen über Blattwerk. Ich atme noch einmal tief durch und will schon weiterziehen, als ich diesen markanten Geruch in der Nase habe und mir auffällt, dass ich vor einem Loch zu einem Bau stehe. Doch die Spinnennetze, Laub und der ausgewaschene Weg verraten mir, dass er wohl unbenutzt ist. Aber ein Eingang kommt selten allein. An einem anderen, nicht weit entfernt, tief unten, wo der Regen nichts verwaschen hat, kann ich frische Fuchsspuren erkennen, die herausführen – Ausgang also. Ist er mittlerweile wieder zu Hause, oder ist er in der Umgebung? Beobachtet er mich gerade? Ist er allein? Ist er eine Sie? ... Das herauszufinden, ist jetzt Eure Aufgabe. Viel Spaß!

Übung 6: Einheimischer Fährtenleser

Ab jetzt musst Du selbst rausgehen und dort weiterlesen. Entdecke Deine eigenen Geschichten. Dokumentiere Dein Wissen und erweitere den Anhang. Heb dabei immer wieder die Nase aus der Spur, sonst stehst Du plötzlich vor dem Fuchs und merkst es nicht. Meiner Meinung nach liegt es in der Verantwortung eines Einheimischen, die Natur um sich herum zu verstehen und zu erhalten. Er lebt schließlich selbst darin. Mir wurde einmal gesagt: »Das erste Mal ist leicht, zweimal auch. Ein Jahr lang ist auch noch leicht, ein Leben lang ist allerdings schwer.«

Füchse laufen gern auf Baumstämmen entlang.

Der Fährtenleser-Knigge

Ausrüstung: *Zeit, Geduld, Neugier, Taschenmesser, Block und Bleistift (vielleicht Kamera, Fernglas).*

Am besten gehst Du auf die Suche, wenn die Sonne nah am Horizont steht.

Vorgehensweise:

1. *Begib Dich an den Rand des Gebietes, in dem Du lesen möchtest.*
2. *Verharre kurz und aktiviere Deine Sinne: Fühlen, Schmecken, Riechen, Hören, Sehen. Schau Dich kurz um, bestimme die Windrichtung und halte nach Wegen Ausschau.*
3. *Wenn Du Dich bereit fühlst, gehe vorsichtig, langsam und ruhig los. Sei mit allen Sinnen in alle Richtungen aufmerksam auf interessante Indizien.*
4. *Falls Du etwas findest, stürme nicht blind darauf zu, sondern überlege Dir jeden Schritt und beachte, auf was Du trittst. Bring die Spur zwischen Dich und die Lichtquelle.*
5. *Beachte die Spur aus verschiedenen Blickwinkeln und stell die W-Fragen. Suche ohne viel Bewegung im Umkreis von Körperhöhe, Schrittlänge, Körperlänge nach weiteren Indizien. Erweitere den Umkreis langsam.*
6. *Wenn* ***wer*** *erkannt, versuche die Richtung zu bestimmen.*
7. *Wenn* ***wohin*** *oder* ***woher*** *erkannt, kannst Du Dich für eine Richtung entscheiden und musst die nächste Spur in der Fährte, die zum selben Tier gehört, erkennen.*
8. *Dokumentiere die wichtigsten Merkmale oder vermutete Anzahl mithilfe von Fährtenstock, Block und Bleistift.*
9. *Versuche jetzt, das Verhalten zu antizipieren und die Gangart zu erkennen.*
10. *Versuche, das Alter der Fährte stetig einzuschätzen.*
11. *Falls die Spuren erst vor kurzem entstanden sind, hast Du nun wohl eine frische Fährte aufgenommen – Glückwunsch! Versuche, ihrem Verlauf Schritt für Schritt zu folgen. Achte besonders auf Richtungswechsel oder Veränderungen der Gangart. An diesen Stellen kannst Du entweder die Fährte weiterverfolgen oder im Umfeld nach Auslösern der Veränderung suchen und beginnen, eine Geschichte zu lesen.*

ANHANG: STECKBRIEFE (AUSGEWACHSENE TIERE)

Hundeartige

In allen variablen Körperformen mit starken Größenunterschieden, Einzelgänger oder Rudeltier, Pirsch- oder Hetzjäger, Primärsinn: Nase.

(Quelle: Joe Vogel)

Bei Hundeartigen sind stets die Krallen sichtbar.

Fuchs

- *Trittsiegel:* Breite 4–5 cm, Länge 5–6 cm
- *Schrittlänge:* 20–30 cm, schneller mehr als 30 cm, Sprünge bis zu 3 m
- *Höhe:* 35–45 cm
- *Paarungszeit:* Dezember–Februar
- *Tragzeit:* etwa 50 Tage
- *Wurfgröße:* 3–5 Jungtiere
- *Lebensraum/Lebensweise:* unspezifisch; eher Einzelgänger, Pirschjäger
- *Nahrung:* Allesfresser (Aas, Amphibien, Fische, Mäuse, Kaninchen, Regenwürmer)
- dämmerungs- und nachtaktiv

Wolf

- *Trittsiegel:* Breite 6–9 cm, Länge 8–11 cm
- *Schrittlänge:* ca. 1 m im Trab, Gang 80–90 cm
- *Höhe:* 70–150 cm (Schulterhöhe europ. Wolf)
- *Paarungszeit:* Januar–Februar
- *Tragzeit:* 60–75 Tage
- *Wurfgröße:* 1–10 Jungtiere
- *Lebensraum/Lebensweise:* Halbwüsten, Kältesteppe, Wälder; Hetzjäger, Rudeltier
- *Nahrung:* Fleischfresser (Hirsche, Kaninchen, Mäuse, Rinder, Schafe, Wildschweine)
- tag- und nachtaktiv

(Wild-)Katze

Krallen einziehbar, normal nicht zu sehen, Ballen unterscheidet sich vom Hund, Pirschjäger mit sehr guten Nachtsichtfähigkeiten, tag- und nachtaktiv.

- *Trittsiegel:* Kreis mit Durchmesser 2,5–6 cm (Hauskatze); Kreis mit Durchmesser 4–6 cm (Wildkatze)
- *Durchschnittliche Schrittlänge:* Wildkatze 20–30 cm beim Gehen
- *Höhe:* 25–40 cm
- *Paarungszeit:* Januar–März
- *Tragzeit:* 60 –70 Tage
- *Wurfgröße:* 2–5 Jungtiere
- *Lebensraum:* naturbelassene Wälder (Wildkatze)
- *Nahrung:* Fleischfresser (Mäuse, Wanderratten, kleine Amphibien)

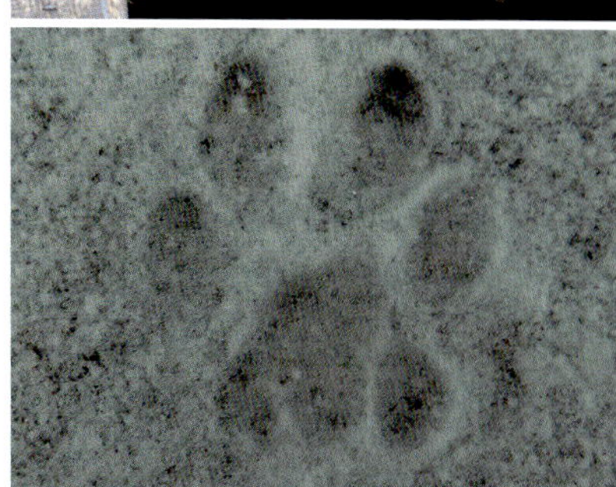

Katzen können ihre Krallen einziehen.

Reh.

Dachs.

Reh

Scheu, bellt, wenn gestört, selten sichtbar, da es verharrt und gut getarnt ist; Fellwechsel Ende Mai und Ende September, dämmerungsaktiv, Geäft oder Afterklauen innerhalb der Schalenbreite und nur selten in Matsch oder Schnee zu erkennen

→ *Trittsiegel: Breite 2–3 cm, Länge 4–6 cm*

→ *Schrittlänge: 30–50 cm*

→ *Höhe: 60–90 cm*

→ *Paarungszeit: auch Blattzeit Mitte Juli–August*

→ *Tragzeit: ca. 9,5 Monate: Eiruhe August–Dezember, dann 5 Monate Tragzeit*

→ *Wurfgröße: 1–2 Jungtiere*

→ *Lebensraum: von Küste bis Hochgebirge*

→ *Nahrung: Pflanzenfresser, sehr wählerisch: nährstoffreiche Pflanzenteile*

Dachs

Kann sich mit Fuchs Bau teilen oder darum streiten; Bauch schleift leicht auf dem Boden, besonders am Baueingang zu erkennen, 5 Zehen zu erkennen, nachtaktiv

→ *Trittsiegel: Breite 5–5,5 cm, Länge 5–6 cm*

→ *Schrittlänge: 25–40 beim Gehen*

→ *Kopf-Rumpflänge: 64–88 cm*

→ *Höhe: 50–80 cm*

→ *Paarungszeit: Februar bis März, Juli bis August*

→ *Tragzeit: ca. 5–12 Monate: erst Eiruhe, dann 45 Tage Tragzeit*

→ *Wurfgröße: 1–5 Jungtiere*

→ *Lebensraum: Feuchtgebiete, Laub- und Mischwälder, Sumpfgebiete*

→ *Nahrung: Allesfresser (Beeren, Insekten, Schnecken, Obst, Würmer, Sämereien)*

Aaskrähe

Aasfresser, vertreiben Raubvögel im Schwarm, jagen u.U. mit Wölfen im Rudel; sehr intelligent, tagaktiv

→ *Trittsiegel: Breite 4 cm, 7–8 cm*

→ *Höhe: ca. 50 cm*

Spuren der Krähe im Schnee.

- *Paarungszeit:* Februar–April
- *Brutzeit:* 21 Tage
- *Gelegegröße:* 3–5 Eier
- *Lebensraum:* Grünanlagen, Parks, Mischwälder
- *Nahrung:* Allesfresser, Nahrungsopportunist (Aas, Insekten, Würmer, Obst, Singvögel)

Wildschwein

Heimlich, aber wehrhaft, wohl durch den Menschen nachtaktiv geworden, Geäft oder Afterklauen außerhalb der Schalenbreite und meist zu erkennen

- *Trittsiegel:* Breite 7–8 cm, Länge 9–11 cm; starke Schwankungen innerhalb der Spezies
- *Schrittlänge:* 40 cm beim Gehen
- *Höhe:* 60–100 cm
- *Paarungszeit:* November–Januar
- *Tragzeit:* 100–120 Tage
- *Wurfgröße:* 4–12 Jungtiere
- *Lebensraum:* unspezifisch, bevorzugt Laub- und Mischwälder
- *Nahrung:* Allesfresser (Aas, Rehkitze, Bucheckern, Eicheln, Früchte, Sämereien, Insekten, Pilze, Wurzeln)

(Quelle: Joe Vogel / Vivalranger.com)

Trittsiegel verschiedener Tiere: Wildschwein, Hund/Fuchs, Reh/Hirsch jeweils ziehend *(links)* und flüchtend *(rechts)*.

Wildschwein: Die Afterklauen sind meist zu erkennen. *Rechts:* Aufgebrochene Wiese, Fraßspuren.

INDEX